John M. Kirk is a Lecturer in English
at the Queen's University of Belfast.

J.D.A. Widdowson is Professor of
English Language and Director of the
Centre for English Cultural Tradition
and Language at the University of
Sheffield.

Stewart Sanderson is Harold Orton
Fellow at the University of Leeds.

Studies in Linguistic Geography

PE
1700
·S7
1985

STUDIES IN LINGUISTIC GEOGRAPHY

The Dialects of English in Britain and Ireland

Edited by
JOHN M. KIRK, STEWART SANDERSON AND J.D.A. WIDDOWSON

WITHDRAWN

GOSHEN COLLEGE LIBRARY
GOSHEN, INDIANA

CROOM HELM   London • Sydney • Dover New Hampshire

© 1985 John M. Kirk, Stewart Sanderson and J.D.A. Widdowson
Croom Helm Ltd, Provident House, Burrell Row,
Beckenham, Kent BR3 1AT
Croom Helm Australia Pty Ltd, Suite 4, 6th Floor,
64-76 Kippax Street, Surry Hills, NSW 2010, Australia

British Library Cataloguing in Publication Data

Studies in linguistic geography
    1. English language — Dialects — Maps
    I. Kirk, John M.   II. Sanderson, Stewart F.
    III. Widdowson, J.D.A.   IV. Series
    427   PE1705

ISBN 0-7099-1502-0

Croom Helm, 51 Washington Street
Dover, New Hampshire, 03820, USA

Library of Congress Cataloguing in Publication Data
Main entry under title:

Studies in linguistic geography.

   Contents: Introduction, principles and practice
in linguistic geography / J.M. Kirk, S.F. Sanderson,
J.D.A. Widdowson — Linguistic geography in England /
S.F. Sanderson and J.D.A. Widdowson — On producing
a linguistic atlas / D. Parry — [etc.]
    1. English language — Dialects — Great Britain —
Addresses, essays, lectures.   2. English language —
Dialects — Ireland — Addresses, essays, lectures.
3. English language — Maps — Addresses, essays, lectures.
4. Linguistic geography — Addresses, essays, lectures.
I. Kirk, John M.   II. Sanderson, Stewart F.
III. Widdowson, J.D.A. (John David Allison)
PE1700.S7   1985   427′.941   84-23118
ISBN 0-7099-1502-0

Typeset by Columns of Reading
Printed and bound in Great Britain
by Billing & Sons Limited, Worcester.

Contents

List of Figures   vi
List of Maps   vii
Locality Codes: England   viii
Locality Codes: Wales   xiii
Abbreviations   xv
The International Phonetic Alphabet   xvi
Contributors   xvii
Acknowledgements   xviii

1. Introduction: Principles and Practice in Linguistic Geography
    John M. Kirk, Stewart Sanderson and J.D.A. Widdowson   1

2. Linguistic Geography in England: Progress and Prospects
    Stewart Sanderson and J.D.A. Widdowson   34

3. On Producing a Linguistic Atlas: The Survey of Anglo-Welsh Dialects
    David Parry   51

4. The Tape-recorded Survey of Hiberno-English Speech: A Reappraisal of the
    Techniques of Traditional Dialect Geography
    †G.B. Adams, M.V. Barry and P.M. Tilling   67

5. Linguistic Atlases and Sociolinguistics
    Paul A. Johnston, Jr   81

6. Linguistic Atlases and Dialectometry: The Survey of English Dialects
    Wolfgang Viereck   94

7. Linguistic Atlases and Generative Phonology
    Beat Glauser   113

8. Linguistic Atlases and Grammar: The Investigation and Description
    of Regional Variation in English Syntax
    John M. Kirk   130

9. Linguistic Atlases and Vocabulary: The Linguistic Survey of Anglo-Irish
    P.L. Henry   157

10. Linguistic Maps: Visual Aid or Abstract Art?
    R.K.S. Macaulay   172

Figures

		Page
1.1	The Position of SED in Dialectology	2
1.2	The Mapping Triangle: Properties	12
1.3	*SLG* Map Profiles	13
1.4	The Mapping Triangle of Map 7.1	14
1.5	The Mapping Process	14
1.6	The Mapping Triangle: Properties and Maxims	17
4.1	TRS Questionnaire, p. 1	69
5.1	A Model of Stylistic Formality Levels	84
5.2	Age and Sex Characteristics of Traditional Survey Informants	85
5.3	Middle-class Informants in Traditional Dialect Surveys	88
5.4	Number of Middle-class Dutch-speaking Informants by Region, Population of Town, and Frequency of Dialect Use	89

		Page
5.5	The Variables (r), (η), (ee), (ii), (oo), (uu) in Pittsfield, Massachusetts, by Class	90
6.1	Eastern Verb Forms with a Distinctively Regional Distribution (USA)	97
6.2	Identity Values: Lexis	101
6.3	Identity Values: Morphology	101
7.1	Rounding Adjustment in the English Midlands	127
8.1	Recent Studies of Regional Syntax	144
8.2	English Syntax in Britain and Ireland	146

Maps

Page

1.1 SED Localities Arranged by New County Boundaries 4
1.2 SED and SAWD Localities Arranged by New County Boundaries 6
1.3 Rounding Adjustment in the Midlands 31
3.1 SAWD: *rabbits* (*R*-quality) 54
3.2 SAWD: *root* (*R*-quality) 55
3.3 SAWD and *SED*: *cow-house* 59
3.4 SAWD and *SED*: *gangway in a cow-house* 60
3.5 SAWD and *SED*: *cart-shed* 61
3.6 SAWD and *SED*: *gate* (vowel) 62
3.7 SAWD and *SED*: *spade* (vowel) 63
3.8 SAWD and *SED*: *tooth* (vowel) 64
4.1 The Northern Counties of Ireland 68
4.2a Grid Map of the Northern Counties of Ireland 71
4.2b Location of TRS Informants in Sample Square 71
4.3 TRS: *boil* (vowel) 75
4.4 TRS: *pony* (vowel) 75
4.5 TRS: *third* (initial consonant) 75
4.6 TRS: *cat* (final consonant) 75
4.7 TRS: *cat* (initial consonant) 77
4.8 TRS: *horse* (vowel) 77
4.9 TRS: *door* (vowel) 77
4.10 TRS: *door* (syllabicity) 77
6.1 *SED* the Midlands and the South: RCM Lexis 98
6.2 *SED* the Midlands and the South: RCM Morphology 99
6.3 *SLG* 46.3 (36 Co 3): GIV (RIV) Lexis 102
6.4 *SLG* 46.3 (36 Co 3): GIV (RIV) Morphology 103
6.5 *SLG* 40.1 (39 Ha 1): GIV (RIV) Lexis 104
6.6 *SLG* 40.1 (39 Ha 1): GIV (RIV) Morphology 105
6.7 *SLG* 23.3 (17 Wa 4): GIV (RIV) Lexis 106
6.8 *SLG* 23.3 (17 Wa 4): GIV (RIV) Morphology 107
6.9 *SLG* 21.7 (21 Nf 9): GIV (RIV) Lexis 108

Page

6.10 *SLG* 21.7 (21 Nf 9): GIV (RIV) Morphology 109
7.1 *SED*: *goose* (vowel) 115
7.2 *SED*: *quarry* (vowel) 117
7.3 *SED*: *wasps* (vowel) 119
7.4 *SED*: *wash* (vowel) 121
7.5 *SED*: *water* (vowel) 123
7.6 *SED*: *swath* (vowel) 125
7.7 *SED*: Rounding Adjustment in the English Midlands 126
8.1 *LAE* S1: *give it me* 132
8.2 *SED*: *give it me* 135
8.3 *LAE* S9: *did not do* 136
8.4 *SED*: 'obligation' 140
8.5 Regional Grammar in Britain and Ireland 148
9.1 *Smallest and weakest piglet of the litter* — Ireland 160
9.2 *LAS* vol. 1, map 65: *the youngest of a brood* 162
9.3 *LASID*, map 34: *smallest pigling of a litter* 163
9.4 *LAS* vol. 2, map 60: *last corn sheaf cut at harvesting* 165
9.5 *Last corn sheaf* — Ireland 167
9.6 *Last corn sheaf* — Scotland 168
10.1 *AES*, p. 9: ME /ī/, *died* (p.p.) 173
10.2 *LAE*: Ph 69b: *make* 174
10.3 *AES*, p. 227: ME /ŭ/ collective map 1 176
10.4 *LAS* vol. 1, map 4: *splinter* 177
10.5 *Splinter*: Alternative Local Responses 178
10.6 *Skelf*: Percentage Tokens of Occurrences in Scotland 179
10.7 *LAUM*, fig. 14.4: *frying pan* 181
10.8 Transition Zone between East Anglia and the East Midlands: Distribution of Lectal Types 181
10.9 Uvular /r/ in Europe 183
10.10 *LAE*: Ph 242: *tongue* 183
10.11 *LAE*: Ph 243: *tongs* 183
10.12 Percentage Occurrences of Final Voiced Velar Stops in the West Midlands 184

Locality Codes: England

SLG	SLG Grid Ref.	Locality	SED	SLG	SLG Grid Ref.	Locality	SED
1. Northumberland				6.4	SD 9198	Muker	6 Y 6
1.1	NU 0139	Lowick	1 Nb 1	6.5	SD 9491	Askrigg	7
1.2	NU 2322	Embleton	2	6.6	SE 4289	Borrowby	9
1.3	NU 0202	Thropton	3	6.7	SE 2688	Bedale	8
1.4	NZ 2792	Ellington	4	6.8	SE 6183	Helmsley	10
1.5	NY 8576	Wark	5	6.9	SD 8574	Rillington	11
1.6	NZ 1366	Heddon-on-the-Wall	8	6.10	SD 6572	Burton-in-Lonsdale	12
1.7	NY 7064	Haltwhistle	7	6.11	SD 8172	Horton-in-Ribblesdale	13
1.8	NY 8455	Allendale	9	6.12	SE 5269	Easingwold	16
2. Cumbria				6.13	SE 1565	Pateley Bridge	15
2.1	NY 3768	Longtown	2 Cu 1	6.14	SE 0064	Grassington	14
2.2	NY 1750	Abbeytown	2	6.15	SD 9354	Gargrave	17
2.3	NY 5835	Hunsonby	5	6.16	SE 3650	Spofforth	18
2.4	NY 0830	Brigham	3	6.17	SE 6050	York	19
2.5	NY 3225	Threlkeld	4	6.18	SE 5737	Cawood	24
2.6	NY 5522	Great Strickland	4 We 1	**7. Isle of Man**			
2.7	NY 3915	Patterdale	2	7.1	SC 4199	Andreas	6a Man 1
2.8	NY 7410	Soulby	3	7.2	SC 2472	Ronague	2
2.9	NY 0603	Gosforth	2 Cu 6	**8. Lancashire**			
2.10	SD 3097	Coniston	5 La 1	8.1	SD 5074	Yealand	5 La 3
2.11	SD 4697	Staveley-in-Kendal	4 We 4	8.2	SD 5153	Dolphinholme	4
2.12	SD 7087	Dent	6 Y 5	8.3	SD 4048	Pilling	6
2.13	SD 3778	Cartmel	5 La 2	8.4	SD 3247	Fleetwood	5
3. Tyne and Wear				8.5	SD 4037	Thistleton	7
3.1	NZ 3272	Earsdon	1 Nb 6	8.6	SD 6435	Ribchester	8
3.2	NZ 3056	Washington	3 Du 1	8.7	SD 7634	Read	9
4. Durham				8.8	SD 5216	Eccleston	11
4.1	NZ 1055	Ebchester	3 Du 2	8.9	SD 4404	Bickerstaffe	13
4.2	NY 8539	Wearhead	3	**9. Humberside**			
4.3	NZ 1431	Witton-le-Wear	4	9.1	TA 0559	Nafferton	6 Y 20
4.4	NZ 3231	Bishop Middleham	5	9.2	SE 9136	Newbald	25
4.5	NZ 0023	Eggleston	6	9.3	TA 3421	Welwick	28
5. Cleveland				9.4	SE 9816	Saxby	10 L 2
5.1	NZ 6518	Skelton	6 Y 3	9.5	SE 8016	Eastoft	1
6. North Yorkshire				**10. West Yorkshire**			
6.1	NZ 1908	Melsonby	6 Y 1	10.1	SE 3034	Leeds	6 Y 23
6.2	NZ 5208	Stokesley	2	10.2	SE 1430	Wibsey	22
6.3	NZ 8006	Egton	4	10.3	SD 9827	Heptonstall	21
				10.4	SE 2418	Thornhill	26

SLG	SLG Grid Ref.	Locality	SED
10.5	SE 4618	Carleton	6 Y 27
10.6	SE 0915	Golcar	29
10.7	SE 2210	Skelmanthorpe	31
10.8	SE 1106	Holmbridge	30
11. Merseyside			
11.1	SD 3419	Marshside	5 La 10
11.2	SJ 4585	Halewood	14
12. Greater Manchester			
12.1	SD 7411	Harwood	5 La 12
13. South Yorkshire			
13.1	SK 3393	Ecclesfield	6 Y 32
13.2	SK 5993	Tickhill	33
13.3	SK 3587	Sheffield	34
14. Lincolnshire			
14.1	TA 1610	Keelby	10 L 3
14.2	SK 9293	Willoughton	4
14.3	TF 1590	Tealby	5
14.4	TF 1378	Wragby	6
14.5	TF 3877	Swaby	7
14.6	TF 3564	Old Bolingbroke	8
14.7	TF 0658	Scopwick	9
14.8	SK 8753	Beckingham	10
14.9	SK 9450	Fulbeck	11
14.10	TF 2835	Sutterton	12
14.11	TF 0123	Swinstead	13
14.12	TF 4323	Lutton	14
14.13	TF 2310	Crowland	15
15. Derbyshire			
15.1	SK 0092	Charlesworth	8 Db 1
15.2	SK 2083	Bamford	2
15.3	SK 0472	Burbage	3
15.4	SK 2164	Youlgreave	4
15.5	SK 4159	Stonebroom	5
15.6	SK 2050	Kniveton	6
15.7	SK 2333	Sutton-on-the-Hill	7
16. Nottinghamshire			
16.1	SK 7685	North Wheatley	9 Nt 1
16.2	SK 5671	Cuckney	2
16.3	SK 8270	South Clifton	3
16.4	SK 6351	Oxton	4
17. Cheshire			
17.1	SJ 5475	Kingsley	7 Ch 1
17.2	SJ 9575	Rainow	2
17.3	SJ 8067	Swettenham	3
17.4	SJ 4154	Farndon	4
17.5	SJ 6543	Audlem	5

SLG	SLG Grid Ref.	Locality	SED
18. Staffordshire			
18.1	SK 0858	Warslow	12 St 1
18.2	SJ 8557	Mow Cop	2
18.3	SK 0742	Alton	3
18.4	SJ 8938	Barlaston	4
18.5	SJ 8426	Ellenhall	5
18.6	SK 1223	Hoar Cross	6
18.7	SK 0817	Mavesyn Ridware	7
18.8	SJ 8713	Lapley	8
18.9	SK 2112	Edingale	9
18.10	SK 2106	Wigginton	10
18.11	SO 8891	Himley	11
19. Salop			
19.1	SJ 2835	Weston Rhyn	11 Sa 1
19.2	SJ 5533	Prees	2
19.3	SJ 2620	Llanymynech	3
19.4	SJ 6716	Kinnersley	5
19.5	SJ 4114	Montford	4
19.6	SO 2598	Chirbury	6
19.7	SO 4395	All Stretton	7
19.8	SO 7795	Hilton	8
19.9	SO 5085	Diddlebury	10
19.10	SO 3081	Clun	9
19.11	SO 7180	Kinlet	11
20. Leicestershire			
20.1	SK 7431	Harby	13 Lei 1
20.2	SK 5022	Hathern	2
20.3	SK 6117	Seagrave	3
20.4	SK 3614	Packington	4
20.5	SK 7414	Great Dalby	6
20.6	SK 4810	Markfield	5
20.7	SK 9408	Empingham	14 R 1
20.8	SK 3201	Sheepy Magna	13 Lei 7
20.9	SP 7598	Goadby	8
20.10	SP 6997	Carlton Curlieu	9
20.11	SP 8797	Lyddington	14 R 2
20.12	SP 5087	Ullesthorpe	13 Lei 10
21. Norfolk			
21.1	TR 7637	Docking	21 Nf 1
21.2	TF 9434	Great Snoring	2
21.3	TG 1728	Blickling	3
21.4	TF 7221	Grimston	4
21.5	TF 9820	North Elmham	5
21.6	TF 3818	Ludham	6
21.7	TF 9607	Shipdham	9
21.8	TF 5104	Outwell	7
21.9	TF 7602	Gooderstone	8
21.10	TG 4201	Reedham	11
21.11	TM 1397	Ashwellthorpe	10
21.12	TM 2185	Pulham St Mary the Virgin	12
21.13	TM 0081	Garboldisham	13

SLG	SLG Grid Ref.		Locality	SED	SLG	SLG Grid Ref.		Locality	SED
22. Cambridgeshire					**29. Buckinghamshire**				
22.1	TL	5284	Little Downham	20 C 1	29.1	SP	6533	Tingewick	26 Bk1
22.2	TL	3080	Warboys	19 Hu 1	29.2	SP	8525	Stewkley	2
22.3	TL	0967	Kimbolton	2	29.3	SP	8812	Buckland	4
22.4	TL	3163	Elsworth	20 C 2	29.4	SP	6908	Long Crendon	3
					29.5	SU	9495	Coleshill	5
23. Warwickshire					**30. Oxfordshire**				
23.1	SP	2393	Nether Whitacre	17 Wa 1	30.1	SP	4725	Steeple Aston	25 Ox 2
23.2	SP	3272	Stoneleigh	3	30.2	SP	2523	Kingham	1
23.3	SP	4661	Napton-on-the-Hill	4	30.3	SP	5214	Islip	3
23.4	SP	1359	Aston Cantlow	5	30.4	SP	4309	Eynsham	4
23.5	SP	3355	Lighthorne	6	30.5	SU	3497	Buckland	33 Brk 1
23.6	SP	2540	Shipston-on-Stour	7	30.6	SU	6695	Cuxham	25 Ox 5
					30.7	SU	3089	Uffington	33 Brk 2
24. West Midlands					30.8	SU	7478	Binfield Heath	25 Ox 6
24.1	SP	1572	Hockley Heath	17 Wa 2	**31. Gloucestershire**				
					31.1	SO	8729	Deerhurst	24 Gl 1
25. Northamptonshire					31.2	SP	0029	Gretton	2
25.1	TL	0791	Warmington	18 Nth 1	31.3	SP	1714	Sherborne	5
25.2	SP	6480	Welford	2	31.4	SO	8307	Whiteshill	4
25.3	SP	8771	Little Harrowden	3	31.5	SO	6005	Bream	3
25.4	SP	6959	Kislingbury	4	31.6	SO	7303	Slimbridge	6
25.5	SP	5545	Sulgrave	5	**32. Hertfordshire**				
					32.1	TL	3337	Therfield	28 Hrt 1
26. Suffolk					32.2	TL	2118	Codicote	2
26.1	TL	7371	Tuddenham	22 Sf 1	32.3	TL	1713	Wheathampstead	3
26.2	TM	3968	Yoxford	3					
26.3	TM	1065	Mendlesham	2	**33. Essex**				
26.4	TL	7046	Kedington	4	33.1	TL	5042	Great Chesterford	29 Ess 1
26.5	TM	0044	Kersey	5	33.2	TL	8240	Belchamp Walter	2
					33.3	TL	6836	Cornish Hall End	3
27. Hereford and Worcester					33.4	TL	5428	Henham	4
27.1	SO	9679	Romsley	16 Wo 1	33.5	TL	9527	West Bergholt	6
27.2	SO	8470	Hartlebury	2	33.6	TM	1125	Little Bentley	7
27.3	SO	5267	Brimfield	15 He 1	33.7	TL	8024	Stisted	5
27.4	SO	7162	Clifton-on-Teme	16 Wo 4	33.8	TL	8916	Tiptree	9
27.5	SO	9662	Hanbury	3	33.9	TL	6214	High Easter	8
27.6	SO	3356	Lyonshall	15 He 7	33.10	TM	0414	East Mersea	10
27.7	SO	4051	Weobley	2	33.11	TL	4509	Netteswell	11
27.8	SO	7347	Cradley	3	33.12	TL	7807	Little Baddow	12
27.9	SP	0546	Offenham	16 Wo 6	33.13	TL	9903	Tillingham	13
27.10	SP	0943	Bretforton	7	33.14	TQ	5998	Doddinghurst	14
27.11	SO	8642	Earls Croome	5	33.15	TQ	8994	Canewdon	15
27.12	SO	5938	Checkley	15 He 4					
27.13	SO	3228	Longtown	5	**34. Wiltshire**				
27.14	SO	5417	Whitchurch	6	34.1	SU	0494	Ashton Keynes	32 W 1
					34.2	ST	9478	Sutton Benger	2
28. Bedfordshire					34.3	SU	0969	Avebury	3
28.1	SP	9452	Turvey	27 Bd 1					
28.2	TL	1352	Great Barford	2					
28.3	TL	0330	Harlington	3					

SLG	SLG Grid Ref.		Locality	SED
34.4	SU	2261	Burbage	32 W 4
34.5	SP	9056	Steeple Ashton	5
34.6	SU	1448	Netheravon	6
34.7	ST	9041	Sutton Veny	7
34.8	SU	0028	Fovant	8
34.9	SU	2423	Whiteparish	9
35. Avon				
35.1	ST	6684	Latteridge	24 Gl 7
35.2	ST	7266	Weston	31 So 1
35.3	ST	2118	Blagdon	2
36. Middlesex				
36.1	TQ	3585	Hackney	30 MxL 2
36.2	TQ	0577	Harmondsworth	1
37. Berkshire				
37.1	SU	4682	West Ilsley	33 Brk 3
37.2	TQ	0175	Horton	26 Bk 6
37.3	SU	3564	Inkpen	33 Brk 4
37.4	SU	7264	Swallowfield	5
38. Surrey				
38.1	TQ	2255	Walton-on-the-Hill	34 Sr 1
38.2	TQ	0651	East Clandon	2
38.3	TQ	1444	Coldharbour	3
38.4	TQ	3244	Outwood	4
38.5	SU	9039	Thursley	5
39. Kent				
39.1	TQ	8275	Stoke	35 K 1
39.2	TQ	5566	Farningham	2
39.3	TR	2756	Staple	3
39.4	TQ	9253	Warren Street	4
39.5	TR	2146	Denton	5
39.6	TQ	7337	Goudhurst	6
39.7	TQ	9529	Appledore	7
40. Hampshire				
40.1	SU	3450	Hatherden	39 Ha 1
40.2	SU	5650	Oakley	2
40.3	SU	5832	Alresford	4
40.4	SU	3631	King's Somborne	3
40.5	SU	6414	Hambledon	5
40.6	SU	2103	Burley	6
40.7	SZ	5277	Whitwell (Isle of Wight)	7
41. Somerset				
41.1	ST	4348	Wedmore	31 So 3
41.2	ST	6848	Coleford	4
41.3	SS	9343	Wootton Courtenay	5
41.4	ST	2042	Stogursey	31 So 6
41.5	ST	0937	Stogumber	7
41.6	SS	8435	Withypool	8
41.7	SS	9531	Brompton Regis	9
41.8	ST	3426	Stoke St Gregory	10
41.9	ST	7023	Horsington	11
41.10	ST	2119	Pitminster	12
41.11	ST	4412	Merriott	13
42. Devon				
42.1	SS	6744	Parracombe	37 D 1
42.2	SS	6230	Swimbridge	2
42.3	SS	4721	Weare Giffard	3
42.4	SS	7112	Chawleigh	4
42.5	SY	1398	Gittisham	5
42.6	SX	6593	South Zeal	6
42.7	SX	9186	Kennford	7
42.8	SX	5177	Peter Tavy	8
42.9	SX	7176	Widecombe	9
42.10	SX	6059	Cornwood	10
42.11	SX	8050	Blackawton	11
43. West Sussex				
43.1	TQ	1633	Warnham	40 Sx 1
43.2	SU	7820	East Harting	2
43.3	SU	9715	Sutton	3
44. East Sussex				
44.1	TQ	4323	Fletching	40 Sx 4
44.2	TQ	5717	Horam	5
44.3	TQ	4707	Firle	6
45. Dorset				
45.1	ST	9917	Handley	38 Do 1
45.2	ST	7603	Ansty	2
45.3	SY	3995	Whitchurch Canonicorum	3
45.4	SY	6085	Portesham	4
45.5	ST	7509	Kingston	5
46. Cornwall				
46.1	SS	2511	Kilkampton	36 Co 1
46.2	SX	2281	Altarnun	2
46.3	SX	0071	Egloshayle	3
46.4	SW	9745	St Ewe	4
46.5	SW	5937	Gwinear	5
46.6	SW	4025	St Buryan	6
46.7	SW	6719	Mullion	7

Note

The *SLG* base map is based on National Grid references to SED localities on the Ordnance Survey maps. These references are listed above, and where necessary were supplemented from *Bartholomew's Gazetteer of Britain*. A difference of one unit in the figure references represents one kilometre on the ground. These references are inevitably approximate averages but within this degree of tolerance they are for all practical purposes accurate and form the unequivocal basis for the strict North-South allocation of locality numbers. The *SLG* base map revises both the grid references in SED and the base maps of SED and *LAE* so that the sequentially higher North-South locality numbers within a county parallel the progressively lower North-South grid references. The grid references are reinforced by careful plotting of each locality dot, although it should be borne in mind that in the scale of reproduction here a locality dot itself represents about ten kilometres.

Locality Codes: Wales

SAWD		Grid Ref.		Locality	SAWD		Grid Ref.		Locality
Gn				*Gwynedd*	P	22	SO	1646	Painscastle
Gn	1	SH	3779	Trefor	P	23	SO	0040	Upper Chapel
Gn	2	SH	6079	Llangoed	P	24	SN	8729	Trecastle
Gn	3	SH	7777	Gyffin	P	25	SO	1534	Talgarth
Gn	4	SH	7667	Dolgarrog	P	26	SO	1122	Talybont-on-Usk
Gn	5	SH	4954	Talysarn					
Gn	6	SH	7956	Betws-y-Coed	Dy				*Dyfed*
Gn	7	SH	2632	Botwnnog	Dy	1	SN	6895	Furnace
Gn	8	SH	5935	Llanfihangel-y-Traethu	Dy	2	SN	5979	Rhydyfelin
Gn	9	SH	9039	Fron-Goch	Dy	3	SN	5167	Llanon
Gn	10	SH	7922	Rhydymain	Dy	4	SN	6759	Tregaron
					Dy	5	SN	5045	Drefach
Cl				*Clwyd*	Dy	6	SM	9438	Goodwick
Cl	1	SH	9269	Llanfair Talhaiarn	Dy	7	SN	2038	Boncath
Cl	2	SJ	0879	Trelawnyd	Dy	8	SN	2641	Cenarth
Cl	3	SJ	2764	Buckley	Dy	9	SN	6136	Llansawel
Cl	4	SJ	1355	Llanfair Dyffryn Clwyd	Dy	10	SN	7730	Myddfai
Cl	5	SJ	0541	Cynwyd	Dy	11	SM	7525	St David's
Cl	6	SJ	3741	Overton	Dy	12	SM	9627	Wolf's Castle
Cl	7	SJ	0061	Nantglyn	Dy	13	SM	9220	Camrose
					Dy	14	SN	0218	Wiston
P				*Powys*	Dy	15	SN	1623	Login
P	1	SJ	0526	Llangynog	Dy	16	SN	3724	Newchurch
P	2	SJ	1820	Llanfechain	Dy	17	SN	5919	Gelli Aur
P	3	SH	9911	Foel	Dy	18	SN	6115	Llandybie
P	4	SJ	1112	Pont Robert	Dy	19	SM	7908	Marloes
P	5	SJ	2111	Guilsfield	Dy	20	SM	9909	Llangwm
P	6	SH	8204	Cemmaes Road	Dy	21	SN	3011	Laugharne
P	7	SN	8892	Staylittle	Dy	22	SN	3610	Ferryside
P	8	SN	9696	Carno	Dy	23	SN	5601	Llangennech
P	9	SO	0999	Tregynon	Dy	24	SR	8603	Angle
P	10	SJ	2201	Forden	Dy	25	SN	0801	St Florence
P	11	SO	0288	Llandinam					
P	12	SO	1490	Kerry	WG				*West Glamorgan*
P	13	SO	2694	Churchstoke	WG	1	SN	7000	Glais
P	14	SN	9080	Llangurig	WG	2	SN	8202	Resolven
P	15	SN	9668	Rhayader	WG	3	SS	4291	Llangennith
P	16	SO	1073	Llanbister	WG	4	SS	4992	Llanrhidian
P	17	SO	2574	Knucklas	WG	5	SS	4785	Horton
P	18	SO	3372	Stanage Park	WG	6	SS	5889	Bishopston
P	19	SN	9656	Llanafanfawr					
P	20	SO	2161	New Radnor	MG				*Mid Glamorgan*
P	21	SN	8647	Llanwrtyd	MG	1	SN	9408	Penderyn

SAWD		Grid Ref.		Locality
MG	2	SN	9595	Porth
MG	3	SS	8974	St Brides Major
SG				*South Glamorgan*
SG	1	SS	9577	Llangan
SG	2	ST	0876	Peterston-super-Ely
SG	3	SS	9768	Llantwit Major
SG	4	ST	0570	Llancarfan
Gw				*Gwent*
Gw	1	SO	3322	Pandy
Gw	2	SO	1703	Manmoel
Gw	3	SO	3109	Llanofer
Gw	4	SO	4814	Rockfield

SAWD		Grid Ref.		Locality
Gw	5	SO	3701	Usk
Gw	6	SO	5300	Tintern
Gw	7	ST	3395	Llanddewi Fach
Gw	8	ST	2582	Marshfield
Gw	9	ST	4386	Undy

Note

It is from these references, which are reproduced from information supplied by David Parry in collaboration with John Kirk and based on the Ordnance Survey National Grid, that the SAWD localities have been plotted in Map 1.2.

Abbreviations

AES   *Atlas of English Sounds*, E. Kolb, B. Glauser, W. Elmer, R. Stamm (Francke, Bern, 1979)

AIr   Anglo-Irish

ALE   Atlas Linguarum Europae

ALE   *Atlas Linguarum Europae*, vol. 1 — cartes, premier fascicule, and vol. 1, premier fascicule, par M. Alinei *et al.* (Van Gorcum, Assen, 1983)

AW   Anglo-Welsh

EDD   *English Dialect Dictionary*, J. Wright (ed.) 6 vols. (Oxford University Press, London, 1898-1905)

EDG   *English Dialect Grammar*, J. Wright (Frowde, Oxford, 1905)

Ir   Irish

L   Latin

LAE   *The Linguistic Atlas of England*, H. Orton, S. Sanderson, and J. Widdowson (eds.) (Croom Helm, London, 1978)

LANE   *Linguistic Atlas of New England*, 3 vols., in 6 parts, H. Kurath *et al.* (Brown University Press, Providence, 1939-43)

LAS   *The Linguistic Atlas of Scotland*: Scots Section, 2 vols., J.Y. Mather and H.-H. Speitel (Croom Helm, London, 1975-77)

LASID   *Linguistic Atlas and Survey of Irish Dialects*, 4 vols., H. Wagner (ed.) (Dublin Institute for Advanced Studies, Dublin, 1958-69)

LAUM   *The Linguistic Atlas of the Upper Midwest*, 3 vols., H.B. Allen (University of Minnesota Press, Minneapolis, 1973-6)

LGW   *The Linguistic Geography of Wales*, A. Thomas (University of Wales Press, Cardiff, 1973)

LSS   The Linguistic Survey of Scotland

ME   Middle English

OE   Old English

OED   *Oxford English Dictionary*, with supplement, ed. J.A.H. Murray *et al.* (eds.) (Clarendon Press, Oxford, 1933)

ON   Old Norse

pp   Past participle

RP   Received Pronunciation

SAWD   The Survey of Anglo-Welsh Dialects

SAWD   *The Survey of Anglo-Welsh Dialects*, vol. 1: *The South-east*, vol. 2: *The South-west* ([privately published], Swansea, 1977-9)

SED   The Survey of English Dialects

SED   *The Survey of English Dialects (B): The Basic Material*, 4 vols., each in 3 parts, H. Orton *et al.* (E.J. Arnold, Leeds, 1962-71)

SEU   The Survey of English Usage

SLG   *Studies in Linguistic Geography*

SND   *The Scottish National Dictionary*, 10 vols., W. Grant and D.D. Murison (eds.) (The Scottish National Dictionary Association, Aberdeen and Edinburgh, 1929-76)

TLS   The Tyneside Linguistic Survey

TRS   The Tape-recorded Survey of Hiberno-English Speech

WGE   *A Word Geography of England*, H. Orton and N. Wright (Seminar Press, New York and London, 1975)

THE INTERNATIONAL PHONETIC ALPHABET

(Revised to 1979)

CONSONANTS (Pulmonic air-stream mechanism)

	Bilabial	Labiodental	Dental, Alveolar, or Post-alveolar	Retroflex	Palato-alveolar	Palatal	Velar	Uvular	Labial-Palatal	Labial-Velar	Pharyngeal	Glottal
Nasal	m	ɱ	n	ɳ		ɲ	ŋ	N				
Plosive	p b		t d	ʈ ɖ		c ɟ	k g	q ɢ		k͡p g͡b		ʔ
(Median) Fricative	ɸ β	f v	θ ð s z	ʂ ʐ	ʃ ʒ	ç ʝ	x ɣ	χ ʁ		ʍ	ħ ʕ	h ɦ
(Median) Approximant		ʋ	ɹ	ɻ		j			ɥ	w		
Lateral Fricative			ɬ ɮ									
Lateral (Approximant)			l	ɭ		ʎ						
Trill			r					ʀ				
Tap or Flap			ɾ	ɽ				ʀ				

CONSONANTS (non-pulmonic air-stream)

	Bilabial	Dental, Alveolar, or Post-alveolar	Velar
Ejective	p'	t'	k'
Implosive	ɓ	ɗ	ɠ
(Median) Click	ʘ	ʇ	
Lateral Click		ʖ	

VOWELS

	Front		Back
Close	i y	ɨ ʉ	ɯ u
	ɪ ʏ		ʊ
Half-close	e ø	ə	ɤ o
Half-open	ɛ œ	ɐ ɞ	ʌ ɔ
Open	a ɶ		ɑ ɒ

Unrounded   Rounded

OTHER SYMBOLS

- ɕ, ʑ Alveolo-palatal fricatives
- ʃ, ʒ Palatalized ʃ, ʒ
- ɼ Alveolar fricative trill
- ɺ Alveolar lateral flap
- ɧ Simultaneous ʃ and x
- ʄ Variety of ʃ resembling s, etc.
- ɩ = ɪ
- ʊ = ʊ
- ɝ = Variety of ə
- ɚ = r-coloured ə

DIACRITICS

- ̥ or ̊ Voiceless n̥ d̥
- ̬ Voiced s̬ t̬
- ʰ Aspirated tʰ
- ̤ Breathy-voiced b̤ a̤
- ̪ Dental t̪
- ̣ Labialized ṭ
- ̡ Palatalized t̡
- ˔ Velarized or Pharyngealized ɫ, t̴
- ̩ Syllabic n̩ l̩
- ̯ or ͜ Simultaneous sf (but see also under the heading Affricates)
- ̇ or · Raised ẹ, ẹ, ̣w
- ̣ or ˛ Lowered ẹ, e̡, ɛ̣ʁ
- ̈ Advanced u̟+, ̣
- ̠ or ̱ Retracted i̠, i-, ̱t
- ̈ Centralized ë
- ̃ Nasalized ã
- ˞ ̣, ɚ r-coloured aʴ
- ː Long aː
- ˑ Half-long aˑ
- ̆ Non-syllabic ŭ
- ̜ More rounded ɔ̜
- ̹ Less rounded yʿ

STRESS, TONE (PITCH)

ˈ stress, placed at beginning of stressed syllable : ˌ secondary stress : ˉ high level pitch, high tone : ˊ high rising : ˎ low level : ˏ high falling : ˋ low rising : ˆ low falling : ˇ rise-fall : ˇ fall-rise.

AFFRICATES can be written as digraphs, as ligatures, or with slur marks; thus ts tʃ dʒ : t͡s t͡ʃ d͡ʒ. c, ɟ may occasionally be used for tʃ, dʒ.

Contributors

The late G.B. Adams was Dialect Archivist at the Ulster Folk and Transport Museum

M.V. Barry is Senior Lecturer in English, The Queen's University of Belfast

Dr Beat Glauser is Privatdozent for English Philology, University of Basel

P.L. Henry is Professor of Old and Medieval English, University College, Galway

Dr Paul A. Johnston, Jr. is Lecturer in English Language, University of Edinburgh

John M. Kirk is Lecturer in English, The Queen's University of Belfast

R.K.S. Macaulay is Professor of Linguistics, Pitzer College, Claremont, California

David Parry is Lecturer in English, University College, Swansea

Stewart Sanderson, former Director of the Institute of Dialect and Folk Life Studies, is Harold Orton Fellow, University of Leeds

P.M. Tilling is Lecturer in English, The New University of Ulster, Coleraine

Wolfgang Viereck is Professor of English Linguistics and Medieval Studies, University of Bamberg

J.D.A. Widdowson is a Professor of English Language at the University of Sheffield and Director of the Centre for English Cultural Tradition and Language

Acknowledgements

The editors wish to express their gratitude to various institutions and individuals for their generous assistance and support in the preparation of this volume.

Our major debt is to the Universities of Leeds and Sheffield, who have provided research facilities and secretarial assistance, and have contributed to the costs of materials and travel during our editorial work. The University of Leeds has freely given us access to the collections of the Survey of English Dialects, while the University of Sheffield has provided two of the editors with specific research grants for travel. The Queen's University of Belfast has also contributed generously to the costs of cartography and photography.

We owe a considerable debt to our cartographers, Mrs Pauline Duncan of Sheffield and Mrs Gillian Alexander of Belfast, for their skill in translating draft maps into the finished products. Professor Viereck's maps were drawn in Bamberg by H. Sohmer. We are especially grateful to Mrs B.C. Moore for her exemplary typing of a difficult draft. Our thanks are also due to Mrs S.E. Donnelly and Mrs J. Wardman for typing assistance, and to Miss J. Alexander for her help in preparing final copy for printing.

Above all, we are indebted to the contributors for their patient co-operation over a long period, and to a number of colleagues who, while not contributors to the volume, have given us the benefit of their advice.

Our publishers, Croom Helm, have encouraged us throughout and have been generous in their financial provision for the costly process of producing the finished maps. We are indebted to them for permission to reproduce maps 8.1, 8.3, 9.2, 9.4, 10.2, 10.4, 10.10 and 10.11 and for examples 8.19c, 8.19d and 8.19e, and also to Francke Verlag, Bern, for maps 10.1 and 10.3, to Cambridge University Press for maps 10.8 and 10.9, to Gale Research Company, Detroit, for map 10.7, to the University of Michigan Press, Ann Arbor, for figure 6.1, and to the International Phonetic Association for the chart of the International Phonetic Alphabet.

But thou at home, without tide or gale,
Canst in thy map securely sail,
Seeing those painted countries, and so guess
By those fine shades their substances;
And from thy compass taking small advice
Buy'st travel at the lowest price.

Robert Herrick

1

Introduction: Principles and Practice in Linguistic Geography

JOHN M. KIRK, STEWART SANDERSON
AND J.D.A. WIDDOWSON

The ultimate origin of this volume of papers lies in the continuing debate between so-called 'traditional' dialectologists and those socio-linguists who have developed new approaches to dialect study in recent years. The initial impetus for the work came from John Kirk who has also been the principal architect of its direction and scope, the prime mover in assembling the papers and the overseer of the cartography. Kirk recognised that the publication of *The Linguistic Atlas of England* marked not only the fulfilment of the central aim of the Survey of English Dialects, namely to make the bulk of its primary data available, but also constituted the starting-point for the investigation of this unique resource at a secondary level. His interests in contemporary and historical dialectology at Edinburgh, Bonn and Sheffield led him to explore possible new lines of enquiry which might be developed further from the present state of the art. At this point Stewart Sanderson and John Widdowson were drawn into the project, since they were working on similar lines in a series of projects based on the SED and arising from their co-editing of the *LAE*. This broadening of the editorial team did not, how-ever, materially alter the original scope of the book, and indeed the sharing of editorial responsibility brought benefits not only in the deepening of the analytical level but also in achieving a consensus among the three editors, thus capitalising on their very different exper-ience and contributing to a wider and more representative view of the subject as a whole.

It soon became clear that primary investiga-tion, using refined techniques based on the methodology of the SED, was continuing in Northern Ireland, the Irish Republic and in Wales, revealing both the strengths and weak-nesses of the traditional approach. At the same time, the SED came increasingly under attack from sociolinguists, mostly on the grounds of its supposedly outmoded approach.

The Basic Material volumes of the SED provided researchers with an opportunity to study the data in depth, and the interpretive maps in the *LAE* offered an alternative comple-mentary approach to the data based on Harold Orton's conception of the analytical role of linguistic geography. The Basic Material had already generated scholarly interest on the Continent, notably at the universities of Bamberg, Basel, Bergen, Bonn, Copenhagen, Erlangen-Nürnberg, Heidelberg, Helsinki and Stockholm, among others. At the same time, a number of younger scholars both on the Continent and in the British Isles, began to explore the material. Once the very substantial databases in the basic material and atlases of the linguistic surveys of England and Scotland became fully available their potential for further investigation became an immediately apparent and exciting prospect. Since scholars were responding to the data in different ways and in widely scattered locations, it was felt that to bring their work together in a single volume would provide them with a more specific focus and also reveal significant trends in current research which would be of interest not only to linguists but also to a wider audience.

Thus what this volume conveniently embraces is the scholarly tradition initiated and inspired by

Harold Orton and devoted to the acquisition and custodial charge of primary dialect material. In addition to those trained by Harold Orton, or following directly in the tradition he established, a number of other dialectologists have been anxious to study the SED material not only to discover its character and regularities but also to sample the contribution which the SED can make both to our overall knowledge of language and to the history and description of regional English in England during the mid-twentieth century. We also feel that there is a need for a volume which focuses on the drafting, coding and general production of linguistic atlases and on their analysis, decoding and general reception. Such a volume would create a context for comparison in which the principles and techniques of linguistic cartography could be discussed, refined and developed.

This volume therefore takes the SED as its starting-point, recognising the seminal influence of the Survey and its architects, Eugen Dieth and Harold Orton, whose pioneering endeavours, initiated in the 1930s, not only resulted in the only nationwide survey of English regional dialects but also provided the model for sister and daughter surveys in the British Isles and elsewhere. Among these one might note the Linguistic Survey of Scotland, the Survey of Anglo-Welsh Dialects and the Tape-recorded Survey of Hiberno-English Speech. Further afield, the Survey has always both looked to and drawn from similar work in the USA and Continental Europe. It has parallels with the fifty-year-old project the *Linguistic Atlas of the United States and Canada* (cf. Orton 1971), surveys and atlases in the United States and Canada, as well as in the research of Guy Lowman on both sides of the Atlantic, and in the surveys by other scholars in Europe. The definitive record of the genesis of the SED is to be found in the Introduction to *LAE* pp. 1-4, and the Survey's influence and interaction may be summarised in Figure 1.1.

The prominent position of the SED as the focal point for much dialectological research for some forty years has not always been an advantage. It would be naive to imagine, for example, that a methodology devised in the 1930s could stand the test of time without revealing certain shortcomings when measured against more recent developments. The important new approaches to dialectology which emerged in the late 1960s and the 1970s drew attention to the SED's concentration on the oldest stratum of the rural population. Fired with the voguish new enthusiasm to investigate urban usage across a randomly-chosen representative sample of age, sex and socio-economic class it was all too easy for a younger generation of dialectologists, with the benefit of hindsight, to point out what they saw as defects in the earlier methodology, whether in fieldwork or analysis. However, it must be said that, whatever its shortcomings, the Survey achieved what it set out to do. To expect it to alter course and attempt to absorb new and different methodologies is both misguided and unrealistic. It is to questions such as these that the contributors to this volume have turned their attention. Although they do not claim to answer the questions, they indicate the extent of the problems encountered in using the *SED* data, at the same time revealing its indispensability to English dialectology and its virtually unexploited potential for further investigation.

Large-scale dialect surveys require decisions about the presentation of their material in a convenient form for publication and reference. Although a number of such surveys present data by means of maps, the cartographical techniques lack uniformity, and often reflect the somewhat arbitrary and *ad hoc* basis on which localities were selected for fieldwork. The absence of a standard practice in choosing the locality network, and the considerable variety of techniques used, make it difficult to compare information and draw reliable conclusions. The problem is compounded by the tendency for individual surveys to be carried out independently, without

Figure 1.1: The Position of SED in Dialectology

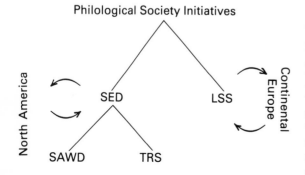

Philological Society Initiatives

North America

Continental Europe

SED   LSS

SAWD   TRS

reference to others, so that even those which have grown naturally out of the SED differ from it to some degree both in principle and in practice.

The editors of this volume had to face these problems afresh and explore ways in which linguistic cartography can be developed, not only to work towards more standardised procedures but also to take account of recent innovations. It is obviously desirable, for example, that data from such surveys as SAWD and TRS which utilise and extend the techniques of SED should be mapped in comparable ways. However, while this in principle should be straightforward, it is complicated by numerous factors, not least of which are the changes in county boundaries introduced by the recommendations of the Maude Commission in 1974. These changes alone suggest the need for a radical revision of older cartographical techniques and the production of a new map in which the SED fieldwork localities can be presented in the context of the new English counties. While it is of course obvious that county boundaries rarely coincide with isoglosses and seldom if ever constitute a reliable guide to patterns of dialect coherence, the network of fieldwork localities for the SED was drawn up county by county, not only for ease of reference but also with the aim of making its coverage as representative as possible. Since the SED constitutes the starting-point and the essential focus for several more recent surveys, it is important that the methods of presenting its wealth of material should be updated and, where possible, improved. Above all, such techniques should aim for greater clarity and accessibility, and establish a logical and comprehensive framework within which the data can be studied to the best effect in its present-day context.

In designing a new map of the SED localities we have been particularly concerned with techniques for numbering both localities and counties in a logical sequence. Alphabetic arrangement, for example, is inappropriate, and no single set of procedures has been devised which other surveys have uniformly adopted, each survey being idiosyncratic. Existing criteria governing the sequence of numbering have ranged from the visual (e.g. the convenience of geographical shape) to the practical (e.g. Harold Orton's plan for the SED locations, or the chronological ordering of the fieldworker as he makes his way, site after site, through his territory). In the

absence of uniformity we feel it is useful to propose a set of procedures for labelling localities on linguistic maps. These will be used in several of the papers presented here and constitute a logical system for such labelling in the future.

Map 1.1 displays the SED localities as they are now to be found in the post-1974 county system. The new counties have been numbered in strict order from North to South, the point of reference being the most northerly point of each county. The North-South principle ignores any implications arising from an East-West axis. The sequence thus begins in Northumberland (no. 1) and terminates in Cornwall (no. 46), the most northerly point of the sequence being further north than all other northernmost county points. The identification numbers of counties have been placed in the topmost corner of each so far as space permits.

Locality dots follow a similar pattern of allocation, with strict North-South ordering always giving precedence to the more northerly of two. Our authority for the location of the dots rests on the national grid references of the *Ordnance Survey*, supplemented occasionally by *Bartholomew's Gazetteer of Britain*, and these grid references are listed by locality number on pp. viii-xii (Locality codes: *England*). It follows from this principle that where two grid references are identical in respect of their North-South position, both dots will be correspondingly level on the map. There are twenty-one such instances in Map 1.1. We recognise, of course, that in drafting this new base map, it is impossible to achieve the ultimate degree of accuracy, since at this scale of reproduction a locality dot itself represents approximately ten miles on the map whereas one unit in the grid references comprises less than one mile. What John Kirk and the cartographers have achieved, however, is a much more accurate and satisfactory base map than that of the *LAE*. When two locality dots appear virtually or actually level on the map the eastern locality number is positioned fractionally lower, so as to reinforce the principle of strict uninterrupted North-South succession of grid references. As a general rule, the number of a given locality has been placed to the right of the dot, the mid section of the number being on the same level. Where this has not been possible, the number has been placed in the next best available position. The two SED

Map 1.1: SED Localities Arranged by New County Boundaries

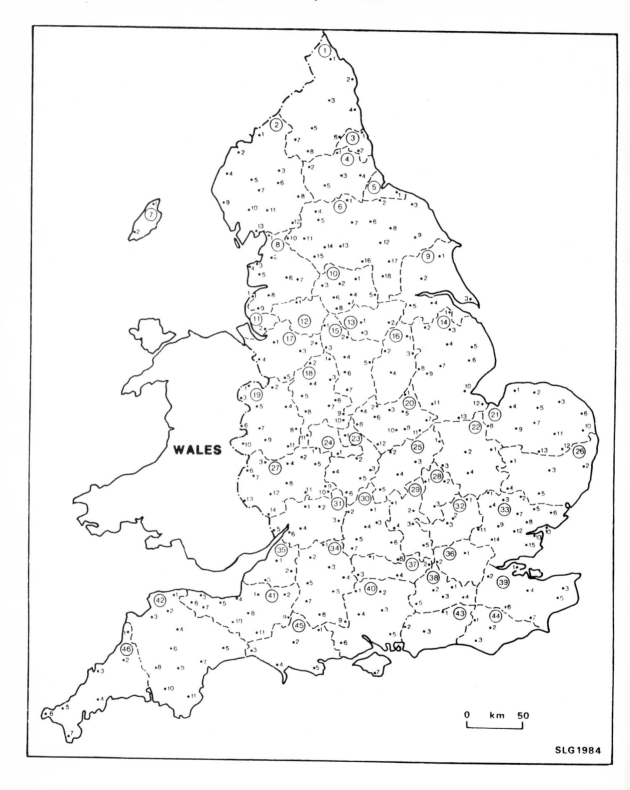

WALES

0 km 50

SLG 1984

localities in the Isle of Man are incorporated at the appropriate points on the North-South axis.

In addition to the grid references, on the basis of which the new numbering system was allocated, the list of locality codes for England includes the original SED locality numbers. It is hoped that the *SLG* code styles will clarify references to the new base map and allow comparison with *SED*, *LAE* and in due course with the *Atlas Linguarum Europae*.

Although the North-South principle is followed for most county and locality numbers in SED, it has never been stated and merely remains implied. Close scrutiny reveals that the principle is occasionally breached in the SED, and the *LAE* has retained these slight anomalies so as to be consistent with the county and locality listings of the Basic Material. When the SED was conducted, arrangements for social administration were different from what they are today. Just as the *LAE* is based on maps which reflect the local arrangements at the time of its preparation, so the new base map and a number of other maps in this volume reflect those of the present day, the English county and locality numbers fully conforming to the North-South principle. We do not think anyone should find these arrangements confusing or have any difficulty in following the numbering scheme.

No doubt after more research has been carried out along the lines discussed by Professor Wolfgang Viereck in this volume or by utilising the techniques of single-link cluster analysis and maximum spanning trees as Byron Morgan and David Shaw (1982) have done in a recent issue of *Lore and Language*, it will eventually be possible to draw a map of local dialect areas in England based entirely on internal evidence from the SED. Such research should, for example, confirm the presence and nature of significant linguistic diversity within the old county boundaries, especially in larger counties like Yorkshire and Lincolnshire. The lumping together of such features under a given county name allows insufficient discrimination and hampers comparison with localities in neighbouring counties. The new administrative districts tend to break up such large areas into smaller units which may prove helpful in identifying the range of dialect variation, and the developing techniques of dialectometry may also confirm the existence of dialect forms peculiar to some of the smaller counties.

The drafting of the new base map has been the responsibility of John Kirk who recognised the importance not only of updating the cartography to take account of the boundary changes but also of establishing a new logical principle for the sequence of county and locality numbers for the SED network. After the completion of the new map for England, our correspondence with David Parry made us aware that the extensive fieldwork undertaken in the SAWD was sufficiently advanced for the network of Welsh localities to be presented cartographically. It was therefore agreed that with the co-operation of David Parry the counties and localities covered by SAWD would be added to the new base map to represent English and Anglo-Welsh forms simultaneously. The advantages of Map 1.2 (new base map England and Wales) are obvious, since it allows comparability of SED and SAWD data and reveals how the two surveys are complementary and interdependent. The list of locality codes for Wales (pp. xiii-xiv) gives the locality codes for SAWD together with their national grid references. It is the first time that this complete list of Welsh localities has been published, and these codes also have their own style which has been used in Parry's paper. Several SED localities, however, were not included in the SAWD network. Firstly, the SED locality of Hanmer, formerly in Flintshire (SED locality 7 Ch 6) now in the county of Clwyd, is not among the seven SAWD localities in Clwyd. The data for Hanmer nevertheless remains compatible even though it was investigated some twenty years earlier. Secondly, the former county of Monmouthshire, now Gwent, originally investigated by SED, has now been surveyed afresh by SAWD using a different and denser network of localities. These complications illustrate the importance of bringing references to administrative boundaries up to date.

A minor drawback to the amalgamation of the maps for England and Wales is the fact that the locality numbers for Wales had already been decided, based on SED principles. While they for the most part follow a North-South axis, this principle is modified by the superimposition of an East-West axis as the eye scans down the page. Thus while the general progression of county abbreviations and locality numbers is from North to South, the principle established on the base map for England is not adhered to

Map 1.2: SED and SAWD Localities Arranged by New County Boundaries

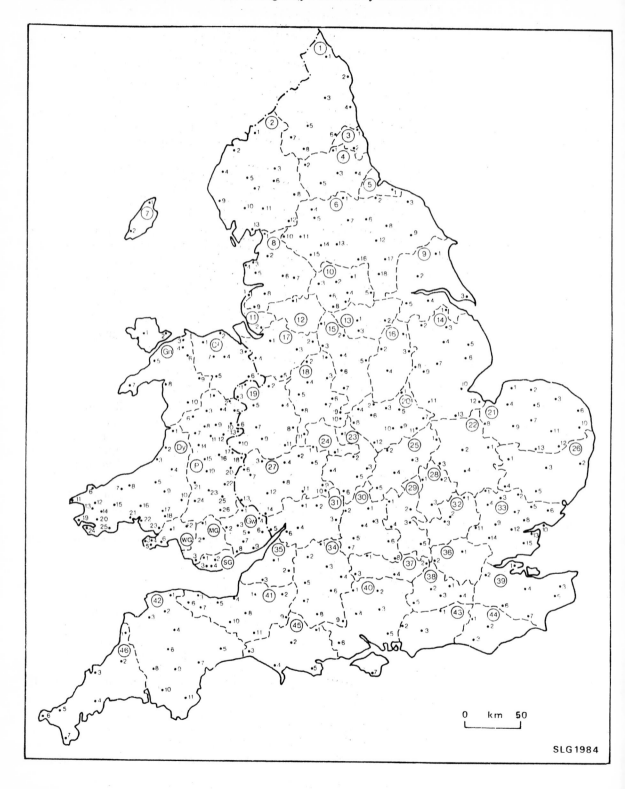

SLG 1984

strictly for Wales. However desirable it might be for the Welsh locations to follow a strict North-South principle it was clearly not practicable to change them at this late stage in the progress of SAWD, and indeed David Parry strongly defends the North-South + East-West system he employs. We are indebted to him for permission to use the SAWD county and locality references in Map 1.2 and for his assistance at every stage of the drafting process.

This volume also displays a diversity of cartographical coding techniques. This is hardly surprising as these techniques have been employed for a wide range of purposes, including a number of new ways of presenting dialect data analyses on the map. These are of course innovatory only in so far as their application to dialect is unfamiliar and therefore new. Although we hope that some of the horizons in linguistic mapping have been extended by the maps in this volume, we are aware that we are merely drawing on a much wider set of more or less well-established methods of coding and drafting no doubt familiar to geographers in other fields. Nevertheless, dialect geographers have been extremely reluctant to talk about the particular techniques they have employed in the past, appearing to take these techniques, as a *Hilfswissenschaft*, very much for granted.

It may be helpful at this point to remind ourselves of the two basic approaches adopted by linguistic geographers in the past. The first is to present the raw data on the map, either by printing the forms directly — the pioneering *méthode classique* of Gilliéron — or by coding the data by means of symbols which are printed at the map localities. The latter obviously conforms better to sound cartographic practice as the symbols, if compact in design, display the material evenly more or less where it is reported, whereas lexical items printed on maps suggest to the eye wider-spread distributions for longer words than shorter. The second approach, typified in the work of an earlier pioneer, Prince Bonaparte, is to indicate the general distributional area of a feature (or set of features in the Prince's dialect maps of England) by enclosing it with lines or hatching. From these two approaches, the use of symbols and of isoglosses, either separately or in conjunction, the methods of linguistic cartography have evolved, too often it seems without discussion.

As all drafting is a matter of deliberate choice,

we believe that the mapping process right up to the finished cartography should be made more explicit. One of the objectives of this volume is to draw attention to the functions which different coding techniques perform when it comes to mapping linguistic data, and to how the same technique may perform a broad range of functions. Quite apart from the need for greater explicitness in coding practice, it should now be possible to work towards the formulation of basic principles and maxims underlying all aspects of the mapping process in linguistic geography. Since the editors had the privilege of being party at some stage to the drafting of most of the 62 maps in this volume it seems appropriate to put on record some of the essential decisions taken in coding linguistic maps — decisions rarely discussed and all too easily taken for granted. They represent a much more complex set of choices than has been acknowledged hitherto. The following summary of coding options applies not only to individual maps in this volume but may also prove useful as general categories in linguistic geography as a whole.

Closed Symbols

Closed or black symbols normally represent the occurrence of a specific item at a particular locality. They are usually arbitrary, invariably small, and their use for representing contrastive variants or outliers in isoglossic and impressionistic mapping is well known. There are a number of variations on this basic principle of use, mostly when closed symbols co-occur with other types of symbol in the same map. In this volume the following variations on standard closed symbol practice are found:

i) In paper 7, Glauser uses the closed symbol in a negative sense to represent a form which is not interpreted in the map, sometimes the form of a cognate but historically different reflex, sometimes a form of doubtful origin. In these maps, the closed symbols actively contrast with numbers and open symbols.
ii) In Map 9.5 'Last corn sheaf — Ireland', euphemisms occur as responses instead of the basic lexical item itself. This contrast in response type is shown by the use of an open symbol for the euphemisms.
iii) In Map 9.6 'Last corn sheaf — Scotland',

some closed symbols represent localities whereas others represent the occurrence of the item over a large area, often a whole county or more. This contrast is brought out by using large, open symbols for the latter. The intention is to suggest, through the openness of the symbol, wider spatial implications than the actual extent of the symbol itself on the map.

iv) Map 8.5 refines this last technique through the use of hatching in the otherwise large open symbols.

v) Map 3.7 illustrates the use to which *SAWD* puts the active contrast between closed and open symbols when dealing wth outliers. This is one of the very few respects in which *SAWD* differs from *LAE*. The closed symbols represent the occurrence of the outlier instead of the prevailing local form, whereas open symbols represent the occurrence of both the outlier and the prevailing form. This contrastive use serves to reinforce what might usefully be thought of as the reductionist and expansionist sense of contrastive closed and open symbolisation. In this map the closed symbol cuts through the isoglossic representation of another item, whereas the open symbol, besides recording its own presence, lets the prevailing form cut through it.

vi) In Maps 9.1 and 9.5 closed symbols are contrasted with numerals. In both these maps so much data was to be presented in a symbolic style that it was necessary to classify the information by response type. Minor types occur once or in a few localities only, the uppermost limit being five; they are thus very local and are indicated numerically. These numbers, of course, have no absolute value. Major types consist of items which occur more than five times and which are more or less widespread; they are represented by closed shapes. Thus the distinctions between numbers and shapes may be taken as indicators of the frequency and distribution of the items they represent.

Open Symbols

Apart from the specific instances discussed above, our general practice in these papers is that open symbols are used to designate the absence of an item in a given locality, especially when the presence of the item elsewhere on the same map is indicated by the closed version of those symbols. Open symbols are mostly used in active contrast, and although in this volume they

do not occur exclusively in any map their use is demonstrated in the maps in paper 6 for localities 21.9 and 37.2. Their function is similar to closed symbols and many geographers seem to use both interchangeably. In linguistic geography, however, there is much to be said in favour of their being used contrastively. A modified version of this usage occurs in Map 8.2 where the open symbol represents the historical form which is being replaced by the reflex indicated by the closed symbol. Thus the areas with closed symbols are those where innovation is advancing, and those with open symbols are as yet uninfluenced by the newer forms. The replacement of open symbols by closed ones is a method of presenting historical expansion by substitution. Glauser, however, uses the open symbol as one of a number of additive styles. In his maps, an open circle, which represents optional /r/ insertion, may be added to the circumference of any other symbol.

Divided Symbols

i) A number of closed symbols do not merely contrast with open ones. Both closed and open symbols contrast with partially closed/partially open symbols as well. The TRS, for example, uses closed symbols to represent the oldest age-group of informants, open symbols for the youngest, and divided circle symbols for the middle-aged. This use contrasts with Kirk's historical choices which in his maps allow the older, open symbols to receive the newer and innovatory closed symbols, thus imparting some sense of direction to linguistic progression through time. Such an interpretation, however, is hardly possible from the present TRS maps, since their symbols represent two types of outliers for any one item across an otherwise isoglossic border: Northern forms in the Southern area, Southern forms in the Northern area.

ii) The other main variety is where the degree of closedness and openness is not equal, and possibly varying from symbol to symbol. Such an instance is Map 8.4 which makes use of symbols which can vary in their significance for an item for which as many as five types of response were recorded. Thus the occurrence of any one of these possible five responses, as well as the co-occurrence of more than one, can be indicated conveniently within each circle.

Crosses

i) Following *LAE* the St Andrew's cross represents the absence of data in the SAWD maps of paper 3.

ii) The St George's cross is used by Glauser as one of his additional markers to represent the occurrence of a form similar to the one already mapped but which differs from it by being one stage behind in its phonological development.

Letters

Letters are used as symbols in *SAWD* maps to represent lexical items, usually by taking the first letter of the particular item. This is a further distinction between SAWD and SED.

Numbers

Numbers may be symbols of their own value or may be arbitrary symbols of some other value. Usually the former are not in contrast with other types of symbolisation within the same map. An example is Map 7.7 where the numbers represent discrete and equally distributed points on a gradient of change within a transition zone. In Maps 9.1 and 9.5, by contrast, the numbers have no value of their own and merely contrast with closed symbols to represent very local minor types. An intermediate use of numbers is also employed by Glauser in Maps 7.2 to 7.6, whereby numbers represent the various stages of scaling or development in a unified phonological process. Other types of symbol would not have captured the linearity of this process.

Glauser's maps display considerable active contrast in the deployment of other types of symbolisation in addition to the numbers of his main line of analysis. Viereck's maps adopt a similar technique. Actual arithmetical scores by locality are mapped directly within open symbols which, like those described above, may be multi-valued. Not only do these symbols contain a statement of an actual data count, they are also hatched in various styles — the hatching representing the relative value of this actual number for either coherency or identity. In short, these maps provide both the data and an interpretation of its value side by side.

Lines

Lines on maps conventionally represent the explicit spatial distribution of the data. They appear to subdivide the map and denote both the extents or ranges and the outer limits of data distribution. Lines summarise distributional information about response types which are common or identical in one area, but differ from those in another. They are a convenient means of displaying the size of each area and the relationships between areas. However much a line on the map might suggest a line on the land, linguistic geographers are at least agreed that this is not their intention and that what the lines represent on the map are transition zones surrounding or between areas of data distribution. As several papers in this volume confirm afresh, transition zones are themselves anything but monolithic and are likely to have a complex structure and extend over a considerable geographical area.

Dialectologists are accustomed to distinguishing, and sometimes confusing, two main types of line: isoglosses and heteroglosses. Both are somewhat controversial (cf. Freudenberg 1966, Speitel 1969) and, although similar in function, they differ in a number of ways.

i) *Isoglosses* demarcate contiguous areas in which contrasting forms occur. The isogloss is an arbitrary arrangement which is open to revision by many factors, as David Graddol has demonstrated by the use of overlays in his Open University course book *Language Variety and Diversity* (Graddol 1981: map 24). The use of isoglosses as a mapping technique raises a number of problems. For instance, as 'lines' they appear explicit but in reality they represent decisions about data. The direction they follow on the map, however, is usually midway between contrastive points among the data in question, and in that sense is arbitrary. Whereas localities determine the course of the isogloss, it is perhaps worth noting that it is not necessarily possible to draw conclusions from the position of an isogloss about localities on either side of it. Other devices are required to represent that information. The isogloss merely offers an interpretation of spatial distribution and thus is explicit only in so far as it generalises distributions.

Revisions of its direction might result from decisions about analysis (such as foregrounding some forms at the expense of others) or from network densening. When the use of isoglosses is accompanied by other types of symbolisation, as in a number of maps in this volume and in *LAE*, the force of its generalisation might be better thought of as a simplification.

ii) *Heteroglosses* simply state (or induce) the distribution for which there is mappable evidence. It is useful to think of them as the outermost limits, or the perimeter, of concentricity, such as the line delimiting /a/ in *porridge* in Map 7.2. Like isoglosses they usually demarcate the spatial distribution of contiguous occurrences but, unlike isoglosses, they need not. Further, whereas isoglosses are overt and prominent, inclined to draw attention to themselves, heteroglosses are covert and recessive, inclined to draw attention to the concentric distribution of the homogeneous data within their perimeters.

Hatching

This usually denotes the occurrence of a particular item in a locality or a number of contiguous localities. It is symbolic, and unless otherwise constrained is similar to the heteroglossic mapping style in that it displays the extent of contiguous occurrence for each item as seen, for example, in *LAS*. An extreme but mimetic form of hatching is used in Map 7.7 where blanket scores of 0 per cent and 100 per cent are separated by a transition zone. The transition zone is delimited by the boundaries (or heteroglosses) of these northern and southern areas, each area being totally black. Area hatching can occur in conjunction with symbols for individual localities. This has been one of Glauser's techniques for mapping the absence of data in Map 7.1. One problem with its deployment in this way is that it tends to draw attention to itself, whereas the use of the St Andrew's cross for the same function elsewhere might be thought less obtrusive. Maps 10.5 and 10.12 include straightforward mapping of percentage occurrences for which conventional hatching is sufficiently functional to show the contrast between the clearly defined distributions. Hatching is also deployed in Viereck's maps to represent the contrast of a relative value with an absolute value. In these choroplethic maps the hatching represents degrees of an interpretation which have been statistically permutated and denotes a number of different classes as well as their intervals.

The Absence of Data

Maps based on large surveys should not ignore

any material without acknowledging the fact. There are all sorts of reasons why data is sometimes omitted for particular localities in specific maps. In these instances the use of the St Andrew's cross, a mark of cancellation established in *LAE*, seems both simple and serviceable, although a variety of other symbols is employed, including open symbols and hatching, among the maps presented here. Clearly this is a case where consistency and uniformity of practice would be advantageous.

Quantitative Maps

This volume presents a number of quantitative analyses of dialect material. As they are all unfamiliar ground to the linguistic cartographer and as we expect that further maps along these lines will be drafted in the future, it seems useful to summarise the mapping techniques employed in the quantitative maps in this volume. We distinguish categorically between numbers as symbols representing data (which may be used arbitrarily) and numbers (or statistics) as data to be symbolised. For actual low scores, usually under 10, numbers have been used directly, in full mimesis of their own value. For percentages of a single and non-contrastive item, without further complications, conventional lined hatching has been employed impressionistically. For computational permutations where all the numbers are relative to each other, but related to specific actual numbers for each locality, both these actual numbers and a hatch are combined within an open locality symbol. The interplay in this volume between statistics, quantification and cartography represents the first sustained attempt to investigate the structure of regional English in Britain and Ireland along these lines.

The craft of map making has long been taken for granted by linguistic geographers. It is all too easy to plot a map without fully considering its preparation and reception. Although not all the maps in this volume were drafted specifically for it, it contains a total of 62 maps, mostly new and innovative, and all recent. The presentation of such a substantial number, with their varied styles, merits more detailed consideration of the mapping processes involved, particularly along more theoretical lines than hitherto and on a more formal level of linguistic description.

Certain factors were clear at the outset. For instance, all the maps obviously deal with data of one kind or another. They present, analyse, contrast, and interpret the data. In so far as they induce an understanding in the reader, they also make a statement about the geographical distribution of the material. A map has to fuse these clearly differentiable activities into a single communicative transaction or exchange by means of coding.

Earlier in this Introduction we detailed the range of graphic coding techniques employed in this volume, not all of which have hitherto been associated with linguistic mapping. Some devices share a number of functions. In certain maps, for instance, the coding appears to have a straightforward and relatively unsophisticated function, representing data unencumbered by analysis or without an implied contrast, whereas in others it represents a much deeper level of analysis, in some cases even combining more than one layer or dimension of analysis, and with clear contrastive implications. A given map may be drafted in a single cartographical style, whereas others may combine more than one style to reproduce a greater analytical sophistication by means of active contrast. Thus what induces a reader's understanding of the mapper's intentions is as much *what* mapping styles are employed as *how* these styles are deployed in relation to each other.

During John Kirk's discussion of the draft maps with the contributors, it became clear that there were a few features which kept recurring and about which questions were frequently asked. He began to think of them as 'principles', and found that despite the range of coding decisions and the various alternative coding practices, there were certain other, deeper, underlying characteristics of the language map which always seemed to be present. In a sense, this was simply a response to what most linguistic geographers had happily taken for granted for years; in another sense, however, faced with the present agglomeration of very heterogeneous mapping styles, the editors became conscious of a need to make the process of linguistic mapping more explicit. In conceptualising this process Kirk drew on a number of models used in other areas of linguistic description, notably the semiotic triangle (as between words and their sense referents) and the set of maxims used to characterise the behaviour of conversation which

were first put forward by the philosopher H.P. Grice and further developed by the linguist Geoffrey Leech.

Kirk's suggestions may be reduced to two basic principles:
1. That the process of language mapping, as well as the map itself, could be represented as a triangle, each of its points representing a different but essential aspect of the map.
2. The coding of the map could be linked to a set of basic cartographical maxims.

The triangle and the maxims, taken together as a pair of operative principles, constitute a convenient model in so far as they appear to be sufficiently formal to be generally applicable. In essence, the properties of every map should be coded in a way that is at once clear, coherent and defensible.

Of the three essential properties which may be represented by the points of the triangle model, the first is *data*. Every language map is data-based, even though the data which is mapped need not itself be of a linguistic kind. Clearly, it should always be possible to answer the question, 'Of what data is this map a representation?' What it is not possible to do, however, is to map data of any kind directly, since data is of one substance (often phonic) and maps are of another (invariably graphic).

It is axiomatic that all data has to be analysed before it can be mapped, and thus the second essential property of maps is *analysis*. Nowadays, British linguistic geographers would not normally present data in a raw unanalysed state. Even the allocation to locality after locality of different kinds of symbol for different response types (as in *AES*, for instance) constitutes a certain level of analysis. It is, of course, also self-evident that the amount of analysis can vary and include (or exclude) various kinds of interpretation, by external or internal criteria, but the fact remains that so-called interpretive maps do not differ from other kinds in respect of this essential property. Even unlabelled areas (for instance, in Maps 3.3 to 3.8) or maps displaying the minimal interpretive techniques result from analysis, not from its absence. Thus all maps are analytical to some degree, and interpretive maps merely display the analysed data in particular ways. The unsubstantiated distinction between display and interpretive maps and between direct and indirect maps made in recent textbooks is hard to maintain. It should always be possible to answer the question, 'In what manner does this map analyse the data it represents?' That is to say, 'What analysis does this map offer?'

The third property every map has is *distribution*. This is the property which distinguishes maps from other communicative modes of display such as lists of basic material or dictionaries. Just as data and the choice of a suitable analysis must be decided upon before the mapping process can begin, so the prior existence of a base map is also essential. There is no limit to the possibilities for base maps, from those displaying simple physical or political boundaries to detailed maps of localities for a specific area, large or small, such as those for England (Map 1.1) and for England and Wales (Map 1.2) presented in this volume. It is of course conventional in dialectology to use a base map which relates more or less explicitly to the localities from which the data originated. The function of the base map is to receive the data in the manner which has been decided upon by the analysis and to allocate the data to the localities in such a way that it will give the mapped material a structure from which the geographical distributions may be inferred. In short, to distribute is to structure. While it is self-evident that a base map of localities is itself a structured map, the same is not true of data until it is analysed *and* distributed. The actual structure of the geographical distribution emerges from the coding, with different distributions emanating from different styles of coding. Whatever the style, it should always be possible to answer the question, 'What is the geographical distribution of the data in this map?'

A few further remarks on distribution may be useful here. Once the map has been coded and structured, a 'full' or 'finished' map may be said to have emerged. The map has acquired its structure from the analysis of the data distributed — if that is the case — by localities. Just as the structure induces an understanding in the reader's mind of the spatial relationships within the data, so also the reader infers the geographical distribution of data from isomorphic structure and coding of the map. This isomorphism allows the map to mediate between the structure of both base map and analysis on the one hand and a set of mental concepts and images about the geographical distribution of the data on the other. If the finished map can be thought of as participating in a process for which there is an end product, then it may be regarded as a mediator in representing geographical distribution in graphic form — a function which maps alone can perform.

The way in which a reader comes to understand a map is a remarkable phenomenon. Most maps in this volume have been produced from a basis of a limited set of highly precise linguistic data. Yet from them a virtually unlimited number of geographical facts of similar precision may be deduced. Some maps yield a structure composed of heterogeneous parts and coding styles but which creates among these parts and styles a meaningful relation as a whole. Other maps may be seen as having a structure which is more meaningful than the aggregate of its parts. Although distribution is the fundamental distinguishing property of maps, it is by no means the only factor through which the complex cognitive process of reading maps may be understood.

These three properties — data, analysis and distribution — are essential to the mapping process, as is demonstrated, for example, in the *LAE*. They are functional in that without them no map could be drafted, but they are also substantive in that without them a map is unable to make a statement or induce an understanding in the mind of the reader. Ideally, none of these properties should predominate, and the equality of their relationship might be represented as in Figure 1.2.

Figure 1.2:   The Mapping Triangle: Properties

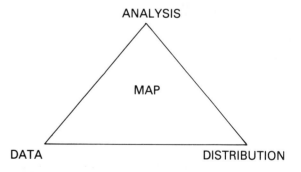

As the properties are both functional and substantive, they may be regarded as a set of mapping principles which:

1. display data,
2. display analysis,
3. display distribution.

While these properties may be too obvious to be thought of as principles, it is hard to deny their constant recurrence. Their usefulness as a set of principles, however, could hardly be better demonstrated than in terms of the maps in the present volume. To this end it might be worthwhile to recall some of the ways in which the properties have been realised in these maps. Besides numerous linguistic items, *data* for maps also comprises numbers, classes of informants, and research projects. As for *analysis*, there are three main types: (i) analysis on external grounds such as phonological or quantitative; (ii) analysis on internal grounds such as by type categories; and (iii) the minimum of analysis, as when restricting oneself simply to the presentation of basic material. Lastly, there are two main types or styles of *distribution:* (i) implicit distribution, where the distribution of the material is stated (or inferred) implicitly, through suggestive styles such as symbols or hatching; (ii) explicit distribution, where the distribution is stated (or inferred) explicitly, through directly expressive styles such as heteroglosses or isoglosses.

All these properties are readily exemplified in the maps in this volume. Further, a comparison of the mapping techniques of *AES* and *LAE* in terms of their presentation of data reveals that while their analyses are constant they differ in the degree to which they state the regional distribution of forms or leave these to be inferred.

At this point it seems useful to summarise the

Figure 1.3: *SLG* Map Profiles

1. *Maps 3.3 – 3.8*
   data = reflexes of single items
   analysis = internal, by different response types
   distribution = explicit of the Welsh forms in both Wales and England, implicit of outliers

2. *Maps 4.3 – 4.10*
   data = reflexes of single items for three age groups
   analysis = internal, by different response types, by age-group
   distribution = explicit of divergence between age-groups for each item, implicit of outliers

3. *Maps 6.1 – 6.10*
   data = absolute values for coherence and identity
   analysis = external, by percentage relative values for coherence and identity
   distribution = implicit of regional groupings of these relative values

4. *Map 7.1*
   data = reflexes of ME /ọ̄/ as in *goose*
   analysis = external, by stages of phonological development
   distribution = explicit of internally receding areas of each stage of development

5. *Map 7.7*
   data = numerical scores for rounding adjustment
   analysis = no further analysis (actual numbers are mapped)
   distribution = implicit of extent and structure of focal areas and transition zone as well as direction of its development

6. *Map 8.4*
   data = responses elicited for 'obligation'
   analysis = internal, by different response type
   distribution = implicit, both of type, and of localities with more than one response type

7. *Maps 9.1 and 9.5*
   data = responses for two separate items
   analysis = internal, by different response type and by frequency of occurrence
   distribution = implicit, of different kinds of major and minor types

principal types of map in the present volume, and provide a set of profiles of the principal features of each, so as to illustrate the formal distinctions in more detail (see Figure 1.3).

These brief profiles are sufficient to demonstrate the mapping triangle in action, and to provide further evidence substantiating the usefulness of the triangle as a model of representation (analysis) of things (data) in space (distribution on a base map). The relationships represented in the triangle operate in a clockwise direction. Data has first to be analysed before it can be mapped and its geographical implications inferred. It is not possible to move directly from data to distribution; analysis is obligatory for it influences the mapping style and determines what that style should be. Figure 1.4 illustrates the relationship between the triangle and map 7.1.

Figure 1.4:   The Mapping Triangle of Map 7.1

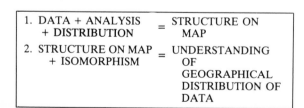

ANALYSIS
(by stages of regular phonological development)

MAP 7.1

DATA
(reflexes
of *goose*)

DISTRIBUTION
(of data in terms of
structural relationships)

As a set of equations, Kirk's theory may be restated as follows:

1. DATA + ANALYSIS + DISTRIBUTION	=	STRUCTURE ON MAP
2. STRUCTURE ON MAP + ISOMORPHISM	=	UNDERSTANDING OF GEOGRAPHICAL DISTRIBUTION OF DATA

Having outlined the principles of the mapping triangle we now turn our attention to cartography. No two maps make the same statement because the properties combine differently on each occasion. It falls to the coding, however, to

make these differences clear. Not only does the coding unify a map's properties, it also forms the vehicle for their communication. Thus it is less by its properties and rather more by its coding that a map may be judged to be more or less successful. All maps, of course, employ some cartography. As coding is a matter of degree, it is useful to conceptualise the process along the analogous lines of conversation, particularly in terms of conversational maxims set out in other work and most recently from G.N. Leech's *Principles of Pragmatics* (1983). Coding techniques apply variably to different maps and in variable degrees. Thus, as in conversation, cartographical maxims in linguistic geography are either upheld to a greater or lesser extent, so far as circumstances allow, or are breached or contravened, but never so severely as to prohibit the production of a map of some description.

So far as linguistic mapping is concerned, different types or sets of maxims may be distinguished. Following Grice, these may be termed maxims of *quantity* and *quality*, but here there is a difference of context since the task of these maxims is to optimise the communicative effectiveness of a linguistic map. Thus, the maxims are applied simultaneously to all three properties of data, analysis and distribution. It will be clear from our earlier remarks that there is a tendency for distribution to be foregrounded in the mapping, but this is an inevitable result of, and not at the expense of, the analysis of the data. This productive relationship between the properties and the map may be represented schematically as in Figure 1.5.

Figure 1.5:   The Mapping Process

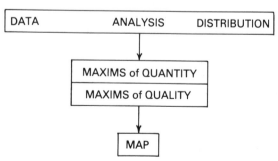

| DATA | ANALYSIS | DISTRIBUTION |

MAXIMS of QUANTITY

MAXIMS of QUALITY

MAP

Let us now consider the maxims of quantity and quality in more detail. Taken together, their function may be said to be the optimising of the map's basic properties. By 'optimising' we have in mind the simultaneous minimising of quantity and maximising of quality, which is to say that that map should be as clear as possible with regard both to the statement it makes (or understanding it induces) about its subject, and the manner in which it makes that statement. By 'quantity' we mean the full or accumulated statement which the map is intended to make — in other words, the map's proposition about a certain item (or larger set of data) within a certain geographical area as a result of a particular analysis — in a word, its informativeness. By 'quality' is meant the clarity with which such a statement or proposition is presented and communicated.

There are all too many published linguistic maps in which the intended statement can only be deduced from the cartography with difficulty, or in which the cartography is clear enough but one is left bewildered about the map's propositional force. If linguistic geographers could agree on a set of cartographical maxims, the coding of such maps could then be judged for its effectiveness and compared with other maps or alternative codings. Obviously, the breadth of scope within which such maxims operate will vary quite considerably, making it difficult to breach them in certain circumstances but comparatively easy to breach them in others. No doubt there are other reservations about introducing maxims into linguistic cartography at all. Even so, the absence of a formal mechanism by which linguistic maps could be compared encouraged Kirk to consider drawing up a model of his own as a basis for future discussion.

It has already been suggested that the maxims of quantity and quality might share the instruction 'Be clear'. Within each maxim Kirk has posited a number of similar instructions, each of which might be thought of as a separate maxim in its own right, so that the maxims of quantity and quality might better be thought of as a pair of super-maxims. His suggestion is that the maxims should govern certain specific decisions in drafting a given map:

Maxims of quantity

1. make the map as informative as possible
2. do not make the map more informative than is required
3. state nothing for which there is inadequate evidence

Maxims of quality

1. make the map as mimetic as is required
2. make the map as topologically significant as is required
3. avoid obscurity
4. avoid ambiguity
5. be orderly

If the maxims of quantity relate to propositional force and a map's degree of informativeness, the maxims of quality may be said to relate to those parts of the map which communicate that force and make it coherent. In others words, there is a link between the substantive role of the properties and the maxims of quantity, and the functional role of the properties and the maxims of quality. Democratic and equally applied as the maxims may be, their application inevitably creates some polarisation, with quantity preferring the map's properties (how much?) and quality the cartographic coding (how?). Although we have already discussed how the cartography acts as the exponent of the properties, that relationship might now be further refined by the maxims, their preferences and their application to optimise these various kinds of data, analysis and distributional styles on the final map. Although the maxims can be shown to contrast, they inevitably share the same coding devices, except that the maxims of quality are as much concerned with the graphic as with the visual aspects of the map.

The degree of quantity involved will vary, quite apart from any constraints imposed by a mapping scale. Some aspects of the maxims may be illustrated in a negative way. For instance, the *LAE* has no map for 'left-handed' (*SED* questionnaire, VI.7.13). The *SED* records no fewer than 89 response types (from the 313 localities), many more than are mapped here for 'the smallest piglet' in Map 9.1 for example. Such a map would have been so overcrowded as to breach both maxims. The distribution of such massive amounts of data on an *LAE* page size would have made the map neither informative nor topologically significant. A similar difficulty arose over 'freckles', the data for which had to be presented on two maps (L50a and L50b); the same is true of 'a loose piece of skin' (maps L49a and L49b), 'sad' (of dough) (maps L35a and L35b) and 'snack' (maps L56a and L56b). At the other extreme, there is no map for 'right-handed' (*SED* questionnaire, VI.7.13) either. As there was only one response universally in this case. a map would have nothing to add (cf. that for /n/ in *AES*, p. 156). Thus these examples show how, in terms of Kirk's model, the data in these cases resisted both analysis and distribution and so was never coded.

Let us now consider some of the ways in which the maxims of quality aid the exponence of these properties in terms of specific coding devices. The maps in this volume have used a range of devices to represent basic properties. For instance, alphabetic letters or numbers are used to represent the presence of data, without further analysis; St Andrew's crosses (originally suggested by John Widdowson for use in *LAE*) denote the absence of data. But these same symbols have been used elsewhere in conjunction with other coding devices to form an active contrast, which, of course, could not have been mapped without an analysis. Thus, in summary, open symbols contrast with closed; open and closed with half-open; large with small; small and closed with large and open; small and closed with large and hatched; symbols with arbitrary numbers; symbols with lines; lines with lines, and so on. Coding techniques are also used as exponents of different *distributions* such as the combination of symbolic techniques, or of symbolic and isoglossic styles, or of complete black hatching and number symbols (most notably for the explicit distribution of the focal areas vis-à-vis the transition zone in Map 7.7) and large symbols which are contrastively hatched (as in Maps 6.1 to 6.10).

This summary of coding practice shows that by considering the specific coding devices in terms of particular properties we are able to validate the effectiveness of any given map. It makes clear that there is no one-to-one relationship between coding devices and properties. Some devices are employed to represent data quite unencumbered by analysis, others (or even the same) may represent some analysis or interpretation, and even deeper levels of interpretation, sometimes on external grounds, are also possible. As far as the reader is concerned, different maps may be read at different levels of analysis. If a map is unclear, the chances are that some of these maxims have not been sufficiently applied. Where the maxims are demonstrably breached one might conclude that the map could have been better drafted.

Some further comments are called for in respect of the maxims of quality which may provide some fresh insights into a number of aspects of map making. Nothing could be more relative than the first maxim, 'make the map as mimetic as is required.' One could imagine a very different version of Map 9.6 'last corn sheaf — Scotland' where icons of corn sheaves were actually drafted on the map. It is doubtful, however, whether their inclusion would induce a better understanding of the item. Map 8.5 maps dialect projects. Here again, one could imagine such a map on which photographs of the individual researchers were included, but that would be rather indulgent, perhaps.

In drawing up this maxim Kirk had two further distinctions in mind. Firstly, what was not mimetic would be arbitrary, and there are plenty of illustrations of arbitrary symbolisation in this volume. Secondly, even within mimetic symbolisation a distinction can be made between those symbols which are broadly or maximally mimetic and those which are narrowly or minimally mimetic. Thus, the absolute number values in Map 7.7 are broadly mimetic, since this is the optimal means of stating that actual number, whereas Parry's use of alphabetical letters is narrowly mimetic in that it is his practice to use the first letter as the symbol for each lexical item. Both numbers and letters contrast with Parry's use of IPA phonetic symbols to represent sounds, which are completely arbitrary. It is hard to know where to draw the line between these points, for it is in the nature of maxims to be indeterminate continua, and the mimetic-arbitrary continuum in cartographical symbology is no exception. Perhaps a working hypothesis for the distinction between mimetic and arbitrary symbols might be the degree of dependence for meaning on an associated label, or set of words, which are usually known as the map's 'key'. Even with the mapping of *LAE*, which is clearly arbitrary, a distinction of this sort may be drawn between the phonetic symbols used for prevailing forms and the symbols used for outliers. Possibly the only mimetic part of many maps is the base outline of its territory. It is mimetic not because it is that territory (which, plainly, it is not) but because it shares a basic similar structure to that territory, which the reader is then able to recognise.

The second maxim of quality states that the map should be as topologically significant as is required. This refers to the relative positions and spatial relationships between the positions of the items drafted on the map and determined by the analysis. Topological significance is balanced as much between the propinquity of individual items as the areas of separation between them. We noticed earlier that Viereck's maps and Kirk's Map 8.5 fully satisfied this maxim of structure by drawing attention to those areas for which there was no coverage. Topological significance refers to relations or, in the case of quantitative maps, equivalences between items, their being bounded or connected in some way, rather than to the size, shape, angularity, straightness, openness, closedness or other such feature of the symbols themselves. Thus, this maxim specifically refers to the visual rather than the graphic aspects of the map. Clear breaches are not hard to find: Map 10.4 might suffice as an example, with its dense, overlapping hatching. In Map 7.1 if the heteroglosses had fallen together, they too would have been in breach of this maxim, for they would not have revealed the order of spatial succession. The point is that clarity of quality is as much constructed visually as graphically. The reader must be able to see a map. If his view is impaired, the map is correspondingly inhibited from inducing its intended communication.

If the second maxim of quality had to do with a map's visual contiguity, the final maxim, 'be orderly', is intended to work in two ways, both of which may be thought of as having to do with a map's coherence. What Kirk has in mind is that items on a map should be seen to cohere in an orderly fashion. Items can fail to cohere by being too few or too sparsely distributed, or too many, or too densely distributed, or by conflicting with the base map. Some of the references in Henry's paper to other maps of the 'last corn sheaf' in Northern Ireland were excluded from illustration on the grounds that the sparseness of their data made the items appear isolated and the map incoherent and (as far as distribution is concerned) in breach of this maxim. Map 4.2b is a *physical* map, but if it had been a *linguistic* map, it too would have been disorderly on the grounds that items of data on the map appeared isolated from each other. Map 10.4, the *LAS* map for 'splinter', exemplifies the other extreme.

The relationship between the maxims and the properties can be represented in terms of the mapping triangle (see Figure 1.6).

The bipartite model of a triangle and maxims

Figure 1.6: **The Mapping Triangle: Properties and Maxims**

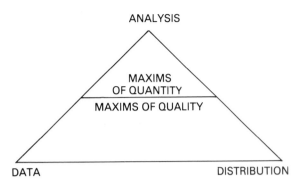

has attempted to make explicit the mediating role of maps. This role has probably been governed by intuition up until now, certainly so far as linguistic geographers are concerned. Intuition might explain why mapping practices appear to be universally accepted and so readily taken for granted. This is hardly surprising, of course, since mapping depends on a number of human systems including logic and cognition and makes other assumptions concerning the reader, such as his familiarity with maps generally. One could not deny that maps succeed in accomplishing their function because individuals interact with them in a range of simultaneous cognitive and perceptual activities. However, while intuition cannot be substituted for or excluded, it does not preclude an attempt to investigate its particular application and to comment on the characteristics of both map production and reception in a formalised manner. In drawing the reader's attention to this versatile means of communicating information about dialects we hope to provide a focus against which linguistic maps generally may be checked and compared.

In preparing these papers for publication, the editors have co-operated with the contributors to produce acceptable and innovatory maps. The maps are a focal point of the whole volume. As far as possible, we have tried to formalise in a pragmatic way how a linguistic map accomplishes (or fails to accomplish) what it is supposed to do. Maps may be singular phenomena, but they can be very complex, and there are no doubt gaps and flaws in this preliminary discussion which will become apparent in due course. It is only one approach; in some respects, the model is ideal, with the maxims simply to be aimed at, and this is substantiated by examples of maps in this volume. The model may not be neutral between production and reception, even though we have tried to take account of both. We have tried to demonstrate that the mediation created by the map is induced by the cartographer but discovered by the reader. Understanding a map remains a truly remarkable communicative phenomenon.

At the outset the editors envisaged an even broader scope for this volume. For example, there could have been fuller treatment of historical and diachronic aspects of English dialects. More importantly, it has not been possible to represent recent work in Scotland on a scale which matches its great significance both intrinsically and in advancing the analytical and cartographic techniques of linguistic geography. Happily, the record for Scotland is readily accessible in volumes I and II of *LAS*, to be completed shortly by volume III. Its editor, Dr Hans Speitel, although unable to contribute to the present collection of papers because of his major commitment to *LAS*, has significantly advanced the technique of linguistic cartography, and in particular the study of lexical isoglosses along the English-Scottish border (Speitel 1969, 1978; cf. Chambers and Trudgill 1980: 116-20). His accounts of phonological variables and discussion of the relationship between isoglosses and linguistic boundaries explore similar ground to some of the parallel studies presented here.

The contribution which *SED* is making to historical language research has also not been represented in this volume as adequately as we originally envisaged. With notable exceptions such as Professor Ernst Burgschmidt's ingenious study of the semantic development of prepositions in Middle English entitled *Koexistenz, Distribution, Äquivalenz, Synonymie: Studien zur Beschreibung der mittelenglischen Lokal- und Temporalpräpositionen* (Burgschmidt 1976), for which he extracted as much *SED* material as was suitable and mapped in particular the responses for *that over there, out of it, whole of it, to stay at home, upstairs, any time, only, than* and *older than, near, to* and *to whom, give it (to) me, from, in front of, between, among, beside, with me, without, tomorrow morning, a week ago, half past seven,* and *till,* the applications of SED data to historical linguistics have largely been confined to phonological studies, of which we would

single out two contrastive but complementary approaches. Members of the Dietz Oberseminar on Historische Englische Sprachwissenschaft in Bonn during the mid-seventies regularly discovered that *SED* evidence would confirm earlier often impressionistic observations about regional dialect distributions, most notably of all by Karl Luick in his monumental *Historische Englische Grammatik*, evidence in itself to vindicate SED's (as well as Luick's) critics. Much of this research by, and inspired by, Klaus Dietz unfortunately remains unpublished. *SED* data has also been exploited by historical linguists interested in theories and explanations of language change. These include Roger Lass who was able to draw on the evidence of the nationwide Survey in his *English Phonology and Phonological Theory* (Lass 1976) and so claim unequivocally, for instance that, (a) there are no English dialects with undiphthongised ME /ī/; (b) there are many dialects which have undiphthongised ME /ū/, normally represented by [u(:)]; (c) in general those Modern English dialects which show the 'expected' reflex of ME /ū/ (i.e. a nucleus of the [aʊ] type or something similar) have a high back vowel or upgliding back diphthong for the reflex of ME /ō/; (d) but those dialects which have [u(:)] for ME /ū/ have a front nucleus for ME /ō/: either a monophthong (like [i:]) or a diphthong with a front syllabic (like [iə]); and (e) there are no modern English dialects with consistent unraised ME /ē/. A more detailed study of (b), Lass's paper 'Mapping Constraints in Phonological Reconstruction: On Climbing Down Trees without Falling out of Them' (Lass 1980: section 6), sets out the evidence to show that each small stage in this development of ME /ū/ is recorded in *SED*: in other words, there seems to be nothing in Lass's phonological reconstruction which is not based on *SED* material. With its meticulous detail, his phonological 'tree' of the development of ME /ū/ (Lass 1978: 268) is remarkable for the way it not only highlights the primacy of SED data but also combines recent generative with traditional neogrammarian approaches in the application of that data as evidence for diachronic description — in this case for aspects of the so-called Great Vowel Shift — as much for theoretical and explanatory models in phonology. At the same time, Lass has also been able to use *SED* material to confirm the observations on dialect diversity and contemporary phonological developments made in their grammars and other handbooks by sixteenth-century grammarians such as John Hart (see also Lass 1980).

Following the Introduction, the second paper in this collection considers the progress and achievements of dialect study in England over the last hundred years, paying particular attention to the problems of presenting data in cartographic form. After reviewing the recent history of English dialectology, Sanderson and Widdowson respond to criticism of the SED and the *LAE*, discuss the merits and shortcomings of 'traditional' dialectology, and place on record a fuller account of the operational strategies of the SED than has been given hitherto. Their championship of the achievements of the Dieth-Orton vision reminds us that the data generated by the Survey is a massive and permanent resource, recorded at a crucial point in the history of the English language, against which other studies can be measured. Much can be learned from the data now available and new strategies may be planned to take account of the Survey's shortcomings. Equally important is the data as yet unexploited, particularly the incidental material and the extensive field recordings on tape which also testify to Harold Orton's willingness to incorporate new technology at a time when the portable taperecorder was still in its infancy. The incidental material includes very substantial information on linguistic variation, and on the social, temporal and spatial context of the whole range of collected data. The taperecordings provide vital evidence with which the Survey's much criticised impressionistic field transcriptions can be compared.

Dialect studies have been stigmatised by some sociolinguists, and the term 'traditional' when applied to such studies has become pejorative. Yet one might ask whether the techniques of modern linguistics are in fact so different from those of 'traditional' dialectology and whether the linguists' claim to greater rigour is justified. Further, one might question whether diachronic and synchronic approaches are necessarily opposed, and whether dialectology, or indeed any linguistic study, can be ideally rigorous and objective. Indeed, the identification of 'traditional' dialectology with the work of Harold Orton and his successors tends to ignore the farsightedness and entrepreneurial zeal of the scholar who singlemindedly planned, executed

and made available in published form the only large-scale survey of dialects ever attempted in England. The SED substantiates many of the theoretical arguments concerning language behaviour in which sociolinguists are interested; for example it provides extensive information on diffusion, erosion, merger and simplification, not to mention a wide-ranging sample of the speech of a specific reference-group, namely older men and women in predominantly rural areas of England in the mid-twentieth century. Notwithstanding the shortcomings which hindsight reveals, the SED compares favourably with equivalent projects in the rest of Europe and in North America and provides a very substantial database from which new surveys and studies may evolve.

Paper 2 concludes by suggesting ways in which dialectology might move forward. An essential part of this development is the need for a rapprochement between the various approaches to the task. Increased co-operation and pooling of resources are essential prerequisites for progress towards more comprehensive studies of the complex interrelationships between social, regional, urban and rural dialects.

There then follow two accounts of the SED's daughter surveys now in progress, the Survey of Anglo-Welsh Dialects and the Tape-recorded Survey of Hiberno-English Speech. The former, which adheres strictly to SED principles, provides valuable complementary evidence. It completes the dialect record for the South of mainland Britain and shows for the first time how patterns of variation revealed by the SED fieldwork sweep through Wales to the coast in the West. While *SAWD* demonstrates that SED methodology can be usefully extended to areas outside England, the data of both surveys being fully compatible, the Tape-recorded Survey of Hiberno-English Speech incorporates significant new methodological strategies. These are designed to take account of criticisms levelled against 'traditional' surveys, and include the taperecording of all data, the eliciting of lengthy specimens of free conversation in addition to questionnaire responses, the establishment of a systematic network of fieldwork localities based on the National Grid and the representative sampling of informants across three specified age-groups. These strategies indicate directions in which new surveys can take account of recent developments by extending and improving older methodologies, while still remaining compatible in terms of their data and analysis.

David Parry outlines the Survey of Anglo-Welsh Dialects (SAWD), which, though fully compatible with the SED, and employing an identical methodology and questionnaire, also differs from it in certain fundamental ways. The first of these is the co-existence of Welsh and English. While Welsh is regarded by some SAWD informants as their first language, it is eschewed by others, so that the English of Wales varies from individual to individual in the extent and frequency of its use. Such factors as the social penetration and institutionalisation of Welsh are responsible for the predominant Welsh-like quality of English in Wales, so that the label 'Anglo-Welsh', unlike 'Anglo-Irish', on which we comment below, has rarely been called into question and is now well established. Contact between English and its Celtic neighbours in these islands has attracted attention recently and it is a matter of regret that discussion of some of the wider issues of cross-cultural and interlingual influences has had to be left aside in this present volume.

With the completion of SAWD, the SED data for the West of England may now be extended to the Welsh coast and it is now possible to add Anglo-Welsh data to complement that of both SED and *LAE*. A new base map for England and Wales has been drawn up and is presented here as Map 1.2. The map is an important contribution to this volume, not least because its use in paper 3 shows how *LAE* isoglosses can be seen to sweep round into Wales and through to the coast in ways which provide new evidence in defence of this particular mapping technique. Notwithstanding the criticisms made separately by Kirk and Macaulay elsewhere in this volume, we know of no other isoglossic maps in which the data of two surveys is mapped together in this way. Other mapping techniques would be less effective in making clear the compatibility of the two different sets of data. What the isogloss is able to state is the continuity of occurrences irrespective of national or survey boundaries. It is equally effective for both lexical and phonological items. Had SAWD departed from the methodology of SED, such useful and impressive results would have been a lot harder to achieve.

Despite the Welshness of SAWD data overall, Parry's maps reveal much about the extent and direction of the Welsh influence, as far as these particular items are concerned. The phonological maps show that there are no sounds exclusive to Wales, and the extent of their distribution in England makes it hard to accept that the influence has spread eastwards and beyond from Wales. By contrast, the lexical maps show that forms which in England are exclusively restricted to the West are well attested in Wales, so that in this case the influence has come from Wales and spread eastwards.

The maps also reveal other new and important information. As Alan Thomas (1973, 1980) has shown in his work on Welsh, Parry now demonstrates for Anglo-Welsh that Wales, with its convenient rectangular shape, lends itself enviably to cartographical interpretation of geographical linguistic variants. Who would have predicted, for example, that retroflexion of /r/ would have been so clearly demarcated between East and West Wales? Or that *shippon* (from OE *scypen*) would have occurred exclusively in the North of Wales, forming a neat division between North Wales and the English Midlands? Or that the realisation of [u:/ɒ] as in *tooth* would be sharply and almost exclusively divided between North and West? Or that there would be a belt of diphthongisation in the centre of Wales which contrasts with an identical monophthong to the North and South? Some of the questions raised by these maps relate to Parry's distinction between strongly Welsh-influenced Anglo-Welsh dialects (SWAWDs) and highly anglicised Anglo-Welsh dialects (HAAWDs). The two most extensive sections of his paper are devoted to descriptions of the Welsh and English elements in Anglo-Welsh.

Parry's data reveals one set of items which we believe has never been identified previously — a list of Anglo-Welsh forms which he maintains have been recorded hitherto neither in Welsh nor in English. They were not recorded in *SED*; we are indebted to Professor John Braidwood for his confirmation that he has no record of any of these items in his extensive files of dialect material gathered over decades for his *Ulster Dialect Dictionary*, and also to Professor A.J. Aitken, Editor of the *Dictionary of the Older Scottish Tongue* and of the *Concise Scots Dictionary*, for confirming that these items in the senses quoted by Parry are all unknown to him. To discover new types of lexical items in English with long-established uses is a remarkable achievement.

The basic features of Parry's mapping techniques are discussed elsewhere in this Introduction. Because of the separate influences from Welsh and English, Parry speculates that SAWD data lends greater scope for interpretation and analysis than SED. One area where such scope lies is the question of transition areas. As new findings on transitional areas by Beat Glauser and Ronald Macaulay are included in this volume, we are particularly looking forward to seeing the maps and details Parry proposes for those areas which he has found to be transitional, not only on the grounds of co-occurrence, but also of identity. This identity he takes to be the result of the conflation of separate internal and external linguistic and extralinguistic influences. It has been the custom of sociolinguists to highlight patterns of variation in regional dialect data. Parry's paper, although still speculative, suggests that the interests of social dialectologists may also be accommodated by the occurrence of regional forms which on the surface appear identical. It is often forgotten that the significance of SED data in social terms was already being investigated by the SED team in Leeds during the 1960s. In continuing to work within the SED framework, which has already produced such impressive results, Parry feels confident enough to recast his material in terms of other categories, including those which take account of cultural and ethnographical variation, and he is constantly aware of such lines of enquiry. His paper provides further proof that the SED framework does not inhibit further analysis along similar, but refined, lines. On the contrary, the framework is able to accommodate a wide range of additional interests and investigations.

The SAWD atlas, when it appears, will also contrast with *LAE*, in that in addition to the maps a commentary is to be provided which, Parry claims, will inform *any* reader about probable explanations of current Anglo-Welsh sounds. At once scholarly in detail and popular in presentation, this is a further innovation and achievement to which we particularly look forward. One cannot but admire the way he has singlehandedly and selflessly directed, financed and executed this remarkable project. Now that the fieldwork is complete we hope that his paper will set his work in a broader perspective and bring it to the attention of a wider audience.

In their account of the ongoing Tape-recorded Survey of Hiberno-English Speech, Brendan Adams, Michael Barry and Philip Tilling discuss the genesis, methodology and findings of the Survey in considerable detail. Like SAWD it draws heavily on the SED in its approach but focuses specifically on the gathering of material which is felt to be phonologically revealing. In several other important respects, however, it extends the SED methodology. Firstly, as the Survey's name implies, it was decided that all data would be taperecorded to enable the analysis to be verifiable and consistent and so avoid the obvious shortcomings of impressionistic transcription in the field for which the SED has been criticised. Secondly, a lengthy specimen of free conversation elicited from each informant was also to be recorded on tape in addition to the use of a questionnaire; the questionnaire itself incorporated as many keywords from SED and LSS as was both practicable and relevant for a phonological investigation and to allow correlation of the data from the three surveys. Thirdly, the network of fieldwork localities, although following SED principles, is more systematic. Based on the Irish National Grid this network not only has the advantage that it can be densened by stages for the investigation of specific areas in more detail but also that it will simplify any eventual production of computerised maps. Fourthly, the TRS departs significantly from the SED and other regional surveys in the selection of informants. The complete questionnaire will be answered by three individuals in each locality, the informants being drawn from three age-groups representative of the first generation (9 to 12 years), the 'parental' generation (35 to 45 years) and the older generation (65 to 75 years) so as to make the sample as representative as possible while at the same time complementing and extending the data of the SED.

The information emerging from the TRS outlined in the paper demonstrates the scope and success of these new and improved methods of fieldwork and analysis. The situation in Ireland is particularly interesting because the boundary area so far investigated by TRS corresponds with a historical Celtic-speaking area into which two distinctive varieties of English were to move, one heavily influenced by immigrant southern British English, the others by Ulster Scots. This boundary is linguistically complex and, as the clustering of phonetic isoglosses shows, it invites comparison with the Scottish-English linguistic border which Glauser (1974) and Speitel (1978) have examined from the lexical viewpoint. However, the TRS is primarily concerned with the correlation between linguistic variation and geographical distribution, rather than between standard usage and dialect; it does not concern itself at this stage with the occurrence of standard forms or the co-occurrence of standard and dialect forms. The mapping of phonetic evidence from the TRS furnishes us with a fuller and more convincing picture of the situation than lexical data could provide, and reveals, for example, intriguing patterns of functional substitution and merger which characterise the boundary. The technique of clustering various isoglosses together to establish such a border is clearly preferable to relying on the inevitably generalised, impressionistic and somewhat subjective interpretation of a single isogloss which is all too easily identified as a rigid line of demarcation. A notable feature of the bundles of isoglosses is that they are evidently not clustered by item or age-group. Although at this stage the material mapped is phonetic and no attempt has been made to phonemicise the data or to subject it to further abstraction, this paper makes a significant contribution to the debate concerning the grading of isoglosses. Grading presents problems both for the cartographer and for the potential user of the maps, but experiments with different mapping techniques may lead away from the rigidity of the single isogloss and permit more detailed analysis. It is interesting to note, for example, that this paper lends some support to the view that isoglosses representing the usage of different age-groups might reveal something about the nature and direction of linguistic change. The evidence presented also suggests that the Irish border area could profitably be analysed in quantificatory terms of mixed, fudged and scrambled lects along the lines put forward by J.K. Chambers and Peter Trudgill and discussed by Macaulay in paper 10. From this viewpoint alone it is to be hoped that the basic material of the TRS may be published in due course, thus making it accessible for others interested in comparative analysis.

The unnatural enforced separation of 'traditional' dialectology and sociolinguistics in recent years has made it more difficult to recognise that each has much to offer the other. The newer and more rigorous methodologies of sociolinguistics, whether in sampling, elicitation techniques, analysis or presentation, represent important advances which cannot be ignored. On the other hand, despite recent evidence of rapprochement, notably in an article by K.M. Petyt entitled 'Who is Really Doing Dialectology?' (Petyt 1982), sociolinguists have been reluctant to acknowledge the achievements of 'traditional' surveys. It is all the more surprising, then, that they have not embarked on a new nationwide survey which would not only vindicate them but also provide the ideal database which they vainly seek in the material currently available. Although more than willing to draw extensively on the resources of the *SED* for exemplification and comparison in their research and publications, none has seriously searched the data in any depth in order to discover whether it offers more insights than their superficial criticisms suggest it can. If any proof were needed that the SED can provide scope for sociolinguistic investigation, even from the published material alone, it is to be found in Johnston's paper 'Linguistic Atlases and Sociolinguistics'. In a wide-ranging survey of comparable projects in Europe and North America, he demonstrates that 'traditional' dialectology is useful not only in suggesting further avenues of sociolinguistic research but also in clarifying the results of sociolinguistic surveys themselves. This seminal paper, with its clear grasp of the full range of subject matter, spans the artificial gulf between the two disciplines with a firm new bridge and invites both dissident factions to meet in the middle.

Johnston compares the aims and techniques of large-scale surveys such as the SED and LSS with those of Labovian and Trudgillian sociolinguistics. He demonstrates how and where data collected by the SED and other surveys corresponds to the demands of a sociolinguistic model, particularly with regard to factors such as class, sex, age and style. Thus he shows how survey data such as that from the SED can be used for comparison with sociolinguistic studies, and how linguistic variation due to sociolinguistic factors can be studied within a survey such as the SED. By drawing parallels between the data of the traditional dialectologist and the analytical approach of the sociolinguist, Johnston translates the SED into sociolinguistic terms as a corpus of data approximating to lower-working-class speech of the generation older than the present oldest in some formal style comparable with word list style.

Using the now familiar sociolinguistic typology, Johnston is able to classify the SED responses in terms of their style. He suggests that by presenting a picture of formalised local dialect what the SED may actually be revealing is an individual's phonology — what Bolinger (1975: 84) has called 'canonical forms' — which are free from any kind of reduction that could otherwise be caused by speech rate in connected performance. He then comments on the ranking of variables and the examination of age variant patterns for native sound changes or substitutions.

He supports his arguments by an analysis of historically bimoric vocalic clusters, based on a comparison of his own fieldwork in Northumberland with that of the SED, and by an exhaustive survey of some 22 European linguistic atlases. Some very revealing comparisons emerge. The broad statistical basis of his survey serves to highlight the very favourable coverage actually given by the SED to sociolinguistically sensitive variation.

This paper fully answers recent criticisms of traditional dialectology by sociolinguists and suggests that such criticism in some recent sociolinguistic textbooks on dialectology may require qualification. He demonstrates unequivocally that the material collected by the SED and similar other surveys seems to be very helpful to sociolinguists studying dialects of any area of Britain in that it more or less defines the localised speech of a community of speakers in all its aspects, including the lexical, and provides a plentiful corpus of data for comparison. Harold Orton had always envisaged that his work would be beneficial to social dialectology, and this paper is a major step in that direction.

Just as sociolinguistics has established itself in recent years as a major innovatory force in linguistic analysis, so also there have been rapid developments in computational linguistics. This is an area in which our thinking has greatly advanced and technology quickly overtaken events since the inception of the SED, particularly in the use of the computer for the sorting of the vast quantities of data generated by linguistic surveys. In another pioneering paper, Wolfgang Viereck brings this new technology to bear in his dialectometric analysis of SED material. The sudden transitions and the illusion of firm boundaries which isoglosses tend to suggest in linguistic cartography have remained an intractable problem in the graphic presentation of dialect material. Viereck shows how, with the use of the computer, statistical techniques for testing coherence and identity are invaluable in revealing areal patterns in the Survey's data. These techniques allow us not only to discern complex and detailed patterns of distribution but also to dispense with cruder subjective assessments on which it has been necessary to rely in the past.

Viereck examines recent innovations in quantitative methodologies devised by continental dialectologists of romance languages, notably by Hans Goebl (especially 1982 and 1984) of the University of Salzburg, and sets out to test them against two subsets of data from the SED. He subjects the data to two new tests. Firstly, he tests some 80 lexical and 60 morphological items for the measure of their agreement with the standard language in all the localities in 28 new counties in the South and interprets the results as evidence for the structure of the linguistic coherency of the area. Secondly, he tests the same amount of data at four selected localities in this southern area to establish the amount of agreement between them and all other localities and interprets the results as evidence for patterns of relative homogeneity and heterogeneity in the structure of the language. The results are transferred onto maps, the actual figure for coherency and identity being recorded in a symbol at each location. From these figures their statistical significance is calculated and the location symbols are then hatched for each of the different statistical grades of relative identity in what is conventionally referred to as a choroplethic style. The areal distribution of these fairly abstract relative grades may then be taken as evidence for identifying likely dialect areas.

The results are preliminary and somewhat relative as only the southern part of the country and a subset of data has so far been investigated. The objectives and methodology, however, are clear, and Viereck introduces us to the new terminology. With the use of a computer, which will be able to take account of all the SED data, it will soon be possible to interpret the internal evidence of the SED in ways which will be suggestive of dialect areas, thus replacing previous impressionistic and rather subjective assessments of their actual extents with one of exhaustive objectivity. Viereck opens up dialectometry as a further field of enquiry into the SED from which much more may be expected in the future.

Turning now to papers 7, 8 and 9 we have three varied contributions which emphasise the value of interrelated nationwide dialect surveys. Despite their different approaches, such surveys have gathered a wealth of information on phonology, lexis, grammar and syntax, and although it is possible to include only a sample of the contributions which the surveys have made, and continue to make, to our knowledge of regional and social varieties of English, these three papers indicate something of what may be discovered from the collected material. Phonology is the most developed discipline within dialectology and phonological variation is the principal feature differentiating one dialect from another. Drawing on some of the recent solid foundations within generative phonology Beat Glauser is able to establish patterns of phonological variation throughout England, from North to South. The resulting generalisations represent a remarkable fusion of model building and data exegesis, again proving how new techniques can be used profitably in analysing the SED data. One of the authors of the *AES*, Glauser is also well known for his work on the lexis of the Scottish-English border, and has recently completed an extensive phonological study of the dialect of Grassington, North Yorkshire. In paper 7 he traces how, with generative rules, original data on maps can be phonologically related. He first investigates various realisation rules for late ME /ă/ and the implications of their mapping, and then proceeds to explore how phonological mapping processes lend themselves to cartographical presentation. Using five further examples of a rule-governed change by which a low short vowel is rounded and raised, he compares their different environments and finds there is a general discrepancy in vocalic output between the North and South. In the South all postvocalic consonants cause the vowel to adjust its roundness features (/ă/ — /ɔ̆/); in the North there is no adjustment at all, whereas in the North Midlands after /w/ only back consonants allow it. After collating the material, Glauser analyses the effect of roundness adjustment in the Midlands. The map of this transition zone between minimum and maximum roundness adjustment is a fascinating example of what a dialectologist can achieve by using the generative approach. Glauser is able to

show that through the direct correlation between mapping and phonological rules generative phonology helps us to understand the implications of these mapping rules deployed in the atlas which otherwise would have remained hidden. He is of course ready to admit that his paper is far from a full statement about generative phonology and linguistic atlases, but he has certainly pointed us in the right direction. His maps are methodologically innovatory, refreshingly interpretive and genuinely uphold the value of the map as an analytical tool in regional dialectology.

In paper 8 John Kirk introduces the hitherto rather neglected study of regional variation in syntax by drawing a contrast between syntax on the one hand and lexis and phonology on the other so as to establish at the outset some of the former's distinguishing features. The syntactic maps of the *LAE* have been given scant treatment in reviews and in recent textbooks even, although they had been discussed by Stewart Sanderson in a series of articles in *New Society* ('Wordmaps 4 and 5', 7 and 14 September 1978). Kirk offers some specimen analyses.

As we have already discussed, all maps are about data, and the implications which emerge from the *LAE* maps make it necessary for Kirk to go back to the fieldwork which collected the data and examine afresh the details of the Survey's methodology including the questionnaire and the manner of its deployment. Syntax is unquestionably complex; there are many factors to be taken into account, and Kirk deals with each of them in turn, adducing further examples for comparison where they usefully illuminate the SED data and set its findings in a much rounder and deeper linguistic context. At the same time he constructs an argument to demonstrate that by borrowing the onomasiological approach to which the investigation of lexis is accustomed the SED methodology is inadequate in its investigation of the variety and variability of syntactic data. It is, for instance, insufficiently discriminating between different syntactic functions in identical features or between identical syntactic functions in different features, as Kirk is able to show from examples of modal verbs and the copular verb *to be*. Whereas the SED contains a wealth of syntactic (as distinct from morphological) information, few examples are actually systematically comparable, so that it is difficult to discover anything about their specific communicative function in a particular dialect, or how the realisation of that function varies from region to region.

Since the SED was published, investigators have tended either to limit the focus of their investigation to the syntax of a particular place or region to give a much fuller description of the local repertoire, as for example in the studies of Farnworth dialect by Graham Shorrocks (1980) and of Eaton-by-Tarporley, Cheshire by Peter Anderson (1977), or alternatively they have preferred to develop fresh methods of investigating syntax in which the approach is often theoretical and much more sophisticated and usually follows a sociolinguistic or variationist methodology, with the result that such studies as those of Reading by Jenny Cheshire (1982) or of the Wirral by Mark Newbrook (1982) are unique in scope and much less readily comparable.

Kirk's paper brings all these various individual and regionally isolated studies together and shows by means of Map 8.5 that despite certain typological incompatibilities the network is now sufficiently dense throughout Britain and Ireland for some practical comparisons to be possible. He points out that the study of regional syntax now also stands to gain from the progress which continues to be achieved from corpus-based investigations of Standard English. Moreover, he leaves little doubt that it would be beneficial in the future to investigate conversation and other discourse exchanges rather than isolated examples. In short, what he establishes is that the SED's unit of investigation for syntax was too constrained to be useful for comparative work and that the investigation of the syntactical level of language should be considerably expanded in future work to allow for informant interaction and contextual ramifications. The anecdotal evidence he adduces from communicative breakdown in conversational exchanges across isolects is particularly valuable to his argument, and he draws attention to the advantages of testing the data not only with the local informants but also among those ordinarily resident in other parts of the country as well.

The question of non-isomorphous dialects raises important and much deeper issues, and Kirk concludes by raising such fundamental issues as the question of communicative competence in the language. He reviews the syntactic evidence which might shed light on the differences between active and passive competence

and helps us to decide whether competence is mono- or polylectal.

This paper covers a great deal of ground, from the North Channel, through the Cheviot Hills to the Watford Gap. It represents a pioneering attempt to come to terms with regional syntax by taking the *SED/LAE* as its starting point and linking these with subsequent work, thereby creating a context in which methodologies can be compared and into which data from all English-speaking parts of these islands can be integrated. With this use of data, as accumulative as it is eclectic, Kirk succeeds in building another bridge which stretches forward from the SED over some perplexing and virtually unnavigated waters on to the shores of newer investigations and beyond, thus overcoming some of the difficulties which have bedevilled the study of regional syntax. At the same time, he also builds outwards and upwards from the data to recognise some of the key types or markers of syntactic variation summarised in Figure 8.1. It is a positive and optimistic paper. Like others in the volume, Kirk points the way ahead by using a dynamic approach to his material, expressing dissatisfaction with those views of dialectology which all too often label it backward-looking and static. His use of multi-variable symbols as a mapping technique for SED material represents one of the many cartographical innovations which his energy and enterprise have contributed to the volume as a whole.

It has long been recognised that the study of lexis in a systematic way has not been developed as fully as that of phonology or grammar for want of suitable analytical models. Nowhere could this be truer or more demonstrative of the belief that every word has its own story to tell than in Leo Henry's article on linguistic atlases and vocabulary. His discussions of 'the smallest pig of the litter' and 'the last corn sheaf' in particular make it clear that localised words relate to universal notions for which the full set of recorded variations falls little short of linguistic history in miniature, and the reader will be indebted to Henry for tracing the words for these concepts via a tour that goes round in a circle from England to Ireland to Scotland. Few dialect studies have fused the Celtic and non-Celtic based vocabulary of these islands in quite such a precise and illuminating way.

The paper begins by commenting on tricky terminological questions such as the labels

'Hiberno-English' and 'Anglo-Irish'. It is our experience that the linguistic arguments in favour of each of these designations for the distinctive Irish variety of metropolitan World English are irresolvable. There are arguments in favour of each, and their usage has become idiosyncratic and established as a matter of personal preference. However, Henry's article itself offers fresh support for the term 'Anglo-Irish' as he proceeds to discuss certain Modern English loanwords from Irish which throw light on characteristic differences between the two civilisations at the points of contact. What is so valuable about the discussion is the way it is able to display semantic and lexical parallels and distinctions between Anglo-Irish and mainland British English, particularly in Scotland. Every word certainly has its own story, and although Henry is able to examine only two items in great detail — 'the smallest piglet', which has attracted attention before, and which suitably lends itself to comparative treatment, and 'the last corn sheaf', which is of considerable interest for sociologists and folklorists as well as linguists — he has advanced the comparative treatment of both these items considerably. The maps also represent a significant advance and are based on materials collected variously from Wagner's Survey of Irish Dialects to the Lexical and Linguistic Questionnaires deployed in the Linguistic Survey of Anglo-Irish, from printed sources, and from archival material held by the Irish Folklore Commission. They show the distribution of all occurrences or recordings of these items in Ireland. They have been drawn according to major and minor types of occurrence, using symbols for the major, numbers for the minor forms, with cognate tokens of major types subsumed, and with Celtic and English forms side by side. By mapping items which have been thus weighted, they represent a further instance of the analytical style of mapping for which Ronald Macaulay is to express a preference in the following chapter and which is evident throughout this volume. It is worth noting that in his lexical survey, which is continuing with the assistance of Dr Seamus Ó Maolín, Henry is particularly interested in finding speakers who not only have good local dialect and are available, but also have an interest in local lore.

The final paper presents something of a contrast to the other contributions both in tone and subject matter. In characteristically relaxed and persuasive style Ronald Macaulay reviews the major linguistic atlases in terms of a well-established typology of their mapping techniques, and goes on to suggest ways in which the material could be presented more analytically. His own preference is for the introduction of a much higher degree of quantification and statistical rigour in linguistic mapping, since so much of the data cries out for this kind of treatment. In addition to evidence from recent work by J.K. Chambers and Peter Trudgill on transitional zones in East Anglia, Macaulay provides some fresh analyses of his own. Among these is a detailed discussion of the Scots lexical item *splinter*, comparing its occurrence with a supra-regional term, *skelf*, which is variable in frequency, along with other much more restricted regional words. Another telling piece of quantitative analysis focuses on the word-final voiced nasal velar stop /g/ in the West Midlands as a percentage of its occurrence by locality.

Like other contributors, Macaulay demonstrates not only the importance of quantifying frequencies of occurrence in analysing the significance of particular forms but also a desire for developing techniques that will reveal underlying patterns of behaviour in the language which existing methods of atlas presentation have ignored or kept in the dark. A further preoccupation is his interest in how a linguistic atlas should be read and what it should be read for — questions asked by a number of readers of the *LAE* from outside the discipline who found this, and no doubt other linguistic atlases, difficult to penetrate.

In assessing the merits of different types of linguistic map Macaulay first deals with general issues, usually with a critical eye. He then analyses specific aspects, and here his approach is highly constructive. He challenges the whole concept of the linguistic atlas and raises questions about its purpose and intended readership. He also identifies a number of criteria by means of which he compares existing atlases and which he is to uphold in his own maps later, and exemplifies the now well-established types of cartographical technique — symbolic (e.g. *AES*), impressionistic (e.g. *LAS*) and isoglossic (e.g. *LAE*). In criticising linguistic atlas editors for restricting their presentation usually to one of these types, he draws attention to specific instances where different mapping techniques could have been used to advantage. One of the ways in which the TRS is reappraising the methodology of the SED, for instance, is in deploying different mapping techniques, as its volume of working papers has shown (see Kirk 1983).

Even though it is the function of linguistic maps to convey information or describe data, Macaulay prefers lists rather than maps of basic material. He is not alone in finding linguistic atlases anything but straightforward. Each map usually contains very little information about a specific locality, so that detailed study requires a considerable amount of extrapolation and collation (see, for example, Widdowson 1984). Although the authors of the *AES* have experimented with summary maps, they confine themselves to an individual item as it occurs in a number of tokens and environments, and for that reason would not answer this criticism.

Furthermore, Macaulay chastises atlas editors for their stubbornness in refusing to interpret or explain the data which they are presenting and of which they alone are knowledgeable. He finds linguistic atlases in their present formats to be fundamentally flawed by their lack of analysis. The TRS directors may have diversified their mapping techniques for description, but they have yet to demonstrate this effectiveness in explanation. Explanation in dialectology is still a rather nebulous concept, and even in recent textbooks such as J.K. Chambers and Peter Trudgill's *Dialectology* (1980) which is generally reliable and authoritative, such explanations as are offered tend to be elliptical and unsatisfactory.

It is salutary to have these criticisms of the conventions and practice of linguistic atlases in this volume, and especially in this final paper which draws together various lines of enquiry running through this collection of papers as a whole. Although much referred to and seemingly taken for granted, both *LAE* and *LAS* are represented here on the grounds of their mapping techniques alone. This enables researchers to see them in a very different light, and suggests how scholars outside such projects may find them frustrating to use. On the positive side, Macaulay then offers suggestions for improving the situation, and his proposals serve to justify the various innovations found elsewhere in the volume. As primary investigation gives way to

secondary analysis, it is reassuring that there is a measure of agreement on the way forward.

The thrust of his argument is that linguistic atlases should move away from description and use the map as a vehicle for explanation. He points out that what is important is not the absolute number of occurrences but ratios of occurrences between standard and dialect forms or between more or less predominant dialect forms. The map should make a statement about how items relate to each other in a geography.

Taking a lead from the quantitative techniques developed by J.K. Chambers to establish transition zones and patterns of variation within such areas, for instance, in the regions to the west and south of the Wash, Macaulay identifies other distinctive areas along similar lines — a West Midlands relic area in England on phonological grounds, and Ayrshire in Scotland on lexical grounds. Incidentally, readers who admire the Ayrshire dialect of Robert Burns will be delighted to discover that the evidence gathered by the LSS shows it to be every bit as distinctive and pervasive today.

It is also important to realise that Macaulay's results are subjective, and because his maps deal with one item at a time, and with its quantitative distribution of occurrence, they are also extremely clear. What makes them so significant here is that they demonstrate both the kind of analytical approach and the type of interpretive result which are possible in utilising the vast amounts of data which the regional surveys of England and Scotland have made available, and to which we have drawn attention above. They further show how particular analyses are able to interpret different sets of data irrespective of the method of collection — a fitting culmination of the methodology and objectives on which this volume is based. They confirm our belief that secondary investigation cannot fail to be rewarding — a belief which this book aims to demonstrate. Although trenchantly critical of atlas editors' unimaginative presentations, the results derived from Macaulay's analytical techniques end on a positive note which unequivocally reaffirms the primacy and value of all survey data.

Finally, Macaulay points out that the data gathered by the LSS is accompanied by a linguistic as well as a social profile and lends itself to investigation along both lines. There is no better substantiation of his point than Paul

Johnston's paper in this volume. Both would agree that it takes a lot of hard work to identify and above all to count occurrences for a given distribution. Using his own techniques, Macaulay is able to preview the types of interpretation likely to become possible with the eventual computerisation of all the SED material. It has long been known that a careful analysis of the parts can justify the whole. Macaulay's analyses and illustrations do this for linguistic atlases as they stand. As his suggestions relate to analyses of particular items, they are on a different scale from those advocated in this volume by Wolfgang Viereck, with which they provide an interesting contrast. They may also conveniently lend themselves to further investigation of other items along similar lines. By drawing attention to the great variety of published linguistic maps and discussing their merits and shortcomings, Macaulay invites the reader to explore them and judge for himself.

Having discussed the techniques of the cartography employed in this volume and the essence of the individual contributions, we now turn, by way of exemplification, to more detailed comments on certain of the new maps. Readers will no doubt wish to carry this process further in relation to all the maps presented. Our intention here is to make the interpretations which they offer more explicit and to point out the ways in which they bring about those interpretations. Furthermore, we suggest how the diverse mapping techniques, data presentations and interpretations can be brought together as a set of underlying principles of linguistic cartography.

Some aspects of Viereck's maps in paper 6 may be usefully compared with other maps in the volume. For instance, Kirk's Map 8.5 represents research projects on regional English in Britain and Ireland. Its mapping style, however, makes it clear just how extensive those regions are where no comparable research has been undertaken. Secondly, whereas editors of linguistic atlases are usually concerned with making explicit their primary data in as unambiguous a manner as possible, Viereck has shown that it is not incompatible to present as well as to interpret information on one and the same map. Other instances of this process are Glauser's maps in paper 7 which assume the relevant data originally presented symbolically in the *AES*. Taking an altogether different approach to

Viereck, Glauser is equally interested in establishing relationships within the data.

Instead of looking at all the data in an optimal way, in terms of sets of overall relationships such as identity or coherence, Glauser seeks to find links between different responses in terms of their phonological structure, the result of discrete phonological changes, and then compares the distribution on the map. Put simply, his principle of analysis may be stated in the following way: for a sound to be Z, it had first to be Y, and for it to be Y, it had first to be X. What is especially interesting about Glauser's Map 7.1 is its ability to interpret within heteroglosses the rare and highly localised responses as lying within a larger area which is by one degree less well developed in terms of its sound structure. He then goes on to interpret this latter area as itself lying within an even larger area which, in turn, is by one further degree less well developed phonologically. Thus, to generalise, the most advanced areas are at the same time also the most localised. Glauser has based his interpretation on ideas about phonology which were developed at a time when the SED was well advanced. It is challenging to compare the mapped findings of Viereck and Glauser in respect of the claim that those areas with most differences from the standard language are also those which are the most geographically remote. Although there are two main types of development within the North, neither could be said to be further advanced than the other. As a result of his analysis, and by contrast with the rather democratic maps in *AES*, Glauser is able to weight the data and load the heteroglosses so that some bundle together, and consequently these bundles are of greater importance. The line which the bundles of heteroglosses takes is clear. We can see at a glance from the map that no matter what the details of the reflexes in the North are, all Northern responses are fundamentally different from those in the South and have all undergone the same *minimum* set of sound changes. The difference is quite considerable, however, in terms of phonological structure. The use of heteroglosses on this map focuses on the way in which responses and localities are interdependent — the more responses advance in structure, the more they recede in regional distribution. The regional distribution may be fully local and maximally advanced; it may alternatively be less advanced but representative of the Northern area as a whole. The bundling of heteroglosses in this map constitutes one of the most convincing statements yet made concerning speech differences between the North and South of England.

The significance of Glauser's maps lies in their comparability with the symbolic, uninterpreted maps of *AES* for *wash* (*AES* p. 197), *wasp* (*AES* pp. 198 and 199), *water* (*AES* p. 200), *quarry* (*AES* p. 212) and *swath* (*AES* p. 206). Glauser's maps are both symbolic and interpretive. They interpret the data in terms of structural phonological differences, of which there are several types. The choice of symbols has been determined by these different types, so that variations in mapping symbol correlate directly with these data differences. The symbols are therefore not of equal value (as in *AES*), but show a direct correlation between phonological structure and geographical distribution. Where there has been no development from the historical base form, there is no symbolisation on the map. To this extent the maps are therefore directional rather than static.

Occasionally, forms are not interpreted. In Map 7.6 *swath*, for example, certain forms are marked as being of doubtful origin. The map shows that in an area where rounding adjustment is almost universal, it may seem surprising that a whole set of forms should be recorded as /ɛ:/ by an SED fieldworker; on the other hand, someone working broadly in many localities might tend to pay less attention to minutiae of phonological variation than one who is investigating a specific locality in greater depth. The same fieldworker has been criticised by Peter Trudgill, who usually argues on the grounds of his own fieldwork or his knowledge as a native speaker from the area. What Glauser's map achieves, we believe for the first time, is a criticism or evaluation of the data on internal grounds alone, without recourse to comparative analysis.

The question of trusting the fieldworker, and isoglosses based on fieldwork data, has been raised by Trudgill several times and a whole study was devoted to it (Bothe 1971, reviewed by Kirk 1982). Despite the inherent difficulties, our belief in the primacy of the data as it stands is unshaken. We hold that the data is the best critic of other data, even though it might require a careful analysis for a particular criticism to

emerge. In other words, there is nothing hidden in the data, but our own approach to it may influence our interpretation. In this respect, as well as in many others, Glauser responds to one of the principal challenges facing the contributors to this volume — to open up the data and reveal what is there.

Glauser's paper thus serves as a useful reply to those critics who feel that the fieldworkers have somehow interposed themselves between the actual linguistic situation and any reliable interpretation. To those critics one might reply that without the fieldworkers there would be no reported data. One might also suggest that it is that lack of suitably refined analytical technique which prevents such critics from discriminating between the differences inevitably inherent in the quality of the data.

Glauser has made new contributions and has substantially advanced the interpretation of the SED material as well as the use of maps in that task. Using a very different but complementary approach to that of Viereck, he continues to provide and clarify the information on which his interpretations are based.

Map 7.2 *quarry* gives a clear picture of rounding (or backness) adjustment as a phenomenon which occurs in the South. It demonstrates that the base vowel remains unaltered in the North, that the transition zone is in the Midlands, and that there is relatively more rounding adjustment to the East of this transition zone than to the West. Map 7.3 *wasps* confirms this picture and adds the presence of lengthening of the base vowel in the transition zone. Map 7.4 *wash* shows that in a word which undergoes rounding adjustment in the South, the base vowel may develop differently in the North, namely by raising to [ɛ] and in a few cases by diphthongisation to [ɛi]. The diphthongisation mirrors that which occurs after rounding adjustment in this word in the South. However, in the South diphthongisation is accompanied by some further adjustment in vowel quality. In the South West, where there is no subsequent diphthongisation, the presence of /r/ is recorded. Map 7.5 *water* shows that the development of the base vowel in the North may be initially raised to [e] and in further instances raised further to [i] or lowered again to [ɛ]. It also shows that rounding adjustment may be extended to develop an [ɑ:], a vowel which was not interpreted in Map 7.3. Further, it reveals a few instances of /r/-

insertion. Map 7.6 *swath* does not interpret reflexes of ME /ā/ which occur in the word and which *AES* distinguishes by mapping in red. This is the item for which Glauser queries some of the reflexes which have been discussed above. In these cases rounding adjustment would have been expected. By his accumulation of examples relating to the same phenomenon, Glauser is able to reveal some of the problems inherent in this data.

Map 7.7 combines the responses of Maps 7.2 to 7.6 and identifies a transition zone in which degrees of rounding adjustment are recorded. We have already referred to the discussion of transition zones by Chambers and Trudgill which prompted Macaulay to investigate in paper 10 the behaviour of post-nasal velar stops in word-final position. Glauser's study of the transition zone created by the rounding adjustment, however, is more ambitious than that attempted by Chambers and Trudgill, in that it comprises no fewer than 118 localities. Certainly only five items were investigated, compared with 65 in some 31 localities surrounding the Wash in Chambers and Trudgill's work. But by limiting himself to only five variables, Glauser is able to give exact scores for every possible dimension of variation of rounding adjustment occurring in these items. Whereas Chambers and Trudgill let localities with 0 per cent and 100 per cent determine the external limits of their investigation, Glauser at least investigated each locality in all the 15 counties in which there is evidence for neither complete presence nor complete absence of rounding adjustment, and which *de facto* constitute this transition zone. A different picture emerges if only those items are considered which display some degree of variability with regard to rounding adjustment. In the terminology of Chambers and Trudgill these localities display 'mixed lects', and around a mid-point of 50 per cent display scores of either more rounding adjustment or less. They may be thought of as 'mixed Southern lects' and 'mixed Northern lects', respectively. This structure of the transition zone has been drafted by Kirk in Map 1.3. The map reveals that the line which separates mixed Southern from mixed Northern lects runs from the Severn estuary to the centre of the Wash in a South-west to North-east direction. From this isogloss it may be inferred that rounding adjustment has not only been innovatory from the Midlands southwards, but

that, within the North-South transition zone where it is not fully established, it is also notably more established in the East than in the West.

Thus, Glauser and Macaulay agree about the importance of investigating the structure of transition zones. Rounding adjustment, the development of ME /ǭ/, or the occurrence of post-nasal velar stop consonants may be singular or individual phenomena, but their distribution is anything but monolithic. The use of contrastively graded hatched areas, of absolute number symbols and the progressive bundling of isoglosses are new ways of overcoming some of the difficulties concerning variation in linguistic data. These cartographical techniques not only benefit from comparison but may also serve to meet some of the criticisms of existing maps which are reiterated by Macaulay himself in the first section of his paper.

Macaulay's Map 10.12 of voiced velar stops after velar nasals may be compared with Glauser's Map 7.1 of the reflexes of ME /ǭ/ as in *goose*. Macaulay identifies a relic area with a 100 per cent occurrence rate. Surrounding this area there is a concentric distribution of decreasing percentages of occurrence of the item, until finally it is absent altogether. By contrast, Glauser identifies a particular set of localities — for example, those he numerically symbolises as 4 or 6 or 8 — which are the result of an additive process which has slight variations in each case. Macaulay's relic set may also be thought of as displaying 100 per cent resistance to a singular additive process — that is, loss of the final stop. Just as Glauser's areas are surrounded by others to a degree less advanced, so Macaulay's area is surrounded by one to a degree less resistant, and so on, until the pattern in each case coincides with the general standard form. The approaches reverse each other, Glauser arguing from the general to the specific, Macaulay from the specific to the general, even though the one is based on an analysis of phonological structure and the other on frequency distribution. Both approaches depend on the map to reveal the particular nature of the data. It is the cumulative comparability of the new maps in this volume which lends itself to such critical assessments.

Some comments may also be appropriate on Macaulay's other cartographical innovations, as they break similar ground with very different data. He takes as an example the *LAS* map of *splinter*. Following the lead of the editors of the

Map 1.3: Rounding Adjustment in the Midlands

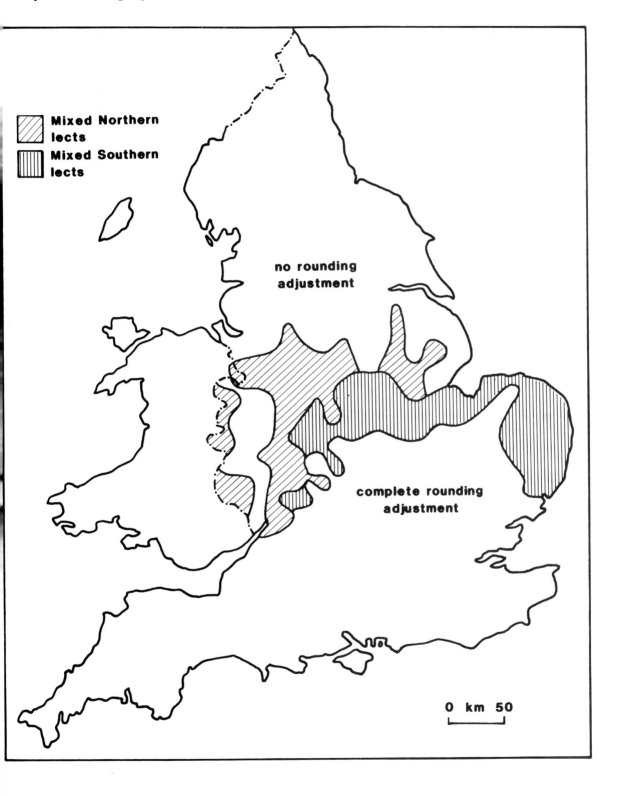

atlas, he proceeds to reduce the items on the map by merging etymologically related forms. Two patterns emerge in the data. One is that *skelf* itself is the commonest as well as the most widely distributed type, and usually occurs in addition to any one of some four other more localised types. Two maps are produced, one (by hatching) of *skelf* as a percentage of all responses; the other (by heteroglosses) of the regional limits of the other types, with their tokens subsumed: *spelk*, *spall*, *splice* and *spilk* which are alternatives to *splinter*. The two maps are set out on facing pages for ease of comparison, and follow a reproduction of the *LAS* on which they set out to improve. A combination of the two new maps was originally proposed but it was felt that it would be unsatisfactory to superimpose heteroglosses of the otherwise undifferentiated geographical limits of certain types on to the hatched percentage occurrences of the geographically predominant type. However, as Macaulay is concerned in a general way about the relationship of items in a geography, the maps should properly be considered together.

Since this collection of papers is breaking new ground, especially in the cartography, it is difficult to maintain complete consistency in terminology or cartographical technique. Wherever possible, however, we have attempted to interrelate the various approaches and the wide-ranging nature of the contributions. Nevertheless, flexibility is essential in responding to and interpreting the maps, bearing in mind that many of them are innovative and experimental. The interrelationships between the papers re-emphasise the continuing importance of the SED as a focus for further research. This common ground shared by all the papers contributes significantly to the coherency and integration of the volume as a whole. Collectively they demonstrate that many different approaches to the data, its analysis, interpretation and mapping yield remarkable new information. Moreover, they suggest that the SED and other linguistic surveys amply repay detailed investigation and have much to offer which as yet remains unexploited.

Part of the original conception of this volume was that it should act as a forum for the cross-fertilisation of ideas in the mapping of linguistic data. It is our hope that the papers presented here will fulfil that aim. Many of the maps had a long gestation, and although new maps emerged from discussions between editors and contributors, the contributors have worked independently and are to that extent uninfluenced by each other's papers.

While the maps are of course integral to specific papers, their innovatory nature and the opportunities which so many new maps offer for comparison, not only among themselves, but also with others, make them particularly significant. In suggesting some possible ways forward within the discipline, the papers and maps in this collection are primarily intended to stimulate new responses and further investigation. We believe that, in spite of recent dissension, linguistic geography as it has been traditionally practised has never been in a healthier or more buoyant state, and has many fresh insights to contribute to the study of language, both now and in the future.

References

Anderson, P. 'The Dialect of Eaton-by-Tarporley (Cheshire): A Descriptive and Historical Grammar', 2 vols., unpublished PhD thesis (University of Leeds, 1977)

Bolinger, D. *Aspects of Language*, 2nd edn (Harcourt Brace Jovanovich, New York, 1975)

Bothe, D. *Direkte und indirekte Transkription — Ein Vergleich zwischen dem phonetischen Notationsmaterial des 'Survey of English Dialects (Worcesteshire)' und Magnetbandtranskripten* (Francke, Bern, 1971), (The Cooper Monographs, vol. 16)

Burgschmidt, E. *Koexistenz, Distribution, Äquivalenz, Synonymie: Studien zur Beschreibung der mittelenglischen Lokal- und Temporalpräpositionen* (privately published, Nürnberg, 1976)

Chambers, J.K. and P. Trudgill, *Dialectology* (Cambridge University Press, Cambridge, 1980)

Cheshire, J. *Variation in an English Dialect* (Cambridge University Press, Cambridge, 1982)

Freudenberg, R. 'Isoglosse: Prägung und Problematik eines sprachwissenschaftlichen Terminus', *Zeitschrift für Mundartforschung*, vol. 33 (1966), pp. 219-32

Glauser, B. *The Scottish-English Linguistic Border* (Francke, Bern, 1974), (The Cooper Monographs, vol. 20)

—— *A Phonology of Present-Day Speech in Grassington*

(*North Yorkshire*) (Francke, Bern, 1984) (The Cooper Monographs)

Goebl, H. *Dialektometrie — Prinzipien und Methoden des Einsatzes der Numerischen Taxonomie im Bereich der Dialektgeographie* (Verlag der Österreichischen Akademie der Wissenschaften, Wien, 1982), (Denkschriften der philosophischen-historischen Klasse, vol. 157)

—— *Dialektometrische Studien*, 3 vols. (Niemeyer, Tübingen, 1984), (Beihefte zur *Zeitschrift für Romanische Philologie*, vols. 191-3)

Graddol, D. *Language Variation and Diversity* (Open University Press, Milton Keynes, 1981), (E263 Language in Use Block 1 Course Book)

Grice, H.P. 'Logic and Conversation', in P. Cole and J.L. Morgan (eds.) *Syntax and Semantics 3: Speech Acts* (Academic Press, New York and London, 1975), pp. 41-58

Kirk, J.M. Review of Bothe (1971), *Lore and Language*, vol. 3, no. 7 (July 1982), pp. 88-91

—— Review of M.V. Barry (ed.) *Aspects of English Dialects in Ireland* (1981), *Lore and Language*, vol. 3, no. 8 (January 1983), pp. 107-10

Lass, R. *English Phonology and Phonological Theory: Synchronic and Diachronic Studies* (Cambridge University Press, Cambridge, 1976)

—— 'Mapping Constraints in Phonological Reconstruction: On Climbing Down Trees without Falling out of Them', in J. Fisiak (ed.), *Recent Developments in Historical Phonology* (Mouton, The Hague, 1978) pp. 245-86

—— 'John Hart *Vindicativus*? A Study in the Interpretation of Early Phoneticians', *Folia Linguistica Historica*, vol. 1 (1980), pp. 75-96

Leech, G. *Principles of Pragmatics* (Longmans, London, 1983)

Luick, K. *Historische Grammatik der Englischen Sprache*, 2 vols. (Blackwell, Oxford, 1964)

McDavid, R.I. 'Retrospect' (paper originally presented at a symposium celebrating the fiftieth anniversary of the Linguistic Atlas of the United States and Canada, 1979), *Journal of English Linguistics*, vol. 16 (1983), pp. 47-54

Morgan, B.J.T. and D.J. Shaw. 'Graphical Methods for Illustrating Data in the Survey of English Dialects', *Lore and Language*, vol. 3, no. 7 (July 1982), pp. 14-29

Newbrook, M. 'Sociolinguistic Reflexes of Dialect Interference in West Wirral', unpublished PhD thesis (University of Reading, 1982)

Orton, H. 'LANE and LAE: Lexical Links', in L.H. Burghardt (ed.), *Dialectology: Problems and Perspectives* (University of Tennessee, Knoxville, 1971), pp. 3-37

Petyt, K.M. 'Who is Really Doing Dialectology?', in D. Crystal (ed.), *Linguistic Controversies* (Arnold, London, 1982), pp. 192-208

Shorrocks, G. 'A Grammar of the Dialect of Farnworth and District (Greater Manchester County, formerly Lancashire)', unpublished PhD thesis (University of Sheffield, 1980), (available from University Microfilms International, no. 8170023)

Speitel, H.-H. 'An Areal Typology for Isoglosses', *Zeitschrift für Dialektologie und Linguistik*, vol. 36 (1969), pp. 49-66

—— 'The Word Geography of the Borders', *Scottish Literary Journal*, Supplement no. 6 (1978), pp. 17-37

Thomas, A. *The Linguistic Geography of Wales* (University of Wales Press, Cardiff, 1973)

—— *Areal Analysis of Dialect Data by Computer — a Welsh Example* (University of Wales Press, Cardiff, 1980)

Widdowson, J.D.A. *From Hunter to Newspeak: Dialect Study in the Sheffield Region, 1829-1984* (unpublished paper presented as an Inaugural Lecture, University of Sheffield, 21 March 1984)

2

Linguistic Geography in England: Progress and Prospects

STEWART SANDERSON AND
J.D.A. WIDDOWSON

Dialectology, the study of regional and social variations within a language, has a long and interesting history. In Britain it has progressed from the word lists of the early antiquarians and the glossaries of eighteenth-century and nineteenth-century collectors through the increasingly more analytical studies of the philologists to the survey-based investigations of the mid-twentieth century. These last have included both the circumscribed area studies of sociolinguists and the more widely ranging studies conducted by 'traditional' dialectologists.

Whereas the former have tended to publish analytical studies of the speech of specific localities, the latter have preferred to publish the full results of their enquiries both in the form of comprehensive and classified lists of their data and also by means of dialect atlases. These, as Bloomfield observed in 1933, comprise 'collections of maps of a speech area with isoglosses drawn in', and 'are an important tool for the linguist'.[1]

While identifying the importance of such atlases for the linguist, today Bloomfield would no doubt have added to his statement other means of symbolising data on maps, even though the isoglossic method remains one of the main current techniques in linguistic cartography. As this volume demonstrates, dialect geography, which Bloomfield defines as 'the study of local differentiations in a speech area',[2] has made considerable advances in the last fifty years. These advances are to be seen for example in theoretical approaches to the subject, in fieldwork and sampling methods, in analysis at all levels — phonological, lexical, grammatical and syntactical, including of course quantitative

evaluations — and not least in cartographic techniques.

At the present time the detached observer could not fail to notice the high level of popular interest in the dialects of the British Isles and Ireland, an interest matched by an equal degree of scholarly activity and research which has been sustained for more than a century. This is not surprising, since the study of dialects is relevant to much wider linguistic research than might be construed from the concept of 'dialectology' as it is popularly and narrowly envisaged.

The results of dialect investigations can fruitfully be applied to many other branches of language study, and indeed to an impressive range of cultural studies including history, literature, anthropology, folklore and social studies in general. Its applications may be extended beyond British cultural boundaries also, for example in helping students of English as a second language to appreciate and differentiate between the manifold variations of both social and regional speech. Indeed it is perhaps only dialectologists and TEFL researchers who are obliged to come to grips with important nuances of idiomatic expression, in both writing and speech, at all levels of usage. English is particularly rich, for example, in its extraordinary variety of individual words and their synonyms for all sorts of everyday notions; and these are distributed both regionally and socially. One of the highest achievements in communicative skill, especially for the foreigner, is to become fluent in choosing the appropriate language form in any given context of communication, from formal written or spoken usage to the colloquial, the intimate, and the jocular — not to mention the skilful use of persuasive, ironic, or deliberately patronising modes of address, and even on occasion the deployment of subtly insulting innuendo.

Many writers, and especially novelists working within the tradition of the English social novel, are experts in deploying these multifarious linguistic registers, which are especially important when manipulating the subtleties of contrasting social backgrounds. In lighter fiction, on the stage, in radio and television drama, in popular song and in the stories and jokes of professional comedians or ordinary people on social occasions, these delicate nuances of usage often have a humorous role to play, a role which has received singularly little serious attention from academics. In an earlier period also one might note among the English classics, for example, the accurate representation of regional dialect in Hardy's novels, in *Wuthering Heights*, and in the works of Scott, to say nothing of the long historical tradition of poetry written in vernacular Scots, in a line stretching from the so-called Scottish Chaucerians through Douglas, Lindsay, Fergusson and Burns to Hugh MacDiarmid, Robert Garioch and others. Nor should we omit such English poetry as William Barnes's work or the bravura of Tennyson's *Lincolnshire Farmer*.

Turning to spoken English, the regional dialects continue to preserve a range of grammatical forms which were originally part of the standard language and which today, although on the losing side when competing with modern Standard forms, can still be studied in the context of living speech rather than as fossils to be quarried from printed sources. The SED reveals, for example, a remarkable number of auxiliary verb forms, most of which have now been superseded in Standard usage — for example, the use of *do*, both present and past, as a non-emphatic tense marker as in *he do take* (cf. *SED* IX.3.7 'take': 31 So 4, 7; 32 W 1, 5, 8; 36 Co 5, 6, 7; 38 Do 2, 3, 4-5). Then there are the strong and weak past participle forms (e.g. *tret* and *bet*); the survival of the 2nd and 3rd singular verb inflections *-est* and *-eth* (familiar also because of the widespread influence of the legacy of the Authorised Version); the survival too of the pronouns *thee, thou, ye* and plural forms such as *youse*; double negatives; and the adverbially modified demonstrative as in *thick there there* = 'that one there' (*SED* IX.10.3 'that over

there' 31 So 13).

Despite extremely rapid erosion in the late twentieth century, the dialects continue to preserve numerous older grammatical and syntactical usages, whereas Standard English continues to shed inflexions and other distinctive features. While the regional dialects still have the double comparatives and superlatives used in Shakespeare's day, the Standard language is losing the old distinction of duality in the comparatives, so that Standard speakers no longer always insist upon using 'taller', 'better', and so on, when only two referents are being compared. The educated insistence upon the use of the relative 'whom' in oblique cases, which appears rarely if ever in regional dialects, is nowadays in decline, while the use of 'to him and I' and the hypercorrection 'to he and I' are gaining ground though they still jar on the ears of the purist.

Much of this range is unrecognised as dialectal by the man in the street, who normally associates the word *dialect* only with vocabulary, whereas of course the words themselves represent only one level of variation, and dialects also exhibit wide ranges of pronunciation, grammar and syntax differentiation. The educational system has tended to perpetuate the myth that Standard English is the oldest and purest English. What we now call Standard English, however, is merely the development of one variety of English which appeared as late as the fourteenth century. What the layman has been led to believe is that other regional forms of English have less historicity, whereas in truth they have more and can claim unbroken lineages from the distribution patterns of the settlement of the Germanic tribes in these islands as early as the fifth century.

In fact English has never been a single homogeneous language. The various dialects of the Low Germanic invaders from the fifth century onwards, superimposed on the original Celtic dialects of Britain, of which there were several, inevitably produced a complexity of linguistic usage, and even the earliest Old English records manifest variation and patterns of distribution which are the ultimate origins of all successive regional dialects.

From medieval times writers have occasionally commented on the way language differs in various parts of the country. These observations, coming as they do from literary figures, no doubt reflect a much more acute sense of such differences than might be apparent to the population at large. They often reveal social attitudes, including the regional and group chauvinism which is mirrored today in the affirmation of solidarity by rival factions through linguistic means. These dimensions, of which historians of the language have long been aware, have more recently become a particular focus of attention for sociolinguists.

Despite these early hints of social and regional differentiation, however, the nineteenth-century philologists preferred to concentrate on evolving a descriptive system of the development of English sounds and of features of grammar and vocabulary, which first identified the evolution of forms in the Standard language as filtered through the writing system. They recognised broad dialectal differences and consequently assigned the texts to certain geographical regions and to specific historical periods. These assignments were made on somewhat tentative, not to say crude, principles, and indeed it is only in recent years that more precise information on both regional distribution and dating has been achieved through more refined methods, as for instance in the *Atlas of the Dialects of Later Middle English* currently being prepared under the direction of Professor Angus McIntosh.

Once the territory of the literary documents had been charted and rules for sound changes in the Standard language established, scholars turned their attention from the dusty documents to the vivid presence of the range of speech forms heard around them every day. This shift of focus brought with it the realisation that many regional forms of English did not follow the same rules of sound change as those of the Standard language.

This concentration on phonology was continued with the development of early phonetic alphabets such as those devised by A.J. Ellis, but concurrently the formation of the English Dialect Society in 1873 generated renewed interest in lexis, leading to the production of numerous local dialect glossaries, many of which indicated pronunciation by means of the new alphabets. These glossaries themselves have a distinguished lineage; they descend from the word lists and vocabularies compiled by seventeenth- and eighteenth-century antiquarians such as John Ray, Edward Lhyd and Francis Grose. Unfortunately they do not cover the whole country systematically; nevertheless they remain a valuable record of late-nineteenth-century usage.

As confidence grew in the accurate transcription of the sounds of speech, dialectologists were able to move away from the philologists' preoccupation with the evolution of the Standard language. In so doing, and despite their neglect of social context and their universal tendency to study older forms merely as 'survivals' — a stance equally shared by the social scientists of the day — they nevertheless began to reveal a wealth of data and its attendant problems which concentration on Standard English had failed to bring to light.

Concurrently with this, the idea of representing English dialectal features in cartographic form emerged in 1876 when Prince Louis-Lucien Bonaparte published the first dialect map of England.[3] His linguistic interests were wide-ranging and led him to act as an energiser of others in the compilation of vocabularies and glossaries in many tongues, including Manx Gaelic, Orkney Norn and Cornish, amongst other languages spoken in Britain. His travels 'amongst the uncultivated peasants' (as he put it) in rural England made him unusually aware of the rich variety of regional usage throughout the country and led him to the farsighted notion of representing dialectal features in the form of maps. He thus became a pioneer of linguistic geography as we know it today, identifying thirteen distinct dialects in England, composed of groups of closely related 'sub-dialects' and 'principal varieties', which he depicted on a map by plotting the varieties and drawing lines to link them together into dialect areas.

While Prince Bonaparte seems to have regarded county boundaries and groupings as possible constraints on dialectal variation, A.J. Ellis in his extraordinarily influential study first discerned English dialect distributions on a larger geographical scale.[4] His maps were the first to attempt to demonstrate these larger groupings of regional features through the use of what he called 'transverse lines' — what later generations of dialectologists were to refine into the more flexible concept of 'isoglosses'. Even today Ellis's suggested dialect areas continue to serve as useful points of comparison for the distribution of the material collected by later surveys.

After these early attempts, linguistic cartography in Britain made no further progress for over half a century. Attention shifted to the compilation of a dictionary of English regional dialects which would incorporate information from the various English Dialect Society glossaries. This work, Joseph Wright's monumental *English Dialect Dictionary*,[5] drew also on both printed popular material and the responses of local correspondents in various parts of the country. Together with its *Supplement* and accompanying *English Dialect Grammar*[6] it stands as the only lexicon of English dialects to date and also provides an essential basis for further research of many kinds. For example, it provides information on the geographical distribution of the entries, which allows comparison with data from later surveys not only within the British Isles but also in all those parts of the English-speaking world where settlers from the Old Country have brought their regional usage as part and parcel of their transplanted culture.

After the flurry of activity which led to the publication of *EDD*, although a few monographs were written on the dialects of individual parishes or localities,[7] no extensive survey was to be made for forty years, though Harold Orton embarked on a small regional survey in Northumberland and Durham in the 1930s[8] and the American Guy Lowman did the same in the South of England.[9] Nevertheless, the need for a large-scale survey of spoken English dialects was raised from time to time, most notably by Joseph and Elizabeth Mary Wright in 1923[10] and by the American linguistic geographer Hans Kurath in 1935,[11] in both instances within the context of the historical reconstruction of English dialect boundaries in earlier periods. For the Wrights, such a survey would help to fix more precisely the boundaries of Middle English dialects, of which they could provide only an approximate classification in their *Elementary Middle English Grammar*; for Kurath, on the other hand, the study of North American dialects of English must needs be built on the foundation of a reconstruction of the various English dialects of the seventeenth century, a task which in turn would have to be based very largely on 'a linguistic atlas of English folk speech of the present day'.[12] The advocacy of such an atlas should no doubt be seen within broader European horizons. Though we can detect a line of continuity in the United Kingdom all the way from the first pioneering efforts to the atlases

published in the 1970s and 1980s, this continuity is by no means insular, for it has absorbed both inspirational spirit and some technical innovations from continental scholars; in particular, Eduard Gilliéron's *Atlas Linguistique de la France* (1902-10), though outmoded in its cartographic technique, was specifically referred to in 1923 by Joseph Wright, and later inspired John Orr, a Romance philologist from Tasmania, to play a cardinal role from his Edinburgh Chair in the foundation of the Linguistic Survey of Scotland. Nor has this been a one-way traffic, as is attested by the field research and publications of many European and other scholars who have based their work on, or collaborated in, dialect research programmes in Britain. One can nonetheless trace a scholarly apostolic succession in the study of dialectology in England, especially from A.J. Ellis to Joseph Wright, and so through H.C. Wyld and Harold Orton to the younger scholars concerned today with surveys of the English speech of Wales and Ireland. Orton in particular stands out uniquely in Britain as carrying the torch of dialect studies from the 1920s to his death in 1975, a torch whose light, though periodically flickering, blazed steadily from the later 1940s not only in his hands in England but also in others' hands elsewhere. A scholar of international renown and very much the innovator, Orton's archetypal historical study of his home village of Byers Green was the model for dialect studies in England for over thirty years until synchronic approaches became fashionable in the 1960s. Forward-looking and a skilled entrepreneur from the outset, he remained remarkably vigorous and young in mind with the advancing years and enthusiastically encouraged a new generation of dialectologists.

As a result of Kurath's suggestion in his address to the Second International Congress of Phonetic Sciences in 1935, a small committee was formed to prepare a memorandum on a linguistic atlas of Britain; but this initiative was unfortunately frustrated by the approach of the Second World War. However, as the war drew to an end, Harold Orton, who had been a member of the committee, revived the idea, eventually inviting Eugen Dieth of Zürich University (a participant in the 1935 Congress who during the war years had interested himself in the work of Swiss linguistic geographers) to visit him in England in order to discuss co-operation in a new attempt to organise such a venture. Orton, who had been a member of the Philological Society since 1932, sponsored Dieth's membership of the Society and arranged that they should present a joint paper in December 1946, outlining their proposals for a new survey of English dialects. At the same time Orton persuaded the Society's Council to set up a planning committee to promote such a survey, with such good effect that by March 1947 the Council resolved to carry out a pilot survey in a few selected areas with a view to compiling a methodological handbook and questionnaire to be used in a more ambitious and comprehensive exercise. Harold Orton in Leeds, John Orr in Edinburgh, and C.L. Wrenn in Oxford were appointed as the Survey's directors, each one to be responsible for the pilot scheme in his own region. To their names were later added those of Angus McIntosh, by now Forbes Professor of English Language and General Linguistics at Edinburgh, and — at Orton's instance — of Eugen Dieth. These pilot survey proposals also proved in the longer term abortive. This was partly because the Philological Society had neither the funds to finance them nor the machinery to seek such substantial funding, and partly because the Universities of Leeds and Edinburgh — Oxford with its collegiate structure was differently circumstanced — were not only in a position to finance major projects but also, through the energetic advocacy of their respective professors, resolved to give high priority in their academic development plans to the institution of surveys for both England and Scotland. Nevertheless, much credit must be given to the Council of the Philological Society for seizing imaginatively on Orton's and Dieth's proposals and for giving moral encouragement to those who were to conduct the new English and Scottish surveys.

Looking back, it seems in some ways regrettable that the Survey of English Dialects and the Linguistic Survey of Scotland were not more closely and systematically co-ordinated in the topics covered by their fieldwork and questionnaires; a greater overlap between both these and the North American questionnaire items could perhaps have led to more integrated publication and comparison of the materials in atlas form and otherwise. On the other hand, it is not surprising that the two sets of scholars had differing views on both theoretical and methodological matters besides certain pragmatical

divergences — the Linguistic Survey of Scotland, for one thing, was faced with a wholly different linguistic situation both historically and contemporarily and was itself organised in two sections for Scots and Gaelic, with three directors at the University of Edinburgh in the persons of Angus McIntosh, Kenneth Jackson of the Chair of Celtic, and David Abercrombie as Head of the Department of Phonetics. Nevertheless, the papers in the present volume amply demonstrate that scholars have not in fact found it impossible to discuss material from the various surveys in Britain and Ireland on a comparative basis.

Confining our attention for the moment to the SED and the Scots section of the LSS, the main differences between the two Surveys, apart from details of questionnaire items, are to be found in fieldwork methods and the forms of publication. The SED relied on a questionnaire placed in the hands of fieldworkers who recorded the responses in IPA script, supplementing this with sound recordings of free conversation on a range of topics; the LSS on the other hand gathered its material both through direct fieldwork recordings and two postal questionnaires constructed in such a way that the respondents could themselves return the information. As regards publication, the SED took the more expensive route of publishing in the first place all its Basic Material in numbered and geographically keyed lists, following this with an aspectually comprehensive linguistic atlas as a separate and later exercise. The LSS on the other hand has adopted the stratagem of publishing its data in list form accompanied by a smaller number of selected maps, in volumes covering first the lexical aspects and eventually phonology. Both approaches have their merits; both also represent pragmatic decisions reached in the real world of fluctuating academic resources of both personnel and finance, a point disregarded, and one suspects unimagined, by some critics who have complained that these publications do not tally with the ideal plans they themselves would have preferred to see realised. One also suspects that the editors who have not only wrestled with financial and managerial problems but also with the technical problems of presenting their data cartographically in readable and assimilable forms, may be at least as fully aware as their critics of the compromises that have had to be made and the shortcomings that have had to be accepted.

It is of course true that both SED and LSS, both as field surveys and in their publications, leave something to be desired, not least in minor but irritating inconsistencies in the presentation of their material. But if the methodology and fieldwork sampling of the SED, for instance, now look out of date, and its resulting analysis consequently rather hidebound, it may be argued that they were both rigorously conceived and indeed forward-looking when they were established nearly forty years ago. Nor are they as unsatisfactory as has sometimes been suggested by a later generation of linguists. The Dieth-Orton questionnaire is often dismissed as being rurally oriented and deployed on a restricted and unrepresentative sample of informants, mainly men and all agricultural workers, neatly but misguidedly characterised by Chambers and Trudgill as NORMs (nonmobile rural older males).[13] But a closer examination reveals that lengthy sections of the questionnaire are concerned with anything but farming topics; that there are quite a number of female respondents; that the male respondents' occupations are wide-ranging; and that certain urban localities were included on the Survey network, though admittedly it is not easy to detect more than fortuitous reasons for their selection. Further, one must reaffirm that SED has fulfilled its primary objectives, which were, firstly, to establish a linguistically comprehensive database for the speech of one particular stratum of society at an especially critical period of social and technological change; secondly, to make the data available to the scholarly world so that major statements could be made about dialectal speech across the whole of England; and thirdly, to enable new comparative studies to be undertaken, both temporally and spatially, in the future. Together, the SED and LSS constitute baselines for such studies over the past eighty or so years since the publication of the *EDD*, continuing to focus attention on the unbroken development of dialectal speech.

The institution of such surveys of English speech in both Wales and Ireland, and of a regional survey in Cornwall which has already published data in map form,[14] go some way towards fulfilling these last objectives, as do other smaller projects, mainly in the form of postgraduate research, in Leeds, Sheffield and other universities over the past 35 years.[15] These

exhibit considerable variety. They are urban as well as rural in orientation, and explore grammar, syntax, and morphology as well as phonology, lexis and lexical erosion, and occasionally also the material culture referents of lexical items. But these achievements, together with free-standing but unco-ordinated investigations of the speech of such cities as Norwich, Liverpool and Leeds,[16] cannot be substitutes for a new nationwide survey. Furthermore, there has been no publication of the data, let alone analysis, of the ambitious and innovative Tyneside Linguistic Survey initiated nearly twenty years ago. It explored a number of new techniques, methods of fieldwork and sampling, but regrettably the collected material may never be published because of the untimely death of the Survey's founder, Professor Barbara Strang.[17] The major resources of the Survey of English Usage, initiated by Professor Randolph Quirk in 1959, have been drawn upon in a number of important studies in recent years. However, scholars have not yet availed themselves of the opportunity, for example, of comparing the SEU's massive body of data on spoken English with the material currently available on social and regional dialects. Thus, while it can be said of this whole area of academic effort that it has been fruitful in producing competing methodologies — which is no bad thing — it fails to add up to any kind of national policy for the investigation of regional and social varieties of spoken English throughout the country in the closing decades of the twentieth century, when English language and culture are experiencing some of the most fundamental changes since medieval times.

Until the industrial revolution the basic culture of the British peoples was essentially rural and agricultural; and indeed, as industrialisation and urbanisation gathered pace, it was the peasant and yeoman population which maintained the traditional British way of life in all its aspects including the language which is a mirror of that life. In the burgeoning towns and cities, this rural stock adapted to urban living but still continued to nurture its new growth from the traditional cultural roots. Urban dialects should therefore be viewed not as separate and distinct from their rural counterparts, but as directly developed from them and as part of the continuing evolution of language within a historic culture. Even those villages which have been absorbed into urban areas continue to maintain a surprising independence which is reflected in all sorts of ways, from the village store to the church, the pub, community life and even local features of linguistic usage.

The Standard language is of course the medium through which maximum communicability is best achieved; and such a standard is still the norm for instance in the courts, the professions, business, the armed forces, broadcasting, and the presentation of a unified model of usage for second language learners. However, in primary education in recent years stress has been placed on the development of oracy and the achievement of confidence in self-expression: there is less effort than formerly in our more flexible education system to suppress regional dialect features, particularly at the outset. At the secondary level children are made aware of the various social strata of linguistic usage and have some degree of freedom in choosing the styles and registers which they think may be appropriate not only for specific occasions but also in projecting their own view of themselves or their lifestyle. Speech therapists, for example, are especially aware of these aspects of language acquisition and social correction in addition to the physical problems of articulation.

But can we be certain that these welcome innovations in educational practice rest on sufficiently secure foundations? It is an axiom of linguistic research that if it is to have real validity it must be based on reliable and verifiable data. Surprisingly, there are comparatively few extensive databases for the study of varieties of English, and especially of social and regional dialects. Just as the Tyneside Linguistic Survey concentrated on a specific geographical region, a number of individual studies of specific aspects of local speech and language variation have recently emerged which are usually also limited to single topic areas, either socially or geographically.[18] Utilising techniques and sampling methods drawn from sociolinguistic research, they are not directly referable either to each other or to 'traditional' studies in methodology, in content, or in presenting a comprehensive overview of a broad span of material in published form. What they do, essentially, is to examine in depth the social stratification of linguistic usage in specific urban areas, revealing patterns of usage in the various constituent reference groups of age, sex, socio-economic class, and so on. While each of these investigations breaks new ground, they do not constitute a unified database for detailed comparisons, as each methodology necessarily differs according to the investigative method and constraints imposed by the particular local conditions of any such survey. An untenable dichotomy has been set up between 'traditional' dialectology and that area of sociolinguistics which sees spoken dialects as its field of study. Yet it remains to be proved whether the overtly plausible profiles of urban speech typical of recent sociolinguistic analyses are necessarily more reliable than SED as a database for extrapolation.

The few surveys in the British Isles which can claim extensive coverage, whether geographical or social, have been undertaken quite recently, as is also true of their counterparts in North America. The Survey of English Usage and the SED both attempt to assemble representative corpuses illustrating the range and complexity of the English language as it is commonly used.

The SED Database and its Potential

Even the most trenchant critics of *LAE* acknowledge the importance of the SED data and note, for example, that 'The materials will undoubtedly serve for decades to come as a major research tool for those interested in dialectology and the processes of language change.'[19] Yet those critics demand far more than might reasonably be expected of *WGE* and *LAE*, given that these two atlases were principally intended to present a representative selection of the collected material to reveal some of the main patterns of distribution and to offer some basic interpretations of the data in cartographical form. With hindsight, and especially taking account of more recent advances in both mapping technique and analysis, the two atlases could have presented the material to better effect. In McDavid's words: 'The case could be even more convincing: clearer cartography, more explication, and an emphasis on pattern rather than item would not only be more useful for synchronic comparison but make a stronger diachronic case.'[20] If constructive comments such as these are accepted, they may be taken as important starting-points for further research. The same is true of a number of criticisms of

LAE, which seems to have been singled out for particular critical attention. The investigation of fieldwork methods, for example, and especially discrepancies between the transcription practices of the same fieldworker in different localities, or between one fieldworker and another, would no doubt yield valuable insights, as Bothe[21] and Kirk[22] have already suggested. The *LAE* editors were aware that in some SED localities, notably in North Norfolk and Leicestershire, the data caused particular difficulties in mapping, but whether the superficial singularity of these areas was due to discrepant transcription or simply to actual dialect differences has yet to be established. The investigation of individual methods of transcription would be a major and lengthy task which the *LAE* editors could hardly have been expected to undertake themselves, though, as McDavid has pointed out,[23] the Basic Material provides ample evidence for such a study in the future, including the calibration of transcriptions. When we noted in the Introduction to *LAE* that our practice had been to adhere faithfully to the transcriptions in the *Basic Material* we were deliberately relying on its integrity as published, especially as Harold Orton and his co-editors had fully noted in those volumes any modifications to the fieldworkers' transcriptions, but we also allowed for the possibility of a degree of reappraisal in the light of more detailed study of the field recording books and tapes in due course. Our central aim was to permit close comparison between the atlas and the published volumes of Basic Material. Few dialect atlases have presented a critical appraisal of transcription practices, even though discrepancies are not infrequent even among expert phoneticians.[24] Those which have given an account of transcription methods, usually very cursorily,[25] can rarely claim that all the fieldworkers were trained by one individual nor that all the transcriptions came under the same editorial scrutiny, which was the case with Harold Orton's close supervision of the fieldwork, analysis and publication of the SED.

We were also very much aware of the arbitrary nature of isoglossic mapping and that in positing certain transition zones between distributional areas we were perhaps suggesting a greater degree of complexity than might actually be the case if the locality network were densened. However, we were careful also to map every individual variant occurring within a given isogloss, so that while areas within isoglosses show the dominant form, alternative patterns of distribution may be inferred from the presence of individual variants. Isoglosses are intended not so much to attract attention to themselves as to identify contrastive forms on either side of a notional divide. Thus we are not claiming any greater status for the isoglosses than is implicit in our interpretation of the Basic Material, and while recognising the complexity of such *LAE* maps as Ph193 'four' we fail to see why the reasonably trained eye of any dialectologist finds them 'virtually impossible to decipher'.[26]

In condemning our isoglossic practice as 'the spaghetti approach to dialect cartography'[27] one critic at least is evidently unable to see not only that the long loops of spaghetti on his plate are carefully and systematically placed, but also that individual and specific alphaghetti symbols are clearly identifiable among the loops. By contrast, the simple transference of data to maps locality by locality (what might be termed 'the bean approach') offers no opportunity for comparison between groups or clusters of contrasting forms. Paradoxically, those who find the spaghetti approach too complex to assimilate seem to find the plethora of near-identical beans on non-isoglossic maps easy to read. While the bean approach is inevitably static and non-interpretive, the use of isoglosses, in spite of its limitations — especially its inability to indicate gradient phenomena — identifies contrasting distribution areas and suggests possible paths of extension or retreat of a specific form. The controversial extension of narrow tongues of isoglosses to encompass one or two outliers, often along a valley or a path already identified by the presence of other outliers, prompts further enquiries in depth to determine whether the feature is advancing, in retreat or merely pointing to a possible earlier link with a cognate area from which it has since become separated. Harold Orton's contention in such cases was that the interpretive authority of the isogloss should match the authority of information in the Basic Material. Certainly the tendency is to maximise the extent of non-standard features, the intention being to offer an interpretation and at the same time to stimulate alternative readings of the data and/or the collection of fresh evidence through more fieldwork. Many of the more vociferous critics of both SED and *LAE* identify actual or potential shortcomings, all worthy of further investigation, but singularly fail either to offer more acceptable alternatives or, more significantly, to actually tackle the enormous critical problems faced by editors and produce maps of their own. Useful though many of the criticisms may be, they expect too much and frequently misrepresent the more limited aims of both the Survey and the atlas.

Many of the more recent techniques of analysis and cartography presented in this volume demonstrate these limitations and suggest ways of overcoming them. At the same time, however, they reveal numerous fundamental problems faced by all those who wish to interpret and present this vast and complex body of data in the most meaningful and accessible manner. To take just one example: in summarising data for maps, the *LAE* editors were at times obliged to present a slightly more generalised account of specific variants, notably by subsuming minor phonetic variants. Anyone who attempts the same task will quickly recognise the difficulties of presenting the full range of variants available in the detailed phonetic transcriptions in the field notebooks. The editors had to decide how best to interpret and present the evidence, relying to a great extent of course on Harold Orton's own experience and expertise. The practice of subsuming minor variations (usually of a phonetic or phonological nature) within major forms was adopted in order to make the maps more readable, the details being invariably presented in the notes accompanying each map, revealing the editors' practice in each case. The evidence of the maps and legends, along with the published *Basic Material*, remains available for others to interpret.[28]

While much of the SED data may be consulted in print and offers numerous opportunities for further exploration, few have taken up this challenge prior to the papers presented here. In addition to the directions in which these papers lead in their various individual responses to the SED, the LSS and other surveys, it is useful to point out some additional ways in which the SED material may be exploited and/or extended. These include:

The Basic Material

The rich resources of the Basic Material, comprising some 404,000 responses, remain remark-

ably unexploited. For example, the detailed phonetic record of the speech of 992 individuals in 313 localities[29] has been examined only in very general terms. The locality network was carefully planned by Harold Orton to reflect the variety of usage in selected communities optimally some 15 miles apart from each other throughout the country, the exact distances between each being modified to some extent by the disposition of suitable fieldwork locations on the map and on the ground. Consequently the localities constitute a systematic base for eliciting a representative range of data from the target population. The data has virtually unlimited potential, not only for the analysis of individual pronunciation and its representativeness for a given locality but also for a more refined examination of distribution patterns than has been carried out hitherto, taking account of the information available on socio-economic status, age, sex and social context. Such investigations would allow comparison with other accounts of regional pronunciation not only in numerous dissertations and published studies but also in more recent surveys, both rural and urban, whether local or more broadly based. The complexity of detailed phonetic variation makes it inevitable that such studies as those of Anderson, Shorrocks, Storr, Wakelin and Widdowson[30] are limited to specific localities, but it is to SED that their authors turn in order to set their data in a fuller regional context. The time-consuming nature of both the transcription process and the analysis of such variation also militates against their being undertaken on a larger scale, yet such evidence is to be found in abundance in the published material of the SED.

Above all, the SED is a unique record of regional lexis at a crucial stage in the evolution of English dialects when the last vestiges of the older pattern of rural life were still discernible. The fullness of this lexical record is astounding, revealing as it does as many as 89 different words for a single notion. It is difficult enough to decide when to identify a given variant as distinctive (e.g. VI.7.13 'lefthanded' responses *keggy*, *kaggy*, *kecky*, *cacky*, and III.8.4 'weakling' responses *rickling*, *ritling*, *rinklen*, *rinkling*, *recklien*, *reckling*, *rutling*), but virtually impossible to present all the responses for 'lefthanded' satisfactorily in cartographical form except in such a large-scale map as would be much too unwieldy for publication and not amenable to reduction to a smaller scale. Much work remains to be done, for example, on the precise point of demarcation between two simple phonological variants and between two recognisably distinct lexical items. This demarcation is complicated by historical considerations too, as for instance in *LAE* map L50a 'freckles' where the forms presented are all derived from ON *freknur*, yet some (e.g. *frackens*, *frettles*, *feckles*) might be regarded as lexically distinct while others (e.g. *vrackles*, *vreckles*, *vrickles*) could be regarded simply as pronunciation variants. It is to such fundamental problems as these that the *LAE* editors had to address themselves, and their decisions will stand until more acceptable solutions are proposed. Commentators on *LAE* all too often underestimate such problems, and fail to appreciate that compromises must be reached and pragmatic decisions taken if material is to be made accessible in published form.

Whereas the SED provides a full and representative inventory of lexis drawn primarily from the rural agricultural population, it must be borne in mind that only two of the nine books of the questionnaire deal exclusively with farming. The questions in the remaining seven, comprising the bulk of the questionnaire, are such as may be answered equally well by people of all ages and classes, urban as well as rural. The claim that such an approach is ' "traditional" dialectology with a vengeance' and that there is 'exclusive emphasis on the antiquarian and agricultural'[31] is manifestly unjust, not to say inaccurate, and takes no account of the fact that at the time of its conception and application the questionnaire was both up to date and farsighted. Nor should we forget that the tape-recorder, especially in portable form, was still in its infancy after the field survey had begun, making it all the more necessary to rely on trained fieldworkers. According to one critic[32] their sole function was 'to select informants and then to perform as recording machines' — no mean tasks, as anyone who has undertaken fieldwork will readily attest. Can we be sure, moreover, that a team of transcribers working from taperecordings will necessarily and invariably be more accurate and unanimous in their transcription than someone actually working, albeit impressionistically, in the field with a personal knowledge of the informant and the interview context?

When the lexical inventory is used as a basis for comparison with material from later surveys, as for example with the findings for the onomasiological section of the *Atlas Linguarum Europae*, its breadth and depth become even more apparent. What little preliminary work has been done[33] suggests, for example, that there has been a dramatic erosion of regional lexis during the intervening thirty years or so, again underlining the timeliness of the SED fieldwork. Much remains to be done on the erosion and also the retention of dialectal vocabulary from the time of the early glossaries to the present day. The rediscovery of many early studies, and especially the exciting prospect of evaluating the detailed and painstaking Glossic transcriptions of Thomas Hallam,[34] reminds us forcibly that all sources of evidence for dialect study, properly evaluated, may assist in piecing together a fuller record of usage.

The lexicon also has immense potential for the study of special vocabularies. Among these, of course, words concerning farming and country life are very fully represented in the data. Equally interesting, however, are the responses to questions which reveal aspects of folklore, folklife and cultural tradition in general, from proverbs and sayings, through children's traditions, to custom and belief, and of course material culture and traditional arts and crafts. This productive vein of material is virtually unexploited.[35] The SED also provides evidence against which to set new surveys of special vocabularies. It is unfortunate, for example, that the locality network virtually ignored the coastal perimeter. Harold Orton was very conscious of this and planned a nationwide survey of localities on the coast, to complement the SED data with linguistic information on maritime lifestyles and occupations.[36] The few available studies of coastal communities by English researchers[37] reveal remarkably persistent patterns of usage preserved in what can only be seen as a series of relic areas whose language until recently remained markedly distinct even from that in the immediate hinterland. A survey of such localities would probably even now reveal an extensive range of older regional usage which escaped the SED net and would certainly also demonstrate the recent changes consequent upon the rapid incursion of more Standard usage into relic areas.

The Basic Material has as yet been analysed and exploited mainly in general ways, and the papers in this volume, together with useful pointers from the more constructive commentators and critics, are the first attempts to carry the analysis further. Before this could be done, however, it was necessary for the Basic Material to be published and for the *LAE* to present a modest selection of the data in cartographical form. The SED is a child of its own time and could not be expected to adopt methodologies which had not then been developed. Moreover, its so-called 'historical bias' is of value to historians of the language, even though the *LAE* offers a phonetic rather than phonological interpretation. Anyone who has ventured to work out from the Basic Material even the basic phonology within a single locality will readily agree that this is by no means an easy task, let alone any attempt to map phonological variation nationwide. Phoneticians have shown a remarkable reluctance to investigate transcriptions in the field notebooks of both Basic and Incidental Material, to say nothing of the taperecordings, preferring instead to base their comments on the published data.

One of the most neglected aspects of the SED data is the information on morphology and grammar. While the SED questionnaire elicited a range of grammatical features, notably in Book IX but also scattered through the earlier Books, they have received virtually no attention until now. It is especially surprising that linguists, preoccupied as they tend to be with grammar, have not taken advantage of this data. Its strengths lie for the most part in the extraordinary diversity of verb forms, elicited by carefully phrased questions to maximise the variety of functions and to permit detailed comparisons to be made of these functions and of their distribution, not to mention their potential for the study of linguistic evolution. The responses for *do*, *go*, *have* and *be* in particular will repay further investigation. The inflections of nouns and pronouns also deserve attention. Analysts and commentators shy away from such thorny questions as precisely how morphological variation might best be classified. Since, for example, verb forms may simply vary phonologically (e.g. past tenses of strong verbs), according to lexical choice (e.g. the various historical conglomerations in the dialectal paradigms of *be*), according to their respective pronominal antecedents (e.g. second person singular present tense forms) or because of the introduction of negative particles, and so on, the distinctions between them are not amenable to rigid classification within the accepted levels of analysis. The SED furnishes numerous examples of these and many other aspects of morphological and grammatical variation, not to mention a remarkable set of verb paradigms which await further study.

It must be acknowledged that the Basic Material of the SED reveals comparatively little information on syntax, since this was not central to its aims, and indeed the detailed and systematic study of syntax is a more recent development. Nevertheless, the Basic Material provides some useful insights, notably when responses consisted of a phrase or clause, the data being sufficient for nine syntactical maps to be included in *LAE*. These maps pose tantalising questions about the underlying reasons for the regional distribution of syntactic features. To take just one example, *LAE* map S7 conclusively demonstrates the predominance of *five-and-twenty* (to three), archaic in Standard English, among the surveyed sample and at the same time challenges scholars to discover why the Standard *twenty-five to three* is found in seven smaller areas separated from each other by the predominant form. There is no simple answer to such questions on social or synchronic grounds alone; the historical and diachronic perspectives for this reference group at least are essential. The investigation of such features in the speech of other reference groups would make a fascinating comparative study in which different patterns of distribution, contemporary and social rather than historical and regional, would no doubt emerge. Much fuller evidence about dialect syntax, however, is to be found in the Incidental Material and of course in the taperecordings. The questionnaire method is unsuitable for eliciting syntactical data as those who have used Book IX of the SED Questionnaire in the field are well aware. The recording of free conversation, as the SED tapes demonstrate, is much more productive in this respect. The *LAE* inevitably presents its selection of the data in a somewhat simplified way, leaving later scholars, including the contributors to this volume, to develop and reinterpret the material in more detail and with the benefit of more recent techniques.

The Incidental Material

While critical attention has focused on the published data, the very substantial information contained in the Incidental Material has remained virtually untouched, except in its illumination of individual items in the editing of the Basic Material and its contribution to the biographical profiles of informants. These profiles incidentally await analysis and reveal a much greater variety of occupation, age, sex, and social and educational background than is often recognised. While farmers and farm-workers inevitably bulk large, other occupations include: agricultural engineer, baker, black-smith, bricklayer, builder's labourer, butcher, cabinet-maker, carter/carrier, coal-merchant's assistant, coal-miner, cobbler, cutler/insurance agent, estate worker/hunt-master, ferry skipper, foreman clay-worker, fustian cutter, game-keeper, greengrocer/smallholder, grocer/draper, groom/chauffeur, hurdle-maker, joiner, licensed victualler, miller, overlooker in cotton mill, painter and decorator, plasterer, plumber, policeman, quarryman, potato merchant, railway-crossing keeper, railway engine driver, road-sweeper, saddler, sailmaker, schoolmaster, seed merchant's representative, shopkeeper, shrimper, steam-roller driver, steel-worker, steward/forester, stone-mason, tailor, thatcher, transport worker, water-works man, weaver, wheelwright, wood-haulier/smallholder, wood-turner, workman in bleach factory. Many informants had had more than one occupation, the first often being on the farm but later ones usually involving somewhat higher social status. Contrary to the suggestion that the informants are virtually all male,[38] no less than 118 women were interviewed, and several were tape-recorded. Although housewives predominate, the female interviewees have a variety of occupations from domestic servant to carrier, factory-worker, school-cleaner, cook, smallholder and singer.

Even a cursory examination of the Incidental Material demonstrates its importance, not only in setting the data in context, but also in supplying numerous additional forms and synonyms (frequently couched within a fuller utterance), phrases, and information on temporal and spatial distribution. Elicited in free conversation, it is by its very nature heterogeneous and diverse, complementing and extending the more controlled questionnaire responses of the Basic Material. Without an extensive knowledge of and frequent recourse to the Incidental Material it is impossible to analyse the SED data as a whole. It is equally unwise to make sweeping critical statements when commenting only on the published data, or to base ambitious new projects on the Basic Material alone. Clearly there is considerable scope here for further research and indeed Harold Orton proposed four companion volumes of selected Incidental Material to complete the published record.

The Taperecordings

By far the least exploited SED resource is the collection of taperecordings made in the field. The editors have already commented on its fundamental importance for syntactic studies, for example, in the Introduction to this volume. It is also potentially perhaps the most important legacy of the SED, not only as a unique historical record at a time when the taperecorder was only just coming into general use in this country, but also as a means of checking and evaluating the fieldworkers' impressionistic transcriptions. As with the Incidental Material, Harold Orton habitually referred to the recordings during the editing process, both to check the fieldworkers' transcriptions and to seek information which might help to resolve various editorial problems. To attempt a full transcription, analysis and comparison of all the taperecordings would indeed be a daunting task, but steps must be taken in that direction if we are to capitalise on this vital resource. Initially, working copies of the tapes themselves must be made available so that at least we shall know the extent of the task.[39]

The SED material as a whole offers many other opportunities for further study. In addition to individual papers such as are presented in this volume, and more extensive studies in the form of books and monographs, current research is continuing in several directions. For example, a dictionary of the Basic and Incidental Material[40] which will provide an alternative means of access to the lexical data is now in the planning stage, a preliminary study of the entries being almost complete. Moving in a somewhat different direction, a popular atlas, based on SED material, is

GOSHEN COLLEGE LIBRARY
GOSHEN, INDIANA

now in the final stage of preparation.[41] Further, the fact that 66 SED localities were investigated for the onomasiological section of the *Atlas Linguarum Europae*, together with 15 English-speaking localities in Scotland, 16 in Wales and 4 in Northern Ireland allows additional opportunities for comparison, especially in England where the erosion of the rural lexicon during the intervening 30 years is nothing less than devastating.[42] In the light of this discovery the SED was indeed timely in recording the range and variety of older rural usage when sufficient members of that historically important linguistic stratum, the 'old prior culture'[43] were still able to pass on their knowledge, which, like much of their speech, was relatively uninfluenced by secondary education and by book-learning in general.

Future Prospects

Beyond these immediate projects which derive directly or indirectly from the SED, dialectology in the British Isles and Ireland is poised to move forward in other directions. Among these one might suggest the following:

1. The mutually beneficial development of a rapprochement between 'traditional' dialectologists and sociolinguists, leading to an exchange of ideas and methods which give equal prominence to both the diachronic and the synchronic approach.
2. The instigation of new fieldwork, drawing on recent advances in sampling, data collection, analysis and presentation.
3. The redressing of the research balance by extending the trend towards the investigation of urban usage, not only in the larger conurbations but also in smaller towns where the interface between urban and rural speech is often more apparent and a representative survey more feasible.
4. The systematic study of social dialects and the social context of usage, whether urban or rural. While sociolinguists have studied this usage in cities they have been much less inclined to extend their investigation to rural communities. Conversely, with very few exceptions,[44] neither they nor 'traditional' dialectologists have examined exclusively regional features in larger conurbations.
5. The new and systematic fieldwork so urgently needed should in due course lead to the possibility of a new national survey of both social

and regional dialects. Such a survey will be in the fortunate position of avoiding the shortcomings of the SED and other surveys and also of reaping the benefits of newer, more refined approaches to the study; it is essential to the establishment of an adequate database for generating major statements concerning language variation throughout the country.
6. In seeking to document linguistic change dialectologists and sociolinguists should join forces to investigate the speech of immigrant communities at this early stage of their undoubted and increasing influence on English language and culture. Conversely, such studies will also reveal the influence of English usage on that of the immigrants.
7. Renewed interest in the work of nineteenth-century dialectologists and glossarists, notably such pioneers as Thomas Hallam, offers fresh opportunities for the reinstatement of historical studies of dialect as an essential part of the discipline as a whole. In extending the boundaries of knowledge and advancing the study of all aspects of dialectology, it is inevitable that researchers must take account of previous work. However inadequate such earlier studies may be, they offer useful insights which we cannot afford to ignore. In redressing the balance from diachronic studies of the older rural mainly working-class population towards synchronic studies of a broader more representative sample of the urban population according to age, sex and socio-economic class we must guard against the danger of exclusive concentration on the latter approach at the expense of the former. While modern synchronic investigations have been undertaken in only a handful of urban areas, evidence for the history and development of regional speech in rural areas is not only extensive but reaches back much further in time. This fact alone indicates its potential for historical and comparative research — a potential still largely unexploited.
8. The collation and comparison of the many continental European studies based directly or indirectly on the *SED* or relating to it in some way, in order to take account of the considerable number of such studies, many of them little known to British dialectologists, and to draw attention to the important contribution which European scholars continue to make to the discipline.[45]
9. The comprehensive study of the lexical and phonological data of the fieldwork in England

and Wales for the onomasiological section of the *ALE* to enable a detailed comparison to be made not only with the 66 English localities which ALE and SED have in common, but also with that from a number of localities covered in SAWD and *LGW*. Such a project would identify trends in the rapidly changing patterns of usage in specific communities and in rural dialects as a whole.

10. The investigation in depth by folklorists of the substantial data on traditional culture in both the Basic and Incidental Material. In the absence of a national folklore survey this material offers valuable evidence on the form, function, provenance, distribution and persistence of this aspect of our heritage. More important, it constitutes the only extensive record of the linguistic means through which such material is transmitted both spatially and temporally.

Co-operative projects such as those outlined in (6), (7) and (8) above should also lead to more effective and broadly-based financial support for future work. Hitherto, such support has been sporadic and unpredictable, and notwithstanding the generous funding of the SED much of the ensuing research and publication has been undertaken with the minimum of financial backing.

As long as our efforts in these fields remain on a small scale, fragmented and unco-ordinated, they are unlikely to attract the necessary support from national institutions, particularly at a time of severe economic restraint.

Beyond these more immediate channels into which dialectologists might usefully direct their endeavours, there are a number of challenging major projects which merit serious consideration. Among these are:

1. The computerising of the SED data — a process already under way — and that of other more recent surveys, to facilitate collation, comparison and analysis.

2. The production of computer maps with the aim of minimising the simplification and distortion of presenting data cartographically, even though, as in (1), the results will depend on interpretation and coding, so that the ideal of a fully objective analysis may well prove elusive.

3. The development of more accurate acoustic means of analysing speech, eliminating a considerable degree of the inconsistency inevitable even in the concerted transcriptions of tape-recorded material by several trained linguists. Again, ideal objectivity is hardly achievable since human speech is by its very nature inconsistent, anomalous and gloriously fallible when measured against absolute norms. Even so, much greater objectivity is both desirable and necessary if the level of accuracy and comparability is to be improved.

4. The creation of a national databank of information on English dialects from the earliest work to the present day, to be continuously updated and made accessible for reference and research. This resource would include data from surveys, glossaries, monographs and other studies from all sources, including of course the work of continental European and North American scholars. The establishment of such an ongoing national repository would greatly facilitate the eventual synthesis of this huge body of information, much of which has hitherto remained undervalued and unused.

In conclusion, it is clear that over the last hundred years the various dialect surveys and studies, each operating in relative isolation, have generated massive quantities of data, most of it uncollated and unexplored. Recent developments in sociolinguistic and quantitative analysis, coupled with the potential for transferring data onto computers for both storage and comparison, offer exciting prospects for the future. By co-operating in utilising these resources, dialectologists and sociolinguists have a unique opportunity to combine the strengths of their respective disciplines — disciplines which are not as far apart as they may seem. In bridging the gap between older-established and more recent approaches, a useful first step would be to acknowledge the rightful place of the SED in the evolutionary chain of English dialectology and of English language studies in general. Just as the sociolinguistic approach to dialect study has its obvious merits and has substantially advanced the discipline in recent years, 'traditional' dialectology can also claim its own justification. Data-based and empirical in its approach and verifiable in its data from its field recordings, it is also comparable, within its terms of reference, over the country as a whole and is a baseline for subsequent research. Far from being static and backward-looking the so-called 'traditionalists' are flexible in approach and willing to adopt new techniques. The 'modernists', on the other hand, have often in their proselytising zeal felt the need to dogmatise in defence of their concept of the only true faith. Attitudes of this kind are counter-productive, especially since in response to Petyt's recent question, 'Who is really doing dialectology?'[46] the answer is, 'All of those who study dialects'. It is only through a concerted effort to capitalise on all their respective resources and expertise that the two related disciplines can positively advance the study of the rich diversity of our dialects both spoken and written, and pass on the fullest possible record of them to future generations.

Notes

1. Bloomfield, L. *Language* (Holt, New York, 1933), p. 51.

2. Bloomfield (1933), p. 321.

3. Bonaparte, Prince L.L. 'On the Dialects of Eleven Southern and South-Western Counties, with a New Classification of the English Dialects' *English Dialect Society Series D, Miscellaneous*, Miscellanies II (1876), pp. 13-24.

4. Ellis, A.J. *On Early English Pronunciation*, Parts I-V (Early English Text Society, London, 1867-89); see especially Part V: *The Existing Phonology of English Dialects*.

5. Wright, J. (ed.) *The English Dialect Dictionary*, 6 vols. (Oxford University Press, London, 1898-1905).

6. The Grammar was also separately published: Wright, J. *English Dialect Grammar* (Frowde, Oxford, 1905).

7. See for example Cowling, G.H. *The Dialect of Hackness (North-East Yorkshire)* (Cambridge University Press, Cambridge, 1915); Reaney, P.H. *A Grammar of the Dialect of Penrith (Cumberland)* (Manchester University Press, Manchester, 1927).

8. Orton, H. 'Northumberland Dialect Research: First Report', *Proceedings of the University of Durham Philosophical Society*, vol. VII (1937), pp. 127-35. The material for this survey was deposited by Harold Orton in the Institute of Dialect and Folk Life Studies at the University of Leeds.

9. For an account of Lowman's work see Viereck, W. 'Guy S. Lowman's Contribution to British English Dialectology', *Transactions of the Yorkshire Dialect Society*, vol. XII, part LXVIII (1968), pp. 32-9; *Lexikalische und grammatische Ergebnisse des Lowman — Survey von Mittel- und Südengland*, 2 vols. (Fink, Munich, 1975); 'The dialectal structure of British English: Lowman's evidence', *English World-Wide*, vol. 1 (1980), pp. 25-44.

10. Wright, J. and E.M. Wright. *Elementary Middle English Grammar* (Oxford University Press, London, 1923), pp. 2-3.

11. Kurath, H. 'The Linguistic Atlas of the United States and Canada', *Proceedings of the International Congress of Phonetic Sciences*, ed. D. Jones and D.B. Fry (Cambridge University Press, Cambridge, 1936), pp. 18-22 (paper delivered to the Congress in the previous year).

12. Kurath (1936), p. 20.

13. Chambers, J.K. and P. Trudgill. *Dialectology* (Cambridge University Press, Cambridge, 1980), p. 33.

14. North, D.J. *Studies in Anglo-Cornish Phonology: Aspects of the History and Geography of English Pronunciation in Cornwall* (Institute of Cornish Studies, Redruth, 1983).

15. See for example Anderson, P. 'The Dialect of Eaton-by-Tarporley (Cheshire): A Descriptive and Historical Grammar', 2 vols., unpublished PhD thesis (University of Leeds, 1977); Cheshire, J. *Variation in an English Dialect* (Cambridge University Press, Cambridge, 1982); Heath, C.D. *The Pronunciation of English in Cannock, Staffordshire: A Sociolinguistic Survey of an Urban Speech Community* (Blackwell, Oxford, 1980); (Publications of the Philological Society, vol. XXIX); Knowles, G. 'Scouse: The Urban Dialect of Liverpool', unpublished PhD thesis (University of Leeds, 1974); Johnston, P. 'A Synchronic and Historical View of Border Area Bimoric Vowel Systems', unpublished PhD thesis (University of Edinburgh, 1980), summarised in *English World-Wide*, vol. 2 (1981), p. 234; Lawson, M.S. 'An Account of the Dialect of Staithes in the North Riding of Yorkshire', unpublished MA thesis (University of Leeds, 1949); North, D.J. 'Aspects of the Phonology and Agricultural Terminology of the Rural Dialects of Surrey, Kent and Sussex', unpublished PhD thesis (University of Leeds, 1982); Petyt, K.M. ' "Dialect" and "Accent" in the Industrial West Riding: A Study of the Changing Speech of an Urban Area', unpublished PhD thesis (University of Reading, 1977), to be published in *Varieties of English Around the World*, General Series (John Benjamins, Amsterdam); Shorrocks, G. 'A Grammar of the Dialect of Farnworth and District (Greater Manchester County, formerly Lancashire)', unpublished PhD thesis (University of Sheffield, 1980), available from University Microfilms in 2 parts, no. 8170023, and summarised in *English World-Wide*, vol. 2 (1981), p. 238; Storr, J.G. 'Survey of the Dialect of Selston in the Erewash Valley', unpublished MA thesis (University of Sheffield, 1977); Wakelin, M.F. 'Studies in the Linguistic Geography of Cornwall', unpublished PhD thesis (University of Leeds, 1969); Widdowson, J.D.A. 'A Pronouncing Glossary of the Dialect of Filey in the East Riding of Yorkshire', unpublished MA thesis (University of Leeds, 1966); Wright, P. 'A Grammar of the Dialect of Fleetwood (Lancashire). Descriptive and Historical', 2 vols., unpublished PhD thesis (University of Leeds, 1954); for a full listing of relevant studies see Viereck, W., E. Schneider and M. Görlach (comps.) *A Bibliography of Writings on Varieties of English, 1965-83* (John Benjamins. Amsterdam, 1984).

16. See Trudgill, P. *The Social Differentiation of English in Norwich*, Cambridge Studies in Linguistics 13 (Cambridge University Press, Cambridge, 1974); Knowles (1974); Petyt (1977).

17. A number of articles and studies relating to the Tyneside Linguistic Survey have been published, see for example Jones-Sargent, V. *Tyne Bytes: A Computerised Sociolinguistic Survey of Tyneside* (Lang, Frankfurt, 1983), and the entries under Pellowe J.N.H. in Viereck *et al* (1984).

18. Cf. Cheshire (1982); Heath (1980); Knowles (1974); Petyt (1977); Trudgill (1974).

19. Southard, B. Review of *LAE*, *Journal of English*

Linguistics, vol. 15 (1981), pp. 53-62 (p. 53).

20. McDavid, R.I. review of *LAE*, *American Speech*, vol. 20 (1981), pp. 219-33 (p. 229).

21. Bothe, D. *Direkte und indirekte Transkription — Ein Vergleich zwischen dem phonetischen Notationsmaterial des 'Survey of English Dialects (Worcestershire)' und Magnetbandtranskripten* (Francke, Bern, 1971) (The Cooper Monographs, vol. 16).

22. Kirk, J.M. Review of Bothe (1971), *Lore and Language*, vol. 3, no. 7 (July 1982), pp. 88-91.

23. McDavid (1981), pp. 224-5.

24. See Mackey, W.F. *Language Teaching Analysis* (Longmans, London, 1965), p. 57.

25. See for example Kurath, H. *Handbook of the Linguistic Geography of New England* (Brown University Press, Providence, 1939), pp. 48-53.

26. Southard (1981), p. 58.

27. Ibid.

28. For a fuller account of the genesis, aims and methodology of the *LAE* see Sanderson, S.F. 'Language on the Map', *University of Leeds Review*, vol. 20 (1977), pp. 160-71, and the Introduction to Orton, H., S. Sanderson and J. Widdowson (eds.). *The Linguistic Atlas of England* (Croom Helm, London, 1978); see also Sanderson, S. *Wordmap 1-5*, *New Society*, vol. 45, Nos. 828-32 (1978), pp. 357, 409, 463, 515, 577.

29. The full SED locality network comprises 313 communities; the names of two communities, Lyonshall and Newport, were inadvertently omitted from the list of localities in *LAE*, and consequently some reviewers have given the number as 311.

30. Anderson (1977); Shorrocks (1980); Storr (1977); Wakelin (1969); Widdowson (1966).

31. Moulton, W.G. Review of LAE, *General Linguistics*, vol. 20 (1980), pp. 151-63 (p. 153); cf. Milroy, L. *Language and Social Networks* (Blackwell, Oxford, 1980) (Language in Society 2), p. 4.

32. Moulton (1980), p. 153.

33. See for example Widdowson, J.D.A. 'Lexical Erosion in English Regional Dialects', unpublished paper presented at the Sociolinguistics Symposium, University of Sheffield, 1982.

34. For a preliminary account of recent work on Hallam, see MacMahon, M.K.C. 'Thomas Hallam and the Study of Dialect and Educated Speech', *Transactions of the Yorkshire Dialect Society*, vol. XV, part LXXXIII (1983), pp. 19-31.

35. Cf. however paper 9 in this volume in which P.L. Henry demonstrates how data from dialect surveys yields valuable information not only on the distribution of regional linguistic forms but also of traditional aspects of culture.

36. Harold Orton discussed these plans with several of the SED fieldworkers and other researchers during the 1960s, and some preliminary work was undertaken: see Wright, P. 'Fishing Language around England and Wales', *The Journal of the Lancashire Dialect Society*, no. 17 (1968), pp. 2-14; Wright, P. and G.B. Smith. 'A Lancashire Fishing Survey', *The Journal of the Lancashire Dialect Society*, no. 16 (1967), pp. 2-8.

37. See Lawson (1949); Widdowson (1966); Wright (1954).

38. See for example Milroy (1980), p. 4.

39. Stanley Ellis, the principal SED fieldworker who was also responsible for the bulk of the taperecording programme, is preparing for publication on tape/disc an anthology of representative speech from across the country, with transcriptions in normal orthography, providing a foretaste of the taperecorded material as a whole.

40. Hedevind, B., G. Melchers, S. Sanderson, J.D.A. Widdowson and A. Zettersten. *Dictionary of the SED* (in preparation). See Sanderson, S. 'The English Dialect Survey's Dictionary Project', in Hyldgaard-Jensen, K. and A. Zettersten (eds.) *Symposium on Lexicography: Proceedings of the Symposium on Lexicography, September 1-2, 1982, at the University of Copenhagen* (Georg Olms, Hildesheim, 1983) pp. 73-85.

41. Sanderson, S., C.S. Upton and J.D.A Widdowson. *Word Maps* (in preparation).

42. Widdowson (1982); taperecordings and duplicate field recording books for the onomasiological section of the ALE for England and Wales are deposited in the Archives of the Centre for English Cultural Tradition and Language, University of Sheffield.

43. The term is used by George Ewart Evans to designate pre-technological agrarian culture — Evans, G.E. *Where Beards Wag All* (Faber, London, 1970), p. 17ff.

44. See for example Shorrocks (1980); the Survey of Sheffield Usage, preliminary fieldwork for which is already under way, incorporates aspects of older regional usage in its predominantly synchronic investigations.

45. See for example Barth, E. *The Dialect of Naunton (Gloucestershire)*, (Keller, Zürich, 1968); Bothe (1971); Burgschmidt, E. *Koexistenz, Distribution, Äqivalenz, Synonymie — Studien zur Beschreibung der mittelenglischen Lokal- und Temporalpräpositionen* (privately published, Nürnberg, 1976); Edel, A. *Hochsprache und Mundart in Nordengland: Der hochsprachliche Einfluss auf den Wortschatz der Mundart in Northumberland und Cumberland* (privately published, Zürich, 1973); Elmer, W. *The Terminology of Fishing: A Survey of English and Welsh Inshore Fishing: Things and Words* (Francke, Bern, 1973) (The Cooper Monographs, vol. 19); Fischer, A. *Dialects in the South-West of England: A Lexical Investigation* (Francke, Bern, 1976) (The Cooper Monographs, vol. 25); Giffhorn, B. *Untersuchungen zu den englischen Dialekten: Der me. Typus 'waishen'*, (privately published, Bonn, 1978); Giffhorn, J. *Studien am 'Survey of English Dialects'* (Fink, München, 1979); Glauser, B. *The Scottish-English Linguistic Border* (Francke, Bern, 1974) (The Cooper Monographs, vol. 20); Glauser, B. *The Phonology of Present-day Grassington Speech (North Yorkshire)* (Francke, Bern, forthcoming) (The Cooper Monographs); Hedevind, B. *The Dialect of Dentdale in the West Riding of Yorkshire* (*Studia Anglistica Uppsaliensia* vol. 5, Uppsala, 1967); Ihalainen, O. 'Periphrastic *do* in Affirmative Sentences in the Dialect of East Somerset', *Neuphilologische Mitteilungen*, vol. 77 (1976), pp. 608-22; 'Relative Clauses in the Dialect of Somerset', *Neuphilologische Mitteilungen*, vol. 81 (1980), pp. 187-96; 'Grammatical Changes in Somerset Folk Speech', paper presented at the Third English Historical Linguistics Conference (Sheffield, 1983); Melchers, G. *Studies in Yorkshire Dialects based on Recordings of 13 Dialect Speakers in the West Riding*, 2 vols. (Department of English, University of Stockholm, 1972) (Stockholm Theses in English, vol. 9); Påhlsson, C. *The Northumbrian Burr: A Sociolinguistic Study* (CWK Gleerup, Lund, 1972) (Lund Studies in English, vol. 41); 'Stickers, Shifters and Others: Aspects of Dialect Space', paper presented at the Second Nordic Conference for English Studies (Espoo, 1983); Rydland, K. *Vowel Systems and Lexical Phonemic Patterns in South-East Cumbria — A Study in Structural Dialectology* (Department of English, University

of Bergen, 1973) (*Studia Anglistica Norvegica*, vol. 1); Stursberg, M. *The Stressed Vowels in the Dialects of Longtown, Abbey Town, and Hunsonby (Cumberland): A Structural Approach* (privately published, Basel, 1970); Tidholm, H. *The Dialect of Egton in North Yorkshire* (Bokmaskinen, Göteborg, 1979).

46. Petyt, K.M. 'Who is Really Doing Dialectology?', in D. Crystal (ed.) *Linguistic Controversies* (Arnold, London, 1982), pp. 192-208.

3

On Producing a Linguistic Atlas: The Survey of Anglo-Welsh Dialects

DAVID PARRY

Introduction

Fieldwork for the Survey of Anglo-Welsh Dialects (SAWD), conducted from University College, Swansea, is now complete. Two volumes of analysed results are already available (Parry 1977, 1980 dealing with South-east and South-west Wales respectively) and a third, dealing with the north, in preparation. This will be followed by (i) an Anglo-Welsh linguistic atlas and (ii) a glossary and a grammar of the Anglo-Welsh dialects. Methods of investigation in Wales are the same as those used for the Survey of English Dialects, the Dieth-Orton Questionnaire (Orton, 1962) having been employed with only slight modification (described in Parry, 1977: 277-80) since we aimed to collect material maximally collatable with that obtained in England (though of course the latter is on the whole rather older than that collected in Wales, where investigation began only in 1960). As Map 1.2 shows, the Anglo-Welsh (AW) network embraces 90 localities, all rural except for one in the Rhondda Valley, included in order to give industrial Mid-Glamorgan similar coverage to that of other counties, where investigated localities are if possible not more than 15 to 20 miles apart, often less. This policy of including, with the one exception, only rural dialects in the atlas means ignoring some more urban dialects (e.g. Abergavenny, Llanhilleth, Tonteg) that are represented in *SAWD* vol. 1; these will be dealt with in a separate future publication. Middleton in Gower, investigated in 1960, will also be ignored since the surrounding

area was adequately covered in investigations made about ten years later. Unfortunately, time and expense prevent our dispensing with all of the oldest material and we still have to use three *corpora* that are 20 years old (the other 87 dating from 1969 to 1981). These 20-year-old *corpora* all come from one area, having been obtained at Rhayader, Llanbister and New Radnor (P 15, P 16, P 20) in central Powys. But partial reinvestigation of these dialects, along with the evidence of material obtained more recently in neighbouring localities (Llangurig P 14, investigated 1972; Knucklas P 17, 1971; Stanage Park P 18, 1977; Painscastle P 22, 1972), suggests that the conservative dialects of this whole area changed little in the 1960s and early 1970s.

Although it is widely acknowledged that drawing isoglosses on a map is itself an act of interpretation, the projected Anglo-Welsh atlas will aim to do more than that in order to expose, explore, and where possible solve questions concerning the significance of the results of a dialect survey conducted in a country that is partly bilingual. A good deal of introductory and commentatorial material will be required.

Bilingualism and the Welsh Element in Anglo-Welsh Lexis

All our informants were of course able to speak English, but many considered Welsh their first language. That part of the Introduction to the atlas that deals, as it must, with the extent of the use of Welsh in the localities investigated should ideally, for places where Welsh is used at all, provide more information than just the percentage of the local population that is 'able to speak Welsh'. We need to know *who* uses it and in what social contexts — a matter of considerable complexity. In some places, people of all generations regularly speak Welsh; in others, only elderly natives do so. Some parents discourage their children from using Welsh; others seek special schools provided by Local Education Authorities where all instruction is conducted through the medium of Welsh. Some people attend Welsh-speaking chapels but (they say) always use English at home; others say they can read, but not speak, Welsh — and *vice versa*. Occasionally sermons can be heard in which each section of discourse is first given in Welsh, then repeated or summarised in English, and some village-square conversations appear to be constructed according to a similar pattern. One Carmarthenshire-born husband and his Merioneth-born wife speak to each other only in English because, they say, each finds difficulty in the other's dialect of the native tongue. Any A.J. Ellis-type Celtic boundary designed to show the linguistic preferences even of just our informants would be hard to draw and would require complex annotation. Perhaps even when all the available documents on bilingualism in Wales have been consulted, one may be unable to do more than quote bilingual informants' own assertions about their linguistic habits (noted by the fieldworkers) and try one's best to fit these into the broader picture that the documents suggest.

Informants in some localities gave a good many Welsh words in response to the Questionnaire, but SAWD of course is concerned with Welsh only in so far as it influenced the English spoken in the Principality. Welsh sounds used in pronouncing English, and Welsh-derived syntactical constructions, are easily recognised and there is no doubt about their status: they are not Welsh but Anglo-Welsh. Welsh *words* given as responses to questions designed to elicit AW pronunciation and grammar can of course be categorically ignored. But the same cannot be said of Welsh words given in responses to questions designed to elicit AW *lexis*. On the one hand they may be just 'intruders' -– by which I mean 'Welsh words given by an inform-

ant who merely draws on his Welsh word-stock to fill gaps in his English one': from the investigator's point of view the informant is answering in a foreign language, one already documented in Alan Thomas's *The Linguistic Geography of Wales* (Thomas 1973). On the other hand, a proffered Welsh word may be a genuine importation into the AW dialect of the locality: one might cite as examples the continuing currency of *twp* 'stupid', *pentan* 'the hob of a grate', *ach-y-fi!* (an exclamation of disgust) in Gwent, the Gower Peninsula, and other areas that have long been English-speaking. Here the language is so unarguably a dialect of English that no one need hesitate to accord such words the status of completely-established 'Welsh loans into Anglo-Welsh' and proper material for inclusion in the atlas. The difficulty lies in deciding the status to be accorded Welsh lexical items in the bilingual areas. No general principle suggests itself, but where an informant gave both a Welsh word and an English one we shall generally (not invariably — see below) ignore the former and map the latter, even if we suspect this latter to be just the English *translation* (learnt from school, dictionary, radio, and so on) that came most readily to the informant's mind: here of course is where the informants' assertions about their own linguistic backgrounds and preferences may help us assess the status not only of their Welsh words but also sometimes of their English ones. But where a Welsh word was the *sole* elicited response it will have to be accepted, *faute de mieux*, as 'the response' to that question for that locality. Can we attempt to distinguish 'intruders' from 'importations' in cases like these?

There are three ways in which perhaps we can: by using (a) evidence external to the dialect itself; (b) evidence internal to the dialect; and (c) our intuition.

The Welsh word *cardydwyn* was the sole response to the question 'What do you call the smallest and weakest pig of a litter?' at Drefach (Dy 5), where the informants, though amply fluent in English, generally prefer Welsh. But the same word occurs in many localities *surrounding* Drefach: not only the Welsh-speaking localities directly north and south of it but also at, for example, P 15 Rhayader to the north-east (long English-speaking), P 19 Llanafan-fawr to the north-east (even longer English-speaking), P 21 Llanwrtyd as well as the territory, south of the Pembrokeshire landsker, containing localities Dy 13, Dy 14, Dy 19, Dy 20, Dy 24, Dy 25 that have been English-speaking for centuries. Because of this external evidence of the persistence of *cardydwyn* in well-established English dialects in Wales one ventures to assume its future persistence in the developing English dialect at Drefach as well. Now in some of these well-established English dialects around Drefach we find not only *cardydwyn* but also other, non-Welsh, words expressing the same concept. Llanafanfawr, for instance, has additionally *crink, crank* and *cull*. And this, of course, is one of the exceptional cases referred to earlier in which we do *not* disregard a Welsh word in favour of an English one; for Llanafanfawr we shall map them all. *Cardydwyn* in the AW dialect of that locality is 'Welsh' only in the way in which, say, *garage* and *restaurant* in Standard English are 'French'. This analogy is even closer in the case of AW *bwbach* 'a scarecrow', which in some AW dialects retains the traditional Welsh pronunciation ['bubax] and in others is anglicised as ['bɒbə̈k].

The kind of *internal* evidence often at our disposal as an aid to assessing the status of Welsh lexical items is phonetic or, sometimes, syntactical. If the vowels of an AW dialect regularly include [e:], [o:], [ʊu] corresponding to, respectively, RP /eɪ/, /əʊ/ and the /u:/ conventionally spelt *ew, ue*; or if its consonants included rolled [r], clear [l] and [ts] corresponding to RP [ɹ], dark [ɫ] and /tʃ/, then that dialect has a propensity for introducing Welsh sounds into the pronunciation of English (though the [e:] and the [o:] alone, unaccompanied by any of the other items in the list, could result from borrowing of conservative forms from neighbouring dialects in England). A dialect notably rich in such 'Welsh sound-substitutions' may not have moved far from being just English spoken as a foreign language — an AW dialect that has not yet lived very long. For examples of the distribution of AW [r] and [ɹ] see Maps 3.1 *rabbits* and 3.2 *root*. The *grammatical* features of an AW dialect that may be indices of the same thing need treating more cautiously, and are nearly always syntactical rather than morphological. The construction *there's nice!* corresponding to Standard English *how nice!* is a literal translation from Welsh but it may be heard any day in the anglicised county of Gwent. *The name on*, rather than *of*, something is similarly a translated Welsh idiom,

as are *to read it on the newspaper* and *to pull a photograph*, but all are heard in Swansea, not just in the Welsh-speaking villages adjoining that city. More reliable syntactical indices of a strong continuing Welsh-speaking tradition are such items as *It's not very big of a town: OUT we were keeping them* (meaning 'We used to keep them not inside but outside'); *This is the man that his uncle died: They are going to church* (Standard English *They go to church* in answer to the question *What do good people do on a Sunday?*). Unfortunately, apart from the two last examples, most of the items in this category are recorded only as incidental material in the *SED*, hence they may occur in more of the investigated localities than those at which we have them attested; any future questionnaire must cater for systematic investigation of such items.

Now, if a dialect includes a good deal of Welsh sound-substitution and Welsh-influenced syntax and our impressions of these lead us to classify it as what I call a SWAWD (strongly Welsh-influenced Anglo-Welsh dialect), then the chances are that any Welsh word given as sole response to a lexical question will be just an 'intruder' unless external evidence (see above) suggests otherwise. Conversely, a marked lack of Welsh sound-substitutions combined with a dearth of recorded Welsh-influenced syntax suggests that the dialect concerned is a HAAWD (highly-anglicised Anglo-Welsh dialect), in which a Welsh word given as sole response to a lexical question is probably an established importation, whether there be corroborative external evidence or not.

Intuition comes into play in deciding the status of Welsh words, not only in directing us how to use the types of external and internal evidence discussed earlier, but also in directing our recognition of special cases, such as *ty bach*, 'an outside lavatory' but literally 'a little house'. This is used in plenty of dialects where it is hard to believe *lavatory, toilet* or other socially-accepted English euphemisms are unknown. Intuition suggests it is preferred to these latter because its euphemistic character is less eroded than theirs in an area where Welsh is little used, and we classify it as an established importation into the local Anglo-Welsh dialect.

Fieldworkers often asked Welsh-speaking informants for their own judgements whether a given word was Welsh or English. The assertions of the famous 'naive native informant' were not

Map 3.1: SAWD: *rabbits* (*R*-quality)

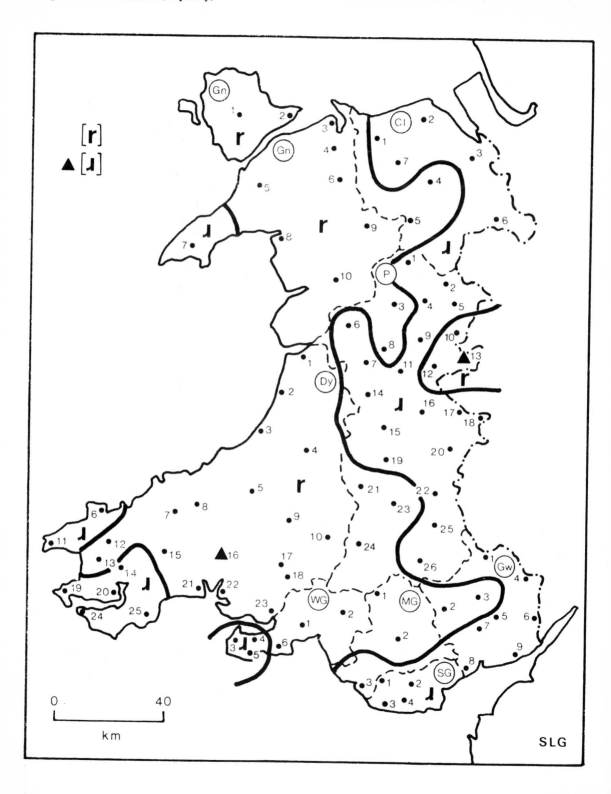

Map 3.2:   SAWD: *root* (**R**-quality)

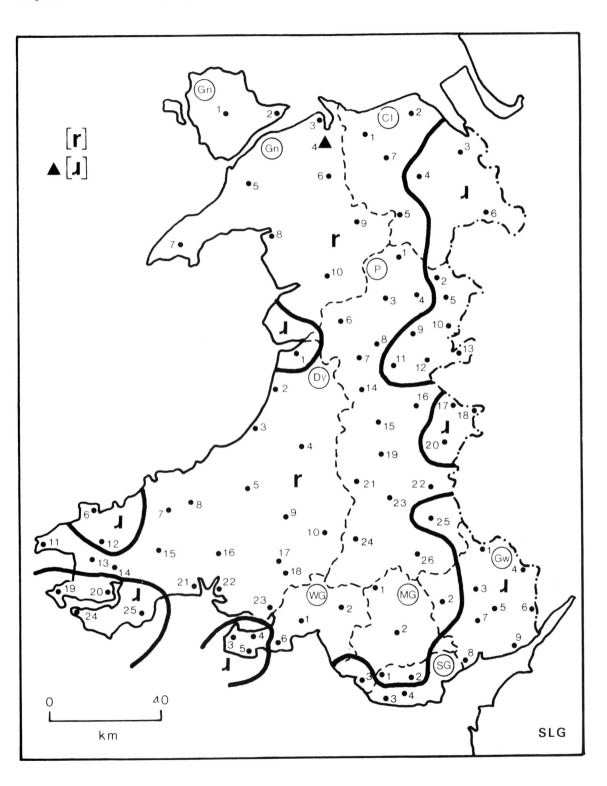

always helpful: *cwtsh* [kutʃ] is popularly designated 'Welsh' but the only thing really Welsh
about this form of English *couch* is its vowel; it
even contains, in [tʃ], a sound completely alien
to Welsh. But they did sometimes provide clues
to the status of words that are, historically,
English importations into Welsh that have 'come
back' into *Anglo*-Welsh. For instance *bowl*
[boul] 'the hub of a wheel', says one informant,
is 'the English word' and *bwl* [buːl] 'the Welsh
word'; in another place, *funnel* is designated
English and *tun-dish* — pronounced ['tundɪs] —
Welsh.

From the foregoing sketch of a rather complex
situation I hope the following principles have
emerged: (a) the term 'AW Dialects' is to
include whatever varieties of English were used
by the informants, and recognises some of the
Welsh words elicited as 'intruders' and others as
'importations', each word being judged on its
own merits in the locality concerned. Generally,
but not always, a Welsh word will be unmapped
if an English one is available. (b) Much introductory and commentatorial material will have
to be added to the maps in order to help the
reader assess their significance. (c) Argument
even from concrete evidence will often remain
impressionistic and even sometimes circular;
mere intuition, too, will not be despised
(provided it is acknowledged as such).

The English Element in Anglo-Welsh

In some areas of Wales the chief influences on
AW dialects are those of neighbouring dialects in
England, as might be expected. 'Neighbouring'
means not only 'adjacent', as in the case of the
dialects spoken near the border with England,
but also 'on the opposite side of the Bristol
Channel', as in the case of AW dialects of the
south coast. Generally speaking, these English
influences are readily identifiable as such from
the information in *LAE* and *SED*, or sometimes
from the older information in *EDD* and *EDG*.
Sometimes these works suggest that dialect
material has spread into AW from *specific* areas
of England; in other cases, an AW form proves
to be in *general* dialectal use in England; but
occasionally we find apparently-English forms
occurring in AW remote from enclaves of the
same form in England, or even that no such
English enclaves are attested.

South Pembrokeshire south of the landsker
(i.e. Dy 13, Dy 14, Dy 19, Dy 20, Dy 24, Dy 25)
and the Gower Peninsula (WG 3, WG 4, WG 5,
WG 6) share many dialect forms with South-west
England (by which in the present context I mean
all or part of Cornwall-Devon-Somerset), though
the extent of the distribution in both countries
varies considerably between one form and
another. *Offis/oavese* 'eaves of a haystack',
recorded in four South Pembrokeshire localities
and two in Gower, but nowhere else in Wales, is
widespread in South-west England, Wiltshire,
Berkshire and Dorset, but nowhere else in
England. Similary with *not-cow* 'hornless cow',
peculiar in AW to South Pembrokeshire/Gower
but in England spreading across not just the
South-west but also into Wiltshire, Dorset,
Hampshire and Gloucestershire. Initial [v]
corresponding to RP /f/ occurs much more
widely in South Pembrokshire and Gower than
elsewhere in Wales and of course has an English
distribution covering more than just the South-
west. How, then, on linguistic, rather than
historical, geographical or sociological evidence,
can we confidently posit a connexion between
South Pembrokeshire/Gower on the one hand
and specifically Cornwall/Devon/Somerset, more
than any other southern English counties, on the
other hand? The answer is of course that a
number of South Pembrokeshire/Gower features
occur in England *only* in the South-west; in some
cases this emerges not only from *LAE/SED*
evidence but from the older record in *EDD* too.
Here are a few examples from South
Pembrokeshire/Gower lexis followed by their
county distribution in England, from *SED* first
then from *EDD*: *culm* 'slack coal' (nil; D, So,
Ha); *frithing* 'wattling used in making hurdles'
(nil; Co, North-west D, West So); *foriers/vuriers*
'headlands of a field' (Co, D; Co); *pilk* 'to butt'
referring to cows (nil; D); *cawel* 'basket for
horse-fodder' (nil; Co); *murfles* 'freckles' (Co, D;
Co, D); *nestletripe* 'smallest pig of a litter' (D,
So, W, Do; D, So). Comparably-distributed
phonetic forms are much fewer, but one good
one is *thistle* with initial [d] (Co, D, So, W; D,
So, He) and an [ai]-type diphthong (Co, D; nil).
Similarly-distributed morphological items are
even fewer, but at Middleton, Gower (not now
included in the AW network, see above) in
1960 one informant had sporadic examples of a
third singular present-tense ending [θ] that is not,
so far as I know, recorded by *SED*, but compare

[ð] recorded in *EDG* (section 435) 'among the older generation of dialect-speakers' in Devon and Somerset.

Of the forms cited in the previous paragraph, most are found in both South Pembrokeshire and Gower, but a few only in the one or the other. The list of lexical items could be expanded considerably — and this applies to all three of the categories 'shared', 'South Pembrokeshire only' and 'Gower only'. Examination of the distribution of all these items in England may perhaps provide a statistical basis for deciding whether there is any significant difference between the English influences operating on the one AW area and those operating on the other in cases where the AW items are *peculiar*, in Wales, to either South Pembrokeshire or Gower.

While talking of forms being peculiar to these two AW areas it should be mentioned that the quest to identify English influences is complicated by the fact that some of these South Pembrokeshire/Gower words — all apparently English, or at any rate not Welsh — are not recorded in England at all. *Lattergrass* 'aftermath' is a case in point that occurs in *both* the AW areas. The list of peculiar South Pembrokeshire words includes *preen* 'to butt' referring to cows; *byholt* 'hired pasturage'; *lonker* 'a shackle'; *looch* 'a porridge-ladle'; *labbigan* 'a gossiping woman', all of which *EDD* records for Pembrokeshire or South Pembrokeshire only, besides others (e.g. *cutty-evver* 'newt', *trapple* 'threshold', *lockses* 'beard') that seem to be unrecorded anywhere but in *SAWD* vol. 2 (Parry 1980), along with others again from the *SED* Incidental Material, sometimes recorded in this area (only) by *EDD* and sometimes unrecorded in England at all though of course these last are outside the scope of the Dieth-Orton Questionnaire, which renders their absence from *SED*'s findings irrelevant in the present context. Some words in these groups defy my attempts to etymologise them, despite research with dictionaries of the languages (Irish, Flemish, Scandinavian, French, English) of groups known to have invaded or settled the area in times past.

I know no cases of AW *phonetic* forms peculiar to South Pembrokeshire and unrecorded in England. But South Pembrokeshire's unique AW enclave of [ɒ] corresponding to RP /ʌ/ has few parallels in South-west England, the figures for the words in this group cited in *SAWD* vol. 2, section 2.19 being as follows: *butter: no* occur-

rences of [ɒ] in Cornwall/Devon/Somerset; *suck:* 5 localities out of the 31 investigated by SED; *doves:* 4; *dust* and *thumb:* 2 each; *dozen, furrow, hundred, thunder* and *uncle:* none. Though all these words appear in the Index to *EDG*, none was apparently recorded with [ɒ] in South-west England. According to *SED*, the nearest areas to Pembrokeshire where [ɒ] consistently corresponds to RP /ʌ/ are in Herefordshire and Gloucestershire.

Items peculiar to the Gower Peninsula and unrecorded in England — all lexical — are few, but include *lead* [li:d] 'gangway in a cow-house'; *snarl* 'prong'; *cluppit* 'broody' referring to hens (all apparently unrecorded in *EDD*), and a few others in the Incidental Material.

Those AW forms that are characteristic of Gwent and the other dominantly English-speaking territory along the national border fall into three chief groups: (a) those that are Welsh-derived, e.g. *twp* 'stupid', raised centralised [ʌ̈] corresponding to RP /ʌ/, and exclamatory *there's* plus adjective; (b) those with very widespread distribution in England, e.g. *tup* 'ram', r-colouring of relatively-open long vowels, *as* (relative pronoun with masculine antecedent), and third singular present-tense forms *he have/haven't, he do/don't*; (c) evident borrowings from specifically West Midland English sources. This last group includes such lexical forms as *wainhouse* 'cart-shed'; *tiddler/tidling* 'orphaned lamb'; *nisgal* 'smallest and weakest pig of a litter'; *beasthouse* 'cow-house'; *pails* 'barley-awns'; *bin(g)* 'gangway in a cow-house' (though this spreads right over to Anglesey in Gwynedd and as far South-west as Resolven WG 2); *tump* 'potato-clamp'; *jibbons* 'spring onions'; *fitchock* 'polecat'; *shield-board* 'the mould-board of a plough' and many others, all of which occur in England in some or all of the counties of Cheshire, Shropshire, Herefordshire and Gloucestershire. In the same category are the morphological items ['anə], ['dɒnə], ['ɒnə] and ['kanə] 'haven't', 'don't', 'won't' and 'can't'. Few border-Welsh forms of English derivation are unrecorded in England, but one that comes to mind is *cow-bay* 'cow-house' that has a small enclave in central Montgomeryshire in North Powys.

Such then are some characteristics of the HAAWDs, the 'highly anglicised' AW dialects. I have not yet fully worked out a scheme for classifying those AW dialects that do not neatly fit either of the categories SWAADs or HAAWDs, but I hope such classification will be aided by the atlas.

How the Atlas is to be Arranged

In a few cases, *phonetic* material need not be mapped at all, since certain correspondences between AW and RP are so regular that statements of the rules, the exceptions and the illustrations will suffice. In stressed syllables, AW [ɛ], [ɑ] and [ɔi] correspond regularly to RP /e/, /ɑ/ and /ɔɪ/, and in final unstressed syllables AW [i(:)] corresponds to RP /ɪ/. In cases like these we shall just give the rule, list the examples in their full recorded IPA form (since *SAWD*, unlike *SED*, has not already published full lists of the Basic Material), and where necessary comment on the probable sources of the regular AW reflexes and of their exceptions. AW final [i(:)] in *ready* must result in some localities from the influence of Welsh final unstressed [i:] as in *Cymry*, in others from South-west English [i] (cf. *LAE* map Ph 204), and in others perhaps from the combined pressure of both influences: the commentary, by noting and examining all the available evidence, will try to sort out which cases are which. The exceptional AW [ʊ] recorded in three localities at the Mid-Powys border with England are no doubt extensions of the [ʊ] enclave of the English West Midlands.

We now turn to the items that are to be mapped. The mapping conventions employed will be basically those of *WGE* and *LAE*, but with the slightly different method of indicating outliers that is exemplified in *SAWD* vols. 1 and 2, and in Map 3.7 below, and which the editors of *SLG* discuss in the Introduction.

In the lexical section, a map of the words for 'cow-house' will display a number of different forms and the commentary, which will include lists showing the distributions of the words as recorded in *SED*, *EDD* or *The Linguistic Geography of Wales* (*LGW*), as applicable, will try to point out how the various importations are typical in the development of the AW dialects generally. The old-established (1300) compound *cow-house* itself spreads into the eastern borders of Wales from the English West Midlands; the modern (nineteenth-century) *cow-shed* is ousting Welsh *beudy* in Dyfed after having securely established itself in the longstanding-English territory of South and South-west Wales; *beast-house* in Mid-Wales extends from a very small Herefordshire enclave of the same (SED found part of Monmouthshire to belong to this enclave, but SAWD has not found the word there); Gower has *cow-stall* that is recorded sporadically in Somerset, Surrey, Dorset and Sussex; North Powys *cow-bay* is apparently unique in the whole of Wales and England. The South-west English enclave of *shippon* has had no apparent influence on South Pembrokeshire/Gower, where it might have been expected, but the Lancashire/Cheshire enclave of *shippon* spreads right across North Wales into Anglesey. A few of these forms are displayed on Map 3.3. Map 3.4 shows *bin(g)* 'gangway in a cow-house' spreading from the English West Midlands as far north as Anglesey and as far south-west as Resolven (WG 2); the same word has a similar distribution in Welsh (see *LGW* pp. 362-3); this and the similar distributions in *SAWD* and in *LGW* of other words for *gangway* (such as *walk*/*wac*, *ranch*/*ransh*/*range*) neatly remind us again of the problems in deciding what we can properly call 'Welsh' and what 'Anglo-Welsh'. A similar question is raised by some of the words for *cart-shed* (Map 3.5), where the distribution of AW *cart-house*, *hovel* and *wain-house* corresponds to, or overlaps with, that of Welsh *certws*, *hofal* and *weinws* (*LGW* pp. 100-11). The Somerset influence on Gwent appears fleetingly in *rinnick* 'the smallest and weakest of a litter' at Undy Gw 9 and the West Midland English influence on Powys in *sally* 'willow'; the map of *willow* will also illustrate the fact that South Pembrokeshire and Gwent sometimes have a common form, in this case *withy*.

The phonological maps seem likely to call for more searching and more speculative interpretive material than the lexical, the *causae rerum* being generally less clear. Often enough, one and the same AW sound may be due to either Welsh or English influences, depending on where it occurs. For instance AW [e:] corresponding to RP /eɪ/ and AW [o:] corresponding to RP /əʊ/ can both be cases of either Welsh sound-substitution or importation from neighbouring dialects in England. For examples of AW reflexes of RP /eɪ/, see Map 3.6 (*gate*) and Map 3.7 (*spade*). If AW [e:] or [o:] spread in an unbroken belt from England across to West Wales, appearing in both HAAWDs and

Map 3.3:   SAWD and *SED*: *cow-house*

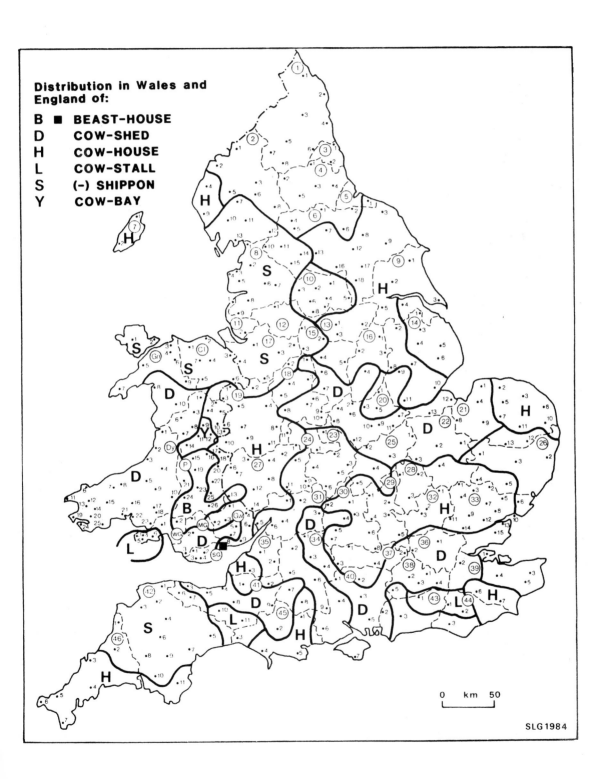

Distribution in Wales and England of:

B ■ BEAST-HOUSE
D   COW-SHED
H   COW-HOUSE
L   COW-STALL
S   (–) SHIPPON
Y   COW-BAY

0   km   50

SLG 1984

Map 3.4: SAWD and *SED*: *gangway in a cow-house*

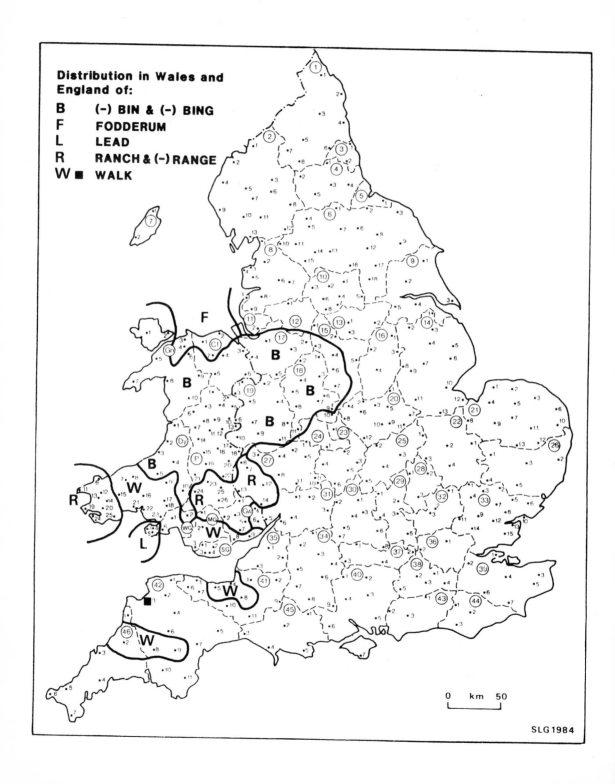

Map 3.5: SAWD and *SED*: *cart-shed*

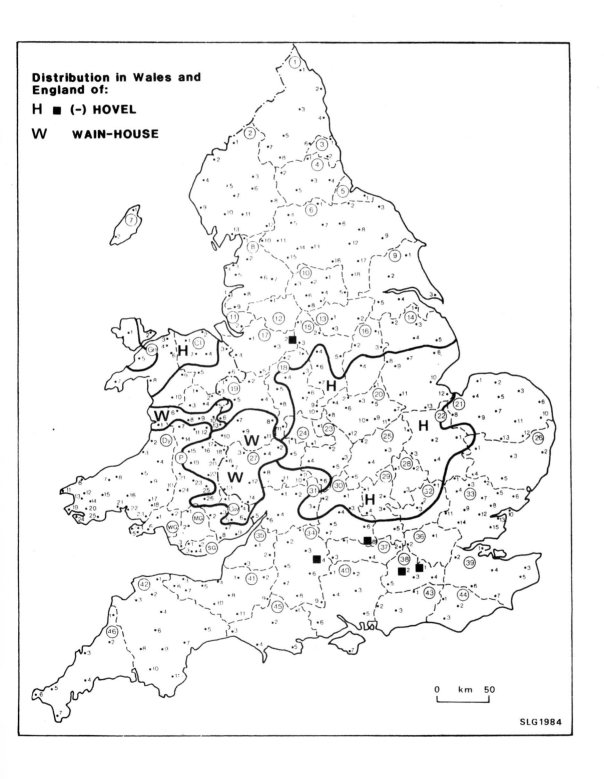

Map 3.6:   **SAWD and** *SED: gate* (vowel)

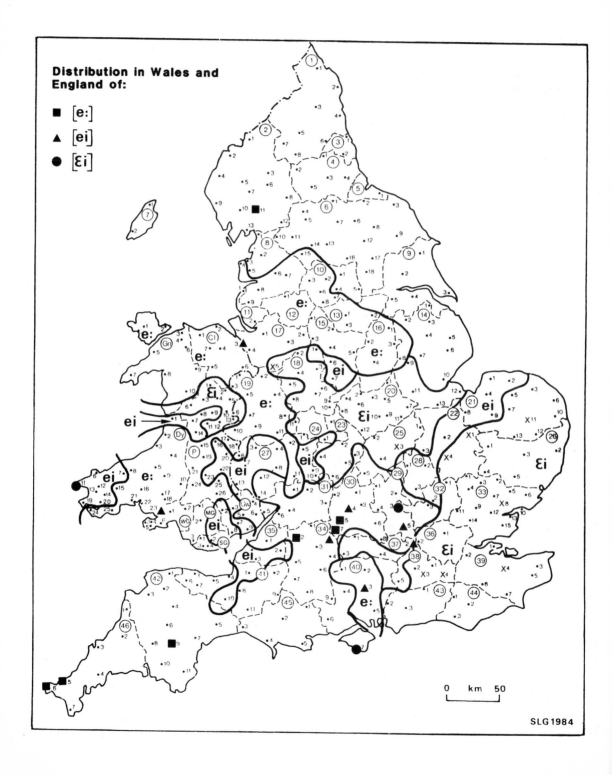

Distribution in Wales and England of:

■ [eː]

▲ [ei]

● [ɛi]

SLG 1984

Map 3.7:   SAWD and *SED*: *spade* (vowel)

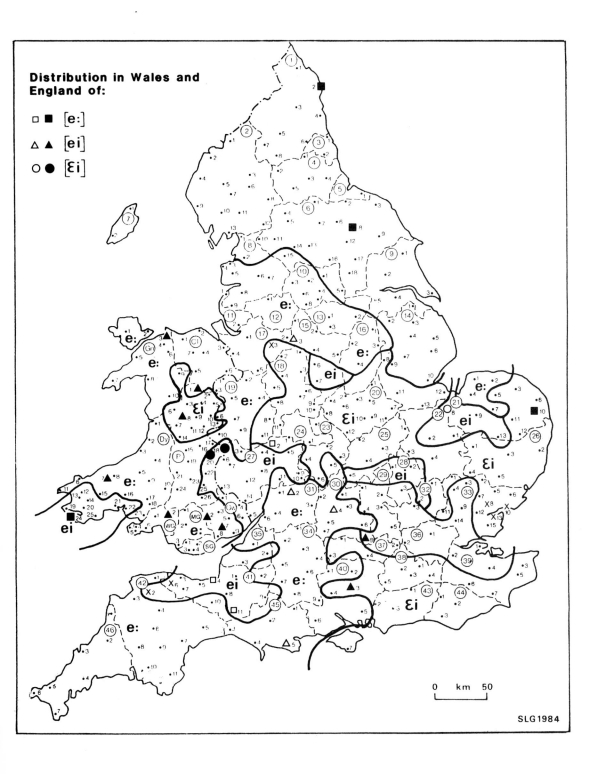

Map 3.8: SAWD and *SED*: *tooth* (vowel)

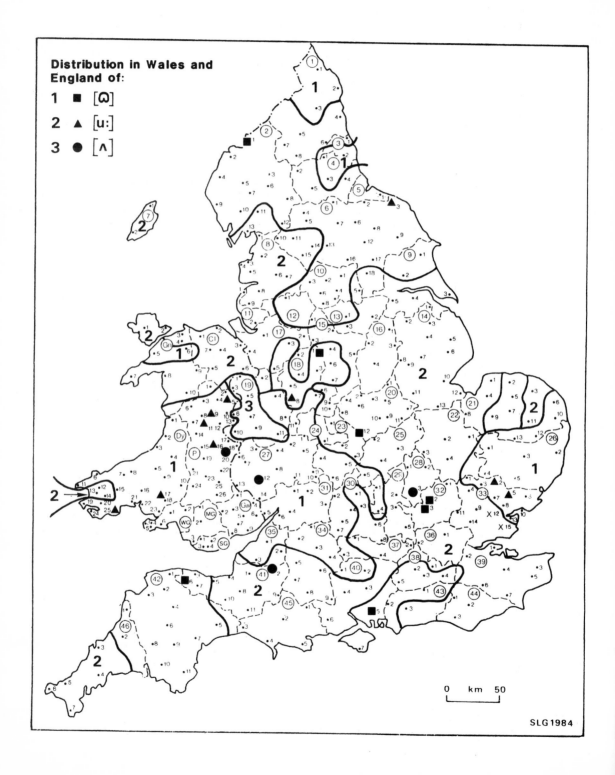

SWAWDs, we shall want to try to establish 'transition areas' not in the sense 'areas where adjacent enclaves overlap' but in the sense 'areas where different originating influences apparently combine to produce the same result', all the known evidence, internal and external, linguistic and extra-linguistic, having been examined. If this endeavour succeeds and maps of 'bundlings of influences' become possible, our investigations may attain something of the sociological significance that some scholars would welcome. One would like also to find out why one sound from neighbouring English territory spreads widely into AW and another not at all: why, for instance, Herefordshire/Gloucestershire [ɒ] in *tooth* is a dominant form in AW whereas Shropshire [ʌ] is hardly replicated in Wales at all, as Map 3.8 shows.

I have spoken of AW sounds as reflexes of RP, rather than ME, sounds because the phonological material will be arranged under main headings determined by the RP sound-system. But the diverse ME origins of many of the RP phonemes will not be ignored since the sub-headings will take account of them. For RP /eɪ/ from ME *ā* and RP /eɪ/ from ME *ai, ei* (to cite one example) do not have identical reflexes everywhere in AW, the latter having diphthongal reflexes rather more often than the former, which may be due to parallel differences in neighbouring English dialects or to Welsh-influenced orthographical interpretations of *ai, ei* in *chain, neighbours* and the like. AW reflexes of RP /ə:/ seem to reflect a number of different historical processes, though none of the diversity seems attributable in this instance to the separate ME sources of the sound in RP. In many dialects we find [œ:], the foreign learner's imperfect imitation of [ə:] that is due to the similar inherent pitch of the two sounds (Sweet, 1906: section 62). The most obvious of the HAAWDS have [əˡ:] from adjacent areas of England. But many of the SWAWDS seem to be undergoing, or to have undergone, developments parallel to those that took place in early Modern English, the dialects where Welsh influences are strongest of all having [ər] and those where they are not quite so strong having 'moved on to' (I think the inference is justified but cannot argue for it here) the [ə:] of modern RP. It is only occasionally that the case for thinking of AW sounds as reflexes of ME sounds rests on the fact that archaic forms are retained in AW, as when, for

instance, we find in the eastern-border dialects [fɪft] 'fifth', [gu:ld] 'gold'; or that we find forms explicable in terms of known sound changes in early English being differently applied in the dialects, for example [gɪs] 'geese', [ku:m] 'comb'. It could even be argued that thinking of AW sounds as reflexes of ME sounds can mislead: for instance [kɔrn] in a SWAWD almost certainly does *not* show 'retention of early English post-vocalic *r*' in *corn*; and the difference between [o:] in *coal* and [ou] in *snow* in such a dialect is hardly likely to be due to the different vowels the words had in ME, except in so far as this produces in the latter a modern spelling that suggests to a Welsh-speaker the diphthong he uses in words like *Owen*. The real case for taking account of ME sources in the atlas is that the latter aims to be as far as possible a continuation of the investigation of *conservative* forms of British English instigated by SED; the layout of the AW atlas seeks to serve the convenience of users of *SED and* that of readers unfamiliar with ME at once; the *commentary* accompanying a map will aim to inform *any* reader what the editor thinks are the probable explanations of the current AW sounds, which are sometimes explanations in terms of ME and sometimes not. Treating the latter cases as exceptions to the former avails us of a ready-made and convenient way of ordering the material under each main heading. Even then, it is only in a commentary that we can bring out some of the *systemic* differences between RP and AW, such as we find in AW dialects where [ä] corresponds to both RP /ʌ/ and RP /ə/ — a case of sound-substitution of Welsh *y* = [ä], [ə] that can occur in both stressed and unstressed syllables.

Where morphology is concerned, influences on AW are almost entirely English. The geographical distribution of even AW *thou, thee, thy* suggests that Welsh *ti* and its related forms, which have the same socially-conditioned restrictions of occurrence as their English counterparts, have had no influence on AW. Syntactical material in the atlas will be sparse, partly for the reason given earlier and partly because many AW items, though interesting responses to the Questionnaire, occur so sporadically as to make mapping them an act of extravagance.

Conclusion

A good deal can be hoped for from the maps, then, provided they are accompanied by interpretive material. But some questions will remain unanswered in either: for example, why is the apparently English *pine-end* 'gable-end of a building' found in only five out of 313 *SED* localities (two with editorial queries) and 42 out of 90 *SAWD* localities? But a more important limit to the usefulness of maps is that mentioned at the end of the previous section. Much material of interest to the English philologist occurs only sporadically and is unmapworthy but ought to be publicly accessible somewhere better than in the byways of *SAWD* vols. 1 and 2. That is why I hope to see not only an atlas but also the glossary and the grammar mentioned in the first section.

References

Orton, H. *Survey of English Dialects (A): Introduction* (E.J. Arnold, Leeds, 1962)

Orton, H. *et al. Survey of English Dialects (B): The Basic Material* 4 vols., each in 3 parts (E.J. Arnold, Leeds, 1962-71) [*SED*]

Orton, H., S. Sanderson and J. Widdowson (eds.) *The Linguistic Atlas of England* (Croom Helm, London, 1978) [*LAE*]

Orton, H. and N. Wright. *A Word Geography of England* (Seminar Press, New York and London, 1975) [*WGE*]

Parry, D. (ed.) *The Survey of Anglo-Welsh Dialects*, vol. 1: *The South-East* (privately published, Swansea, 1977) [*SAWD* vol. 1]

—— *The Survey of Anglo-Welsh Dialects*, vol. 2: *The South-West* (privately published, Swansea, 1980) [*SAWD* vol. 2]

Sweet, H. *A Primer of Phonetics*, 3rd edn (Clarendon Press, Oxford, 1906)

Thomas, A.R. *The Linguistic Geography of Wales* (University of Wales Press, Cardiff, 1973) [*LGW*]

Wright, J. (ed.) *The English Dialect Dictionary*, 6 vols. (Henry Frowde, London, 1898-1905) [*EDD*]

—— *The English Dialect Grammar* (Henry Frowde, London, 1905) [*EDG*]

4

The Tape-recorded Survey of Hiberno-English Speech: A Reappraisal of the Techniques of Traditional Dialect Geography

†G.B. ADAMS, M.V. BARRY,
P.M. TILLING

At the first Annual Colloquium on the English Language in Ireland, held at the New University of Ulster in 1972, it was decided to establish a phonological survey of the English spoken in Ireland (which, it was felt, should more accurately be described as Hiberno-English, rather than Anglo-Irish). In the first instance, the survey was planned to cover the eleven northern counties of Ireland (see Map 4.1) but, as a result of the interest shown by University Colleges Cork and Dublin, it was subsequently decided to extend the survey to cover the whole of Ireland. The authors of this paper were elected to a working-party to examine the feasibility of the project, and subsequently became the survey's directors. The purpose of the survey was to provide a picture of the English speech of Ireland which would complement that provided for England by the Survey of English Dialects (SED) and for Scotland by the Linguistic Survey of Scotland (LSS). From the beginning, therefore, much of the methodology of the Tape-recorded Survey of Hiberno-English Speech (TRS) was determined by these two surveys, and particularly by SED. However, where appropriate, TRS also sought to take advantage of other recent dialect research and to take account of the criticisms made of 'traditional' dialect surveys. The methods finally adopted and the extent to which

they go beyond those of SED (particularly) and LSS are the subject of this paper. Preliminary analysis of the data, also the subject of some discussion here, suggests that the methodology was justified. From the outset, TRS restricted itself to phonology, in order to avoid any unnecessary duplication with the work of the Linguistic Survey of Ireland, at present being undertaken by Professor P.L. Henry of University College, Galway. This survey and its objectives were discussed in Henry (1958).

The Taperecording Method

From the start, it was decided that all data for the survey would be collected on tape. This would speed collection and would permit more accurate transcriptions to be made. Although SED had collected samples of free conversation on tape, most of its data had been transcribed in the field in a phonetic notation which Orton (1962: 18) described as 'impressionistic'. However, the number of fieldworkers employed by SED and the vagueness of the term 'impressionistic' meant that there was an inherent danger that apparent linguistic boundaries would, in fact, be fieldworker boundaries. This criticism has since been levelled at SED (e.g. by Petyt

Map 4.1:   The Northern Counties of Ireland

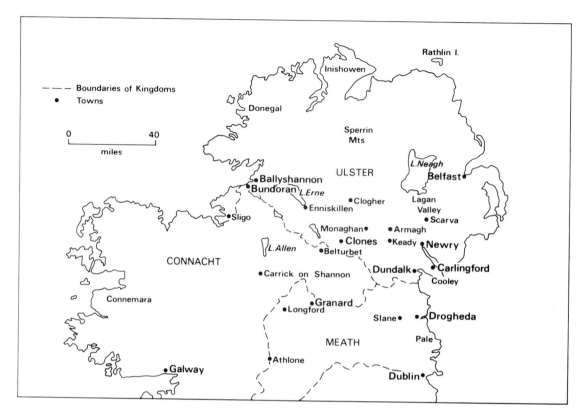

1980: Chapters 3 and 4). It was, in part, in answer to such criticism that the directors of TRS chose to use the taperecording method to collect all its data, which could then be transcribed phonetically in a leisurely and careful manner in studio conditions. This would enable the directors to ensure consistency in the amount of detail shown in the transcriptions and would permit checking and rechecking. Utterances transcribed on the spot in the field could never be checked, although samples of taperecorded speech and other evidence might occasionally suggest doubts about the accuracy of some transcriptions. Of course, transcribers who work from the tapes alone will lose the advantage of being able to observe visually phenomena such as lip-rounding. However, it was felt that the advantages of being able to listen to the recorded responses over and over again (on a tape loop, if necessary), and of bringing in a second listener as a check, outweighed the loss of visual observation of the informant. In any case, a fieldworker who has to transcribe a large amount of data in the field in a limited time is unlikely to have much opportunity to observe his informant closely.

Questionnaire

In common with SED and LSS, TRS adopted the questionnaire method of obtaining data and, like SED, it was further decided to obtain a lengthy specimen of free conversation on tape. In order to permit correlation with the findings of SED and LSS, TRS included in its questionnaire as many of the phonological keywords from the questionnaires of SED and LSS as was practicable. However, it was decided that the questionnaire should be considerably shorter than that used by SED, in order to speed up the collection of data, reduce expenses and, of course, because only phonological information was required. Following SED, questions were arranged thematically, in order to give the interview something of the flow of a natural conversation. Thus the questionnaire (Adams, Barry and Tilling 1976) is divided into four sections (Section A, The Countryside; Section B, The Home; Section C, People; Section D, Miscellaneous), with each section further sub-divided. Again, following SED, most of the questions were of the 'naming' or 'completing' types, none of which included in its wording the required keyword (Orton 1962: 45). In 'naming' questions, a well-known object (the keyword) was described or otherwise indicated and in 'completing' questions the informant was given an incomplete sentence which could only be completed by the required item. A variant of the 'naming' question was a request for a word with the meaning opposite to that of the word given (a sample page of the questionnaire is given in Figure 4.1). Orton's 'conversion' type (by which grammatical and morphological information was obtained) was not often used by TRS. In all, some 379 keywords were listed in the questionnaire. Obviously, since the questionnaire was intended to elicit phonological information from different informants and different localities which could easily be correlated, it was important to avoid questions which would give rise to lexical variation. In this, the survey directors received valuable help and advice from other scholars of English in Ireland and from the published work of Gregg (1972) and Henry (1958). A revised version of the initial questionnaire was finally adopted for use after experimental work in a few widely separated localities mainly in the north of Ireland.

Since the questionnaire was designed for use with children as well as adults (see discussion on Informants below), alternative questions were formulated in some instances. Thus, to obtain the keyword *tree*, informants were asked:

What do you call a tall plant like a poplar,

Figure 4.1: TRS Questionnaire, p. 1

SECTION A
THE COUNTRYSIDE

I *Domestic and Farm Animals*

1. What do you call the animal that barks?	DOG
2. What do you call a dog with a half a dozen breeds in it?	MONGREL
3. If dogs are very pleased, what do they do with their tails?	WAG
4. *Either*: How will a dog hide a bone? He will . . . it.	BURY
Or: What do they usually do with a corpse after the funeral? They . . . it.	
5. What do you call the animal that says 'meow'?	CAT
6. What will a little child call a cat or a kitten?	PUSSY
7. Before they had a tractor to pull the plough, they used a . . .	HORSE
8. When a horse goes quickly, lifting its legs high, you say it has begun to . . .	TROT
9. What's a horse-shoe made of?	IRON
10. If you stand behind a horse you'd better watch it doesn't . . .	KICK
11. To beat a horse is very . . .	CRUEL
12. What do you call the fully-grown female horse?	MARE
13. What do you call a small, stocky horse of either sex?	PONY
14. What do you call the animals that give you milk?	COWS
15. And one of them?	COW
16. What do you call the male of the cow?	BULL
17. What do you call the young cows just born?	CALVES
18. And one of them?	CALF
19. What do you call a young male calf bred for beef?	BULLOCK
20. *Either*: When the milk curdles we get curds and . . .	WHEY
Or: Little Miss Muffet sat on her tuffet,	
Eating her curds and . . .	
21. What do you call a female sheep?	EWE
22. What do you call the creature with feathers that flies (e.g. a Robin, Crow, Thrush, etc.)?	BIRD

oak, pine etc?

As an alternative, children (particularly) could be asked:

If you want some wood, you cut down a . . .
In cases of extreme difficulty, fieldworkers were instructed to display flash-cards spelling the required item.

The questionnaire also included detailed biographical and social information sheets, to provide documentation of the basic facts of an informant's life and to give important information on the nature of the community in which he lived.

The questionnaire concluded with a phonological index which suggested the kinds of variation that might be expected and, at the same time, indicated the reasons for the inclusion of particular items. These 'expected' forms were derived from previously published research (e.g. by Gregg 1972 and Henry 1958). Thus, under *ants*, the probable phonetic realisation of the stressed vowel in Hiberno-English was given as [a] or [ɑː] (both of which were known to occur), while in the case of *any*, it was given as [ɛ], [a] or [ɔ]. This, of course, is not to suggest that these were the only variations encountered in these items by TRS.

In general, the keywords selected were uninflected monosyllables (e.g. *cow*, *wet*, *house*), which it was felt would give the maximum linguistic information in the simplest possible context. It was decided not to base the questionnaire on a system of minimal pairs, because these are generally designed to elicit a single piece of information and also would not permit the thematic arrangement of the questionnaire. The questionnaire also included some of the principal morphs found in polysyllables (e.g. *-er*, *-est*, *-y*), since these give useful information on the pronunciation of sounds in unstressed syllables.

Network

The purpose of TRS (following SED and LSS) was to record the sounds of the English of Ireland, as far as was practicable within the scope of a linguistic survey. Thus, following SED, it was decided to collect data from a systematic network of localities throughout the whole of Ireland. In general, the network of SED required localities to be selected at 15-mile intervals, though in practice this was not always adhered to. Topography and low-density population, for example, occasionally made this impossible. In other cases, fieldwork was conducted by students as a part of their research for a higher degree and they investigated more localities in some areas than was strictly required by SED. Thus ten localities were investigated for SED in Leicestershire, as against five in Nottinghamshire, and 15 were investigated in Essex, as against five in Suffolk. The fieldworkers in Leicestershire and Essex were both collecting material for postgraduate dissertations as well as for SED.

Although the directors of TRS adopted the idea of a systematic network of localities from SED, it was decided to use a more systematic method based on the Irish National Grid. The nature of both the urban and rural settlement of Ireland suggested that this was reasonable. Thus there are really only two large conurbations in Ireland, Belfast and Dublin; both of these have the usual mixing and strong social stratification found in large cities elsewhere and it was felt that these were best treated separately (by such surveys as that for Belfast by Milroy and Milroy 1978). Although there are other significant towns (for example, Cork, Galway, Limerick, Londonderry), these are almost all on the coastal perimeter. The huge, industrial urban sprawls found in England are absent from Ireland and a rural survey may be confidently asserted to be more representative of the whole than would be the case in Great Britain. The rural settlement pattern of Ireland also differs from that of England. Few areas of Ireland are without at least a thin scatter of farms or 'townland' settlements and the nucleated village settlement is not a general Irish feature. This also meant, however, that in some areas the number of informants required by the survey, who were both suitable and co-operative, would have to be looked for in the same general area, rather than at a single geographical point, such as a village. The basis finally adopted by TRS for its network was the Irish ten-kilometre National Grid. In order to speed the progress of the survey, it was decided, in the first instance, to work on the basis of a 20-kilometre grid and to select informants for investigation from the north-western ten-kilometre square within each 20-kilometre square (Map 4.2a). This does, of course, lead to difficulties in plotting data on the

Map 4.2a: Grid Map of the Northern Counties of Ireland (shaded areas indicate the ten-kilometre squares investigated)

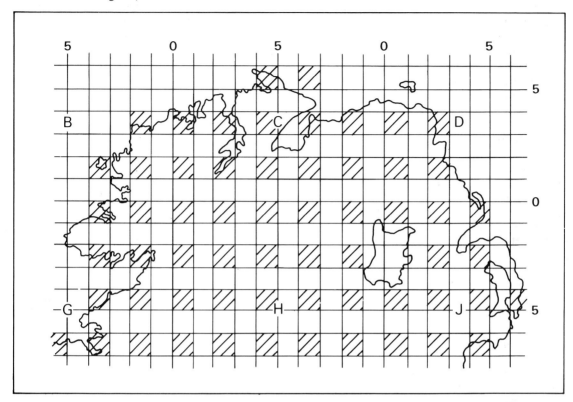

map, and it has been agreed to accept a certain degree of simplification. Thus, data will be plotted from the centre of each square investigated (where this is situated on land), even though this is unlikely to be the exact geographical point investigated. Given the approximate nature of isoglosses established by previous regional dialect survey methods, it was not felt that the minor distortions entailed would be significant. It should be added that fieldworkers were instructed, where possible, to select their informants from a point no further than two and a half miles from the geometrical centre of each square (see Map 4.2b).

The adoption of the grid method has the advantage that the network may be densened at a later stage. Where the data suggests that a particular area is of special linguistic interest, the network can be densened by investigating the south-eastern ten-kilometre square within each 20-kilometre square, and subsequently the north-eastern and south-western squares. Thus the completed survey is envisaged as consisting of

Map 4.2b: Location of TRS Informants in Sample Square

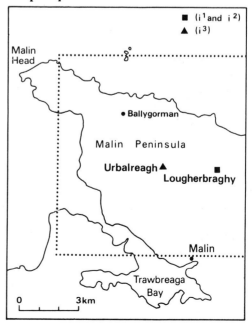

two fieldwork stages: (i) a preliminary collection of data from the whole of Ireland on the basis of the north-western ten-kilometre square within the 20-kilometre National Grid; (ii) a follow-up investigation of the remaining three ten-kilometre squares within the 20-kilometre National Grid where the data previously collected would suggest that this is an area of special linguistic interest and where major boundaries, such as the North-South line (see further below), could usefully be established more precisely. A further advantage of the grid method is that it will simplify the production of computer-compiled maps, since each square can easily be assigned an identifying number.

Informants

A significant difference between SED and TRS concerns the selection of informants. The data for SED was collected from, in most cases, some three to four informants who, between them, answered the survey questionnaire. All the informants were elderly (usually over 60), natives of the locality and of native parents (if possible), mostly working-class, and had spent little time away from the community. Men were preferred to women and urban communities were generally avoided (Orton 1962: 15-16). This aspect of SED (and of other surveys which selected their informants on a similar basis) has provoked unfavourable comment from those dialectologists whose interest is in the total speech of a community, irrespective of an informant's age, status or background, and so on (Petyt 1980: 111-12). Thus SED (and other similar surveys) were seen by some as unrepresentative and hence not so much surveys of dialect as surveys of a restricted kind of speech thought to be in no way typical. Although such criticism seems reasonable enough, it does not do justice to the declared aims of SED, for instance. SED purposely sought to investigate that kind of rural speech which was fast becoming obsolete, firstly, to provide a record of it; secondly, to determine patterns of distribution; thirdly, to relate these dialects to their historical source, thereby illustrating both their historical development and the evolution of English generally. This historical orientation was again the subject of some criticism. The directors of TRS are well aware of the views of sociolinguists and

have attempted, in some way, to reconcile their views with the 'traditional' dialect survey method. Of course, practical limitations make this task somewhat difficult. A nationwide survey cannot do more than collect a limited amount of data from a limited number of informants, and in any case none of the sociolinguists has done a nationwide survey. Time and financial resources do not permit a large-scale investigation of each point throughout the network. TRS, therefore, recalling SED, decided to collect data from three informants in each locality, but, unlike SED, each informant would answer the complete questionnaire. Again, unlike SED or any other regional survey carried out in Europe so far, the informants were to be drawn from three different age-groups: (a) 9-12 years, (b) 35-45 years, (c) 65-75 years. The third group is the one generally sampled by previous regional surveys in the British Isles. The second, middle-aged group (35-45) was chosen as representative of the 'parental' generation (that is, those with children who are old enough to have been strongly influenced by their parents' speech habits, but too young to have had much opportunity to live outside the home). This generation is also the most socially mobile, and the one most influenced by the modern educational system (with its greater opportunities for higher and further education), better transportation, the mass media, and the general twentieth-century increase in living standards. The 9-12 group was chosen as representative of the first generation, at a stage when most children's speech habits are likely to be well developed. This group is under both school and home influence and is old enough to tackle the questionnaire and contribute a little free-speech. This group is still 'local', in that its members are unlikely to be in much contact with the wider teenage world, with its tendency to drift to the city for higher education, employment and entertainment.

Since one of the objectives of TRS was that its data should complement that collected by SED and LSS, it was decided not only to collect data which would give the sound system of each locality, but also to collect data which would illustrate its historical development. Thus, again, informants were preferred who were natives of the area, of native parents (where possible) and who had spent little time away from the community. Important biographical facts were recorded in each case, as were details of the community in which they lived. This would enable a limited number of sociological factors to be taken into account in any explanation of linguistic differences, both between the informants of one locality and the informants of neighbouring localities.

Fieldworkers[1]

In the early stages of the investigation, fieldwork for TRS was undertaken by the three directors of the survey, with the part-time assistance of two volunteers. Although the taperecording method precluded the possibility of fieldworker boundaries, it was realised that a large number of fieldworkers of varying (even non-Irish) backgrounds was in some ways unsatisfactory. This topic received special attention in a sociolinguistic study of a village community in Co. Londonderry, conducted by Dr E. Douglas-Cowie (1978). As a part of this study, one of the TRS directors was recorded in conversation with Dr Douglas-Cowie's informants to determine to what extent (if any) her informants' speech was modified when talking to a stranger who was 'a well-educated Englishman with an RP or modified regional accent'. In some cases (determined, it would seem, by the informant's 'social ambition') there was significant change, usually towards an RP standard. Of course, any stranger (whatever his background) might well have had a similar effect, though, as indicated below, a trained fieldworker can minimise these effects more than perhaps Dr Douglas-Cowie allows. Fortunately, the award of a grant for fieldwork by the Social Sciences Research Council, and additional financial assistance from University Colleges Cork and Dublin, enabled TRS to employ a number of Irish postgraduate students as full-time fieldworkers. Even so, the directors of TRS are aware that fieldwork conducted by any outsider is likely to introduce a degree of formality into the situation. If it is realised that in most cases the data is in the informant's 'interview' style, then this is not felt to invalidate the data. It simply means that the survey is investigating this particular register of an informant's speech. In this respect, the responses in TRS are exactly comparable with those of SED and LSS. Ideally, of course, TRS would have preferred to use one fieldworker for the entire survey, though obviously time and resources would not permit this. It should be noted, however, that a trained and experienced fieldworker can do much to ease the formality of the interview situation, even if that fieldworker is a rank outsider (e.g. British). TRS recordings often show no difference between forms obtained with the questionnaire and those recorded during the conversation period. Also, the questionnaire session is often punctuated by lengthy bursts of conversation.

Editorial Procedure

After the completion of each interview, the taperecordings are returned to the directors for cataloguing and copying. The master tapes for Munster are housed in Cork and those for the rest of Ireland in Belfast; the copies are distributed to participating institutions, where they are readily available for consultation by any interested scholars. Participating institutions are: the Queen's University of Belfast; the New University of Ulster, Coleraine; the Ulster Folk and Transport Museum, Cultra; University Colleges Cork and Dublin. Already a number of scholars have made use of these facilities.

The next stage is the transcription of the taperecorded data into a detailed impressionistic phonetic notation, after Abercrombie (1965). An advantage of the taperecording method, of course, is that transcriptions can be checked and rechecked in the phonetics laboratory, with instrumental aid if necessary. The method adopted has been for a preliminary transcription to be made by one of the directors, which is then checked by the others. At the present stage (1981), transcription is continuing, to be followed later by the transcription of free conversation. It is expected that these transcriptions will be retranscribed in a form acceptable to the computer. Following the editorial practice of SED, data for each informant is transcribed onto sheets which are divided into two columns. Answers to the questions are transcribed into the left-hand column and incidental material of interest into the right-hand column. Correlation of the informants' transcription sheets permits a comparison of the data for each informant to be made even at this stage, and the sheets themselves allow preliminary conclusions to be drawn on the status of the responses as against the incidental material. Thus, an informant who gives [dɒg] as his answer to the question 'What do you call the animal that barks?', but who uses the form [dɔːg] several times in the incidental material, might well be felt to have 'refined' his speech in the questionnaire situation.

Publications

From the beginning, it has been the intention of TRS to publish its data in the form of a phonological atlas of the English of Ireland, thus to some extent complementing the linguistic atlases of England and Scotland. It is felt that this is the most effective publishing method to illustrate linguistic contrasts and the distribution of forms. The mapping methods used will be determined by the data. Thus, isoglosses will be used where appropriate, as also will symbols or hatching. Examples of all three methods were used by TRS in its first volume of working papers. There, isoglosses have been used (Barry 1981: 87-93) to indicate linguistic boundaries; hatching or shading has been used where there is a clearly defined regional distribution of linguistic forms (Barry 1981: 114-16); and symbols have been used (Barry 1981: 117) where distinctive forms occur in a widespread scatter.

Although it is intended that the phonological atlas will be the central publication of the TRS, other publications are also envisaged. It is hoped to publish a series of articles and monographs on topics of particular interest which have been suggested by the survey's data and which may form the subject of further investigation. Possible topics include: the rural background to the dialect of Belfast,[2] the nature and extent of Ulster Scots (that is, the variety of English spoken in heavily Scots-settled areas of Ulster), the interaction of English and Irish in former Irish-speaking communities,[3] the linguistic implications of the Pale, and so on. It is also hoped to publish anthologies of taperecorded material, on both disc and cassette, together with orthographic transcriptions and linguistic commentary. Finally, the directors hope to publish a 'popular' handbook dealing systematically with the English dialects of Ireland, for use in schools and universities, which will use TRS data extensively by way of illustration. No adequate handbook of this kind exists at present.[4]

Summary

It will be apparent that TRS owes much of its methodology to SED (particularly) and LSS. It has adopted the direct (not postal) questionnaire method and many of the keywords of both surveys. Its objective is to record and identify the sounds of Hiberno-English throughout a systematic network of localities, and against the historical development of English in Ireland. (For this reason, the concentration on the 'natives' of a particular locality is especially important.) As with SED and LSS, it is hoped ultimately to publish its data in atlas form, though using computer techniques in the editorial stage. However, TRS has departed from the methodology of SED and LSS in certain respects. All data is recorded on tape and it is concerned almost totally with phonology. Speech samples have been taken from three age-groups and allowance has been made, both in its network arrangement and its publication programme, for a close examination of linguistic topics of special interest.

The North-South Boundary

The most important study to have arisen from TRS so far is an assessment by M.V. Barry (1980) of the boundary between northern and southern varieties of Hiberno-English, a study which has also enabled the TRS directors to assess the effectiveness of the survey's methodology. The material collected by TRS not only made identification and mapping of this boundary possible but, because of the three age-groups selected, suggested to what extent and in what ways it is changing.

Key to maps 4.3 – 4.10

The following indicate the limit and direction of northern forms :

⊥—⊥—⊥	i^1 (child)
⊥·⊥·⊥	i^2 (35-45)
⊥–⊥–⊥	i^3 (65-75)

N forms in S area	S forms in N area
○ i^1	△ i^1
◑ i^2	▲ i^2
● i^3	▲ i^3

Map 4.3: TRS: *boil* (vowel)

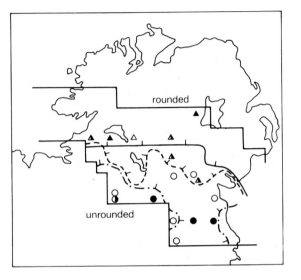

Map 4.4: TRS: *pony* (vowel)

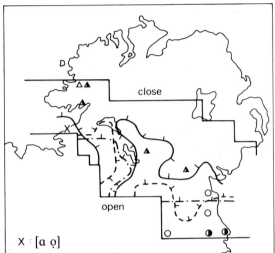

Map 4.5: TRS: *third* (initial consonant)

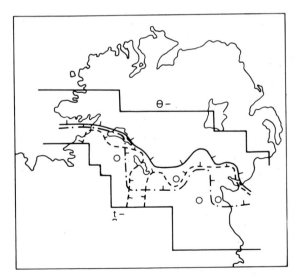

Map 4.6: TRS: *cat* (final consonant)

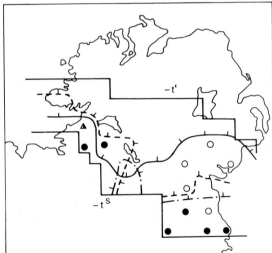

The source of a linguistic boundary between the North and the South of Ireland has been traced to a complex of linguistic, geographical and historical factors (Barry 1980: 105-15). Previous work has suggested that the boundary stretched in a broad band across the country from Dundalk and Drogheda in the east to Bundoran and Sligo in the west (Barry 1980: 112) and that, unlike the dialect diffusion, or gradual differentiation, which usually produced such major boundaries as Ellis's *hoos/house* line from east to west across the North of England, this boundary arose because two very different forms of English were replacing Gaelic in Ireland: one, introduced in the seventeenth century, spread north from the Pale and the other, also introduced in the seventeenth century and heavily influenced by Scots English, spread south and west from east Ulster. The two happened to meet around the area where the older North-South Gaelic dialects divided (that is, approximately along a line from Bundoran in the West to Carlingford in the East). Thus this boundary did not emerge gradually and slowly within a totally English-speaking area, but arose quite suddenly as the two forms of English replacing Gaelic North and South collided in the late nineteenth century. From that time English slowly became the majority, even the only, language in the boundary area.

Professor P.L. Henry (1958: 147-60) had previously suggested a number of criteria (mainly phonetic) for distinguishing between northern and southern speech (eg. northern [æ] v. southern [ɛ/ʉ], as in *neck, get*; northern [ʉ] v. southern [ʉ̈], as in *hook, school, boots*; northern [o̞] v. southern [o̤], as in *home, close*). On the basis of Henry's criteria, together with notes made during the transcription of TRS field recordings, Barry examined 45 phonological features (including those exemplified above) in some 37 words which would seem to show a distinction between northern and southern speech. A number of these features were mapped and their distribution discussed and analysed. Barry was able to show that there clearly is a linguistic boundary, although its position varies from item to item and age-group to age-group (see Maps 4.3 to 4.10 and key). However, when all the material was mapped together, it showed a gradual change from northern to southern forms across the country, centring on a line from Carlingford in the East to Bundoran in the West. The data also suggested the emergence of a sub-dialect in the northern Pale and Dublin hinterland, characterised by northern forms (illustrated by the data for *boil* — Map 4.3 — which shows that, in this area, the northern, rounded realisation of the first element of the diphthong — which recalls RP — was recorded in the speech of Informant 2, contrasting with the southern, unrounded realisations of Informants 1 and 3). It was also noticed that southern forms occasionally appear in South-west Donegal, where they may represent a spread of southern forms into the North-west (illustrated by the data for *pony*, Map 4.4), and that a corridor of northern forms sometimes extended south from the area of Upper Lough Erne (illustrated by the data for *pony* and *third*, Maps 4.4 and 4.5). This could perhaps reflect the direction of old routes from North to South, across the end of the Erne lake system.

Age-groups

The most important difference between Barry's study and previous work on such major linguistic boundaries was his use of data from the three age-groups. The geographical distribution of southern and northern forms was often rather different for each age-group, and the factors governing the choice of either a northern or southern form are not always easily determined (although some clues are provided by the biographical and social information collected for each informant). The distributional maps so far produced suggest some tentative conclusions and create a dynamic, rather than a static, picture of this dialect area. The boundary can no longer be said only to reflect the speech of the oldest, most traditional speakers. Barry's main conclusions are summarised below; they are fully set out and illustrated in Barry (1980).

Thus in general it is true to say that in the speech of Informant 2 (35-45 years), northern forms have a more southerly distribution than is the case with the other speakers. This is probably to be regarded as a southward expansion and is likely to reflect the greater mobility (or the greater linguistic consciousness) of this class of informant. It is surely significant, too, that the relevant northern forms are often closer to RP, in these instances, than are the southern forms. Thus the data for *third* shows that the /θ-/

Map 4.7: TRS: *cat* **(initial consonant)**

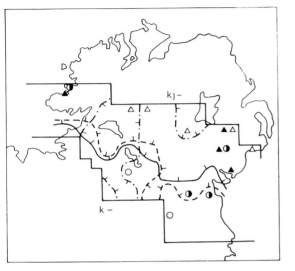

Map 4.8: TRS: *horse* **(vowel)**

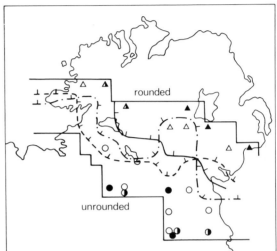

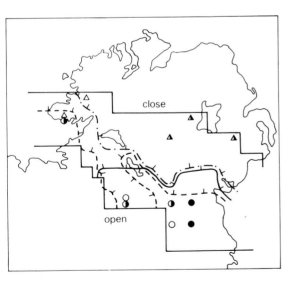

Map 4.9: TRS: *door* **(vowel)**

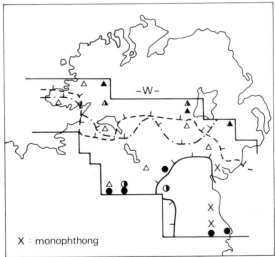

Map 4.10: TRS: *door* **(syllabicity)**

phoneme is realised as [θ] (a northern *and* RP form) in midland and eastern localities well to the South of the area in which this form is used by Informants 1 and 3 (except in the Erne corridor area, where northern forms are recorded for Informant 3); the usual southern realisation is [t̪] (see Map 4.5). The same point is illustrated by the realisation of the /-t/ phoneme, in *cat*, where the affricated realisation [tˢ] (the southern form) is generally avoided by Informant 2 throughout the northern counties (except in the Erne corridor). Again, the northern (aspirated) form [t'] is preferred (Map 4.6). Corroboration of the possibility of RP (rather than northern) influence as the determining factor is suggested by Informant 2's realisation of the initial consonant phoneme in *cat*. A common northern realisation is the heavily palatalised [kj], which is less close to RP than is the common southern realisation [k̟]. In this instance, [kj] would seem to be a stigmatised form and it is recorded in the border area for Informant 2 only in a southward-stretching corridor from East Donegal and West Tyrone (Map 4.7).

Examination of the southern boundary of northern forms recorded from Informant 2 shows considerable North-South undulation. In the East, for example, several northern forms have a southerly distribution which stretches as far as the Pale and the Dublin hinterland. Illustrations are provided by the responses for *boil* (Map 4.3) and *hour*. In *boil* the northern form, in which the diphthong has a rounded first element, extends southwards along a wide East coast corridor, as do the northern forms of *hour*, in which the triphthong is realised without a [-w-] glide between the second and third elements. In this case the wide East coast corridor is penetrated by a corridor of southern forms (with the [-w-] glide).

In *horse* (Map 4.8) the northern form (with rounded vowel) also has a more southerly distribution along the east coast in the speech of Informant 2, yet, by contrast, in the midlands, southern forms penetrate well into the northern area as established by Informants 1 and 3. There is no obvious explanation for this. Thus, while general trends can be noticed and generalisations can reasonably be made, there are exceptional distributions which await explanation. A further example is to be seen in the distribution of the northern forms of *door* (with a close vowel). In this case, the area in which northern forms are recorded from Informant 2 is smaller than is that established by Informant 3. In the West (particularly) the southern boundary of the Informant 2 area lies well to the North of the boundary for Informant 1 and Informant 3 (Map 4.9).

In general, the boundary between southern and northern forms in the speech of Informant 1 (9-12 years) is shown by the data to be closer to that for Informant 3 (65-75 years). Where there are noticeable differences, it is usually because southern forms have a more northerly distribution in the speech of Informant 1 than is the case with the other speakers. Where Informant 1 uses the same form as Informant 3 but not as Informant 2, this may reflect the influence of the elderly on the home-based younger generation. Where Informant 1 uses a southern form, in preference to the northern form used by Informant 2 and Informant 3, possible influences might be Dublin-trained teachers and Radio Telefís Éireann. However, a detailed study of the biographical and social information sheets may suggest other causes.

The data for *third* and *thistle*, for example, shows that the southern realisation of the phoneme /θ-/ as [t̪] has a more northerly distribution in the speech of Informant 1 than in the speech of the other speakers (see Map 4.5). The data from Informant 3 does not differ markedly in its distribution from that of Informant 1, except for a corridor of northern forms which extends southwards from Upper Lough Erne. In the case of final /t/, illustrated by *cat* (Map 4.6), the southern affricated realisation [tˢ] is used by Informant 1 well to the North of the other informants in the eastern half of the area. Other instances where Informant 1 uses southern forms to the North of other informants are illustrated by the data for *cat*, *pony* and *boil*. In *cat* (Map 4.7) the boundary between the northern and southern realisations of the initial consonant phoneme /k/ is roughly similar for Informant 1 and Informant 3, except that the boundary for Informant 3 is extended southwards in the Midlands and eastern half of the country. In this particular case, the data for all informants taken together would suggest that the northern [kj] is here receding, to be replaced by the southern [k̟]. In *pony*, also, (see Map 4.4), where the contrast is between an open vowel (South) and a close vowel (North), the southern form is used by Informant 1 well to the north of both other speakers. In *boil* (Map 4.3) the contrast between the three speakers is of particular interest. Here the contrast is between a rounded vowel (North) and an unrounded vowel (South). Again, the southern form is used by Informant 1 in an area to the North of Informant 3, which suggests an expansion in the use of the southern form. However, in the case of Informant 2, as previously noticed, the northern form (which recalls RP) has spread south to the Pale (which suggests an expansion of the northern form).

Not all the data, however, conforms to the patterns suggested above. As an example, the data for *door* might be cited. In this case, southern forms without an internal [-w-] glide are, in the speech of Informant 1, restricted to the Pale area (Map 4.10).

Conclusion

In summary, consideration of the data from the three age-groups suggests that there are clear distribution patterns which together identify a wide isogloss area dividing a northern and southern speech. However, consideration of each of the age-groups suggests differences in the route of the isogloss. Obviously, a full explanation would require more detailed work in each of the localities concerned. What is clear, however, is that the conclusions would have been quite different (and less accurate) if TRS had concentrated only on the speech of the elderly. At the same time, the directors of TRS are fully aware of the limitations of isoglossic maps, that they suggest too simplistic a picture in that they mask exceptions. However, exceptions can be, and have been, indicated by symbols. An isoglossic map is regarded by TRS simply as a visual record of the forms encountered during fieldwork; other forms could, no doubt, be found. However, if the resulting data produces a pattern, it seems reasonable to suggest that this is evidence of at least the broad, general truth. Three other studies, based on TRS material, have demonstrated the value of the three age-groups. In Lunny (1981) and Ní Ghallchóir (1981), material from the three age-groups was used to illustrate the declining influence of Irish Gaelic in parts of Ireland, while in Adams (1981) it was used to show the recession of an archaic form (i.e. the Ulster Scots [x], as in *lough*). From the above, it is clear that the decision of TRS to examine the speech of three different age-groups was fully justified.

Notes

1. The principal full-time fieldworkers employed by TRS were Miss C. Ní Ghallchóir, who worked in Ulster; Mr P.A. Lunny, in Munster and Leinster; Mr B. Gunn, in Munster; Mr A. McCrumlish, in Leinster; and Miss M. Ní Rónain, in Connaught.

2. See Ann Hollingsworth Pitts, 'Urban Influence in Northern Irish English: A Comparison of Variation in Two Communities', PhD thesis (University of Michigan, 1982) (available from University Microfilms International, ref. no. RPD83-04572), which used material from TRS as evidence.

3. Two of the Survey's fieldworkers have worked on this topic; see Patrick Anthony Lunny, 'Studies in the Modern English Dialect of Ballyvourney', unpublished PhD thesis (The Queen's University of Belfast, 1981), and C. Ní Ghallchóir, 'Linguistic Interplay: English and Irish in Co. Donegal', PhD thesis in preparation, The Queen's University of Belfast. It is hoped that these studies will be published in due course.

4. The work nearest to the approach envisaged here is D. Ó Muirithe (ed.), *The English Language in Ireland* (The Mercier Press, Dublin, 1977), which includes a valuable, though discontinuous, collection of articles (originally broadcast talks) on the English of Ireland.

References

Abercombie, D. 'The Recording of Dialect Material' in *Studies in Phonetics and Linguistics* (Oxford University Press, Oxford, 1965), pp. 108-13

Adams, G.B. 'The Voiceless Velar Fricative in Northern Hiberno-English' in M.V. Barry (ed.), *Aspects of English Dialects in Ireland* (Institute of Irish Studies, Belfast, 1981), pp. 106-17

Adams, G.B., M.V. Barry, and P.M. Tilling. *A Tape-recorded Survey of Hiberno-English, Questionnaire* (privately published, Belfast, 1976)

Barry, M.V. 'The Southern Boundaries of Northern Hiberno-English Speech' in R. Thelwall (ed.), *Linguistic Studies in Honour of Paul Christophersen* (The New University of Ulster, Coleraine, 1980) (Occasional Papers in Linguistics and Language, vol. 7), pp. 105-52

Barry, M.V. (ed.) *Aspects of English Dialects in Ireland* (Institute of Irish Studies, Belfast, 1981)

Douglas-Cowie, E. 'Linguistic Code-switching in a Northern Irish Village: Social Interaction and Social Ambition' in P. Trudgill (ed.), *Sociolinguistic Patterns in British*

English (Arnold, London, 1978), pp. 37-51

Gregg, R.J. 'The Scotch-Irish Dialect Boundaries in Ulster' in M.F. Wakelin (ed.), *Patterns in the Folk Speech of the British Isles* (Athlone Press, London, 1972), pp. 109-39

Henry, P.L. 'A Linguistic Survey of Ireland: Preliminary Report' in *Lochlann*, vol. 1 (1958), pp. 49-208

Lunny, A. 'Linguistic Interaction: English and Irish in Ballyvourney, W. Cork' in M.V. Barry (ed.), *Aspects of English Dialects in Ireland* (Institute of Irish Studies, Belfast, 1981), pp. 118-41

Milroy, J. and L. Milroy. 'Belfast: Change and Variation in an Urban Vernacular' in P. Trudgill (ed.), *Sociolinguistic Patterns in British English* (Arnold, London, 1978), pp. 19-36

Ní Ghallchóir, C. 'Aspects of Bilingualism in North West Donegal' in M.V. Barry (ed.), *Aspects of English Dialects in Ireland* (Institute of Irish Studies, Belfast, 1981), pp. 142-70

Orton, H. *Survey of English Dialects (A): Introduction* (E.J. Arnold, Leeds, 1962)

Petyt, K.M. *The Study of Dialect* (André Deutsch, London, 1980)

Editorial Note

Since this paper was commissioned, similar treatment of the TRS and of the Irish linguistic border has also appeared in M.V. Barry, 'The Methodology of the Tape-Recorded Survey of Hiberno-English Speech' and 'The Southern Boundaries of Northern Hiberno-English Speech' (which repeats Barry 1980) in his *Aspects of English Dialects in Ireland* (Institute of Irish Studies, the Queen's University of Belfast, 1981, reviewed by John Kirk in *Lore and Language*, vol. 3, no. 8, January 1983, pp. 107-10); M.V. Barry, 'Handling Three Age Groups in a Large Regional Dialect Survey in Ireland' in *Papers from the Fourth International Conference on Methods in Dialectology* (Department of Linguistics, University of Victoria, 1981), and in M.V. Barry 'The English Language in Ireland' in R.W. Bailey and M. Görlach (eds.), *English as a World Language* (University of Michigan Press, Ann Arbor, 1982, republished Cambridge University Press, Cambridge, 1984), as well as in M.V. Barry, Final Report to the SSRC on Grant HR 2823.

5

Linguistic Atlases and Sociolinguistics

PAUL A. JOHNSTON, JR.

Introduction

The aim of this paper is to present a guide to the interpretation of traditional (linguistic-geographical) dialect surveys in a sociolinguistic context. I wish to provide a link between traditional surveys and sociolinguistic dialect surveys, such as Labov's (1966) study of New York City speech, Trudgill's (1974) of Norwich, and similar works, and to illustrate the kind of sociolinguistic investigations that can be carried out using traditional survey material.

The two types of dialect survey are often presented as irreconcilably opposed to each other, and, indeed, their aims are different. The purpose of a traditional dialect survey is to examine the most localised speech variety in a large network of communities throughout a linguistic area, although in Kurath (1939) and, to some extent, in Jaberg and Jud (1928), other varieties may also be investigated. The communities surveyed tend to be rural, since conservative speech habits often survive away from cities and large nodes of communication, and the speakers are selected for their knowledge of conservative dialect forms, whether phonological, morphological, syntactic or lexical. The study of lexical variation, including the elicitation of items rather rare in conversation, is of prime importance, and sometimes is the sole focus of investigation, as in Mitzka (1951-80), Thomas (1973), and Mather and Speitel (1975-7). Questionnaires employed are designed for the elicitation of specific forms in response to the appropriate question, and cannot help but focus on the informants' language. The main emphasis in the study is on geographical, not social variation, which is optimally held constant in the selection of informants.

Sociolinguistic surveys, on the other hand, aim to give a representative picture of all varieties (or at least native ones) of speech found in a single community. Informants come from all social strata, are of both sexes and all age-groups, ethnic origins where relevant, and so on, so that correlations between these social factors and choice of linguistic forms may be determined, and are usually selected by use of random sampling. Questionnaires are constructed to provide various degrees of contextual formality, and the study of stylistic variation is also important; the interview, however, is structured largely in the form of a conversation, and the lexis elicited comprises words that occur in normal discourse. The main emphasis is on social and stylistic variation, and geographical variation is held constant.

Note that I do not use the term 'urban dialectology' (unlike Chambers and Trudgill 1980: 54-64) for the latter type of survey. Although most sociolinguistic studies have been carried out in cities, since urban areas exhibit more social stratification than rural ones, and thus more complicated linguistic patterns, sociolinguistic variation does exist in rural districts, and can be discovered *via* the same methods as in cities, as Labov (1978: 143), Douglas-Cowie (1978), and I have pointed out (Johnston 1979). Traditional surveys are not necessarily rural either; the localised speech habits of large cities such as London, Leeds, Sheffield, Boston, Hartford, Paris, Brussels, Amsterdam, Rome,

Naples, Florence, Milan and Venice have all been covered in them.[1]

It is precisely to further rural sociolinguistic research that I aim to put the findings of traditional surveys into sociolinguistic terms, so that future investigators can use them for comparative purposes with the most localised speech they elicit. This necessitates examining the handbooks and introductions to various surveys to determine the *social* characteristics (social stratum, sex and age) of their informants, as well as assessing the *stylistic* characteristics of the dialect survey interview. Because the importance of social stratification variables differs from country to country, I examined fourteen surveys of twelve countries in order to obtain the broadest possible overview.[2] In addition, I furnish examples of the type of comparisons that can be made using survey material.

Style Variation

At the outset, it is necessary to determine the position on the stylistic spectrum occupied by the results of traditional surveys. Sociolinguistic surveys have always been acutely aware of the effect of contextual formality on the forms elicited, and questionnaires are designed to provide examples of various contextual styles of speech. Besides the usual range of questions which can be answered in the *formal style* (FS) typical of the conversational interview, others, such as Labov's (1966: 107-8) 'childhood lore' and 'danger of death' or Trudgill's (1974: 51-2) 'funny experience' questions are added to produce narratives, and to gain access to the informant's *casual style* (CS). It is held that, in telling a story, the informant's mind will be less on his presence at an interview than on the events he recounts, and the formality of the discourse will be lowered accordingly (Trudgill 1974: 41-52). CS, in varying amounts, can also be elicited in response to other questions, or in speech to third parties, speech outside the interview context, and so on, depending on the personality of the informant and the mode of approach of the fieldworker (Trudgill 1974: 51-2). In addition, the stylistic spectrum is often extended towards the formal end by the inclusion of passages or word lists to be read aloud. Here, the informant's mind is directed

towards his language and in addition the mode of discourse is switched, both of which tend to raise the formality of discourse (Trudgill 1974: 41-6), and to produce more formal styles such as *reading passage style* (RPS) and *word list style* (WLS), the last being the most formal due to the words being in isolation.

Let us now examine the process of interview in a traditional dialect survey. To some extent this varies from study to study, but the various investigations can be roughly classified into three main types: the *indirect interview*, the *direct interview with direct questioning*, and the *direct interview with indirect questioning*. In addition they can be classified into surveys yielding answers in word or phrase form on the one hand, and sentences on the other.

The indirect interview method was used by Thomas (1973: 2-7), Mather and Speitel (1975: 14) and Remacle (1953: 12) (in the early stages, although results were later checked by direct interview), and in early studies such as Wenker (cf. Chambers and Trudgill 1980: 18-19). A postal questionnaire is sent out to educated people (often schoolteachers) in each community to be surveyed. These contacts then act as intermediaries, collecting data from suitable informants, and mailing the completed questionnaire back to the survey's office. This approach is often adopted when a large number of communities is to be covered quickly, and seems to be suited to the collection of lexical data (Mather and Speitel 1975: 13-14), although when detailed phonological information is needed, the method is less efficient than direct interviewing, owing to the inadequate phonetic training of the intermediaries.[3]

Most surveys occupied with phonology as well as other features make use of some kind of direct interview. A fieldworker actually visits each community to be surveyed, selects informants himself and interviews them personally, transcribing as he goes. The questionnaire may call for the informant to translate Standard words or phrases into dialect (direct questioning), or employ 'naming' questions (for example, 'A flying animal with feathers is called a . . .'), gestures, photographs and drawings to elicit the item without the Standard equivalent being uttered (indirect questioning). The first type includes surveys such as Gilliéron (1902: 4-7), Blancquaert (1925:11), and Wagner (1958: viii), although the last called for translation from

English to Irish, rather than Standard to dialect of the same language. The second type is used in most surveys, and has become nearly standard procedure; examples are Jaberg and Jud (1928: 175-96), Kurath (1939: 46-8), Gardette, (1950-76: 48), Nauton (1957-63: 88), Navarro and Menéndez-Pidal (1962: 4), Hotzenköcherle (1962: 29-34, 126), and Orton (1962: 25). Indirect questioning was adopted in reaction to one of the failings of the *Atlas linguistique de la France*, namely that informants, in translating from the Standard, may be unduly influenced by the Standard form and give some sort of *Mischsprache* (approximating to the *local* Standard) as a result. Nauton (1957-63: 88; see also Gardette 1950-76: 23-4) gives examples where precisely this seems to have happened in the Massif Central area. By avoiding the Standard word for something while eliciting the dialect word for it, more localised forms can be obtained.

It was also felt that asking questions in alphabetical or random order, as had been done in the direct question surveys, would call the attention of the informant too much to his language (Jaberg and Jud 1928: 196-200). Hence, questions are often grouped together by subject matter — for example, farming terms, parts of the body — since it was hoped that the informant would pay attention to that, rather than his usage, and the answers would thus be more spontaneous. This is a point I will discuss below.

Where do survey results then fit in on the stylistic spectrum? First of all, I do not see any difference in style between the data in direct and indirect interview surveys, since even the latter type entails some kind of face-to-face interview at some point (unless the intermediary fills out the postal questionnaire himself, in which case style is irrelevant). The main difference seems to lie in the employment of an amateur rather than a professional fieldworker, but the techniques in both types of survey otherwise seem to be similar, although some lowering of formality possibly occurs if the intermediary and informant are friends or neighbours.

From all the concern expressed about the methods of questioning, layout of the questionnaire, and so on, traditional surveys seem to be aiming to produce CS. This is made explicit in the use of phrases such as 'How would you say it to a wife or neighbour?' in Kurath (1939: 48), and in other comments about optimally obtaining spontaneous responses (Gardette 1950-76: 48-9). This is natural; sociolinguists have found the most localised forms in CS, with their occurrence decreasing as formality increases.

In CS, the speaker is not being tested for his linguistic ability. He is simply speaking, whether chatting to friends and neighbours or telling a story or whatever; there are no right or wrong answers to what he says. However, in a linguistic interview situation of this kind, as opposed to a more conversationally-based sociolinguistic one, there definitely are, and certain fieldwork techniques allowed in most traditional surveys (Orton 1962: 25; Nauton 1957-63: 92; Hotzenköcherle 1962: 126; Kurath 1939: 145) such as suggesting forms and pressuring informants, make this very clear to the speaker. Hence, despite all the attempts of investigators to reduce formality of context, the informant's focus of attention must surely be on his own language, whatever method of questioning is used. Furthermore, a sociolinguistic interview takes only a short time (less than an hour), while a traditional interview usually takes many hours, spaced over several sessions (see Chambers and Trudgill 1980: 27); the fatigue factor might well lead to greater formality of discourse also. Some CS may appear in 'incidental material' (which is sometimes recorded, see Orton 1962: 25-6), given a skilled fieldworker, but the majority of responses seemingly are in a more formal style than would occur in normal conversation, which I postulate is at the same level of formality as RPS (if connected sentences are elicited) or WLS (if isolated words and phrases), which have the common trait of being styles where discourse is focused on language.

If this is true, linguistic features which occur characteristically in RPS and WLS should also appear in responses in traditional linguistic surveys. I shall illustrate some that do, by comparing data collected in Orton and Halliday (1962) for Lowick (1.1) and Wark (1.5), Northumberland with my data for Wooler and Bellingham (Johnston 1979: 95-103, 170-77) respectively. Each pair of towns (Wooler and Lowick, Bellingham and Wark) is close enough geographically to the other to represent more or less the same subvarieties of Northumbrian.

Words in final /p t k/ show a high incidence (50 per cent or so) of ejective realisations [p' t' k'] in Orton and Halliday's (1962) material for all North and Central Northumbrian dialects,[4] including Lowick and Wark. In Wooler and Bellingham, I found that ejectives were the majority form for working-class speakers only in WLS; in CS and FS, the usual final /t/ realisations were [ʔt] or [ʔ] (Johnston 1979: 95-8).

In Orton and Halliday (1962: I. 8.3; V. 7.13; V. 8.8; VI. 3.2; VI. 9.5) final /ii/ is sometimes realised as [ɧi~ɛ̈ɥ], or even [ɛ̈ɥ], although these are majority forms in neither Lowick nor Wark. I found such diphthongs to be rare at Bellingham in CS or FS, but in WLS, they were found in comparable frequency to *Survey of English Dialects* data (Johnston 1979: 175). Orton and Halliday (1962: III, 4.5; III. 10.2; IV. 11.8; V. 2.5; VI. 2.1) also give [ɔʁ] as the exclusive outcome of vocalised preconsonantal or final uvular /r/ outside Greater Tyneside or Allendale in Northumberland. I found all working-class groups to use a majority of [əʁ] realisations in all styles but WLS; however, at Wooler, [ɔʁ] forms were elicited 79 per cent of the time among the lower-working-class group in this style (Johnston 1979: 152, 159, 170, 174).

It could be argued, as in fact I did (Johnston 1979: 98-9, 175, 224) that speech rate, not stylistic characteristics, accounts for the first two similarities between traditional survey material and my WLS data. Ejective [t'] and diphthongs for /ii/ are conditioned by lento rate, as would occur when reading — or uttering — words in isolation or under emphasis, as might occur in Orton and Halliday's responses. However, I can think of no cogent phonetic explanation for the rounding of [əʁ] to [ɔʁ] due to speech rate. It was pointed out to me at the time by Roger Lass (personal communication; cf. Johnston 1979: 175, 310), that eliciting words in isolation, either as part of a word list or otherwise, may produce something like a speaker's *canonical norms* (forms uninfluenced by surface phonetic modifications that would occur in connected sentences).

There are problems, though, in identifying the style found in traditional survey responses with WLS. One is that there is no mode-switching in the data; the informant did not read his responses aloud. I recognise this, and so refrain from saying that WLS is elicited in survey interviews of this type. Instead, I will call this style *canonical style* (CaS), one in which the focus of the informant is on his usage and canonical norms are produced, but not involving the written medium, although more formal than

FS. Similarities with WLS probably indicate that it is of the same level of formality, however.

What about the style found in the Dutch surveys, where words are elicited in sentences? The definition above excludes it from qualifying as canonical style, yet the focus of the informant is on his language, which indicates a higher formality level than FS. I will postulate that, as CaS is the spoken-mode equivalent to WLS, this style is in the same relationship to RPS (which is also connected), and call it *self-conscious connected style* (SCS).

The model of stylistic formality levels, I conclude, has the Y- shape shown in Figure 5.1, with the style ranges elicited in dialect survey material located along the upper fork of the Y.

Figure 5.1: A Model of Stylistic Formality Levels

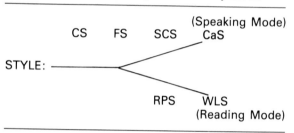

There is another difficulty with postulating such high levels of formality in survey responses. In all sociolinguistic studies, it has been found that, where style-tying exists for a variable, the prevailing tendency is for its realisations to become more Standard-like. A Wooler speaker who uses [u(:)] in *out, house,* or other words descending from Northern Middle English /uu/, in casual speech, would tend to have [ɣɔ] in RPS and WLS. However, in Orton and Halliday (1962: III. 1.1; V. 1.1) only [u(:)] forms are given.

Two reasons can be suggested to explain this. The first is that both fieldworker and informant know that localised forms, even concerning variables such as this one, where the Standard and localised realisations are so different that there is a high level of consciousness of the variable throughout the community, are the only appropriate responses in this context. If the informant produces a diphthongal reflex in this class of word, such as [ɣɔ], he is 'not playing the game' of being a participant in this type of survey, and the fieldworker might very well pressure him until [u(:)] is elicited. To be co-operative, an informant has to employ his CS repertoire in CaS, as far as 'dialect features' in the traditional sense — cf. Petyt (1980: 16-17) — are concerned. Yet, variables to which no community consciousness is directed, such as [t~t'], will appear in the form they would otherwise take, since the speaker is not conscious of them ('accent features').

The second reason why Standard-like forms are found in sociolinguists' reading passages and word lists but not in traditional surveys, is due to difference in mode. The orthography of the texts would tend to influence a speaker's usage where dialect features are involved, particularly if his area has any tradition of dialect literature with a different orthographical system. A Scottish informant from Edinburgh who normally uses [hẹm] for *home* will tend to produce [höm] or the like, when encountering the item in Standard spelling. If [hẹm] is wanted, he would expect the word to be spelled *hame*, as in dialect literature. In a linguistic interview of the traditional kind, since no written material is used, these influences would be absent.

In conclusion, the styles elicited in traditional surveys seem to be the spoken-mode equivalents of the sociolinguists' RPS and WLS, due to the focus of attention of the informants being on their own speech. If the utterances are connected, they are in SCS; if not, in CaS. Features of speech of which there is community consciousness will nevertheless appear in the forms they would take in CS, owing to the appropriateness conditions of this type of interview. The results are best compared to RPS and WLS, as well as CS, responses in sociolinguistic works.

Sex and Age Variation

Sex and age are often found to be relevant factors for linguistic variation in communities studied in sociolinguistic surveys. Labov (1966: 310-14; 318-96; 429-33), Trudgill (1974: 93-5, 107), and others have found many of their variables to be dependent on these two factors, and age variation patterns in particular are found to be indicators of the direction of any linguistic change in progress. The results of previous, traditional surveys have long been used as checks on any age variation patterns discovered in communities where previous study has been carried out, since the informants used in the earlier surveys may often be a generation older than the oldest speakers in the later one which allows the pattern to be extrapolated back. Since age (and sex) characteristics of traditional surveys are listed in the appropriate survey handbooks, this task is a relatively easy one.

But can sex or age variation patterns be discovered *within* a traditional survey's material? According to Chambers and Trudgill (1980: 33), this is highly unlikely, due to 'the majority of informants' . . . in all cases . . . [consisting] . . . of nonmobile, older rural males'. While the majority of informants have indeed been rural and male, at least in all the surveys I examined, they have not necessarily been older, and some studies have used a noticeable minority of female informants. Figure 5.2 lists the sex and age breakdown for a number of surveys.

The statistics in Figure 5.2 show that few surveys were so strict as to exclude women and informants under 60 categorically. In fact, while women are always in the minority, Nauton in

Figure 5.2: Age and Sex Characteristics of Traditional Survey Informants

Survey	Total informants	Women	%	Aged 30-60	%	Aged 0-30	%
Gilliéron	751	63	8.4	462	61.6	95	12.6
Gardette	395	134	34.0	69	17.5	6	1.5
Nauton	218	96	44.0	50	23.9	2	0.9
Jaberg and Jud	433	35	8.2	227	52.3	29	6.7
Remacle	844	186	22.0	345	40.8	45	5.3
Kurath	402	101	25.1	98	24.4	5	1.2
Orton et al.[a]	955	118	12.3	27	2.8	1	0.1
Blancquaert et al.[a]	4,012	912	22.8	1,836	45.3	1,205	30.0

Note: a. Data from all relevant publications combined.
Source: Various survey handbooks.

particular comes close to selecting equal numbers of both sexes, while the various Dutch and Belgian surveys, as well as the New England one (which was not only interested in localised speech) select enough women to make exploration of sex variation within the findings theoretically possible. The middle-aged comprise the majority of Gilliéron's and Jaberg and Jud's speakers, and the oldest group forms only about a quarter of those employed in the Dutch survey, in which some investigators made great use of child informants, since they were felt to be as good dialect speakers as the old in some districts, especially Flemish Brabant and the part of Flanders belonging to the Netherlands (Blancquaert and Vangassen 1931: vi).[5] Age variation therefore also might be recoverable from survey data. In fact, at least a few investigators have apparently noticed age variation, especially where obsolescent forms are concerned; examples occur, for instance, in Orton and Halliday (1962: V. 2.12; VII. 3.11) for Heptonstall, West Yorkshire (10.3), where forms of *light* and *night*, with or without /x/, are contrasted according to currency in modern speech, with the /x/ realisations marked as obsolescent.

However, sex variation is another matter, and remarks concerning its presence or absence are usually confined to notes in survey handbooks. Orton (1962: 15-16) seems to recognise that, in England, women on the whole speak more Standard-like than men, and this was a factor in the selection of so few female informants. From the several instances where informants' wives disapprove of dialect speech in New England mentioned by Kurath (1939: 168, 173, 192, 193), this seems to be true of the United States as well. Since this type of sex variation is so common in these two countries in both rural and urban areas (cf. Johnston 1979: Chapter III), Chambers and Trudgill (1980: 97-8) go so far as to state it as a possible universal for Western nations; this, as I shall show below, is an oversimplification. Some reasons why women are 'Standardisers' relative to men given by Chambers and Trudgill include:

(a) the relative lack of opportunity of achievement in society and the resulting need for women to signal their social status by appearance and behaviour (including linguistic) rather than by what they do;

(b) the relative lack of cohesion of women within social networks due to the existence of fewer occupational opportunities and greater tendency to remain at home, so that they would find themselves in more formal situations more often than men would, and formal speech would result;

(c) the greater sensitivity of women to norms of 'accepted' behaviour, owing to their traditional role in child socialisation;

(d) the greater acceptance of rough, tough, 'rule-breaking' behaviour among men, rather than women, by society.[6]

These reasons may well account for the linguistic situation in societies where localised dialect speech is stigmatised and associated with the usage of lower social strata, where the pressure to use a Standard variety is large, and defined as accepted behaviour. However, in a society where localised dialect is employed by everyone, reasons (a), (c) and (d) above would not apply, since they can depend on the association of speech with social stratification, and implications resulting therefrom. One is left with reason (b), but if a Standard variety is not a norm for formal speech, isolation of women from the mainstream of social networks would not result in greater Standardisation by women, but in a lessened sensitivity to linguistic change, which has been found to be true of class-conscious societies such as Britain as well, in so far as the change is native and not simply in the direction of the Standard.[7] Conservatism of this type in female speech is mentioned by Jaberg and Jud (1928: 189)[8] for Italy, and Hotzenköcherle (1962: 126) for German-speaking Switzerland. (The importance of the association between speech forms and social strata in various European societies will be discussed in greater detail in the next section.) In any case, female informants in traditional dialect surveys would not be selected if they showed Standardising tendencies, so that difference in sensitivity to native linguistic change is the only product of sex variation one can examine these surveys' corpora for (see note 7).

To do this, one must find communities where men and women of similar ages and social classes, where appropriate, have been interviewed, and compare forms known to be undergoing linguistic change, as revealed by the responses of informants or speakers in a different age-group, or by the evidence of later studies. In any case, corroboration by later surveys is essential, since the samples in traditional ones are invariably too small to screen out the problem of idiolectal peculiarities of the speakers; if variation patterns in both earlier and later studies coincide, the possibility of them reflecting sex variation is increased.

Lowick, Northumberland again furnishes interesting and relevant data for this. Orton and Halliday interviewed two men and a woman in the village, all from farming backgrounds and over 60 years of age in 1951. In 1975 I carried out a sociolinguistic survey in nearby Wooler, with seven males and eight females in the sample. Although my primary result was that Wooler women speak more Standard-like than men of the same social class, two variables, known to have undergone change in the early-to-mid twentieth century by comparison with earlier data in Ellis's (1889) survey,[9] agreed in variation pattern in both Orton and Halliday's and my findings. These are (a) the outcome of Northern Middle English /aa ai/ as in *stone*, *name*, *rain*; and (b) that of Northern Middle English /ɛɛ ee uu/ (modern /ii uu/ respectively) in word-final position, as in *me*, *see*, *sea* and *how*, *cow*.

Orton and Halliday elicited 136 items stemming from Northern Middle English /aa/ or /ai/. For all speakers, the majority form is [e:], mentioned as being the usual reflex of these word classes in Northern Northumberland by Ellis (1889: 681-99). However, [eə], used by both sexes, appears also, and there are ten examples of [ɩə], all used by men. There seems to be a change from [e:] through [eə] to [ɩə], which I confirmed (Johnston 1979: 152-6).[10]

In my data, whereas the majority form of working-class men (combined) is [ɩɛ] except word-finally, working-class women always prefer [e:~eɛ] in all environments. There is thus a sex-tying pattern, male [ɩɛ] *vs.* female [e:~eɛ], with the latter being both more conservative with respect to the ongoing change, and (at least for the *name* and *rain* classes) more Standard-like than men.

Another ongoing change suggested by Orton and Halliday's (1962) data is the diphthongisation of final /ii uu/ to nuclei of the [ëɩ] and [ɔu] type. 35 examples of final /ii uu/ were recorded; for the men, 17 out of 27 were diphthongal, as opposed to only three out of eight for the woman interviewed. In my survey, the diphthongisation of final /ii/, at least, was found less than 10 per cent of the time among Wooler women, but 20 per cent in male speech. Again, the sex-tying pattern coincides, with women preferring the pre-change form. The arguments that this is due to the conservative, rather than standardising tendencies of women, are strengthened by the lack of class-tying shown by this variable.[11]

To conclude: sex and age variation can occur within the corpus of data recorded by traditional surveys, although there generally is a preference for males. Age variation is usually noted by the surveyors, since it determines where linguistic change is taking place. Sex variation is not, but can be examined where both males and females were interviewed in a single community, and each informant's responses are clearly marked. Age and sex variation patterns suggested by traditional survey data need corroborative evidence from later surveys of the community with respect to variables undergoing change, since this is where both age and sex differences will appear.

Class Variation

I now turn to another type of variation that sociolinguistic surveys often treat as of prime importance — variation by social stratification, or *class variation*. The profound connection between social class and speech patterns has been explored by all such surveys (especially, but not exclusively, in Britain and America: see Chambers and Trudgill 1980: 98-9), and a regular pattern emerges from their results: that the farther up the social scale one goes, the more Standard-like speakers' usage becomes, and the fewer localised forms appear. Indeed, the speech of the highest-ranking social groups can be said to define the local form of the Standard. Due to the association between localised dialect and low social status, such speech is stigmatised to a greater or lesser degree, and regular stylistic and sex variation patterns result also, so that the Standard is favoured in formal contexts, and in women's speech (for reasons discussed in the previous section). If the force toward Standard-isation is strong enough, or is increased through longer exposure to the Standard through education, increased facility of communication, the

Figure 5.3: Middle-class Informants in Traditional Dialect Surveys

Survey	Total	Informants with occupation specified	Middle-class informants	Percentage middle-class to informants with occupation specified
Gilliéron	751	726	258	35.6
Gardette	395	395	14	3.5
Nauton	218	218	2	0.9
Jaberg and Jud	433	431	103	23.9
Remacle	844	581	277	47.0
Kurath	402	349	132	37.8
Orton *et al.*	955	922	16	1.7
Blancquaert *et al.*	4,012	3,253	1,576	48.5

Source: Various survey handbooks.

influence of the mass media, or any number of reasons, an age variation pattern may result so that the young 'Standardise out' the most divergent characteristics of the local dialect, and these face extinction. Such patterns are found in such profusion in both rural and urban Britain and America, that it is tempting to conclude that all Western societies share them, and that any traditional linguistic geographer who used middle-class people as informants was making a grave mistake.

If so, the mistake is extremely common. Figure 5.3 shows the percentage of people in middle-class occupations (including shopkeepers and non-manual workers of all types, as well as owners of large, well-staffed farms)[12] among the samples of a number of surveys.

If patterns similar to those found to exist in New York City and Norwich are also present throughout Western societies, only the English and regional French atlases can be relied on to contain exclusively localised dialect. Indeed, both Gardette (1950-76: 23-4) and Nauton (1957-63: 38) criticise Gilliéron for his frequent reliance on town clerks and officials as informants, and give examples where (admittedly highly-accented) Standard-like forms were elicited when more localised ones existed. Nauton (1957-63: 25-45) also mentions ties between class and speech patterns, and gives a historical account of the spread of Standard French throughout the Massif Central area. France, it seems, is also a country where localised speech is highly stigmatised, as in Britain and America, with evidence of stigmat-

isation appearing as far back as the sixteenth century (Fox and Wood 1968: 27) so perhaps the criticisms of Gilliéron can stand. But what about the other surveys? One might excuse the 37.8 per cent proportion in Kurath, since he was not looking only at localised varieties, but surely the ratios of middle-class informants in the Walloon and Dutch/Flemish surveys are too high for the studies to be reliable, if class-tying is universal, and possibly even the 23.8 per cent in the Italian survey could lead to large errors?

Luckily for the surveys, there is ample evidence that this is not the case. Pressures to standardise speech vary from country to country, and even from district to district within a language area. In German-speaking Switzerland, localised dialect is used in most contexts by everyone, according to Petyt (1980: 202). Jaberg and Jud (1928: 190) seem to confirm this also for Italian-speaking Switzerland; in Italy proper, some towns, including all large cities, seem to have a class-tied linguistic structure, but others (even in the same district) do not — which type exists depends on the size of town, proximity to major local centres, and percentage of incomers, as well as region. Even in rural southern Scotland, I found that some middle-class speakers used localised dialect in the family group, and could even translate Standard English reading passages into fluent Border Scots. In all cases, however, they had come from working-class backgrounds (agricultural or otherwise), and had many working-class contacts. Unlike other middle-class speakers,[13] they would probably have been excellent informants for a traditional survey.

The Northern Continental situation seems to be in between the Swiss and English/American/French ones, regarding class variation. The various Dutch surveys (Blancquaert *et al.*), in their notes, examine the extent of dialect use both by their own informants, and in each community as a whole in some detail. Although results are complicated by the use of French as a dominant language in some districts of Flemish Belgium, notably the Brussels area (see van de Craen 1980), and by the great lapse of time between the earliest and most recent publications in the series (with the Second World War intervening), one can more or less determine where in the Dutch-speaking area one is likely to find middle-class local dialect speakers, and where class-tying exists.

Figure 5.4 lists the number of middle-class informants, and their frequency of dialect use, by district and by population of their community. Schoolteachers, who were frequently interviewed, tend to use Standard Dutch in some form within the classroom; they are listed here according to their speech in other contexts. Friesland is excluded for the reason that the most localised speech of the area is Frisian, not Dutch; Groningen is also excluded, since little

information about the speakers' dialect use is provided.

The first thing to notice from this table is that the great majority of middle-class members in the survey, except in the North and West of the Netherlands, to which, from remarks made in Sassen (1967), Groningen may be added, are localised dialect speakers in most or all contexts. This is best shown for small towns in the South of the Netherlands or Belgium, but holds also for medium-sized communities in Belgium and Dutch Limburg, and for even larger ones in the extreme South-east of the Dutch linguistic zone and East Gelderland, Twente, and the Veluwe. This fits well with remarks made about where class-tying does exist in various communities; it is found in both Hollands, Utrecht, Groningen, West Gelderland and along the Rhine and Maas to the point where they turn southward; elsewhere it seems restricted to large cities and their suburbs, or to areas where there are many incomers from outside. If a sociolinguistic survey was done in these areas, a British-type pattern would result; elsewhere, the Standard-speaking population would be very small, probably schoolteachers, clergymen, and University graduates, while shopkeepers and businessmen would speak localised dialect. This situation

Figure 5.4:   Number of Middle-class Dutch-speaking Informants by Region, Population of Town, and Frequency of Dialect Use

Population of Town	0-5,000				5,000-10,000				10,000-50,000				50,000+			
Frequency of dialect use[a]	1	2	3	4	1	2	3	4	1	2	3	4	1	2	3	4
Region																
West Flanders[b]	82	17	10	6	21	14	2	1	7	6	1	1	0	0	0	1
South-east Flanders	46	50	7	3	2	11	2	3	2	3	0	1	—	—	—	—
North-east Flanders	27	71	3	24	3	18	3	3	5	11	0	5	0	0	3	4
Flemish Brabant	61	75	8	3	10	10	1	0	4	9	3	4	2	5	1	0
Little Brabant	15	28	7	12	3	5	2	4	2	1	1	1	0	1	0	1
Antwerp	40	24	23	10	6	5	9	2	4	2	6	4	0	0	2	1
South Limburg	97	43	15	0	27	14	6	2	6	8	3	4	2	1	0	0
North Limburg	43	40	15	12	12	12	9	5	7	7	6	2	2	0	2	4
North Brabant	0	9	10	13	1	10	0	9	0	2	0	8	0	2	1	2
Zeeland	18	12	2	9	1	0	1	3	1	3	0	3	—	—	—	—
South Holland[c]	4	5	0	6	0	0	2	5	1	3	2	3	0	1	0	3
North Holland[c]	0	0	0	4	0	0	1	1	—	—	—	—	0	1	0	0
Gelderland	5	47	21	6	0	15	7	1	0	8	6	1	0	5	0	2

Notes: a. Key to frequency numbers: 1 — always; 2 — mostly; 3 — sometimes; 4 — never. b. Excludes Dutch-speaking parts of France. c. Informants' frequency of dialect use rarely recorded.
Source: The various *Reeks Dialect-Atlassen van Nederland* publications.

seems to be the case in Dutch Limburg; when I was there, shopkeepers spoke to me in dialect, even though I was a foreigner, and apparently managers in business offices in Venlo use localised Limburg as their usual speech, also. The pattern here would be more like Switzerland.

It follows that any sociolinguist wishing to use data from traditional dialect surveys for comparative purposes must take account of who, according to the local situation, actually uses localised speech forms in the community to be studied, only restricting his comparison to working-class speech if class is a factor in linguistic variation.

Can class variation be examined within a single survey's findings, as I did for sex variation? The Dutch surveys would seem ideal for this, as many towns were investigated using both middle- and working-class informants. Unfortunately, the published results seem to be a composite picture, and it is impossible to tell which utterance belongs to which informant in most cases.[14] In surveys dealing with societies where class variation *is* a factor in speech differences, middle-class speakers are avoided in order to screen out non-localised responses; otherwise the question of class is irrelevant. However, there is at last one survey on which such studies could be done: the *Linguistic Atlas of New England*, since both localised and non-localised varieties were recorded. There are some seventeen communities where both 'cultured' and 'folk' speaking informants were interviewed; a suitable one for examination is Pittsfield, Massachusetts (242) where the middle-class and working-class speakers are both of the same sex and of similar age, and are found at the

extremes of the social scale, one, a businessman, the other, a labourer.

The localised dialect of Pittsfield is similar to ones in other Berkshire Mountain or South-west Vermont communities; it also (impressionistically) exhibits ties with the Upper Hudson Valley dialects to the west. However, being in Massachusetts, it should be influenced culturally by the Boston conurbation and Eastern Massachusetts, and one would expect the local Standard to have more in common with Boston speech, with variables appearing where the two areas differ. One such difference is in the reflex of pre-consonantal and final /r/. /r/ in these positions is vocalised in Eastern Massachusetts, as in most non-South-western English dialects; in the Berkshires, it is retained as a retroflex (or possibly 'molar') [ɹ] (Kurath 1939: 19-20). Another divergence between Eastern and Western Massachusetts is in the reflex of /oo/ (*coat*), /ee/ (*name*), /ii/ (*see*), and /uu/ (*spoon*). The coastal dialects tend to have diphthongs of the [eɪ oʊ ɪi ɔu] type, whereas many inland Northern (and Canadian) ones tend toward monophthongal [e: o: i: u:]. A third difference, directly attributable to class variation in many dialects of English (Trudgill 1974: 84; Johnston 1979: 68-73) is in the realisation of verbal *-ing*; whereas middle-class speech should favour [-ŋ], that of the working class should show a preponderance of [-ɪn]. All these differences are in fact observable in Pittsfield, with the middle-class speaker showing higher frequencies of the Standard and/or Eastern Massachusetts reflex in every case, as Figure 5.5 illustrates.

The evidence of Pittsfield suggests that, where non-localised varieties are elicited, class-tying patterns may show up in traditional survey data,

Figure 5.5: **The Variables (r), (ŋ), (ee), (ii), (oo), (uu) in Pittsfield, Massachusetts, by Class**

Variable: reflex	Middle-class frequency	Working-class frequency	Variable: reflex	Middle-class frequency	Working-class frequency
(r): Vocalised	86%	11%	(ŋ): [ŋ]	100%	0%
Retained	14	89	[n]	0	100
(ee): [eɪ]	80	59	(oo): [oʊ]	72	44
[e:]	20	41	[o:]	28	56
(ii): [ɪi]	88	50	(uu): [ɔu~ɯ]	78	45
[i:]	12	50	[u:]	22	55

Source: H. Kurath, *Linguistic Atlas of New England* (Brown University Press, 1939).

and can be used to suggest further avenues of investigation. My earlier warning against the possible existence of idiolectal variation within such a small sample still holds; however, corroboration exists in other studies for (r) and (ŋ), at least (Trudgill 1974: 84; Johnston 1979: 68-83; Labov 1978: 145) and points of interest for further study are raised in the other cases.

Conclusion

Traditional surveys present a large corpus of data that can be used for comparison with those elicited in sociolinguistic works, for the appropriate group of speakers in the appropriate styles. Techniques of investigation used in dialect geographies produce a very formal style of speech suitable for comparison with both the equally formal reading styles elicited by sociolinguists, in respect to features which the community has low consciousness of; and with casual speech, where high consciousness exists. Responses of dialect-speaking populations in both types of survey in a single community can be compared also, if indications in the survey handbooks regarding the class, sex, and age

characteristics of localised speakers are heeded. In addition, evidence of earlier stages of linguistic change in progress can often be found in traditional survey data.

Since few dialect surveys have been so strict as to exclude completely females, younger speakers, and middle-class members of a community, the way is open in principle for the study of class, sex, and age variation using traditional survey data alone. However, the following conditions must be met for this to be possible: first, that within a given community, the list of informants includes speakers belonging to all groups to be compared, and that each person's responses be clearly marked; second, that either the survey be concerned with more than just localised varieties, or that all groups compared be viewed as containing speakers of localised dialect; third, that any variation patterns discovered be confirmed by other studies, since the samples used for a single community in traditional surveys are too small to guard against idiolectal variation. If these precautions are taken, traditional dialect studies may be very useful in suggesting further avenues of sociolinguistic research, and in further clarifying the results of sociolinguistic surveys.

Notes

1. H. Orton and W.J. Halliday. *The Survey of English Dialects: Basic Material: The Six Northern Counties and the Isle of Man* 3 vols. (Arnold, Leeds, 1962-3) for Leeds and Sheffield; H. Orton and P.M. Tilling. *The Survey of English Dialects: Basic Material: The East Midland Counties and East Anglia* 3 vols. (Arnold, Leeds, 1969-71) for London; H. Kurath. *The Linguistic Atlas of New England*, 1st edn (4 vols., Brown University Press, Providence, 1939-53) for Boston and Hartford; J. Gilliéron, *Atlas linguistique de la France* 13 vols. (Champion, Paris, 1902-10) for Paris; H. Vangassen. *Dialect-Atlas van Vlaamsch-Brabant* (De Sikkel, Antwerp, 1938) for Brussels; J. Daan, *Dialect-Atlas van Noord-Holland* (De Sikkel, Antwerp, 1969) for Amsterdam; K. Jaberg and J. Jud. *Sprach- und Sachatlas des Italiens und der Südschweiz* (Ringier, Zofingen, 1928-40) for the Italian cities.

2. A full list of surveys consulted follows. For English, Orton and Barry (1969-71); Orton and Halliday (1962-3); Orton and Tilling (1969-71); Orton and Wakelin (1967-8). In Scotland, Mather and Speitel (1975-7). In the United States, Kurath (1939). For Welsh, Thomas (1973). For Irish, Wagner (1958-69). For French, Gilliéron (1902-10); Gardette (1950-76); Nauton (1957-63). In Belgium, Remacle (1953). For the Iberian languages, Navarro and Menéndez-Pidal (1962). For Italian, Jaberg and Jud (1928). For German, Mitzka (1951-80). In Switzerland, Hotzenköcherle (1962). For Dutch: Blancquaert *et al.* (1962); Daan (1969); Entjes and Hol

(1973); Hol and Passage (1966); Sassen (1967); van Oyen (1968); Weijnen (1952). In Belgium, Blancquaert (1925, 1935); Blancquaert and Meertens (1941); Blancquaert and Vangassen (1930); Pee (1947, 1958); Vangassen (1969).

3. Cf. criticisms in Petyt (1980: 40, 45).

4. That is, Lowick and Wark, plus Embleton (1.2) and Thropton (1.3).

5. See criticisms in Weijnen (1952: vi).

6. To which I might add that British or American working-class women might use the status implied in more Standard-like speech as a source of power over their husbands.

7. But cf. the many American and Swiss counterexamples in Labov (1978: 301-3). Greater integration of women in social networks may account for American data, but certainly not those from early twentieth-century rural Switzerland. I am frankly perplexed as to any explanation for these, as they contradict Hotzenköcherle's findings (1962: 261).

8. Men were primarily interviewed, however, because of practical problems; husbands were frequently reluctant to have their wives be interviewed, and often women were too busy with family chores to participate. The proportion of female informants rises the further north one gets.

9. For Berwick. Wooler was included in this survey, but it is quite likely that the informant was a Scot (cf. Johnston 1979: 446).

10. In the reference, I also discussed the conditioning effects of pre-dental environments. All examples of [ɯ] in the Orton and Halliday findings occur before dentals or palatals.

11. At least for /ii/. /uu/ is very class-tied, since the Standard reflex is [aʊ]. Speakers who have this in *cow*, however, will have /uu/ in *do*, and this shows a similar variation pattern to /ii/.

12. The definition follows Trudgill's (1974: 24) occupational index scale; speakers scoring 3 or more are considered middle-class here. No other indices could be used, owing to lack of information in most cases in survey handbooks.

13. Middle-class speakers, if they come from backgrounds of equal status, tend to either Standardise or 'hyper-dialectalise', a process similar to hypercorrection. An example of the latter was given at a meeting of Scots dialect enthusiasts, one of whom constructed the form [rëxt], meaning *write* (on the analogy of [rëxt] = *right*)! (Data from Caroline Macafee, personal communication).

14. Only in a few localities, mostly Belgian, are informants' separate responses mentioned. The differences illustrated, however, are supposed to be geographical in most cases, when dialects in the outlying villages and the central town of a general community differ.

References

Blancquaert, E. *Dialect-Atlas van Klein Brabant* (De Sikkel, Antwerp, 1925)
—— *Dialect-Atlas van Noord-Oost Vlaanderen en Zeeuwsch-Vlaanderen* (De Sikkel, Antwerp, 1935)
Blancquaert, E., J.C. Claessens, W. Goffin and A. Stevens. *Dialect-Atlas van Belgisch-Limburg en Zuid Nederlands-Limburg* (De Sikkel, Antwerp, 1962)
Blancquaert, E. and P.J. Meertens. *Dialect-Atlas van de Zeeuwsche Eilanden* (De Sikkel, Antwerp, 1941)
Blancquaert, E. and H. Vangassen. *Dialect-Atlas van Zuid-Oost-Vlaanderen* (De Sikkel, Antwerp, 1931)
Chambers, J.K. and P. Trudgill. *Dialectology* (Cambridge University Press, Cambridge, 1980)
Daan, J. *Dialect-Atlas van Noord-Holland* (De Sikkel, Antwerp, 1969)
Douglas-Cowie, E. 'Linguistic Code-Switching in a Northern Irish Village: Social Interaction and Social Ambition', in P. Trudgill (ed.), *Sociolinguistic Patterns in British English* (Arnold, London, 1978), pp. 37-51
Ellis, A.J. *Early English Pronunciation*, 5 vols. (Asher, Trübner, London, 1889)
Entjes, H. and A.R. Hol. *Dialect-Atlas van Gelderland en Zuid Overijsel* (De Sikkel, Antwerp, 1973)
Fox, J. and R. Wood. *A Concise History of the French Language* (Blackwell, Oxford, 1968)
Gardette, P. *Atlas linguistique et ethnographique du Lyonnais*, 5 vols. (Centre National de la Recherche Scientifique, Paris, 1950-76)
Gilliéron, J. *Atlas linguistique de la France*, 13 vols. (Champion, Paris, 1902-10)
—— *Atlas Linguistique de la France: Notice* (Champion, Paris, 1902)
Hol. A.R. and J. Passage. *Dialect-Atlas van Oost-Noord-Brabant, de Rivierenstreek, en Noord-Nederlands-Limburg* (De Sikkel, Antwerp, 1966)
Hotzenköcherle, R. *Einführung in den Sprachatlas der Deutschen Schweiz* (Francke, Bern, 1962)
Jaberg, K. and J. Jud. *Sprach- und Sachatlas des Italiens und der Südschweiz* (Ringier, Zofinger, 1928-40)
—— *Der Sprachatlas als Forschungsinstrument* (Niemeyer, Halle, 1928)
Johnston, P.A. 'A Synchronic and Historical View of Border Area Bimoric Vowel Systems', unpublished PhD thesis (University of Edinburgh, 1979)
Kurath, H. *Handbook of the Linguistic Atlas of New England* (Brown University Press, Providence, 1939)
Kurath, H. *et al. Linguistic Atlas of New England*, 3 vols. in 6 parts (Brown University Press, Providence, 1939-43; reprinted AMS Press, New York, 1972)
Labov, W. *The Social Stratification of English in New York City* (Center for Applied Linguistics, Washington, 1966)
—— *Sociolinguistic Patterns*, 2nd edn (Blackwell, Oxford, 1978)
Mather, J.Y. and H.-H. Speitel. *The Linguistic Atlas of Scotland:* Scots section, 2 vols. (Croom Helm, London, 1975-7)
Mitzka, W. *Deutscher Wortatlas*, 22 vols. (Schmitz, Giessen, 1951-80)
Nauton, P. *Atlas linguistique et ethnographique du Massif Central*, 4 vols. (Centre National de la Recherche Scientifique, Paris, 1957-63)
Navarro, T. and R. Menéndez-Pidal, *Atlas lingüístico de la Península Ibérica* (Consejo Superior de Investigaciones Scientificas, Madrid, 1962)
Orton, H. *Survey of English Dialects (A): Introduction* (E.J. Arnold, Leeds, 1962)
Orton, H. and M.V. Barry, *The Survey of English Dialects (B): Basic Material*, vol. II: *The West Midland Counties*, 3 parts (E.J. Arnold, Leeds, 1969-71)
Orton, H. and W.H. Halliday. *The Survey of English Dialects (B): Basic Material*, vol. I: *The six Northern Counties and the Isle of Man*, 3 parts (E.J. Arnold, Leeds, 1962-3)
Orton, H. and P.M. Tilling. *The Survey of English Dialects (B): Basic Material*, vol. III: *The East Midland Counties and East Anglia*, 3 parts (E.J. Arnold, Leeds, 1969-71)
Orton, H. and M.F. Wakelin. *The Survey of English Dialects (B): Basic Material*, vol. IV: *The Southern Counties*, 3 parts (E.J. Arnold, Leeds, 1967-8)
Pee, W. *Dialect-Atlas van West-Vlaanderen en Fransch-Vlaanderen* (De Sikkel, Antwerp, 1946)
—— *Dialect-Atlas van Antwerpen* (De Sikkel, Antwerp, 1958)
Petyt, K.M. *The Study of Dialect* (André Deutsch, London, 1980)
Remacle, L. *Atlas Linguistique de la Wallonie* (Vaillant-Carmanne, Liège, 1953)
Sassen, A. *Dialect-Atlas van Groningen en Noord-Drente* (De Sikkel, Antwerp, 1967)
Speitel, H.-H. 'Dialect', in A. Davies (ed.), *Problems of Language and Learning* (Heinemann, London, 1975), pp. 34-60
Thomas, A.R. *The Linguistic Geography of Wales* (University of Wales Press, Cardiff, 1973)

Trudgill, P. *The Social Differentiation of English in Norwich* (Cambridge University Press, Cambridge, 1974)

van de Craen, P. 'Frenchification Processes in Brussels: a model for verbal strategies', in P.H. Nelde (ed.), *Sprachkontakt und Sprachkonflikt* (Steiner, Wiesbaden, 1980), pp. 399-407

Vangassen, H. *Dialect-Atlas van Vlaamsch-Brabant* (De Sikkel, Antwerp, 1969)

van Oyen, L. *Dialect-Atlas van Zuid-Holland en Utrecht* (De Sikkel, Antwerp, 1968)

Wagner, H. *The Linguistic Atlas and Survey of Irish Dialects*, 4 vols. (Dublin Institute for Advanced Studies, Dublin, 1958-69)

Weijnen, A. *Dialect-Atlas van Noord-Brabant* (De Sikkel, Antwerp, 1952)

6

Linguistic Atlases and Dialectometry: The Survey of English Dialects[1]

WOLFGANG VIERECK

Dialectology has a long and eventful history.[2] It has its strengths and — who would deny? — its weaknesses. But even the theorists who expound their theories while extensively excluding linguistic data — consideration of these would, after all, be bothersome and time-consuming and thus unconscionable — must admit (if only somewhat secretly) that 'even' dialectology, which is so readily accused of being broadly deficient in theories, has done something for theoretical structuralist linguistics.

'Theory-rich' and 'data-poor' have always gone together. Robert B. Lees's famous or rather infamous epithet about the 'dull cataloguer of data' did not at that time lack effect. After all, who would want to be counted as such a functionary? Dialectologists and lexicographers had always belonged to that category, whose importance has, however, increased greatly in the last two decades, so that the 'dull cataloguer of data' nowadays virtually no longer leads a shadowy existence. It should not be overlooked that in the largely empirically-oriented disciplines that have made essential contributions to this growth in prestige — primarily in sociolinguistics and pragmatics — fashionable traits can be seen which will fizzle out. Similarly there is no lack of proposals to expand dialectology in the above two directions, though research into the social dimensions at least of American English is nothing new (see for instance McDavid (1979, 1980) and, on the subject of pragmatics, Schlieben-Lange and Weydt (1978)). On the other hand the value of the new type of dialect studies like those of Labov, Shuy and Wolfram in the USA and Trudgill and others in Britain, should not be underestimated, although traditional dialectologists refuse to be dazzled by such apparently exact figures and statistics as are presented in many works by sociolinguists.

For dialectology there has certainly been no lack of data. As was hinted at above, there are weaknesses in diverse aspects of their collecting methods; we have gone into various details elsewhere (see Viereck 1973a, 1973b). The motto in the interpretation of these masses of data has up until now been *selection*, a principle that carries with it the danger of subjectivity. In his book *Studies in Area Linguistics* Kurath describes the procedure hitherto followed in dialectology as follows:

> When the . . . heteroglosses . . . drawn for the items provided by the sample are assembled on maps, one finds that in some parts of the areas they run in bundles of various sizes — closeknit or spaced. These bundles show the location of major and minor dialect boundaries and thus indicate the dialectal structure of the total area. (1972: 24)

The problem is 'just' that not a few variants either show no unambiguous isoglosses, or heteroglosses, as Kurath more appropriately calls them, or do not show them where one would like them to be. Nevertheless, this procedure has yielded astonishingly good results. Selective indicators of only one language level, which were singled out by experienced researchers often intuitively on the basis of a comprehensive knowledge of the linguistic situation in the relevant area, proved to be quite significant for the classification of dialect areas. For in this field one can definitely 'put things to the test'. This consists firstly in statistically evaluating the *selected* heteroglosses, and secondly in trying to ascertain whether heteroglosses of different language levels agree with each other or not. Furthermore, in interpreting the language evidence one can pursue the question of whether it correlates with extra-linguistic factors characteristic of the overall sociocultural setting as well as those concerning topography. Finally, a further test can be conducted, about which more will be said below.

With reference to the Anglo-American field, it can be established that — insofar as the dialect structure of British and American English has yet been worked out at all — the interpretation adopted may be watertight to the extent that it is supported both by a count and subsequent statistical evaluation of the *selected* heteroglosses, and by the fact that phonological, morphological and lexical heteroglosses are in substantial agreement. For American English we owe this result to Kurath's countless studies of the Eastern States of the USA — (Kurath offers a summary in his book *Studies in Area Linguistics* (1972: 24-38) — but Kurath has also interpreted the phonological parts of the dialect data provided by Guy S. Lowman, Jr., who gathered these more than forty years ago in Southern England and parts of the English Midlands (see Kurath and Lowman, 1970). We have recently evaluated Lowman's morphological and lexical data according to traditional principles (Viereck, 1980a) and have come to the same conclusion — already alluded to — as Kurath did for American English. Here, too, the results for the most strongly fluctuating language level — the lexical — agree with the more stable phonological and morphological levels. In the third and so far most recent summary of British English dialects Wakelin remarks with regard to the data of the *SED* 'that traditional dialect areas may still be traced with some definiteness' (1972: 152), but has nothing to say about their location. The same is unfortunately also true of Orton and Wright's *A Word Geography of England* (1975); Orton, Sanderson and Widdowson's *The Linguistic Atlas of England* (1978); and Kolb, Glauser, Elmer and Stamm's *Atlas of English Sounds* (1979). In these three publications one might well have expected a chapter on the structure of British dialects.

As already mentioned, Kurath's and almost all of our previous interpretations are based on a selection of heteroglosses. The amount of selection is shown for instance in Kurath's *Word Geography of the Eastern United States*, where the author states: 'Figure 3 presents a scheme of the major speech areas of the Eastern States and their subdivisions, which is based upon the isoglosses of more than 400 different words treated in this book' (1949; repr. 1966: 11). The word index in Kurath's *Word Geography* alone includes around 800 words. How many local and regional lexical forms the linguistic atlas fieldworkers actually did note decades ago in the East of the United States can be checked at present only for the New England States (see Kurath *et al.*, 1939-43), since, after a delay of several decades, the *Linguistic Atlas of the Middle and South Atlantic States* is only now in the process of being published. The first two fascicles appeared in 1980 (see McDavid *et al.*, 1980).

The enormous masses of data in linguistic atlases which for various reasons have hitherto been excluded from evaluation, moved the Romance philologist Jean Séguy to develop a quantifying method that allows *all* linguistic atlas data to be taken into account. This dialectological statistics or statistical dialectology was termed *dialectométrie* (dialectometry) by Séguy (1973a), by analogy with other *-métries* such as *économétrie* and *sociométrie*. Surprisingly, the one most intimately connected with linguistics, namely Zwirner's *Phonometrie*, is not mentioned in this connection. Séguy notes that the field itself is not so new and mentions the dialectologist Adolphe Terracher as the first scholar to have used numerical methods in his study *Les Aires Morphologiques des Parlers de l'Angoumois* (Paris, 1914). Yet, earlier still, Hugo Schuchardt had planned to determine mathematically the relationships between neighbouring dialects. Unfortunately, he never executed his plan (see Schuchardt-Brevier: 435). Although Séguy was not in favour of mapping his dialectometric results — he preferred to publish long lists of matrices for different parameters — he did publish maps showing the linguistic distance between localities at the end of Vol. 6 of his *Atlas Linguistique de la Gascogne* (1973b), putting the scores of his five parameters (historical phonetics, phonology, morpho-syntax, verb, lexis) together. Guiter's method of measuring the linguistic distance between atlas sampling points in the Roussillon and other areas, and consequently his maps, are very similar to Séguy's (Guiter 1973). What the maps of both scholars at any rate have in common is that they are complex and confusing; patterns hardly ever emerge.

Dialectometry has been used and further developed by Hans Goebl in several contributions (Goebl 1975, 1976, 1977a, 1977b, 1978, 1984) also with reference to Romance dialect material. As far as can be ascertained, this approach has not yet been taken up in either German or English dialectal studies, with but one exception: our attempt at a dialectometrical analysis of Lowman's lexical and morphological data (collected in England) where we confirmed the results arrived at earlier by traditional methods (Viereck 1980b).

The procedure involving isoglosses/heteroglosses, as outlined, is a sample of a sample, while the dialectometric approach is statistically more objective and exact since it is capable, ideally, of taking into account *all* the available language data by use of a computer. Dialectometry as developed by Goebl sets off the linear approach of traditional dialectology with an areal one. Its methodological procedure is based on the question of identity or non-identity of two linguistic forms. Dialectometry, or dynamic dialectology (Goebl 1976), shows — and this is more suited to linguistic reality — fluid transitions and none of the abrupt boundaries suggested by the term *isogloss*, which is defined as follows by Freudenberg, among many others: 'In a broader sense we understand by the term an imaginary line that separates geographically linguistic phenomena of every kind; more exactly: that encloses *one* linguistic phenomenon and isolates it from its surroundings' (1966: 220).[3] Freudenberg has no great opinion of neologisms such as Kurath's term *heterogloss*, 'since they lack the etymological backing that even modern Greek neologisms need . . .' (1966: 221, fn.7). Nonetheless the conceptual content is more accurately reflected in this neologism. Moreover, traditional Anglo-American dialectology had already demonstrated clearly how difficult, if not impossible, it often is to proceed strictly according to Freudenberg's definition when interpreting dialect data. This is shown for

instance in Figure 6.1 from Atwood's interpretive volume *A Survey of Verb Forms in the Eastern United States* (1953: 40) in which altogether thirty-one verb forms are listed that show a notably regional distribution in the Eastern States of the USA. The criteria applied by Atwood are quite vague ('fairly common to common') and the transitions are gradual rather than abrupt ('Chiefly Northern', 'Chiefly Midland', etc.).

We are in the process of specially coding the whole *SED* material (published between 1962 and 1971) for computer processing. The coding of the lexical items was finished some time ago. Half of these have already been punched on cards and put on magnetic tape. Lexis will be followed by morphology and syntax. Both these aspects will be finished by the end of 1985. In our present project we work with normal spelling, which is quite sufficient for our purposes. It is still undecided what to do with the phonetics. There exists a computer programme, about ten years old (see Keil 1974), but this does not seem to be detailed enough: according to Raven McDavid, Jr., not all the diacritics seem to have been taken care of.[4] The lexical, morphological and syntactic items of the *SED* that we are now concerned with, when computerised, can be used in a variety of ways: a dictionary or a linguistic atlas of a traditional kind, but showing the areal structure of dialectal British English, can be produced, or the results can be quantified and then put on maps.[5] It is for all these projects that programmes are now being written at Bamberg University; they are being tested on the above-mentioned limited amount of data.

In the present study we had to analyse lexical and morphological data of the *SED* without electronic data-processing assistance.[6] This is quite a laborious undertaking and resulted in a restriction of the data sample. The area treated includes the South of England and parts of the Midlands. The northern boundary is constituted by the counties of Herefordshire and Worcestershire, Birmingham, Warwickshire, Leicestershire, Lincolnshire and the southern parts of Humberside to make the area identical with the one investigated by Lowman and to allow comparisons with his results. In this area the *SED* counted 185 sampling points; thus clearly more than half of the localities investigated in the whole of England are included. A total of 80 maps were evaluated for lexis, and 60 for

Figure 6.1: Eastern Verb Forms with a Distinctively Regional Distribution (USA)

/ = fairly common to common . = scattered	North						Midland				South			
	n.e. N. Eng.	s.e. N. Eng.	w. N. Eng.	N.Y.	n. Pa.	H.V.	Pa.	W. Va.	w. Va.	w. N.C.	C.B.	e. Va.	e. N.C.	s.C.
CHIEFLY NORTHERN														
wun't /wʌnt/	/	/	/	/	/									
be for am, etc.	/	/	/	/	/									
hadn't ought	/	/	/	/	/	/								
see (pret.)	/	/	/	/	.						.	/	.	.
dove	/	/	/	/	/	/	.				.			/
et	/	/	/	/	/	/	.	/			/	.	.	/
CHIEFLY MIDLAND														
boilt						.	/	/	/	/		.		.
clum						.	/	/	/	/	/	.	.	/
seen (pret.)	.	.	.	.	.		/	/	/	.	/	.	.	/
dogbit								/	/	/		.	.	/
CHIEFLY SOUTHERN														
he do										.	/	/	/	/
what make†											.	/	/	.
belongs to be†											/	/	.	/
freezed											/	/	/	.
Is I?										.	.	/	/	.
heern								.			/	/	/	.
gwine	/								/		/	/	/	.
div	.							.	/		/	/	/	/
holp†								.	.	/	/	/	/	/
seed								.	/	.	/	/	/	/
mought†									/	/	/	/	/	/
riz	/							.	.	/	/	/	/	/
taken (pret.)								/	.	/	/	.	/	/
tuck								/	/	/	.	/	/	/
might could†						/			.	/	/	/	/	/
NORTHERN AND SOUTHERN														
wan't	/	/	/	.	/						/	/	/	/
clim	/	/	/	/	.		.	.	.	/	.	/	/	.
waked	/	/	.						/	/	/	/	/	.
MIDLAND AND SOUTHERN														
heered							/	/	/	/	/	/	.	/
eat (pret.)						.	/	/	/	/	/	/	/	/
sweated	.	.	.			.	/	/	/	/	/	/	/	/

* The diagonal in the tabulation means that the form is fairly common to common, i.e., relatively more common, in the areas indicated; of course the frequency of some of the forms (e.g. *holp* and *hadn't ought*) is much greater than that of others (e.g. *be* and *div*). The dot means that the occurrence of the form is scattered; this symbol is also used to designate the currency of a form in only part of the territory indicated, as with *holp*, which in W. Va. is current only in the southern part. 'H. V.' stands for the Hudson Valley, approximately as far north as Albany, and 'C. B.' stands for the Chesapeake Bay area, including Delmarva.

† Not recorded in N. Eng.

morphology, all selected at random. Two dialectometrical tests — the coherency test and the identity test — were applied to the data mentioned.

Linguistic atlases are representable as two-dimensional matrices: the variables are points and maps. In the ideal case, the computer instruction for the coherency test is 'Given a point P_1 on the atlas, calculate from a certain number of maps the average size of the surface area to which other points typical of P_1 belong' (Goebl 1975: 34). For this process the commonalities of one point with the other 184 had to be checked for each of the eighty lexical maps examined, which contained numerous variants. The following example serves for clarification.

In Napton-on-the-Hill in the county of Warwickshire *hatch* is recorded instead of *brood*. The same expression is used at 23 other localities. This frequency or coherency score is added to those for lexical overlap in informants' answers presented for the 79 other items on the other maps, thus yielding the absolute coherency value for Napton-on-the-Hill, that is, the total number of identical forms found with regard to all localities and maps. This procedure was adopted for all the sampling points. Then the absolute coherency value was divided by the number of maps to yield the absolute coherency mean for a locality. The proportion of that score compared with the number of localities investigated in the whole area, expressed as a percentage, is called the Relative Coherency Mean (RCM). These RCM scores, in turn, are presented on maps and provide a clear picture of the patterning of a dialectal area: regions with high RCM values are focal areas, those with low RCM scores relic areas. The number of intervals or scales to be mapped should be neither too small nor too high, to avoid underdifferentiation or overdifferentiation of the data. But statistics (that is, numerical taxonomy) can help here and provides a useful formula (see, for example, Nikitopoulos 1976: 22). As regards the range of these scales, we started from the arithmetic mean and ordinal-scaled the distribution above and below the mean. As one moves from the middle of the distribution, the size of the intervals on the scale increases in order to maintain as far as practical the principle that each interval contains the same number of scores as any other. These scales are presented on maps by employing — in the present case — shading techniques which

Map 6.1: *SED* **the Midlands and the South: RCM Lexis**

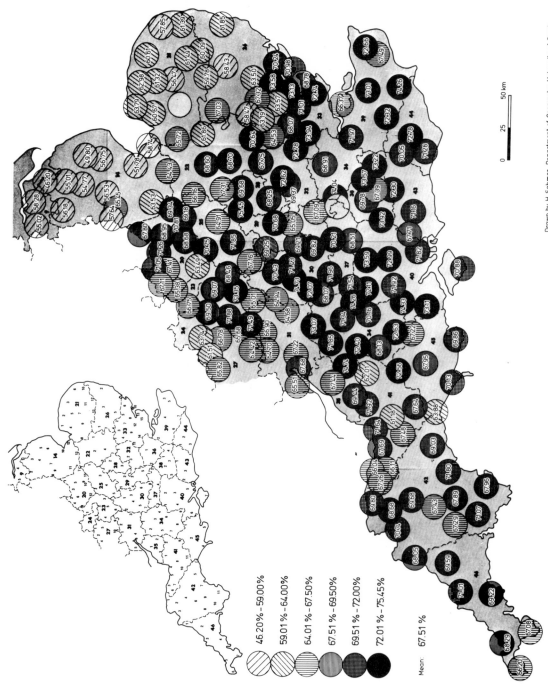

46.20%–59.00%
59.01%–64.00%
64.01%–67.50%
67.51%–69.50%
69.51%–72.00%
72.01%–75.45%

Mean: 67.51%

Drawn by H. Sohmer, Department of Geography, University of Bamberg

0   25   50 km

Map 6.2: *SED* the Midlands and the South: RCM Morphology

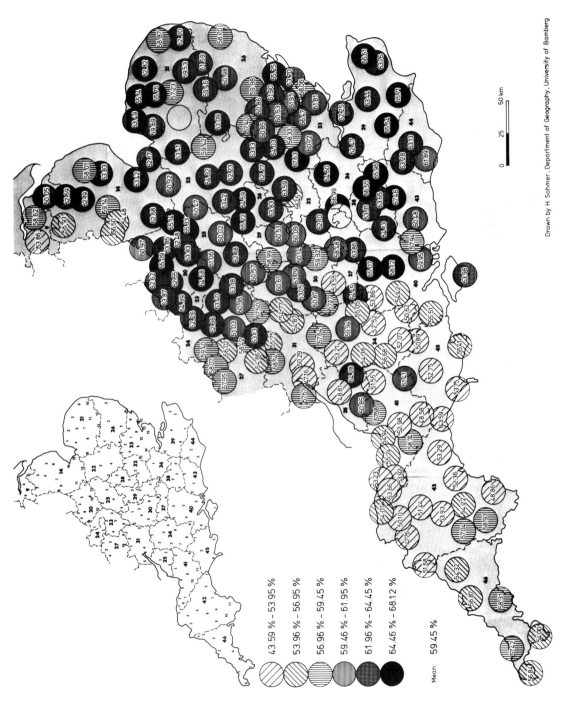

43.59 % – 53.95 %

53.96 % – 56.95 %

56.96 % – 59.45 %

59.46 % – 61.95 %

61.96 % – 64.45 %

64.46 % – 68.12 %

Mean: 59.45 %

Drawn by H. Sohmer, Department of Geography, University of Bamberg

visually highlight the percentage score for the so-called Relative Coherency Mean. The exact significance of these is keyed on the individual maps.

The presentation adopted here tries to combine two aspects: precision and visual clarity. It should be borne in mind that the calculated figures (that is, the precise results) refer only to the respective localities. These figures alone would not show any possible patterning. Consequently larger areas had to be devised which are, of course, only approximations. It is assumed that within the whole locality area the RCM lies within a range of values of which the exact value has been established only for the respective sampling point. The size of the area, here a circle with the locality dot as its centre, is arbitrary. The merits of such circles are considerable, and they are to be preferred to the presentation of fields of varying sizes covering the whole map, as used in Viereck (1980b). The circles contribute in a new way to the evaluation of the *SED* as a whole in that the locality areas not only quantify an area covered, unlike locality dots, but also, more significantly, show up quite considerable areas not covered by the survey. Areas of varying sizes covering the whole map do not suggest this at all. Thus, significant areas of non-coverage emerge such as the gap through the middle of Cornwall, Devon and Dorset or the absence of coverage anywhere near the coast in the South-east or in Suffolk, compared to the apparent density of coverage in the northern areas like Leicestershire and Warwickshire. In this way alone our maps, therefore, offer valuable new criticisms of the original survey.[7] So much for the presentation.

When we look at the two maps that show the RCM for lexis and morphology (Maps 6.1 and 6.2) we see that they exhibit clear parallels, but also differences. On both maps the area with the highest RCM score (the highest level of identity) is in the Home Counties around London,[8] extending to the South-east and showing high RCM score pockets in the North-west of our area (in Northamptonshire, Leicestershire, and Warwickshire). Similarly high RCM score pockets, for lexis only, are found beyond Hampshire as far as East Somerset. The more extreme South-west and the North-east show further differences on the two maps; while the North-east has a low RCM score for the lexis, this score is fairly high for morphology in much

of that area. It is just the other way round in the South-west, which shows fairly high scores in the vocabulary and fairly low ones in morphology. The North-east agrees with the South-west inasmuch as RCM scores clearly decrease in these directions, from the more central and the south-eastern areas, but to differing degrees.

One or two restrictions must be indicated. The quantifying method depends on standard sampling at all locality points. If this does not occur then the dialectometric method cannot be applied optimally. In both the lexis and the morphology two sampling points (localities 21.9 and 37.2) are left blank on the maps because they yielded an insufficient amount of data: the latter showed 69 zero entries for lexis and 56 for morphology, whereas for the former the numbers were 26 for lexis and 54 for morphology. Thus these two localities had to be left out of account, or they would have vitiated the results. The actual number of localities taken into consideration on both linguistic levels for the calculation of the arithmetic mean is therefore 183. Goebl (1977a) discusses the not infrequent zero entries in linguistic atlases. He solves the problem by calculating the identity values for every locality, not on the basis of the total number of maps used but on the basis of the number of maps without zero entries for the locality in question. The same procedure has been followed here.

Double or multiple answers to the questions asked, which in traditional interpretations of dialectal data are of importance since they may indicate transition areas, also cause problems in quantifying data. Goebl does not seem to mention this problem in his writings.[9] Whereas we were faced with that problem in our dialectometrical analysis of the Lowman data, due to the reduction of *SED* data we were able to ignore in the present study items which produced double or multiple responses. In our large-scale computer project such a procedure is, of course, no longer possible. Then a decision must be reached. In order to avoid the effect of distortion only one form could be chosen per locality and the other(s) discarded, if there are certain preferences for a particular form. Perhaps from two forms one is marked as archaic or one form is the only one occurring in the neighbouring area or one form is marked as preferred.

In the second test, the identity test, the *modus operandi* was: 'Given a chosen point P_1 in the atlas, correlate it with each other point in turn, establishing each time how many of the maps in the source data agree in lexical, morphological or syntactic type with the point of departure P₁' (Goebl 1975: 36). The number of maps showing identical forms between point of departure and specific point of comparison represents the General Identity Value (GIV) of the former. Though the calculation of the RCM only makes possible quantitative evaluations, the investigation of the GIV allows us to complement this with a qualitative statement. This is an important point since a frequently encountered misconception is that a quantifying procedure excludes the possibility of reaching conclusions of a qualitative nature. After choosing a departure point, which is 100 per cent identical with itself, one calculates — and illustrates on maps — the linguistic relationship between this locality and the rest of the area investigated in which the GIV is, of course, below 100 per cent, proportionately more so the further a point is linguistically from the initial point of investigation. The GIV was related to the number of maps and thus converted into a Relative Identity Value (RIV). On the maps the scales based on the arithmetic mean are presented by various graphic devices, as with the RCM. Although it is more useful for comparison purposes to establish interval ranges which are the same for all GIV/RIV maps, this could only be done for the lexical maps. Because

of great distributional differences on the morphological maps the interval ranges vary, having been derived separately for each map. Yet the absolute values of the GIV morphological maps are directly comparable since the number of maps is almost always the same (an insignificant exception is locality 23.3 with 59 instead of 60 maps). The comparability between lexical and morphological maps is ensured because of the RIV values added in brackets.

For the identity test, altogether four localities were chosen in the present study, reasonably far away from each other: one each in Cornwall, Warwickshire, Hampshire and Norfolk. The figures given in Figure 6.2 for lexis and Figure 6.3 for morphology supply detailed information. Zero entries on several maps account for the smaller number of maps used at two localities. The calculations both of the range of values and of the arithmetic mean were worked out without taking into consideration the value of the locality chosen as point of departure. Most of the Maps 6.3-6.10 display substantial agreement for both linguistic levels (lexis and morphology).

Maps 6.3 and 6.4 show the General Identity and the Relative Identity Values for lexis and morphology relating to locality 46.3 (Egloshayle, Cornwall). Devon, West Somerset and parts of Cornwall form an independent area. The bordering areas to the East do reveal high agreement

Figure 6.2:   Identity Values: Lexis

Source locality	Number of localities computed	Number of maps	Range of values		Means	
			GIV	RIV	GIV	RIV
46.3	183	80	34-73	42.50-91.25	57.30	71.63
40.1	183	80	35-71	43.75-88.75	58.17	72.71
23.3	183	78	36-68	46.15-87.18	55.18	70.74
21.7	183	75	30-60	40.00-80.00	45.41	60.55

Figure 6.3:   Identity Values: Morphology

Source locality	Number of localities computed	Number of maps	Range of values		Means	
			GIV	RIV	GIV	RIV
46.3	183	60	25-55	41.67-91.67	34.34	57.23
40.1	183	60	21-51	35.00-85.00	32.53	54.22
23.3	183	59	23-47	38.98-79.66	38.42	65.12
21.7	183	60	20-49	33.33-81.67	34.80	58.00

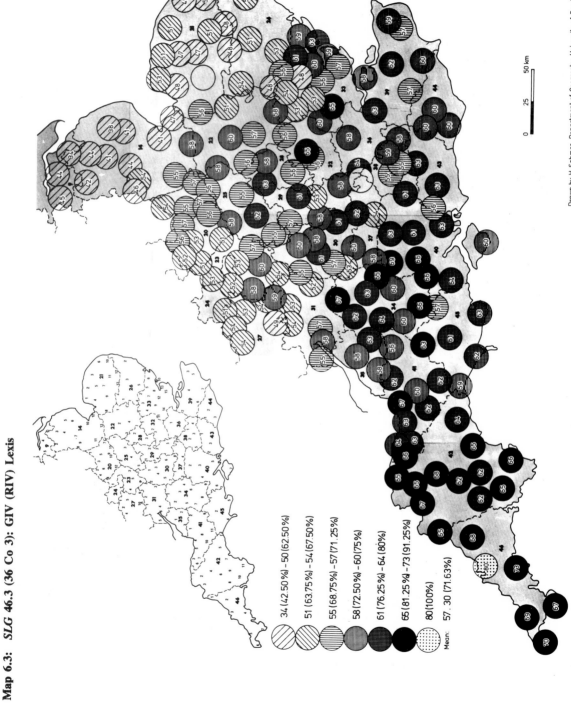

Map 6.3: *SLG 46.3 (36 Co 3): GIV (RIV) Lexis*

34 (42.50%) – 50 (62.50%)

51 (63.75%) – 54 (67.50%)

55 (68.75%) – 57 (71.25%)

58 (72.50%) – 60 (75%)

61 (76.25%) – 64 (80%)

65 (81.25%) – 73 (91.25%)

80 (100%)

Mean: 57. 30 (71.63%)

Drawn by H. Sohmer, Department of Geography, University of Bamberg

Map 6.4: *SLG* **46.3 (36 Co 3): GIV (RIV) Morphology**

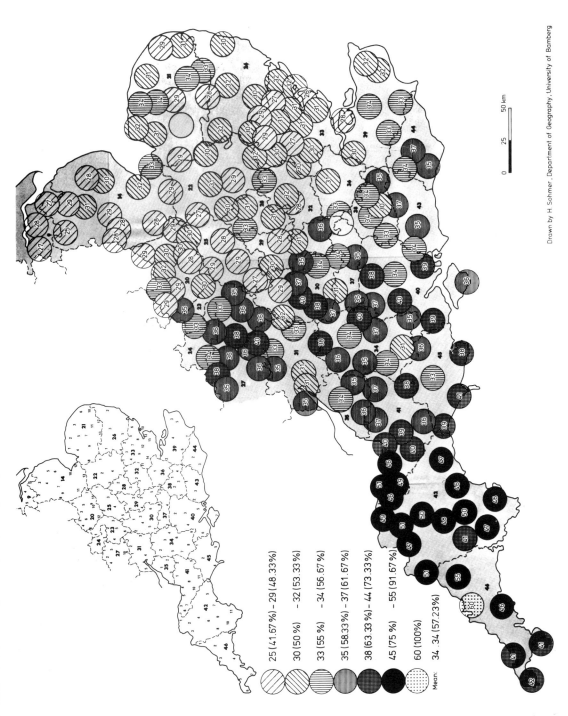

25 (41.67 %) – 29 (48.33%)

30 (50 %) – 32 (53.33 %)

33 (55 %) – 34 (56.67 %)

35 (58.33%) – 37 (61.67 %)

38 (63.33 %) – 44 (73.33 %)

45 (75 %) – 55 (91.67 %)

60 (100%)

Mean: 34 . 34 (57.23%)

Drawn by H Sohmer, Department of Geography, University of Bamberg

50 km

0   25

Map 6.5: *SLG 40.1 (39 Ha 1): GIV (RIV) Lexis*

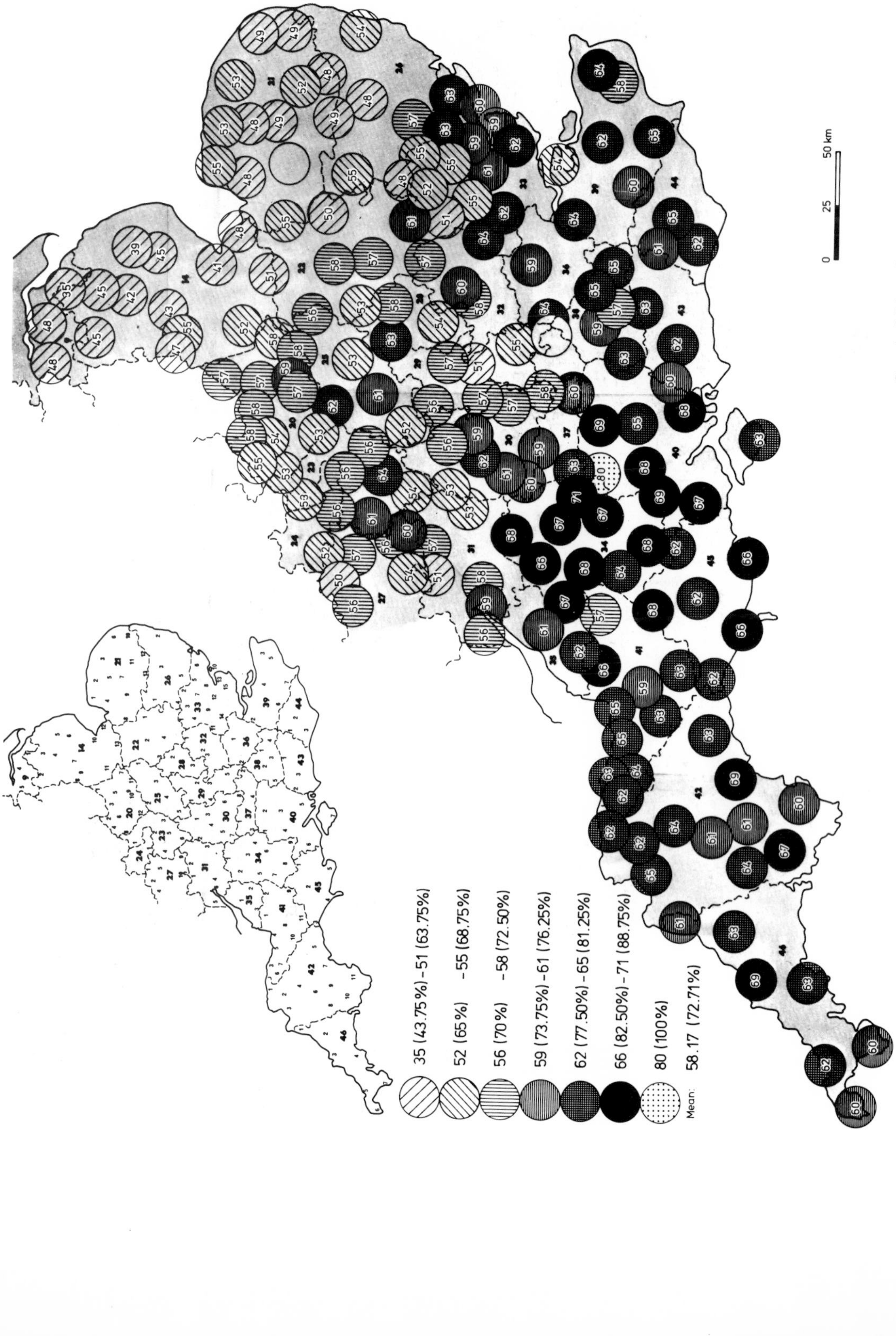

35 (43.75%)–51 (63.75%)

52 (65%)   –55 (68.75%)

56 (70%)   –58 (72.50%)

59 (73.75%)–61 (76.25%)

62 (77.50%)–65 (81.25%)

66 (82.50%)–71 (88.75%)

80 (100%)

Mean: 58.17 (72.71%)

Map 6.6: *SLG* 40.1 (39 Ha 1): GIV (RIV) Morphology

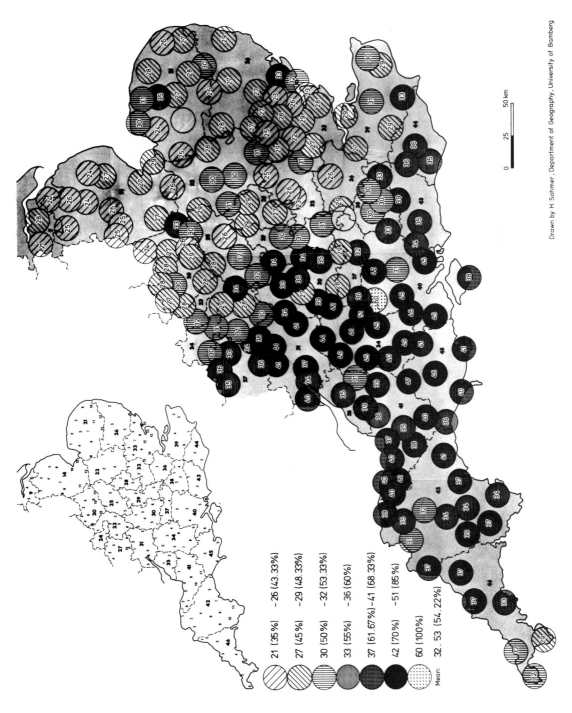

21 – 26 (43.33%)

27 – 29 (48.33%)

30 – 32 (53.33%)

33 – 36 (60%)

37 (61.67%)–41 (68.33%)

42 (70%)

60 (100%)

Mean: 32.53 (54.22%)

Drawn by H. Sohmer, Department of Geography, University of Bamberg

Map 6.7: *SLG 23.3 (17 Wa 4): GIV (RIV) Lexis*

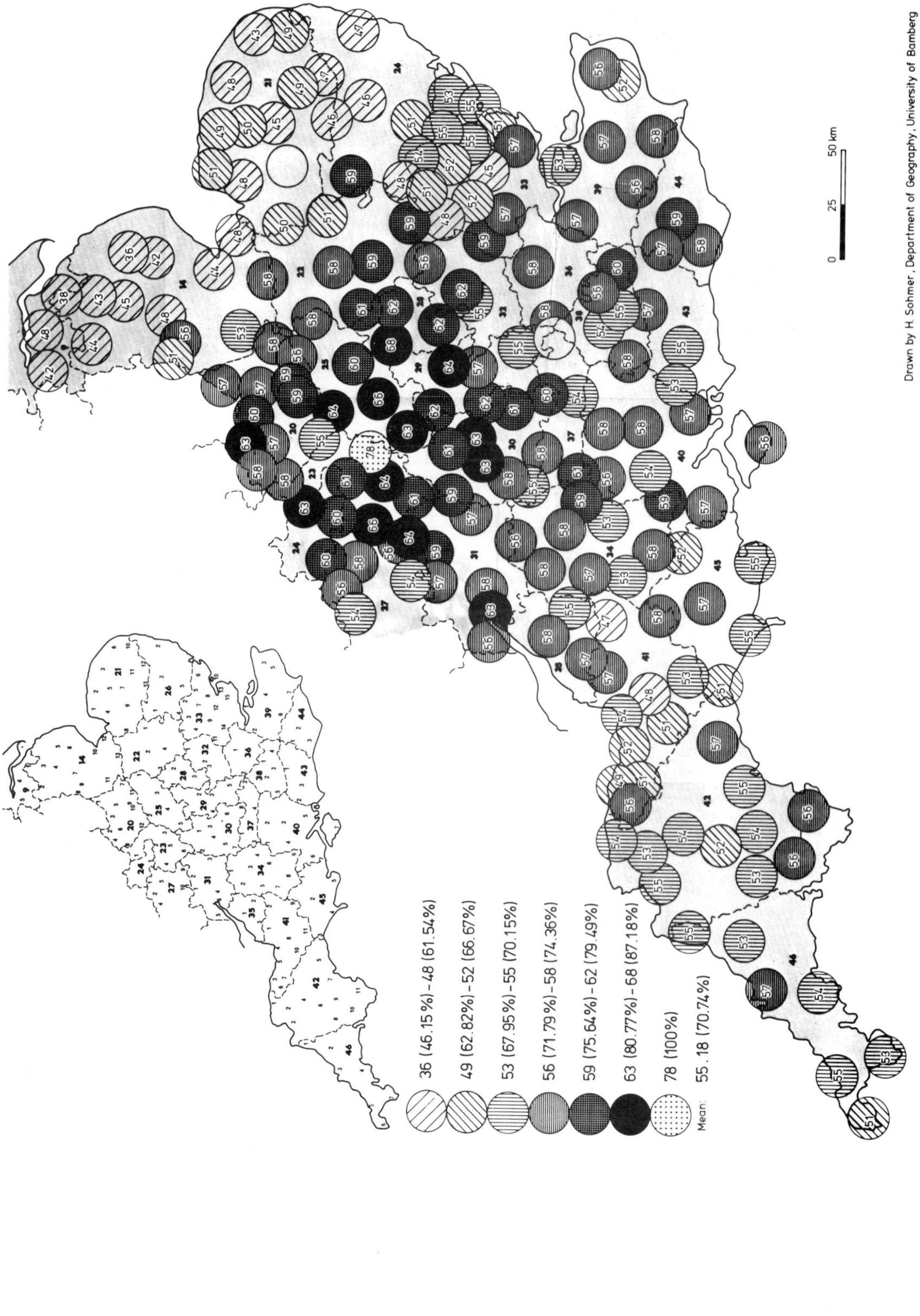

36 (46.15 %) – 48 (61.54%)

49 (62.82%) – 52 (66.67%)

53 (67.95%) – 55 (70.15%)

56 (71.79 %) – 58 (74.36%)

59 (75.64 %) – 62 (79.49%)

63 (80.77%) – 68 (87.18%)

78 (100%)

Mean: 55 .18 (70.74%)

Drawn by H. Sohmer, Department of Geography, University of Bamberg

0   25   50 km

Map 6.8: *SLG 23.3 (17 Wa 4): GIV (RIV) Morphology*

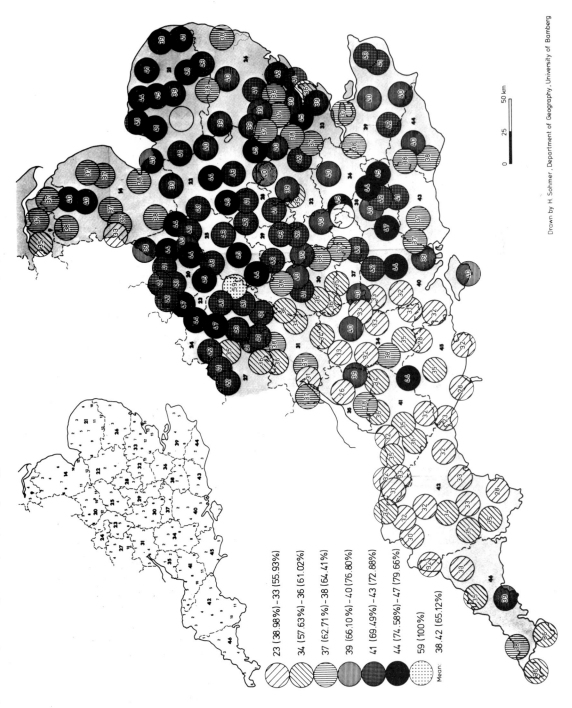

Drawn by H. Sohmer, Department of Geography, University of Bamberg

23 (38.98%) – 33 (55.93%)

34 (57.63%) – 36 (61.02%)

37 (62.71%) – 38 (64.41%)

39 (66.10%) – 40 (76.80%)

41 (69.49%) – 43 (72.88%)

44 (74.58%) – 47 (79.66%)

59 (100%)

Mean: 38.42 (65.12%)

Map 6.9: *SLG 21.7 (21 Nf 9): GIV (RIV) Lexis*

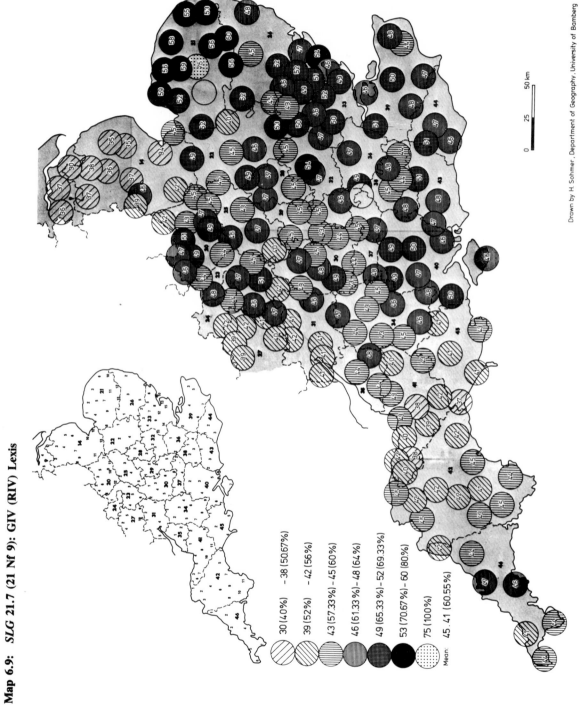

30 (40%) – 38 (50.67%)
39 (52%) – 42 (56%)
43 (57.33%) – 45 (60%)
46 (61.33%) – 48 (64%)
49 (65.33%) – 52 (69.33%)
53 (70.67%) – 60 (80%)
75 (100%)

Mean: 45 .41 (60.55%)

Drawn by H. Sohmer, Department of Geography, University of Bamberg

Map 6.10: *SLG 21.7 (21 Nf 9): GIV (RIV) Morphology*

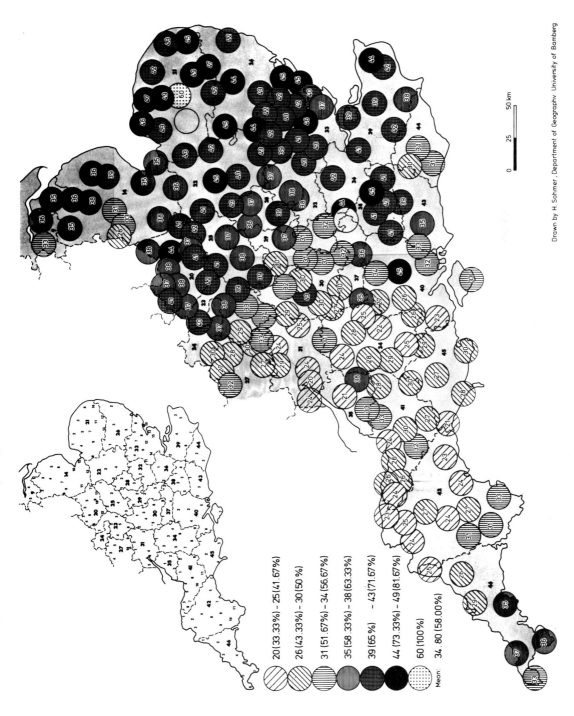

20 (33.33%) - 25 (41.67%)

26 (43.33%) - 30 (50 %)

31 (51.67%) - 34 (56.67%)

35 (58.33%) - 38 (63.33%)

39 (65%)   - 43 (71.67%)

44 (73.33%) - 49 (81.67%)

60 (100%)

Mean: 34 . 80 (58.00%)

Drawn by H Sohmer., Department of Geography University of Bamberg

50 km

25

0

with the region just mentioned, but are clearly separate from them. For lexis some high GIV scores are to be found in Wiltshire and Hampshire — the two in the East are borderline cases. Low identity values are found for both linguistic levels in East Anglia and Lincolnshire, and additionally, for morphology, in the more westerly-situated East Midlands. This whole region is separated by minimum values. Originally another locality had been selected in the South-west, namely 42.4 (Chawleigh, Devon). Owing to limitations of space the results cannot be mapped here but the draft maps clearly confirm that West Somerset, Devon and East Cornwall are an independent area. West Cornwall is set off on both linguistic levels here, whereas in Maps 6.3 and 6.4 this was the case only for morphology. Maps 6.5 and 6.6 show the GIV (RIV) scores for lexis and morphology relating to locality 40.1 (Hatherden, Hampshire). On both linguistic levels Hampshire, Wiltshire, parts of Dorset and East Somerset exhibit the highest values and thus form an independent area. As Map 6.6 reveals, locality point 41.7 (Brompton Regis, West Somerset) belonging also to the highest category is a borderline case. This is not so with the three equally highly rated localities further west of the independent region just mentioned with regard to lexis (Map 6.5). The extreme South-west is in rather high agreement with, yet markedly separated from, West Somerset, parts of Dorset, Wiltshire and Hampshire — again on both linguistic levels. For morphology the South-east shows a lower level of agreement with the extreme South-west, while for lexis the South-east and the extreme South-west reveal identical levels of agreement. For both lexis and morphology, the rest of the region investigated is separated by GIV (RIV) values that almost always belong to the three lowest categories.

For the West Midlands locality 23.3 (Napton-on-the-Hill, Warwickshire) was chosen as the point of departure. The results are displayed on Maps 6.7 and 6.8. On both linguistic levels the highest GIV (RIV) scores are shown in a rather small area surrounding the locality in question. For morphology we find a few pockets of similarly high values in some of the Home Counties. From the small independent area in parts of the West Midlands GIV (RIV) scores decrease in all directions, but with differing degrees for morphology and lexis. For lexis both East Anglia and Lincolnshire are separated by

minimum values, whereas scores decrease more slowly towards the South-east and the South-west, hardly ever reaching the lowest scale point (twice in Somerset only). Morphology shows a different picture in that the whole South-west from Worcestershire in the North and West Hampshire in the South is characterised by very low values.

Finally, Maps 6.9 and 6.10 display the GIV (RIV) values relating to locality 21.7 (Shipdham, central Norfolk). They show East Anglia as a solid independent area for the vocabulary, with minimum scores for close-by Lincolnshire, the western parts of the West Midlands (Worcestershire and Gloucestershire) and parts of the extreme South-west. For morphology the high-score region is also in East Anglia. The few pockets of similarly high values in other areas of the East are almost always borderline cases. Low scores are to be found — as for the lexis, but to a larger extent — in all of the South-west, from Worcestershire in the North to West Hampshire in the South. In this respect Map 6.10 is identical with Map 6.8.

East Anglia, Lincolnshire, parts of the West Midlands and much of the South-west prove to be linguistically independent and conservative areas, even if not always to the same degree as regards the two linguistic levels of lexis and morphology. Generally speaking, the parallels between the two linguistic levels mentioned were greater in our dialectometric analysis of the Lowman data than they are in the analysis of the material of the *SED*. Whether this is due to linguistic changes that took place between the late 1930s when Lowman collected his data and the 1950s and early 1960s when the data for the *SED* were gathered can only be answered once the full-scale computerised analysis of the *SED* data is available.

Because of lack of clerical assistance we had to use fewer maps than the minimum number — 100 — established by Guiter (1973: 80). But Guiter continues: 'Yet we had to content ourselves sometimes with statistics based on less than 100 maps, in the case of the *A[tlas] L[ingüístico de la] P[enínsula] I[bérica I.]* (70 maps published) or the Atlas *Sacaze* (80 maps used out of 83)' (Guiter, 1973:80). These numbers are identical in the case of lexis and rather close in the case of morphology to the number of maps we utilised for this paper and these in turn are almost identical with the number of maps on which our analysis of the Lowman data is based (cf. Viereck 1980b: 342).

We are in full agreement with Goebl when he expresses his concern that

> it should always be borne in mind that, in choosing which methods to use and which fields of discovery to explore, it is better to link up as harmoniously and gently as possible to the results of seventy years of taxonomic dialectology with its attendant problems, than to dig a ditch of division by the full application of modern technology. (1975: 38)

This is relevant also for the reason that 'the dialectometric methods at present available . . . explore completely new territory, throwing up many methodological and linguistic problems that are still unsolved, and these methods are thus to be viewed as a prolegomena' (Goebl 1978: 299).

Unquestionably, dialectometry presents an interesting approach. In the present state of knowledge, however, it also has weaknesses: the areal presentation — in this case the size of the circles, the number of the scales and their distributional ranges, arrived at differently at times (see our comments above), are approximations only. Furthermore, a close scrutiny of the maps will reveal that in several cases neighbouring localities are minimally differentiated. However, since the values come close to interval borders, different shadings suggest greater differences than actually exist. Yet these visual presentations of the data on maps are only of secondary importance; of primary importance is the calculation of the various scores. And here certain preconditions have to be met in the dialect data (cf. our remarks on zero/multiple responses) for dialectometry to be used effectively. A further point is that the expenditure in time and effort in the dialectometric procedure is much larger than in traditional dialectology. Also, this new procedure is not structurally oriented since every item/response receives equal weight. However, on the levels treated here a structural weighting of items would have been impossible or arbitrary. Nevertheless, this new approach merits more attention than it has received up to now. Only when more, and more extensive, analyses have become available will it be possible to appreciate its value fully.

Notes

1. Part of this paper was read at the School of English of the University of Leeds on 24 March 1983.

2. The first pages largely follow Viereck (1980b), but appear here for the first time in English.

3. Throughout this paper, German and French quotations have been translated into English.

4. Personal communication.

5. In American and English dialectology the computer has up to now been used in a variety of ways. These are discussed by Schneider and Viereck (1984).

6. This is why we had to rely on several others without whose help this contribution could not have been written. It is a great pleasure to acknowledge the assistance given at various stages and in various ways by L. Dietel, M. Evans, A. Steinmetz, S. Wiesmann, G. Will and, above all, E. Schneider and H. Sohmer. Schneider worked out the various values as well as the intervals and drew the draft maps accordingly, while H. Sohmer drew the final maps in an expert fashion. I thank my colleague Professor H. Becker for kindly having made the cartographer's help possible.

7. This point was also made by John Kirk in a personal communication. We drew attention to the uneven distribution of the SED localities in Viereck (1973a: 77), and mentioned a few striking examples.

8. In the case of the Home Counties this fact has sociolinguistic implications. Here, high RCM scores point to a close proximity to the Standard language, whereas in investigations excluding the linguistic centre, areas with high RCM scores simply show a considerable linguistic homogeneity in the areas in question. No sociolinguistic conclusions should therefore be drawn.

9. We have not seen his most extensive publication on this topic — three volumes totalling over 1,000 pages (!) — to be published in 1984.

References

Atwood, E.B. *A Survey of Verb Forms in the Eastern United States* (University of Michigan Press, Ann Arbor, 1953, 2nd impression 1967)

Freudenberg, R. '*Isoglosse*: Prägung und Problematik eines sprachwissenschaftlichen Términus', *Zeitschrift für Mundartforschung*, vol. 33 (1966), pp. 219-32

Goebl, H. 'Dialektometrie', *Grazer Linguistische Studien*, vol. 1 (1975), pp. 32-50

—— 'Taxonomische vs. dynamische Dialektologie', *Zeitschrift für Romanische Philologie*, vol. 92 (1976), pp. 484-519

—— 'Rätoromanisch versus Hochitalienisch versus Oberitalienisch: Dialektometrische Beobachtungen innerhalb eines Diasystems', *Ladinia* vol. 1 (1977), pp. 39-71 (Goebl, 1977a)

—— 'Zu Methoden und Problemen einiger dialektometrischer Messverfahren', *Germanistische Linguistik*, nos. 3-4 (1977), pp. 335-65 (Goebl, 1977b)

—— 'Dialektometrie', in H. Berschin, J. Felixberger and H. Goebl. *Französische Sprachgeschichte* (Hueber, München, 1978), pp. 299-303

—— *Dialektometrische Studien*, 3 vols. (Niemeyer, Tübingen, 1984), (Beihefte zur *Zeitschrift für Romanische Philologie*, vols. 191-3)

Guiter, H. 'Atlas et Frontières Linguistiques', in *Les Dialectes Romans de France à la Lumière des Atlas Régionaux: Actes du Colloque National, Strasbourg, 24-28 Mai 1971* (Paris, 1973), pp. 61-107

Keil, G.C. 'Narrow Phonetic Transcription on the Computer: Taking the Phone off the Hook', *Computers and the Humanities*, vol. 8 (1974), pp. 217-29

Kolb, E., B. Glauser, W. Elmer, R. Stamm. *Atlas of English Sounds* (Francke, Bern, 1979)

Kurath, H. *A Word Geography of the Eastern United States* (University of Michigan Press, Ann Arbor, 1949, 2nd impression, 1966)

—— *Studies in Area Linguistics* (Indiana University Press, Bloomington, 1972)

Kurath, H., M.L. Hanley, B. Bloch, G.S. Lowman Jr. and M.L. Hansen. *Linguistic Atlas of New England*, 3 vols. in 6 parts (Brown University Press, Providence, 1939-43; reprinted AMS Press, New York, 1972)

Kurath, H. and G.S. Lowman Jr. *The Dialectal Structure of Southern England: Phonological Evidence* (University of Alabama Press, 1970) (Publication of the American Dialect Society, vol. 54)

McDavid, R.I. Jr. *Dialects in Culture: Essays in General Dialectology*, edited by W.A. Kretzschmar, Jr. (University of Alabama Press, 1979)

—— *Varieties of American English*, selected and introduced by A.S. Dil (Stanford University Press, Stanford, Ca., 1980)

McDavid, R.I. Jr., R.K. O'Cain, G.T. Dorrill, and G.S. Lowman Jr. *Linguistic Atlas of the Middle and South Atlantic States*, vol. 1, fascicles 1-2 (University of Chicago Press, Chicago and London, 1980)

Nikitopoulos, P. *Statistik für Linguisten* (Narr, Tübingen, 1976)

Orton, H. *et al. Survey of English Dialects (B): The Basic Material*, 4 vols., each in 3 parts (E.J. Arnold, Leeds, 1962-71)

Orton, H. and N. Wright. *A Word Geography of England* (Seminar Press, New York and London, 1975)

Orton, H., S. Sanderson and J. Widdowson (eds.) *The Linguistic Atlas of England* (Croom Helm, London, 1978)

Schlieben-Lange, B. and H. Weydt. 'Für eine Pragmatisierung der Dialektologie', *Zeitschrift für Germanistische Linguistik*, vol. 6 (1978), pp. 257-82

Schneider, E.W. and W. Viereck. 'The Use of the Computer in American, Canadian and British English Dialectology and Sociolinguistics', in H. Goebl (ed.) *Dialectology* (N. Brockmeyer, Bochum, 1984), pp. 15-60, (Quantitative Linguistics, vol. 21)

Hugo Schuchardt-Brevier: ein Vademecum der allgemeinen Sprachwissenschaft, compiled and introduced by Leo Spitzer (repr. Wissenschaftliche Buchgesellschaft, Darmstadt, 1976)

Séguy, J. 'La Dialectométrie' dans *L'Atlas Linguistique de la Gascogne*, *Revue de Linguistique Romane*, vol. 37 (1973), pp. 1-24 (Séguy, 1973a)

—— *Atlas Linguistique de la Gascogne*, vol. 6 (Paris, 1973) (accompanied by *Les matrices dialectométriques*, portefeuille joint au vol. 6) (Séguy, 1973b)

—— *Atlas Linguistique de la Gascogne*, vol. 6 (Paris, 1973) (*notice explicative*) (Séguy, 1973c)

Terracher, A. *Les Aires Morphologiques des Parlers de l'Angoumois* (Paris, 1914)

Viereck, W. 'A Critical Appraisal of the *Survey of English Dialects*', *Orbis*, vol. 22 (1973), pp. 72-84 (Viereck, 1973a)

—— 'The Growth of Dialectology', *Journal of English Linguistics*, vol. 7 (1973), pp. 69-86 (Viereck, 1973b)

—— 'The Dialectal Structure of British English: Lowman's Evidence', *English World-Wide*, vol. 1 (1980), pp. 25-44 (Viereck, 1980a)

—— 'Dialektometrie und englische Dialektologie', *Grazer Linguistische Studien*, nos. 11-12 (1980), pp. 335-56 (Viereck, 1980b)

Wakelin, M.F. *English Dialects: An Introduction* (Athlone Press, London, 1972)

7
Linguistic Atlases and Generative Phonology

BEAT GLAUSER

Dialect geographers map comparable reflexes from different dialects in order to show their regional spread. The result of their endeavours is a collection of such maps, a linguistic atlas, which enables them to interpret maps 'internally', that is in comparison with other relevant maps, as opposed to earlier 'extralinguistic argumentation' (Goossens 1969: 14) via geographical and historical factors (see, for example, Kolb 1965, who links up the distribution of certain words of Scandinavian origin with the area of extensive Scandinavian settlement). Even the most advanced interpretation by means of internal evidence, however, is strictly on the level of 'observational adequacy' (Chomsky 1965: 31-2); it is an arrangement of facts.

The generative phonologist, on the other hand, collects data from one dialect and traces the phonological processes that are relevant to the material under scrutiny. His work achieves at best 'explanatory adequacy' (Chomsky 1965: 33), if he succeeds in embedding his findings into a linguistic theory that predicts them.

My argument in this paper is that we should now stop discussing how to arrange reflexes but start dealing with the processes that underlie them. I shall give an example of this by interpreting the reflexes of *goose* (*LAE*: Ph 139; *AES*: 74) and then treat a group of five maps along the same lines, namely *swath* (*AES*: 206), *wasp* (*AES*: 198), *water* (*AES*: 200), *wash* (*AES*: 197), *quarry* (*AES*: 212), their common denominator being rounding adjustment of /a/ after /w/ (Chomsky and Halle 1968: 217) — but see Luick (1964: section 536), who describes the same phenomenon as non-fronting of *a* (whatever its exact quality) after /w/ and subsequent merger

with /o/. In the whole process I will draw heavily on rules that have been established by generativists for Standard English or American, mainly Chomsky and Halle (1968) — the feature catalogue made use of comes from there too, but has been adapted to allow for four vowel heights (cf. Wang 1968) and follows Sommerstein (1977) in treating diphthongs as one unit.

The following analysis of *goose* is based on a triangular vowel system with four heights. We have /ī/ and /ū/ at the highest level, /ē/ and /ō/ at the second, /ɛ̄/ and /ɔ̄/ at the third, and /ā/ at the lowest one. According to this descriptive approach, /ō/, the vowel reflex underlying *goose* (cf. *goose — gosling*), is a [+ back], [+ round], [+ high], [+ mid], [+ long] vowel, the information [+ round] being redundant: English [+ back] vowels are usually [+ round]; [− back] ones are [− round].

The most frequent reflex on the maps *goose* (*LAE*: Ph 139; *AES*: 74) is [gu:s], the form analogous to RP. This sound is related to underlying /ō/ by way of a very simple rule, which we formulate as

$$(1) \quad V \rightarrow [-\text{ mid}] \Big/ \begin{bmatrix} \rule{1cm}{0.4pt} \\ +\text{ high} \\ +\text{ back} \\ +\text{ long} \end{bmatrix}$$

— cf. Chomsky and Halle's vowel shift rule (1968: 187ff.), which contains, amongst other processes, rule (1).

For the present purpose the forms with onglides, [gᵒu:s] and [gᵊu:s], are included here and not differentiated any further. The same thing is true for centralised [gü:s] and the centralised forms with onglide. The risk of arriving at a wrong interpretation is very small, as the distribution of the forms in question is complementary: where one occurs the others are absent.

Immediately after rule (1) follows shortening of [u:]. The process has taken place in a small area near the Welsh border and in a few isolated villages in the South Midlands and the South. According to rule (2), the [+ long], [+ high], [− mid], [+ back] vowel is shortened.

$$(2) \ V \rightarrow [- \text{long}] \ / \ \begin{bmatrix} \underline{\quad\quad} \\ + \text{ high} \\ - \text{ mid} \\ + \text{ back} \end{bmatrix}$$

In the area with vowel shortening there are two instances of [gʌs]. The relation between [gɒs] and [gʌs] is the same as on maps like *butter, cousins, drunk, hungry* (*AES*: 227), which have undergone rule (3) south of a line leading from the forms in question to the Severn and from there to the Wash.

$$(3) \ V \rightarrow \begin{bmatrix} - \text{ high} \\ - \text{ round} \end{bmatrix} \ / \ \begin{bmatrix} \underline{\quad\quad} \\ - \text{ mid} \\ + \text{ back} \\ - \text{ long} \end{bmatrix}$$

The majority of the forms with [ɒ], however, occur in the area which has undergone the change from [ɒ] to [ʌ]. Why these apparent exceptions? There are words in RP, too, which have retained [ʊ], for instance *bush, push, pull, full, butcher,* and so on, but in most of these cases the preceding consonant is a bilabial: lip rounding has prevented the change; *goose* clearly does not belong here.

The only way of accounting for [gɒs] in the West Midlands is to postulate that the change from [ɒ] to [ʌ] (rule 3) preceded shortening (rule 2). This gives special status to the two forms with [ʌ] that appear on the surface completely regular. The two villages that feature it are at the outer limit of the area that has undergone rule (3). This process may have happened fairly recently if we take into account that the higher status of the forms with [ʌ] (by analogy with RP) would have made, and would still make it spread to the North and West.

There is another chain of rules that relates to the [+ back], [+ high], [+ long] vowel. In the south-west and in South Lancashire and Cheshire there occur forms with a rounded front vowel. Rule (4) describes the process that results in [gʏ:s]:

$$(4) \ V \rightarrow [- \text{back}] \ / \ \begin{bmatrix} \underline{\quad\quad} \\ + \text{ high} \\ - \text{ mid} \\ + \text{ round} \\ + \text{ long} \end{bmatrix}$$

We can see that individual dialects feature rounded front vowels, a vowel type that developed several times in the history of English sounds, but has had no bearing on RP.

A reduction of the feature specification $\begin{bmatrix} - \text{ back} \\ + \text{ round} \end{bmatrix}$ is the best way of accounting for the forms [gɪɒs] and [gɒɪs]. The two reflexes are the result of diphthongisations which re-establish the ordinary English state of affairs: long vowels agree in backness and roundness. Rule (5a) results in [ɒɪ], (5b) in [ɪɒ].

$$(5) \ \begin{bmatrix} - \text{ back} \\ + \text{ round} \end{bmatrix} \rightarrow \left\{ \begin{matrix} \begin{bmatrix} +- \text{ back} \\ +- \text{ round} \end{bmatrix} \\ \\ \begin{bmatrix} -+ \text{ back} \\ -+ \text{ round} \end{bmatrix} \end{matrix} \right\} \ / \ \begin{bmatrix} \underline{\quad\quad} \\ + \text{ high} \\ - \text{ mid} \\ + \text{ long} \end{bmatrix} \begin{matrix} (\\ \\ (\end{matrix}$$

There remain four instances of [gɛɒs] in Derbyshire. This is an area where [ɛɒ] occurs also in words that have [ju:] in RP, e.g. *Tuesday, dew, suet* (*LAE*: Ph 175ff.; *AES*: 147ff), so it seems obvious to have rule (6) succeed rule (5b) and to understand the whole process as a lowering of the first component of [ɪɒ].

$$(6) \ \begin{bmatrix} -+ \text{ back} \\ -+ \text{ round} \end{bmatrix} \rightarrow \begin{bmatrix} -+ \text{ high} \\ +- \text{ mid} \end{bmatrix} \ / \ \begin{bmatrix} \underline{\quad\quad} \\ + \text{ long} \end{bmatrix}$$

This hypothesis must be tentative, however, as [ɪɒ] co-occurs in the area, and the [ɛɒ] sounds in words like *dew* might go back to old /eu/.

Map 7.1:   *SED:* *goose*

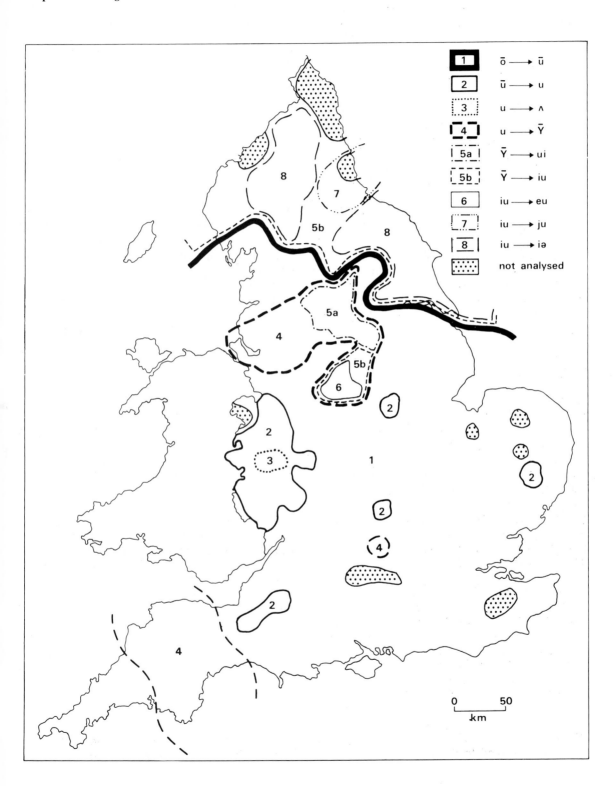

Map 7.1 is a summary of what has been discussed so far. To the South of the thick black line leading from the Humber to the Lune, underlying /ō/ was raised to [u:] (rule 1). In two areas the [u:] sound continued to change: (a) shortening near the Welsh border (rule 2), within this area lowering to [ʌ] (rule 3), and (b) fronting in the South-west and in the North Midlands (rule 4). Within the northern area that underwent rule (4), diphthongisation took place (rule 5), and in Derbyshire the result of diphthongisation (rule 5b) was lowered to [ɛʊ] (rule 6).

The area north of the Humber-Lune line is more complex. Three main types of phonetic reflex occur: [gʊəs], various forms of [gɪʊs] and near Newcastle-Upon-Tyne [gjʊs]. Apart from this we find [gu:s] as a secondary form in the whole North-east and in the extreme North exclusively. These forms do not result from rule (1), however, but are due to RP influence. In the whole area words like *how, now, brown, cow* have the vowel reflex [u:] (*AES*: 21-6; *LAE*: Ph 149-54), so underlying /ō/ could not develop to [u:] because the phonemes would have merged.

If, as we did in Derbyshire, we want to relate the forms of the type [gɪʊs] to a [− back], [+ round], [+ long] vowel, the question is how underlying /ō/ should have developed like that. On historical evidence, Luick (1964: 426ff) actually comes to the conclusion that it did do so in the whole area north of the Humber, but he cannot offer any explanation as to how this happened.

For the present interpretation we omit this problem and start from [gʏ:s] in the area north of the Humber-Lune line. We then asume that this reflex was diphthongised by rule 5b. The remaining development is fairly clear. [gjʊs] in the North-east is the result of a change of accent within the two components of the diphthong, which can easily be formulated by means of distinctive features. The first component lost its syllabicity and is now a glide (rule 7).

$$(7) \begin{bmatrix} -+ \text{ back} \\ -+ \text{ round} \end{bmatrix} \rightarrow \begin{bmatrix} -+ \text{ syll} \end{bmatrix} / \begin{bmatrix} \rule{1cm}{0.4pt} \\ + \text{ high} \\ - \text{ mid} \\ + \text{ long} \end{bmatrix}$$

The sound [ʊə] is the result of a phonemic merger. In the North-west and in the remote Yorkshire Dales [ʊə] from underlying /ō/ is in opposition to [ea] from underlying /ā/ (*AES*: 73, 104; *LAE*: Ph 60-1, Ph 138-40). In a large area north of the Humber-Lune line [ʊə] holds for the two reflexes. Rule (8) shows the change from [ʊɔ] to [ʊə]:

$$(8) \begin{bmatrix} -+ \text{ back} \\ -+ \text{ round} \end{bmatrix} \rightarrow \begin{bmatrix} - \text{ round} \\ -+ \text{ mid} \end{bmatrix} / \begin{bmatrix} \rule{1cm}{0.4pt} \\ + \text{ high} \\ + \text{ long} \end{bmatrix}$$

Summing up the development in the North, we have a sound of the type [ʊɔ] resulting from [ʏ:], the origin of which is not quite clear. In the North-east [ʊɔ] became [jɒ] (rule 7); in two large areas it developed into [ʊə] (rule 8).

Eight process rules are sufficient to show the relations between the reflexes on this rather complicated map. The interpretation appears elegant and phonologically plausible. What probability is there that the developments postulated have actually happened? Basically we have to distinguish between two types of argumentation.

Firstly, the construction on Map 7.1 can be correct to the extent that dialects are the result of sound changes. Even here, however, limitations are to be allowed for. Let us have another look at area 4. The change from /ū/ to /ʏ/ in the West might have occurred much later than in, and independently of, the East. This would mean that we have constructed relations where in reality there are none. In such cases the geographical relevance of the areas constructed might warn us; probably the interpretation of related maps would lead to contradictions in that we would have rules that are mutually exclusive. In other words, the more material we can adduce, the more convincing our construction will be. Secondly, dialects have not exclusively developed from sound changes. This has become clear with regard to [gu:s] in the North-east. The other black dots on Map 7.1 show similar cases. In the South there are three instances of [gɛʊs], with the same vowel reflex as in words like *mouse, louse* (*AES*: 21-8; *LAE*: Ph 149-54) whereas underlying /ō/ is normally [u:]. Maybe a speaker or a fieldworker made a mistake. Maybe a special development has taken place, but the obvious cases of this kind are not so frequent as to throw doubts on the interpretation as a whole. With regard to hidden cases we can only speculate and try to use more material.

Map 7.2: *SED*: *quarry*

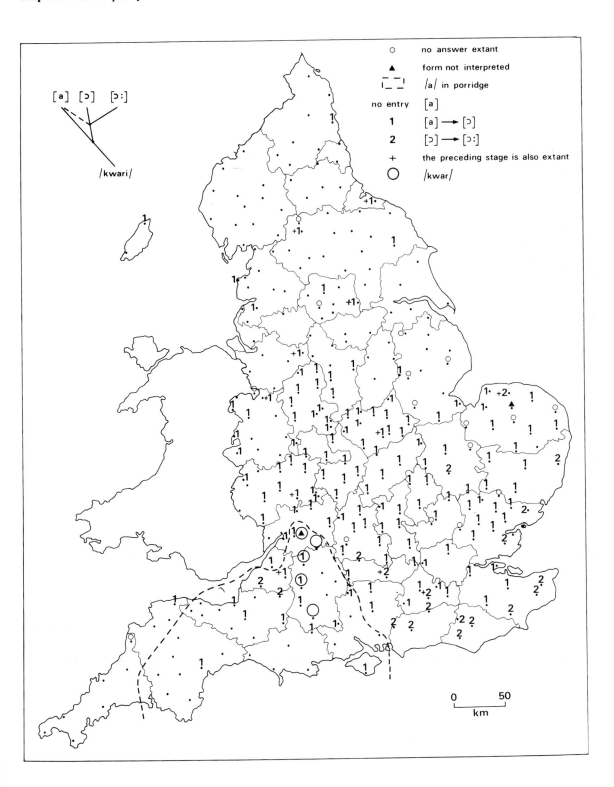

Quarry (*AES*: 212) is a much simpler map (Map 7.2) than *goose*; only three main types of reflex occur, and the processes that underlie them are fairly straightforward, too. [a], the non-back, non-round, low, short vowel, can be found in the whole North as far down as Shropshire and Herefordshire, North Derbyshire, Nottinghamshire and Lincolnshire. In the South-west [a] is also extant — regularly in Cornwall, Devon and Dorset, less so in Somerset, Wiltshire and Hampshire. In the rest of the country /kwari/ has undergone assimilation in roundness and backness after /w/ (rule 9).

$$(9) \quad \begin{bmatrix} + \text{ syll} \\ - \text{ long} \\ - \text{ high} \end{bmatrix} \rightarrow \begin{bmatrix} + \text{ back} \\ + \text{ round} \\ + \text{ mid} \end{bmatrix} / \begin{bmatrix} - \text{ syll} \\ - \text{ cons} \\ + \text{ back} \\ + \text{ round} \end{bmatrix} \underline{\quad\quad}$$

Two simplifications have been made so far. The first one concerns two forms with [ɑ] extant in Northumberland. As this sound does not, as a rule, occur in the two villages in question it has been subsumed under [a]. Secondly the SED material as a whole presents problems with regard to [ɔ] and [ɒ]. For the present purpose [ɔ] will be dealt with and no further distinctions will be made.

Within the area that has undergone rounding, lengthening of [ɔ] occurs in Sussex, along the coast in Kent, Essex and Suffolk, as well as in a few isolated instances. Rule (10) accounts for this change whose immediate reason is not clear; intervocalic /r/ does not usually serve as a lengthening context.

$$(10) \quad V \rightarrow [+ \text{ long}] / \underline{\quad\quad} \begin{bmatrix} + \text{ back} \\ + \text{ round} \\ - \text{ high} \\ + \text{ mid} \end{bmatrix}$$

Map 7.2 sums up what has been discussed so far. Somewhere in the South-east [a] changed to [ɔ] (rule 9), and the process began to spread towards the North and the South-west. In the extreme South-east [ɔ] has been lengthened (rule 10).

Two details on the map are worth mentioning. In Wiltshire four instances are extant in which /kwari/ has lost the final vowel. This brought /r/ to the ultimate position, which has resulted in lengthening of the vowel and /r/-colouring.

Two problematic individual instances remain, [kwaᵗ:] in Gloucestershire and [kwɑ·ɹɪ] in Norfolk. These forms, if we can take them seriously, have quite different status. [ɑ:] in Norfolk is the lengthening product of [a] in words like *chaff*, *grass*, *last* (*AES*: 183; *LAE*: Ph 3-4), *arm*, *barley*, *star*, etc. (*AES*: 285ff; *LAE*: Ph 11, 19-21). [ɑ:] in Gloucestershire, on the other hand, occurs in words like *broth*, *cough*, *cross*, etc. (*AES*: 214; *LAE*: Ph 44-6). In other words [ɑ:] in Norfolk has not undergone rule (9), [ɑ:] in Gloucestershire has. As we are dealing with isolated instances, however, we had perhaps better refrain from attributing to them too complicated a derivation, so on the map they are marked, but not interpreted.

Wasps (Map 7.3) is the same type of map as *quarry*. Again we have rounding adjustment after /w/ in the South-east (rule 9), but the geographical distribution of the process is different: fairly regular in the whole South-west, with a few exceptions in West Somerset, and in a much smaller area of the South Midlands than *quarry*. In fact, forms of the type /wasp/ occur as far south as Monmouthshire, Gloucestershire, Leicestershire, Rutland and Northamptonshire.

As in *quarry*, forms are extant in which [ɔ] has been lengthened. The area is not the same, however, and in addition instances of [a:] occur, too. Rule (11) formulates that short, non-high vowels that agree in backness, roundness and midness (/a/: [− mid, − back, − round]; /o/: [+ mid, + back, + round]) are lengthened before voiceless fricatives.

$$(11) \quad \begin{bmatrix} + \text{ syll} \\ - \text{ high} \\ \alpha \text{ mid} \\ \alpha \text{ back} \\ \alpha \text{ round} \end{bmatrix} \rightarrow [+ \text{ long}] / \underline{\quad\quad} \begin{bmatrix} + \text{ cons} \\ + \text{ cont} \\ - \text{ voice} \end{bmatrix}$$

This process is well documented for the South Midlands and the whole South (*AES*: 182, 214; *LAE*: Ph 3-4, 44-6). *Wasps* differs from the general pattern in that south of a line leading from the Severn to the border between Suffolk and Essex (see Map 7.3) it has not undergone rule (11). This apparent exception falls in line as soon as we consider the consonants. South of the line in question metathesis has led to forms like [wɔpsɪz], [wɔps], [wɔpəz]. This process is in

Map 7.3:   *SED: wasps*

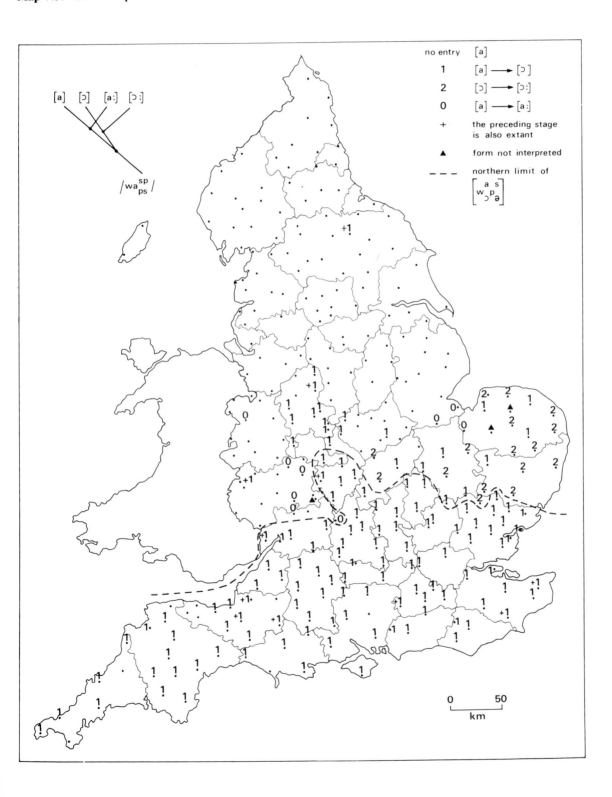

a bleeding relationship with rule (11); it deletes the context responsible for lengthening.

Map 7.4, *wash*, differs from *quarry* and *wasps* in that forms with [a] are rare. Two instances are extant in Lancashire, two in Gloucestershire, two in Yorkshire (beside [wɛʃ]), and one each occurs in Herefordshire, Worcestershire and Lincolnshire. The normal reflex in the area where we would expect [waʃ] is [ɛ] according to rule (12).

$$(12) \quad V \rightarrow [+ \text{ mid}] / \begin{bmatrix} \overline{} \\ - \text{ high} \\ - \text{ back} \\ - \text{ round} \\ - \text{ long} \end{bmatrix}$$

Rule (12) can be evidenced in the whole North as far down as Lincolnshire, Nottinghamshire, Derbyshire, Staffordshire, Cheshire and in a few isolated instances in Shropshire, Herefordshire and Gloucestershire.

South of [wɛʃ] we have the forms that result from rounding adjustment (rule 9). The almost total absence of forms like [waʃ] between the two areas might invite speculation that the present-day boundary between [wɔʃ] and [wɛʃ] coincides with the old line that separated [wɛʃ] from [waʃ]. [wɔʃ] being Standard, the prestige form, we had rather assume that [wɛʃ] was at one time used farther south and that [ɔ] was introduced by analogy with RP and not via [waʃ] and rounding adjustment.

In the area that underwent rule (9), lengthening before voiceless fricative (rule 11) took place in the East (Suffolk and isolated instances in adjacent Norfolk, Essex and Cambridgeshire) and in the South (Somerset, Dorset, Wiltshire and Sussex). Again, the geographical spread is far from being even, but unlike in [wɔpəz] 'wasps' there is no obvious reason for the preservation of the short forms.

In Somerset and Wiltshire the lengthened reflexes have been subjected to an additional development, /r/-colouring, which is here a case of neutralisation. In a large part of the South Midlands and the South [ɔ:] word-internally is the surface reflex of /or/ in the same way that [a:] and [ɑ:] represent /ar/. This means that /a,o/ + /voiceless fricative/ cannot be distinguished from /a,o/ + /r/ + /voiceless fricative/, e.g. [a:s] 'ass, arse'. Where there is retroflex /r/, the contrast should be carried by presence versus absence of

/r/-colouring. In reality instances of intrusive /r/-colouring occur in practically all the words that have undergone lengthening, in other words the structure /a,o/ + /voiceless fricative/ tends to be interpreted as /a,o/ + /r/ + /voiceless fricative/ according to rule (13).

$$(13) \quad \begin{vmatrix} a \\ o \end{vmatrix} + \begin{vmatrix} f \\ \theta \\ s \\ \int \end{vmatrix} \rightarrow \begin{vmatrix} a \\ o \end{vmatrix} + /r/ + \begin{vmatrix} f \\ \theta \\ s \\ \int \end{vmatrix}$$

If [wɔᵗ:ʃ] in the South-west is the result of rounding adjustment (rule 9) and restructuring (rule 13), the two instances of [waᵗ:ʃ] in Somerset may well have a more complicated derivation than straightforward /waʃ/ + restructuring. In an area including Worcestershire, Gloucestershire, Mid and East Somerset, Wiltshire, Dorset and Hampshire, words of the type *fork*, *forty*, *north*, *horses* (*AES*: 291-4; *LAE*: Ph 47) usually have the reflex [aᵗ:]. The back vowel has been fronted before retroflex (i.e. strongly palatal) /r/ according to rule (14).

$$(14) \quad \begin{bmatrix} + \text{ syll} \\ - \text{ high} \\ - \text{ long} \end{bmatrix} \rightarrow \begin{bmatrix} - \text{ mid} \\ - \text{ back} \\ - \text{ round} \end{bmatrix} / \underline{} \begin{bmatrix} + \text{ syll} \\ + \text{ cons} \\ - \text{ back} \\ + \text{ high} \end{bmatrix}$$

In the context /w—r/ rule (14) undoes the effects of rule (9), so [waᵗ:ʃ] might have undergone rounding adjustment, /r/-intrusion and fronting.

The case is difficult to decide on the evidence of two instances, but it leads to second thoughts about the apparently simple Map 7.2, *quarry*, with its unusually large spread of [a] in the South-west. Adducing the evidence from *porridge* (*AES*: 225) we see that fronting has also occurred before /r+C/, so that [kwaᵗɹ] seems to represent old /a/ in Cornwall and North Devon only. In the remaining South-west it is the result of rounding adjustment (rule 9) and fronting (rule 14). This would mean that rounding adjustment has spread to the South-west and that the situation as mirrored in *wasps* is representative.

Map 7.4, *wash*, reflects another process; we have to account for the forms with [ɛɹ] in Lancashire, Yorkshire and Derbyshire and those with [aɹ] and [ɔɹ] in the South-west. The reflexes in question are the result of [ɹ]-introduction before /ʃ/; according to Luick (1964: section

Map 7.4:   *SED: wash*

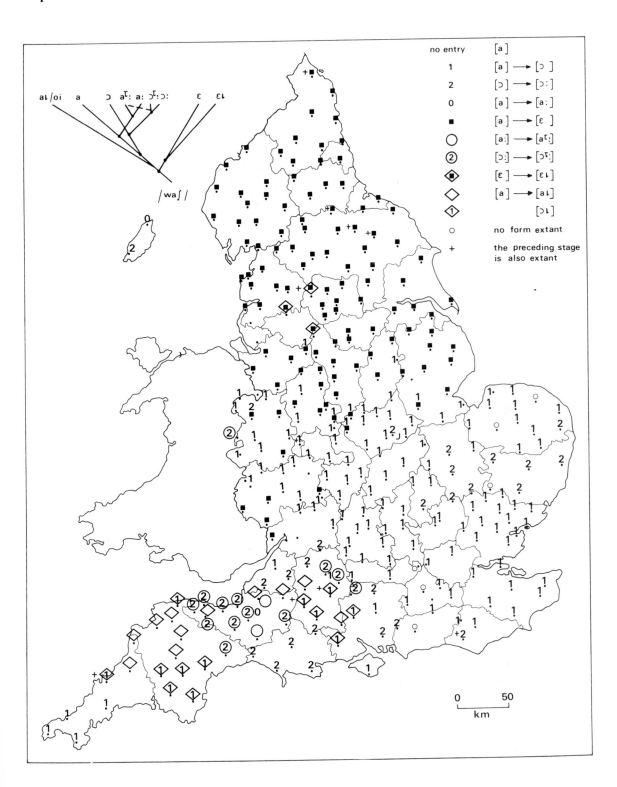

404) this happened in the thirteenth century after /a/ and /e/ (rule 15).

$$(15) \quad \emptyset \rightarrow \begin{bmatrix} + \text{ syll} \\ + \text{ high} \\ - \text{ back} \\ - \text{ long} \end{bmatrix} / \begin{bmatrix} + \text{ syll} \\ - \text{ high} \\ - \text{ back} \\ - \text{ round} \\ - \text{ long} \end{bmatrix} \underline{\qquad} \begin{bmatrix} + \text{ cons} \\ + \text{ high} \\ - \text{ voice} \\ + \text{ cont} \\ + \text{ strid} \end{bmatrix}$$

This process has been dealt with comprehensively by Giffhorn, who confirms the view that [ɔʊ] in the South-west is by no means due to rounding adjustment but an allophone of /ai/ (Giffhorn 1978: 88). Independent evidence for this is the map *white* (*LAE*: Ph 105), which does not have any more forms with [ɔʊ] than for instance *sky, time, writing* (*AES*: 6-8).

Summing up the rules that are responsible for the present-day reflexes of *wash* we have (i) raising to [ɛ] in the North (rule 12), (ii) ʊ-introduction before /ʃ/ in the North Midlands and the South-west, (iii) rounding adjustment (rule 9) in the South Midlands and the South, (iv) lengthening of /a,o/ before voiceless fricative (rule 11) in the same area, (v) /r/-insertion (rule 13) in Wiltshire, Somerset, Devon and Hampshire, (vi) fronting (rule 14) in Somerset, altogether an elegant presentation of a rather complex reality.

Map 7.5, *water*, shows the pattern we are familiar with, apart from forms like [e:], [ɛʊ], [i:] and [ɛ] in the West Midlands (Lancashire, Cheshire, Derbyshire, Shropshire, Staffordshire, Herefordshire, Worcestershire and isolated instances in Gloucestershire), and [ɛ] as well as [e:] in Northumberland. [e:], [ɛʊ], [i:] in the West Midlands fall into line with the evidence on maps like *gable, grave, laces* (*AES*: 104; *LAE*: Ph 60-1), which would have to be analysed as underlying /ā/ + vowel shift, with different vowel shift rules accounting for the individual reflexes. The relation with /water/ becomes clear: lengthening must have taken place so early that the resulting long vowel could undergo vowel shift. We postulate rule (16).

$$(16) \quad V \rightarrow [+ \text{ long}] / \underline{\qquad} \begin{bmatrix} - \text{ high} \\ - \text{ mid} \\ - \text{ back} \\ - \text{ round} \end{bmatrix}$$

and order it before vowel shift, whatever the latter's exact form. The two instances of [e:] in Northumberland mirror the same development; the reflex [ɛ] is best derived from [e:] by way of shortening.

The rest of the country shows again the dichotomy between northern [a] and southern [ɔ:], the boundary between the two areas running from South Lancashire to South Lincolnshire.

Lengthening is very general in the southern area; only Norfolk exhibits a few short forms. This might indicate that it has nothing to do with lengthening of [ɔ] (rule 10) after rounding adjustment (rule 9) encountered in *quarry*. If the West Midlands forms show lengthening + vowel shift, the area to the south and east of it had best be seen as vowel shift + lengthening; in other words there is a difference in rule order. This would mean that rounding adjustment could also affect long vowels (of which there is only one example, *water*). Rule (9) becomes rule (17)

$$(17) \quad \begin{bmatrix} + \text{ syll} \\ - \text{ high} \end{bmatrix} \rightarrow \begin{bmatrix} + \text{ back} \\ + \text{ round} \\ + \text{ mid} \end{bmatrix} / \begin{bmatrix} - \text{ syll} \\ - \text{ cons} \\ + \text{ back} \\ + \text{ round} \end{bmatrix} \underline{\qquad}$$

and must be ordered after vowel shift.

The area with lengthening includes a small region in Monmouthshire, Gloucestershire and Worcestershire in which the reflex is not [ɔ:] but [ɑ:]. Forms like [brɑ:θ] 'broth', [kɑ:f] 'cough', [krɑ:s] 'cross' (*AES*: 214; *LAE*: Ph 44-6) at the same localities show, however, that [ɑ:] is the result of lowering (rule 18) rather than backing. In other words, the forms presuppose rounding adjustment.

$$(18) \quad V \rightarrow [- \text{ mid}] / \underline{\qquad} \begin{bmatrix} - \text{ high} \\ + \text{ back} \\ + \text{ round} \\ + \text{ long} \end{bmatrix}$$

/r/-insertion (rule 13) is rare on this map. Isolated instances occur in Devon, Berkshire, Herefordshire, Monmouthshire and Shropshire. [wɛ:tə] in Staffordshire and Worcestershire may well be the result of /r/-insertion, too. Words like *gable, grave, laces* (*AES*: 104; *LAE*: Ph 60-1) usually have [e:] in this area as opposed to *mare, hare* (*AES*: 317-18; *LAE*: Ph 68) with [ɛ:]. The

Map 7.5: *SED: water*

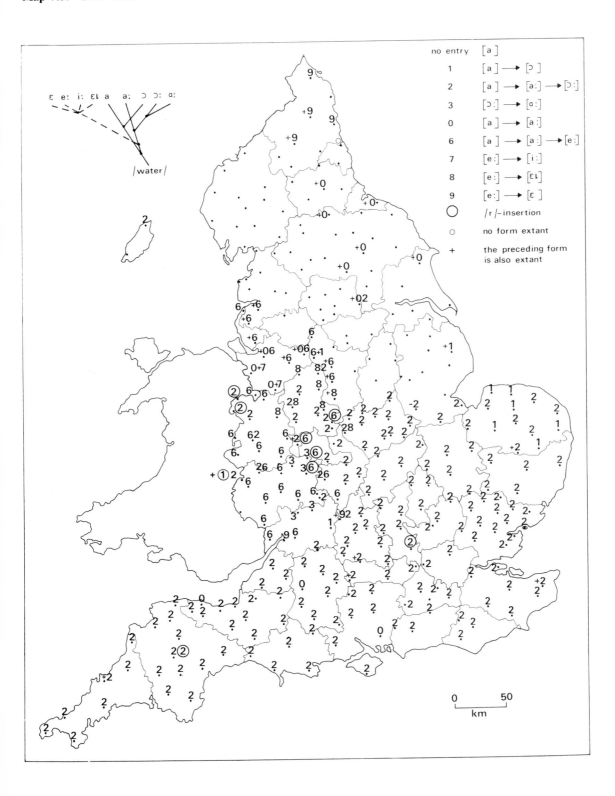

case is not clear in Worcestershire because *water* does not show /r/-colouring, *mare* and *hare* do.

Map 7.6, *swath*, is complex because we are dealing with two variables, the vowel as well as the final consonant, which is basically voiced in the North, voiceless south of Lancashire, Yorkshire and Lincolnshire and absent in Devon and Cornwall.

Voiced consonant following a long reflex, underlying /ā/ as in *gable*, *grave*, *laces* (*AES*: 104; *LAE*: Ph 60-1), indicates that the dialect in question does not distinguish between the noun *swath* and the verb *swathe*, the verbal form has assumed the two grammatical functions. Long vowel reflex usually does combine with voiced consonant, a notable exception being Norfolk and Suffolk, which makes these forms difficult to account for. Has the vowel reflex of the noun been raised, or has the long vowel of the verb been shortened? The case cannot be decided, but quite clearly rounding adjustment (rule 17) has no context here on which to operate.

The remaining forms mirror the processes we have already encountered. [swaθ] is extant south of a line leading from the Mersey to Mid Lincolnshire and north of another line leading from the Severn to the Wash. In this area there are a few isolated instances of rounding adjustment (rule 17) and lengthening (rule 11). To the south of the second line rounding adjustment has occurred regularly, lengthening less so: some short reflexes are extant in Berkshire and Buckinghamshire. In this southern region there are four forms extant with a vowel reflex [ɑ:]. The two instances in Monmouthshire and Gloucestershire are due to lowering (rule 18), whereas [ɑ:] in Norfolk seems to be the result of backing, cf. forms like [tʃɑ:f] 'chaff', [gɹɑ:s] 'grass', [lɑ:st] 'last' (*AES*: 182; *LAE*: Ph 3-4). Rule 19 formulates this process.

$$(19) \ V \rightarrow \begin{bmatrix} + \text{back} \\ + \text{round} \end{bmatrix} \ / \ \begin{bmatrix} - \text{high} \\ - \text{mid} \\ + \text{long} \end{bmatrix}$$

This means that [ɑ:] in the West Midlands is a result of rounding adjustment, [ɑ:] in Norfolk is not.

In the area with loss of final consonant /r/-insertion is general. The four forms with [aᶜ:] are outside the area in which fronting (rule 14) has applied, so we must assume that they have not undergone rounding adjustment.

On the surface the present interpretations of *quarry*, *wasps*, *wash*, *water*, *swath* seem to have confirmed a commonplace: 'Every word has its own history', at best paraphrased in generativist terminology as: 'Individual processes affect words differently in different areas'. Map 7.7 is an attempt to go beyond this. Having established the forms that are direct or indirect results of rounding adjustment, I shall try to look at this particular process in some detail. In 120 localities in the Midlands the individual words have undergone it very unevenly: *swath* 31 times, *wasps* 51 times, *water* 72 times, *wash* 74 times and *quarry* 83 times. Figure 7.1 is an implicational arrangement of this (cf. DeCamp 1971a, b), the localities mentioned first are prone to rounding adjustment, the ones towards the end of the list undergo the process more readily.

The presentation is made complicated by the fact that in many cases rounding adjustment did not take place because the word in question cannot serve as input to rule (17), especially in forms like [wɛʃ] 'wash', but also in [we:tə] 'water' and [swɛ·əð] 'swath(e)'. Secondly all the forms are not extant in every locality but the implication is clear: if rounding adjustment is absent in *quarry*, it tends to be absent in the other words, if it is present in *swath*, it is present in all the other words. The phonological implications become clear if we rewrite rule (17) as rule (19).

$$(19) \ \begin{Bmatrix} a \\ a: \end{Bmatrix} \rightarrow \begin{Bmatrix} ɔ \\ ɔ: \end{Bmatrix} \ / \ w \ \underline{\quad} \begin{Bmatrix} ʃ/ʈ & \text{a)} \\ ʃ & \text{b)} \\ t & \text{c)} \\ s & \text{d)} \\ θ & \text{e)} \end{Bmatrix}$$

In a way that cannot be expressed with binary features, backness of articulation of the following consonant seems to favour rounding adjustment. Between the area that has undergone rule (17) and the one that has not, there are some villages that are subjected to it step by step, first in words of the type (19a), then (19b) and so on until eventually rounding adjustment will be implemented in this area, too.

Looking at Map 7.7 we see that the innovative force of rounding adjustment is strongest in the central Midlands; Shropshire, Herefordshire and Worcestershire are more conservative, one notable exception being the localities along the Welsh border.

In conclusion I should like to come back to

Map 7.6:   *SED: swath*

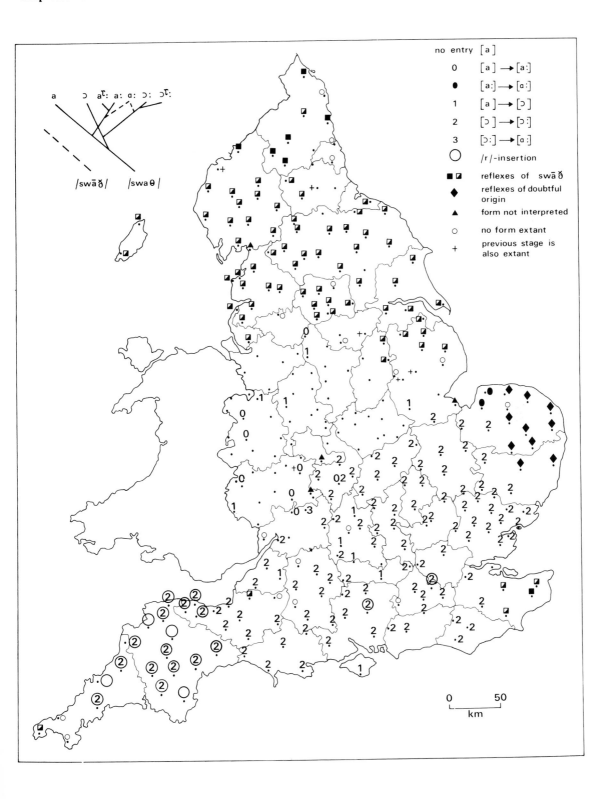

Map 7.7: *SED*: **Rounding Adjustment in the English Midlands**

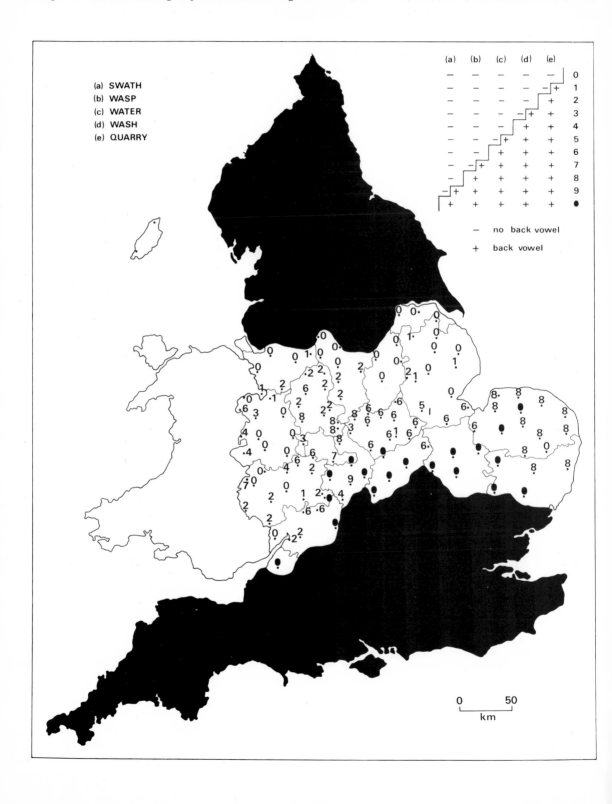

Figure 7.1: Rounding Adjustment in the English Midlands

−	no adjustment
+	adjustment
( )	reflex that cannot be input for adjustment rule
(( ))	no form extant

locality	swath	wasp	water	wash	quarry	mapped value
27.7	−	−	( )	−	−	0
16.2	−	−	−	( )	−	0
16.4	−	−	−	( )	−	0
14.10	−	−	−	( )	−	0
16.1	( )	−	−	( )	−	0
9.5	( )	−	−	( )	−	0
9.4	( )	−	−	( )	−	0
14.1	( )	−	−	( )	−	0
14.3	( )	−	−	( )	−	0
14.4	( )	−	−	( )	−	0
14.5	( )	−	−	( )	−	0
14.7	( )	−	−	( )	−	0
17.1	−	−	(−)	( )	−	0
17.3	−	−	(−)	( )	−	0
17.4	−	−	(−)	( )	−	0
15.4	−	−	(−)	( )	−	0
15.1	−	−	( )	( )	−	0
15.2	−	−	( )	( )	−	0
19.5	−	−	( )	( )	−	0
19.11	−	−	( )	( )	−	0
31.5	(( ))	− +	( )	( )	−	0
15.3	+	−	(− +)	( )	−	0
16.3	( )	−	−	+	−	0
19.8	−	−	( )	+	−	0
19.9	−	−	( )	+	−	0
27.8	−	−	( )	+	−	0
19.7	−	−	(+)	+	−	0
27.3	−	−	(+)	+	−	0
19.1	−	−	+	+	−	0
21.12	( )	+	+	+		0
14.9	(−)	−	−	−	(( ))	1
14.2	( )	−	−	( )	(( ))	1
14.6	(( ))	−	−	( )	(( ))	1
17.2	−	−	−	( )	− +	1
27.11	−	−	( )	+	− +	1
19.2	+	−	( )	+	− +	1
20.9	−	+	+	+		2
27.5	−	−	(+)	−	+	2
31.4	−	+	( )	−	+	2
18.5	+	+	(+)	−	+	2
31.6	+	+	(+)	−	+	2
15.5	−	−	−	( )	+	2
17.5	−	−	(−)	( )	+	2
15.6	−	−	(−)	( )	+	2
14.8	(( ))	−	−	( )	+	2
15.7	−	−	( )	( )	+	2
18.2	−	−	( )	( )	+	2
27.12	−	−	( )	( )	+	2
27.14	−	−	( )	( )	+	2
27.9	−	−	( )	( )	+	2

locality	swath	wasp	water	wash	quarry	mapped value
27.13	−	−	+	( )	+	2
18.3	−	− +	( )	( )	+	2
18.1	−	+	( )	( )	+	2
18.6	−	+	( )	( )	+	2
18.7	−	+	( )	( )	+	2
19.4	−	−	+	( )	+	2
18.11	−	+	(+)	− +	+	3
20.8	−	+	(+)	− +	+	3
23.6	+	+	−	+	+	4
19.6	−	−	( )	+	+	4
19.10	−	−	( )	+	+	4
27.4	−	−	( )	+	+	4
14.11	+	−	− +	(+)	(( ))	5
27.6	−	− +	− +	+	+	5
31.1	−	−	(+)	+	+	6
27.1	−	−	(+)	+	+	6
19.3	−	−	+	+	+	6
18.4	−	−	+	+	+	6
20.1	−	−	+	+	+	6
20.2	−	−	+	+	+	6
20.3	−	−	+	+	+	6
20.6	−	−	+	+	+	6
20.5	−	−	+	+	+	6
20.10	−	−	+	+	+	6
20.7	−	−	+	+	+	6
20.11	−	−	+	+	+	6
27.2	−	−	+	+	+	6
14.12	( )	−	+	+	+	6
21.8	+	−	+	+	(( ))	6
14.13	+	−	+	+	(( ))	6
20.12	+	−	+	+	+	6
25.1	+	−	+	+	+	6
31.2	+	−	+	+	+	6
24.1	+	− +	+	+	+	6
18.9	−	+	(+)	(+)	+	7
20.4	−	+	+	(+)	+	8
21.7	−	+	+	+	(( ))	8
21.3	−	+	+	(( ))	+	8
18.8	−	+	+	+	+	8
18.10	−	+	+	+	+	8
23.1	−	+	+	+	+	8
21.1	−	+	+	+	+	8
21.2	−	+	+	+	+	8
21.4	−	+	+	+	+	8
21.6	−	+	+	+	+	8
21.11	−	+	+	+	+	8
21.10	−	+	+	+	+	8
21.13	−	+	+	+	+	8
26.2	−	+	+	+	+	8
26.3	( )	+	+	+	+	8
23.5	− +	+	+	+	+	8
22.1	+	+	+	+	+	9
26.4	+	+	+	(( ))	(( ))	●
21.5	(( ))	+	+	+	+	●
27.10	+	+	+	+	+	●
23.2	+	+	+	+	+	●
23.3	+	+	+	+	+	●

locality	swath	wasp	water	wash	quarry	mapped value
23.4	+	+	+	+	+	●
25.2	+	+	+	+	+	●
25.3	+	+	+	+	+	●
25.4	+	+	+	+	+	●
25.5	+	+	+	+	+	●
22.2	+	+	+	+	+	●
22.3	+	+	+	+	+	●
22.4	+	+	+	+	+	●
21.9	+	+	+	+	+	●
26.1	+	+	+	+	+	●
26.5	+	+	+	+	+	●
31.3	+	+	+	+	+	●
35.1	+	+	+	+	+	●
rounding adjustment	31	51	72	74	83	

the point of departure. Linguistic atlases present linguistic data in a way that implies their geographical distribution. This distribution is the result of various processes and developments, and only by looking for these processes can we try to understand the linguistic reality the atlases mirror. Generative phonology, with its very insistence on abstract processes, provides an excellent tool for this kind of work. Rounding adjustment in the Midlands is just one example.

Editorial Note

This paper was received in May 1981 and does not take into account Glauser's more recent work on scaling. An expanded version which also dealt with mutated plurals was presented at a Conference on Language Varieties, Centre for English Cultural Tradition and Language, University of Sheffield, in July 1981.

References

Chomsky, N. *Current Issues in Linguistic Theory* (Mouton, The Hague, 1965)

Chomsky, N. and M. Halle. *The Sound Pattern of English* (Harper and Row, New York, 1968)

DeCamp, D. 'Implicational Scales and Sociolinguistic Linearity', *Linguistics*, vol. 73 (1971), pp. 30-43

—— 'Towards a Generative Analysis of a Post-creole Speech Continuum', in D. Hymes (ed.). *Pidginization and Creolization of Language* (Cambridge University Press, Cambridge, 1971)

Giffhorn, B. *Untersuchungen zu den englischen Dialekten: Der me. Typus 'waishen'* (privately published, Bonn, 1978)

Goossens, J. *Strukturelle Sprachgeographie: eine Einführung in Methodik und Ergebnisse* (Carl Winter, Heidelberg, 1969)

Kolb, E. 'Skandinavisches in den nordenglischen Dialekten', *Anglia*, vol. 83 (1965), pp. 127-53

Kolb, E., B. Glauser, W. Elmer, R. Stamm. *Atlas of English Sounds* (Francke, Bern, 1979)

Luick, K. *Historische Grammatik der englishen Sprache* (Bernhard Tauchnitz, Stuttgart, 1964)

Orton, H., S. Sanderson and J. Widdowson (eds.). *The Linguistic Atlas of England* (Croom Helm, London, 1978)

Sommerstein, A.H. *Modern Phonology* (Arnold, London, 1977)

Wang, W.S.-Y. 'Vowel Features, Paired Variables, and the English Vowel Shift', *Language*, vol. 44 (1968), pp. 695-708

8

Linguistic Atlases and Grammar: The Investigation and Description of Regional Variation in English Syntax[1]

JOHN M. KIRK

Linguistic surveys have usually included some study of grammatical items. Reviewers of *The Linguistic Atlas of England*[2] have been remarkably unresponsive in their accounts of its treatment of grammar. 'Syntax is an unwieldy subject which dialectologists have fought shy of', writes the author of one of the classic textbooks on English dialects (Wakelin 1972: 125). Yet it is hard to doubt the experience of Edinburgh dialectologists such as A.J. Aitken (1972: 38), A. McIntosh (1952) and D.D. Murison (1967: 283) when they write that it is from grammatical material, especially the syntactical, that the most interesting results for linguistic variation are to be expected. W.N. Francis has recently confirmed that syntax is one of the challenging areas of dialectology today (Francis 1983: 41). From the outset of the planning of the Survey of English Dialects there was never any doubt in the minds of Eugen Dieth and Harold Orton that grammatical information would be collected. To discuss grammar in a linguistic survey was very much *comme il faut*.

The study of grammar in a linguistic survey presents quite different problems from the study of lexis or pronunciation. For a start, what is meant by grammar has to be carefully defined. The forms of words which denote grammatical class membership and the meaning which all words derive from the environment in which' they occur in the sentence, must be distinguished from their functional behaviour and arrangement in that environment. These crude distinctions

may sufficiently represent the differences between morphology and syntax for our present purposes.

Syntax contrasts with lexis in that syntax never performs its communicative functions through the form of a word alone and rather more through the relationships between words in a sentence. Although Orton talks about 'syntactic features' in the same breath as 'lexical features' (Orton 1960: 340), the two components of language are put to quite different communicative tasks and are hardly equivalent in status.

If an informant in Sheffield or Falkirk or Belfast talked about being left-handed as *dolly posh* or *corrie fistit* or *fjuggy*, or of the youngest member of a litter of animals as the *reckling* or *draidlock* or *deoraidh*, then there would be little else to add, except that each choice was made in preference to a word or expression in the Standard language, or that the option to choose the latter was suppressed; and probably everybody would be happy. Either choice carries stylistic associations which a speaker will undoubtedly draw upon in making his selection in one context of utterance or another. Dialectologists have sometimes confused the stylistic and the regional implications of a linguistic item.

If an informant in Sheffield or Falkirk or Belfast used *never* for 'not', *have got to* or *boun to* for 'must', to express obligation, or was confused by the word order differences between *give it to me*, *give me it* and *give it me*, then probably nobody would be happy if this piece of linguistic description ended there. It might be said, for instance, that any stylistic difference carried by these last choices was blurred for the speaker at the moment of utterance and caused him to say both. From a regional point of view, however, syntactic variation is a complex phenomenon. The delight of the *hapax legomenon* is denied the grammarian.

Without going into detail, and allowing for simplification, lexis might be said to be the study of the whole range of possible relationships between words and things, onomasiological as well as semasiological, so that for each item of reference in experience, and in a particular context of utterance, there exists one appropriate word, or lexeme. Such relationships, their significance and the complexity of their geographical distribution in Britain and Ireland are dealt with by P.L. Henry elsewhere in this volume.

Syntax makes considerably less reference to the existence of things outside itself except perhaps for its notable references to time (as tense), to the durational aspects of activities and experience (as aspect), to the properties of logic, including assertion and denial (as mood and negation), features of discourse such as markers of focus, prominence, attention-seeking or organisation by means of epenthetic qualifiers, particles or adjuncts, such as *as it were*, *what one might call*, in a certain usage *like*, initial *see* in Scotland (cf. *See my man. See fish. He hates it.*), the ubiquitous cognates *(you) know* and *ken*, or the numerical *firstly . . . secondly . . .*

These brief illustrations of some of its formal properties are certainly sufficient to show that syntax is both fundamental and necessary for any form of communication. It is syntax which gives each utterance its particular meaning, its particular semantic identity. There is no way in which meaning may be accurate or successfully exchanged without syntax. It is surprising that regional syntax should be so neglected.

Syntax operates by selection — in each morphological category there are usually a number of elements, or forms, which are available for selection. Only when these individual category choices are formed into a syntagmatic sequence may communication take place. What a person says is determined by what he wants to do with his utterance: what he chooses is what he says; what he says is what gets understood. The choice of any linguistic item or feature is constrained by the social and psychological disposition of the speaker, but as we are primarily concerned with syntactic choice in different parts of the country, these extra-linguistic pragmatic concerns need not detain us here. Syntactic meaning is far from delimitable in the ways in which lexical sense or reference may be considered. There are numerous external constraints on the choice of syntactic variables which necessarily conflate with, but far from fully account for, geographical variants in syntax. This paper will show that syntactic variants need not be referentially equivalent, and that the syntax of the same formal notions (such as obligation or permission) need not be identical in all parts of Britain and Ireland.

Let us now consider the implications of a number of syntactic maps. Map 8.1 reproduces *LAE* S1 and maps three responses:

(1a)   give it to me
(1b)   give it me
(1c)   give me it

to the question which was required to be completed by the informants:

(2)   Jack wants to have Tommy's ball and says to him, not Keep it! but . . . (*SED*, Questionnaire, IX. 8. 2)

In drafting the map, the editors state in the introduction that they were simply concerned with the word order — the position of *me* as one of the two complements after the main verb. The map distributes the three responses within isoglosses which appear to separate them off. At first sight, the isoglosses suggest that some areas have (1a) and not (1b) or (1c), some (1b) and not (1a) or (1c), and others (1c) and not (1a) or (1b), with the apparent implication that (1a), (1b) and (1c) are mutually exclusive, geographically restricted alternatives. While an isogloss is intended to indicate a transition zone, it is all too often interpreted as marking a boundary as abrupt as a march fence, since it appears simply as a line on the map. This may be a naive response, but we have become used to interpreting the line of the isogloss as a marker of abrupt difference in onomasiological maps generally. It is not hard to find phonological maps for localised burrs or twangs, for instance, or lexical maps for local

Map 8.1: *LAE* S1: *give it me*

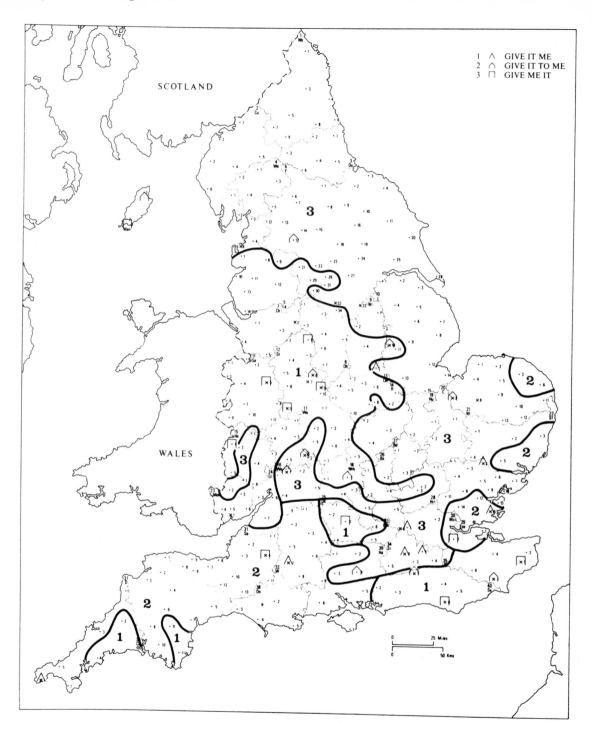

words, which show distributions which appear to stop at a very sharp border. The lexical Maps 3.3 to 3.5 and the phonological Maps 10.10-10.12 in this volume make this point. Although this use of an undifferentiated isogloss in the *LAE* has been criticised, lines on a map have a number of unique advantages over other mapping styles, as the bundling of heteroglosses in Map 7.1, for instance, makes clear.

Syntax is different. Most speakers could readily produce all three of the mapped responses in Map 8.1 whereas no speaker (apart from schooled dialectologists) would be likely to share *dolly posh* and *draidlock* in their vernacular vocabularies. Whereas the use of *dolly posh* and *draidlock* contrast with the use of Standard words or other, probably periphrastic, expressions, no such contrast is possible in the case of, for example, variant word ordering, most modal verbs, or past tense *never*. Our interest in Map 8.1 is not derived from the differences between the grammatical forms of *give*, *it* or *me*, nor from *give* as a lexical item, but rather from the variant linear arrangements of word order, from the regional distribution of these variants, which happens to be quite neat, and from the fact that these responses from across England were but three from what might have been a much larger set of possibilities, such as I shall now suggest.

Although SED did not record an undeleted subject in this context, no matter what its stylistic implications might have been, its occurrence from a syntactic point of view would have been entirely respectable, i.e.

(2a)   you give it to me
(2b)   you give it me
(2c)   you give me it

Had the second person pronoun of direct appeal to an interlocutor not been deleted, it would have been eligible, through other processes of linear arrangement, for a number of positions in the sentence, by inversion:

(3a)   give you it me

or by extraposition:

(3b)   give me it you

These utterances, however, are not so readily interchangeable and are hardly synonymous. The range of options could be further extended by local forms of the second person pronoun, such as *thou* in many parts of England:

(4a)   give thou me it
(4b)   give me it thou

Nor does Map 8.1 provide a systematic account of regional variation within the imperative, even though there was no occasion when imperatives were not elicited. What the map displays is nothing other than the answers to the particular question posed to SED informants. For better or worse, it has no other mandate for the study of synchronic variation in syntax. Variation is available to all speakers as part of their communicative code, but the questions eliciting instances of the variation in word order represented here required of informant after informant only *one* utterance. While the map represents the responses elicited by the survey and this is all it can do, these responses amount to only some of the possible variants. The map does not reveal all the likely variants in an imperative construction with two pronoun complements. It does not identify new variants. It does not explain the regional preferences for one form of word order over another in this one context, nor the different possibilities available for saying the same thing in different parts of the country or in any one place.

If we recall that even the syntactic features were elicited onomasiologically rather than by any other means, as we shall see below, this shortfall of explanation about the syntax in question may hardly be surprising. It is all too easy to criticise the map by overlooking the fact that it has no other mandate than the particular questions which were put to informants and which were thus instrumental in eliciting the data which the maps represent. Some of these questions will now be reviewed here, bearing in mind the intention of the Survey's directors who devised the questions.

In interpreting *LAE* maps we should never forget Orton and Dieth's interest in the historical evolution of the language. The responses on Map 8.1 *give it to me*, *give it me* and *give me it* represent a historical pattern of syntactic evolution. *Give it to me* is the most historical form in that *me*, by its role in the activity of the main verb *give* as the benefactive or recipient, was originally, in Old English, declined like a pronoun in the dative case. *It*, as the object affected by the activity of 'giving' and to which something was done, was in the accusative case. When inflectional endings were eventually lost, their function was assumed principally by prepositions and word order. Thus, out of a dative nominal group '*me* + dative inflection' there emerged a prepositional group '*to me*', with the same function. In the course of time, as this innovative *to* came to be considered as merely the marker of a form rather than of a function, it began to be omitted. The deletion of *to* produced a double complement, in which the form of the pronouns was not differentiated. In due course, as they ceased to be accompanied by any kind of pre- or post-modification, members of the same form class were free to switch themselves around. This switch placed the animate referent of the complement beside the main verb *give*, which denotes an animate activity. What motivated this switch of pronouns could be said to be a conspiracy which was operating to bring items marked for animacy closer together in the sentence.

The dating of these changes is relative, for in the past, as today, there was considerable overlap, but the following sentences from comparable Biblical translations bear out the point:

(5a)   1000 *fæder syle me (DATIVE) minne dæl minre æhta*

(5b)   1400 *fadir ȝyue to me the porcioun of substaunce*

(5c)   1611 *father giue me the portion of goods*

(5d)   1961 *father give me my share of the property*

The history of the construction helps to explain the geographical distribution of responses on Map 8.1. Orton and Dieth's objective was to find the oldest kind of vernacular speech possible. 'Their primary aim therefore must be to compile a corpus of the oldest and most conservative forms of dialect speech, which would both demonstrate the continuity and historical development of the language', wrote the editors in the introduction to the *LAE*, 'and also serve as a historical baseline against which future studies could be measured.' The success of both of these achievements is discussed by Stewart Sanderson

and John Widdowson in paper 2 of this volume.

Compiled from present-day information, Map 8.1 has significant historical implications. In the regional dialects of English the oldest form *give it to me* is confined to the South-west and to sporadic occurrences in East Anglia and the Thames estuary. It can be seen that *give it me*, as the intermediate stage of the historical development, almost invariably occurs on the map in areas between *give it to me* and *give me it*. Thus those areas occupied by *give it me* have some claim to being transitional, where the historical influences had not fully broken down and most recent influences had not fully worked through. What the map presents, in effect, is a neat set of historically evolving paradigmatic choices. To make this process clearer, the responses are redrafted by means of separate symbols in Map 8.2. Apart from a few exceptions, this map shows how the most recent form appears to be intruding into the historical and transitional areas quite forcefully, and thus how the historical forms appear to be receding by taking to the hills or the coast and how the transitional areas are gradually adopting the newer form. Map 8.2 is at once diachronic and diatopic. Location symbols of the same size and order are used. The historical *give it to me* is represented by an open symbol, the most recent *give me it* by a closed symbol, the transitional *give it me* by a divided symbol. By redrafting the responses impressionistically, using location symbols, I have attempted to state this dynamic interplay between history and geography in the development of the grammar of spoken English in England.

Map 8.3, which has an altogether different syntactic interest, reproduces *LAE* S9, and concerns the substitution of *not* by elaborated use of *never* as restricted to simple past tense forms of certain kinds of verb. The map suggests that this function of *never* is not very widespread. In the greatest number of cases *not* is the form recorded, albeit by a range of tokens which have phonological rather than syntactic significance (for instance, whether *not* occurs as a syllabic isolate; whether *not* is cliticised; if *not* is cliticised, whether it is syllabic or non-syllabic; whether the final consonant of *not* is present or absent; all of which need not concern us here). It is generally accepted that the meaning of this use of *never* may be glossed as 'not on one specific occasion'.

Map 8.2:   *SED: give it me*

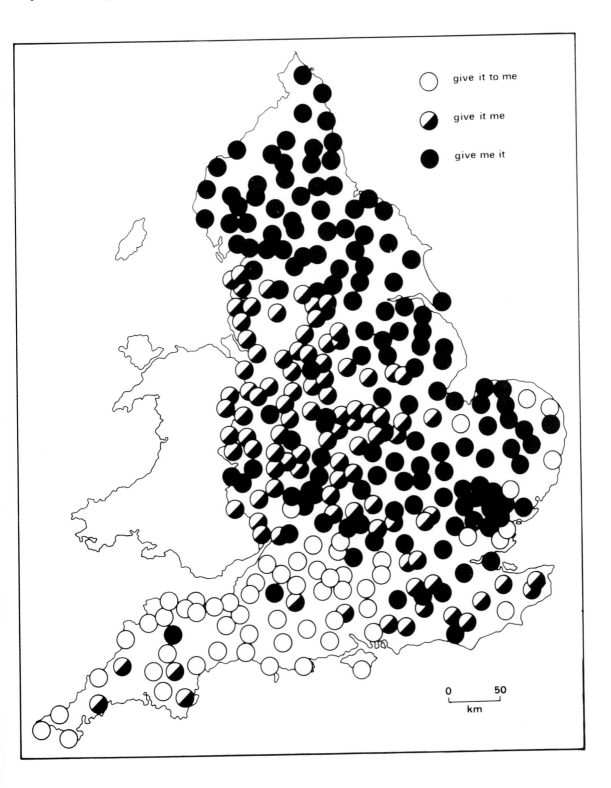

give it to me

give it me

give me it

0   50
km

Map 8.3: *LAE* S9: *did not do*

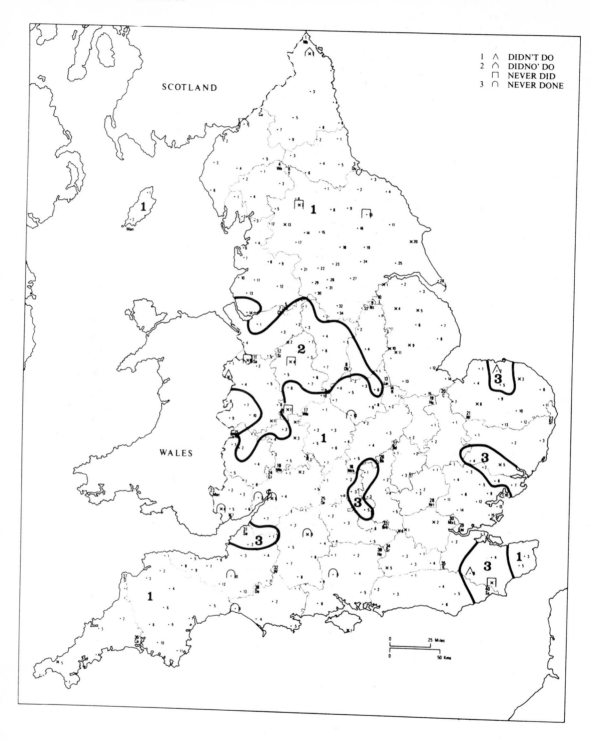

By contrast, in their useful, albeit impressionistically based handbook on *English Accents and Dialects*, Arthur Hughes and Peter Trudgill (1979: 16) state quite assertively that *never* as a past tense negative marker is very widespread and generally British. Recent work in various parts of the country confirms this claim. Jenny Cheshire has found it in Reading (Cheshire 1982), it has been found in Central Scotland (e.g. Miller and Brown 1982) and elsewhere (e.g. in Greater Manchester by Graham Shorrocks (1980), in Cheshire by Peter Anderson (1979), and in Belfast by Jim Milroy (1981)).

As a negative marker there is no question of its extension to other non-past tenses, so that the following *not/never* contrast in present tense examples remains functional:

(6a) I never drink beer, and I'm certainly not starting to do so now.

(6b) I never eat potatoes, and I'm not having any to please you.

Nor are we concerned with *never* as a marker of emphatic denial.

When *never* occurs as a past tense marker of negation it is usually in the context of reporting about or commenting upon an event or activity, for example:

(7a) I got to Woolworths and Boots the Chemists, but I never got to Marks and Spencers.

(7b) If you think it was me who did it, you're mistaken. I never kicked the ball through the window.

Functional contrasts between *not* and *never* may be obscured in the past tense:

(7c) Peter never buys anyone a drink, and he never bought a round last night either.

The use of *never* with stative verbs or with verbs of psychological activity would appear to be avoided. These brief observations might sufficiently establish the behaviour of non-standard *never* for the present.

Let us now consider the SED question which elicited the *never* responses. It meets the above constraints:

(8) Your wife suddenly says to you: The vase is broken and you at once say: Well, I can truthfully say (. . . . .) it. (*SED*, questionnaire, IX, 5, 5)

The question poses an environment which is certainly conducive enough to the occurrence of negative *never*. But as it is so widespread in non-standard speech, why are there so few *nevers* recorded in *SED*? Is elaborated *never* so recent that it has spread itself, like wildfire, all over the country in the course of the past thirty years? Innovatory lexical items may spread very quickly, as for instance *clone*, *preppy*, and *punk* have done. Innovations in the category of polarity markers, however, do not tend to capture the imagination overnight. Lexical epithets, particularly if they or their referents are destined to be shortlived may be interchanged or substituted time and time again. A polarity marker, however, simply redistributes part of the semantics of negation which always was, and always will be, in the communicative system. Perhaps my question should be rephrased: why does SED record so few examples of this redistributed meaning of *never* as 'not on one occasion' in such an apparently telling example?

Cheshire (1982: 70) has offered us one explanation. She bases her point on the claim that there is a certain linguistic process whereby grammatical items change in the direction of the standard language. Thus all *LAE*'s *nots* have undergone this change, leaving the earlier *nevers* as evidence for the language prior to it. In the light of the foregoing, Cheshire's argument is challenging, even though the other available evidence points in the opposite direction. Jespersen (1940), in his historical grammar quoted by Cheshire in other parts of her description of Reading English, does not comment on the matter.

The question may be answered differently. Ever since Labov undertook his work on non-standard American English, sociolinguistic dialectologists have been interested in an individual's possible range of variation among his speech styles. Thus unscripted spontaneous speech among intimate friends and relatives at home is said to be 'casual' or relatively informal. Answers to questions, in particular answers to questions by a stranger, are said to be much more formal. The reading of a list of words is considered to be the most formal speaking style of all, and may be referred to as a person's 'word-list style'. As Paul Johnston has shown earlier in this volume, particularly with pronunciation in mind, many SED questions could be categorised as such, as the informant is only expected to utter one single word at a time.

By the nature of syntax, it would be difficult to elicit its features by questionnaire techniques in such a way that the responses may be taken to conform — or fail to conform — to certain stylistic norms. But if that were possible, responses to questions which required informants to talk about particular topics spontaneously, or even to complete an imagined sentence, would likely be less formal on a bipolar scale of relative stylistic formality/ informality than those to questions which required informants to name an object. In addition, example (8)'s suggested context of familial intimacy, substituting for a communicative exchange with an unknown fieldworker, might imply a further degree of intimacy.

But how is this profile of increasing informality reconciled with the pragmatic status of the imaginary exchanges? The first contains an indirectly implied accusation, the second its refutation, followed by a declaration of innocence. The latter is made more formal by the qualifying adjunct *truthfully*, which not only makes the utterance an emphatic assertion of innocence, but also requires the standard negative form to achieve it. The SED question converts — probably unwittingly — the basic activity of elicitation of a marker of past tense negation, in what was presumably intended to be a straightforward manner, into a short exchange of assumption, refutation and assertion. It is hard to reconcile this exchange to its function. Its parts cut across each other and do not produce a single unified stimulus. No matter how the map is drafted, one is forced to conclude that the data is simply not available with which a revealing, or even a historical, statement about the variation within this particular negative marker might be made.

What might have been explored by the question was the avoidance of a past tense auxiliary *do* in negative sentences. Compare:

(9a) did not speak
(9b) never spoke

where the distinction gets neutralised when *never*

stands for a universal as well as a specific temporal reference. There is increasing evidence from recent work that there is a conspiracy to avoid *do* as an auxiliary verb, and its avoidance in this past tense negative example would be one such type. It is not known how regionally restricted in Britain and Ireland this phenomenon is.

Further, I know of no evidence which suggests that *never* is elaborated in other tenses. Thus there is no neutralisation of function (and so no ambiguity) in the following examples:

(9a) I never smoke
(9b) I have never smoked
(9c) I had never smoked
(9d) I will never smoke

If SED elicits deleted syntactic items, then it is usually accidentally; it did not set out to elicit instances of zero responses where items might be deleted, although it is well known that the definite article, for instance, is deleted in certain functions in many parts of the North. It is not that deleted auxiliaries are a rare phenomenon, rather their absence as a syntactic phenomenon defeated the SED methodology and is only being redressed in corpus-based studies (of hours and, accumulatively, days of spoken English) such as Miller and Brown's survey of spoken Scottish English or my own survey of varieties of the written language. Consider the following examples taken from this latter survey:

(10a) Whit ye gonnae dae wi them?
(10b) Whit ye daein wi that auld thing?
(10c) Whit yese talkin aboot, youse?
(10d) How we gonnae find him?

The use of deleted copulas is clearly idiolectal. Editorial parentheses in the popular national magazine *Private Eye* suggest that the deleted copula is also widespread and acceptable. Consider the following example:

(11a) Academic Press churns out 250 titles a year on obscure subjects like paleo-semantics and anthroposcopy (what they? Ed.) . . . (*Private Eye*, April 1983)

Verbless clauses are also common spoken features of both standard and non-standard.

Compare the following Scottish concessive paratactic clauses:

(10g) an me wi ma bad leg tae
(10h) an her in bed wi' her stomach tae
(10i) an him pushin a wheelbarrow

with

(11)   with Margaret unwell, . . .

From these remarks it may be inferred that non-standard *never* or the deletion of auxiliary verb operators or copulas are more revealing as markers of speech style than as markers of regional speech. Although examples (10a-d) and (11) are from written sources, their reproduction of spoken speech is plausible and highly realistic.

In an article on the modal verbs Gunnel Melchers produces a title-less map, presumably of *must*, based on the responses to the SED question (Melchers 1980: 120):

(12)   You needn't do that job today if you don't want to, but tomorrow you really . . . do it. (SED, Questionnaire, IX, 4, 11)

The variants of *must* displayed on the map are *mun, have to, will have to, shall have to, got to, have got to, boun to*. Only *mun*, and *boun to*, are exclusively regional forms, unknown in the standard language. As Melchers's cartography does not lend itself to reproduction here, I have redrafted these responses symbolically in Map 8.4.[3]

The interpretation of Melchers's map presents some difficulties. Not only has she conflated symbolic with isoglossic mapping techniques, she appears to have overlooked the incompatibility of such coding. Nowhere does she discuss what she attempted to state in the map.

Map 8.4 represents an attempt to capture linguistic variation by introducing multi-valued symbols to British dialect cartography. It is indisputable that the question elicited responses to the notion of 'obligation'. It follows that the subject of the map is 'obligation' and that the map charts its responses throughout England. Five major contrastive types were found: *must, mun, have to, got to*, and *boun to*. Up to three types may be recorded from any one locality, and in fact only three localities were recorded as

displaying more than two types. Either one or two types were found, and in those locations with only one it was usually *must* or *mun*. *Must* is by far the commonest type, but it is not universal, and is frequently replaced in Cheshire, Lancashire and Yorkshire. On the grounds that five types did occur, it follows that, in the mapping, 'obligation' is represented by the location circles, and that each response type is allocated a segment equivalent to one fifth of the circle. The appropriate segment is filled in when each response type occurs.

The map raises a number of questions. Firstly, as the variant forms have all been recorded in the same environment, may they all be taken, at least in these places, as onomasiological expressions of 'obligation'? In other words, are they referentially equivalent? Secondly, where *must* occurs as well as one of the variants, may the two forms be taken to be synonymous? Thirdly, may we infer that, in those, certainly few and northerly, locations where no *must* is recorded, *must* is unknown in the sense of 'obligation', and thus that the modal system has redistributed 'obligation' to another form? Finally, from this one example of modal verb behaviour, and leaving aside the function of modal adjectives and modal nouns, which tend to be less frequent in non-standard speech anyway, may we infer that, for any part of the country, there is a different distribution of modality among locally found modal verbs?

Miller and Brown's work in Central Scotland (1980) has shown that *may* and *shall* are absent, *ought* is missing, that *might*, whilst present, may be adverbial rather than modal in function, and that *must* is purely epistemic. What has happened is that the functions with which these verbs are associated have been transferred in Standard English to other verbs in the modal system or even to a number of verbs usually outside it, all of which express some kind of modality, at least in meaning.

The investigation of syntax through SED questions appears to create a paradox. While the elicitation was carefully controlled by the questions, the responses do not lend themselves to comparison with each other on a one-to-one basis. Even if the present data was gathered into systems for mapping, the systems, certainly for the modal verbs, would not be complete. Difficult though it is to make *ad hoc* comparisons of use with the modals in Standard English, it

Map 8.4:   *SED:* 'obligation'

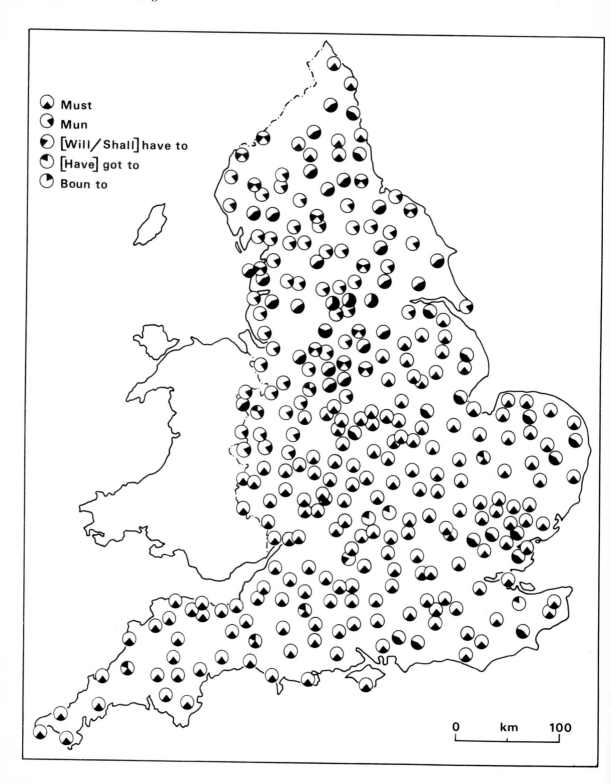

would be very much harder to make comparisons of whole systems between regions based on SED. The quantitative approaches of identity and coherency outlined by Wolfgang Viereck in chapter 6 of this volume — if restricted only to the modals — might be the best attempt that could be made. And as far as maps are concerned, there will be no genuine syntactic maps of the UK until the variables for each have been quantified by region, as H.B. Allen was able to do for lexis in *The Linguistic Atlas of the Upper Midwest*, or by location, as J. Séguy did for phonology in his *Atlas Linguistique de la Gascogne*. Map 8.4 is a first step in this direction.

Some verbs are born modals, some have historically become modals, and dialect surveys such as Miller and Brown's show that some verbs have modality thrust upon them. How else would examples of *get* such as

(13)   as that way I get drinking twice as much

be explained? The point is not that *get* is peculiarly Scottish, but rather that this particular use of *get*, expressing 'permission', is. Not surprisingly, it occurs in the syntactic environment 'get + gerund' which is also extremely rare. I have also heard it from students and office workers in Northern Ireland (e.g. *to get doing something, to get keeping something*). Although there are hundreds of examples of *get* in the Brown Corpus of Standard American English and in the Lancaster-Oslo/Bergen Corpus of Standard British English, there are no examples of this construction or meaning. In the written sources for my survey of Scottish English I have found the 'permission' meaning but with an infinitive, and not a gerund, construction:

(14a)   Did you get to have a look?
(14b)   How would I get to look at the boy?
(14c)   How come I don't get to see my own daughter . . . eh?
(14d)   I never got to sign a form or nothing . . . no.

It is difficult to imagine how many questions would be required to elicit all *gets* and to isolate 'get permission' and 'have got to obligation' in particular, using SED methodology. Such items have not been identified before because our methodologies have prevented us from eliciting

them. Quite apart from identifying their functions, we are still a long way off from drawing isoglosses round meaningful regional patterns. From corpus-based studies of large numbers of lengthy conversations or of written texts, however, particularly through the use of the computer, all occurrences or absences (e.g. no *mays*) of a particular item (e.g. all *gets*) may now be identified, as well as all the environments (e.g. 'get + gerund'). I doubt if elicitive questions would have revealed that most of my written examples of Scottish 'get permission' occur in the interrogative mood.

Traditional dialect studies continue to report that, for instance, in the dialect of Bolton, Greater Manchester, *mun* has the meaning of 'must' (Shorrocks 1980: 599), as Map 8.4 also suggests. The only qualification of this statement refers to the replacement of *mun* by *must* in what the author calls 'modified speech' (Shorrocks 1980: 600). The range of meanings of *must* is not, however, revealed. Despite copious fieldwork, we are not told whether *mun* and *must* are referentially equivalent. That they are stylistic variants is supported by comments made by informants, recorded by SED in its Incidental Material, and excerpted by Melchers.

In a very recent paper Ossi Ihalainen (1983) pointed to the continuing presence of the present tense indeclinable *be* forms in Somerset. While it is undoubtedly true that these forms continue to occur there, it is unlikely that they replace the standard forms of the copula either as a main verb or as auxiliary verbs in every case, or that their occurrence is not in some way affected by mood or polarity. The chances are that these *be* forms are primarily habitual (e.g. *they be going there every day, he be working there thirty years*) and are rare in some environments, and avoided in others, such as positive existential sentences (*there be a God*). Thus, Somerset *be* is a significant local marker, not as a local form, but because it behaves in a locally restricted way. In other words, its syntactic, and so semantic, functions are local. It is not substitutable for all standard forms, nor is it referentially equivalent. Likewise its cliticised forms with the negative polarity marker, as in *them beint nar chickens, them be ducks*. Without a large battery of comparable and contrastable examples, it is hard to establish regional syntactic behaviour conclusively. A lot of dialectology remains impressionistic.

By eliciting only the copula and *to be* as an auxiliary verb, which are nationally distributed, and no other functions, it is impossible to draw conclusions both about the types of localised usages of the verb *to be* and the extent of their distribution. As the editors of *LAE* point out, the thrust of these copula maps is, once again, historical — to show the extent to which the persistence of *be*, *bin*, *bist* forms is socially and functionally restricted, being usually avoided in the serious, permanent or public forms of discourse for which standard forms are considered the norm. Other aspects of Ihalainen's work have also been discussed recently by Bert Weltens (1983).

Possibly the only comparisons which have been tackled between corpora of English are those between the regional standard varieties of British and American English. Although their comparison is beyond the scope of this volume, they offer very useful models. In a study of *shall*, *will*, *should* and *would* in British and American English Inger Krogvig and Stig Johansson (1981) found that *shall* and *should* are more frequent in the LOB Corpus than in the Brown Corpus, and that the higher number of occurrences of *shall* and *should* in the British material is not matched by a corresponding increase of *will* and *would* in the American material. Krogvig and Johansson were able to evaluate the frequencies of occurrences of these verbs in relation to person (the higher scores of *shall* in British English are due to its occurrence with a first person subject), to clause type (independent declarative clauses, questions, and subordinate clauses), and to the type of text (while *shall* is mainly a feature of informative prose, the main difference was found in imaginative prose where LOB had a strikingly higher frequency of *shall*). Variation by clause or text type is prohibited in an oral single-style survey such as SED, although it should perhaps be added that the Brown and LOB corpora represent ideals probably unobtainable in the investigation and description of regional syntax in Britain and Ireland.

Figure 8.1 compares three recent studies with the SED. Cheshire (1979, 1982) is a study of Reading. Miller and Brown (1980, 1982) is a study of Central Scotland, principally Edinburgh. Both have already been referred to.

The third is by Dr Viv Edwards, Professor Peter Trudgill and Dr Bert Weltens.[4] With the support of the Social Sciences Research Council, Edwards, Trudgill and Weltens set out to review all the work that had been done, or was in progress, on non-standard grammar in the UK. They gave prominence to syntax. Their report provides an extremely useful checklist, as well as a summary, both of grammatical features and where they occur, and of areas and what is known about their grammar. While some studies are classified by both grammar and area, most of them are primarily regional. In addition to many examples the authors have added commentaries and made suggestions for areas of grammar which they have identified as repaying further investigation. Their interest is defined as being all aspects of grammar which are at variance with the grammar of Standard English, which of course is well documented. In their survey the authors were not obliged to distinguish between types of non-standard variation, as it was sufficient to assume that the standard language is non-regional in character, in England at least. Some dialectologists, Trudgill himself for one, would hold that the definition of the standard language should exclude pronunciation as a criterion. If this is accepted, then the distinction between standard non-regional language and non-standard regional language is one of analytical bias and lies with the functions to which the two dialects are put. By such functional criteria, the Cheshire and Miller and Brown studies are unquestionably non-standard. I have discussed the relationship between Scottish Standard English and Scottish non-standard English elsewhere (Kirk 1981).

It might be practical to think of the Edwards/ Trudgill/Weltens report as a programme for a new survey of English regional dialects within the UK. Fortunately, they are neither prescriptive nor programmatic. They realise the difficulties of conducting a *nationwide* survey of regional syntax. To my knowledge, Trudgill appears to be alone among *LAE* reviewers to have turned his attention to this matter (see note 2).

Figure 8.1 attempts to characterise current research practice on regional syntax schematically. Its entries show that what is now being investigated are systems of items and functions of items, especially if the latter are semantically significant. With few exceptions, Cheshire and Miller and Brown may be taken to represent the first two case-studies of this new nationwide survey. And there are other candidates for inclusion already. Their findings substantiate much of the Edwards/Trudgill/Weltens blueprint (with, perhaps, the exception of Cheshire's conspicuously absent modal verbs). By producing, in columns 1-3, these syntactic inventories of work completed or of work proposed, my intention is to draw a contrast with the methodology of SED. SED investigated for syntax only a limited number of particular items which had been previously identified from, and in terms of, Standard English, some of them not actually directly. As a basis for a systematic investigation of grammar, it is sufficient to read down column 4 and compare the inventory of any of the eleven classifications with the entries to the left (what was looked for in the Cheshire and Miller and Brown corpora and what emerged from them) to discover the inadequacies of the *SED* compared with the systematic approaches of the newer studies. They report on copious amounts of highly comparable data. Cheshire was able to load her findings formally, Miller and Brown impressionistically, with frequency scores of occurrence, particularly of items within systems, rather than of items over other items. The inventory labels those items which differ in function from the standard language as 'non-standard', which I used above for *never*. But the Scottish *had* + *have* + past participle construction (e.g. *if I hadnae've been able to swim, if I hadna've went*; also *Ah would rather they had've been on the committee, Ah wouldnae of come if Ah had of knew* (Macafee, cf. key to Map 8.5, entry 3)), which may additionally involve the syncretism of past tense and past participle forms, and which has no standard equivalent, need not be so categorised in this way.[5]

Over the SED's random questions the newer studies, based on lengthy amounts of spontaneous, unplanned, free-flowing, purportedly uninhibited conversation on a wider or narrower range of topics, are making significant strides forward. There is no doubt that the fieldwork has thrown up spoken English as it really is, for only in this way may speech-orientated devices be identified, such as the devices which make constituents prominent in discourse. When, collectively, this multifarious contribution to our knowledge is considered, is its inability to match the uniquely nationwide coverage of the SED all that regrettable? However, it remains a disappointment that the conversational material now stored in the copious SED sound archives has never been exploited, particularly by those

fieldworkers whose subsequent university employment was to provide them with such enviable opportunities.

It has already been shown by these newer studies, and others referred to below in connection with Map 8.5, that some non-standard forms are common to a number of different parts of Britain and Ireland — notably *ain't* and *never*. Some forms are also innovatory — such as indeclinable *int-* as a tag element:

(15a) Yer a mucky pup, int' ye?
(15b) They're aa daft, in't they?
(15c) Tar's brilliant stuff, intit?
(15d) It's the truth, in't it?
(15e) Horrible, intit?
(15f) Weird that, intit?

From these findings it is premature to speculate about the emergence of a new non-standard dialect that is sufficiently widespread to be as non-regional in character as the standard. But the more we discover that what is really significant for a regional dialect is not its grammatical forms but the way it redistributes already common forms, the more one might expect such suggestions to be made again and again in the future. For the study of non-standard grammar there are undoubtedly exciting prospects ahead.

Map 8.5 charts the regional distribution of a number of recent studies of regional, non-standard grammar. Of these there are three types: those that are 'traditional', principally concerned with morphology, and usually derivative in their overall approach and scope from the SED. The second are those which investigate social variation in the dialect of a particular place, usually by age, sex and style. The third are more narrowly descriptive, being purely concerned with the identification and a more or less close description of all aspects of the syntax which emerge from the data, although there might be some overlap with the approach of the second type. The three may be thought of as 'traditional', 'sociolinguistic' and 'variationist'. Some are inevitably based on more data than others, some fuller in their description than others, but all of them should prove reliable for comparisons, most likely confirmations, of regional syntax.[6] Each of these types is represented in Map 8.5 by a different symbol. The symbols in turn each have two tokens which

Figure 8.1: Recent Studies of Regional Syntax

1	Features/Source	1 Edwards/Trudgill/Weltens	2 Cheshire	3 Miller/Brown	4 SED
	Negation	multiple negation auxiliaries *to be*, especially *ain't* non-standard *never* negative scope negative attraction	multiple negation negative concord non-standard *never* non-standard *ain't/int* non-standard *weren't*	multiple negation *-n't/-nae* v. *no/not* non-standard *never* non-standard *ain't/int* negative interrogatives	items *he doesn't* (etc) *he did not do* (etc) *he hasn't* (etc) *I haven't* (etc) *aren't you?* (etc) *aren't I? isn't he?* (etc) *wasn't I?* (etc) *I'm not* (etc)
2	Verb forms	present tense endings irregular past tense forms present and past tense forms of *to be* present tense *to do*	non-standard *have, has* non-standard *was, were* non-standard *does, do, dos*, and *done* non-standard *-s* before complements tense in conditional sentences function of tag questions regularisation of past tense and past participle verb forms	regularisation of past tense and past participle verb forms	lexical items variously marked for present, past and pluperfect declarative, negative and interrogative forms
3	Modal Verbs	infinitive modals double modals *must/mun shall/will going to*		possibility modals permission modals obligation modals necessity modals (*will, can, should, would, might, need to, have got to*) non-standard *get* double modals modals after *to*	items *shall* (×3) (+ neg) *should* (+ neg / + perf) *ought* (+ perf) *must* (+ neg) *may might* (+ neg) *won't can't dare not/durst not*
4	Other verb forms and constructions	imperatives infinitives perfective aspect habitual aspect passive voice	tense in conditional sentences complementisers function of tag questions	reference to future time tense in conditional sentences polar tag questions tags *e:?/e: no?* emphatic polar declaratives with *so/neither* behaviour of pluperfect in subordinate clauses *had +have +* past participle number agreement — invariable *is/was there is +* Sg/Pl N	lexical items variously marked for infinitives, imperatives, the gerund, or perfective aspect *used to*

5	Adverbs	without -*ly* intensifiers	adverbial forms comparatives		items *ajar, backwards* *forwards, diagon-* *ally, giddy, head* *over heels, on* *purpose*

6	Prepositions	substitution
		addition of a second
		  preposition
		substitution of *be-*
		  prefix by *a-*
		presence of local
		  forms
		omission
			substitution
			addition of a second
			  preposition
			reduction of com-
			  plex prepositions
			non-standard *round*
				prepositions after
				  passive verbs
				substitution of
				  locative *by*
				addition and dele-
				  tion of case
				  functions
					items
					till, beside, in front
					of, *between, among,*
					off, out of, by, with
					(each with one
					example), also *not*
					in *calf,* on *heat,* bit
					of, *whole* of it, on
					Friday week, a lot of
					money, what kind
					of?, *married* to, *so*
					old as, and *about*

7	Noun Plurals	unmarked plurality plurals in -(*e*)*n* mutated plurals zero plurals	zero plurals nouns of measurement	items — *wolfs,* *knifes, leafs*	lexical items

8	Pronouns	personal
		possessive
		relative
		interrogative
		reflexive
			non-standard *us*
			relative — *who*
			  which, that, what
			  and zero
			interrogative *what?*
			reflexive *meself*
			  hisself, ourself,
			  theirself
			non-standard *-self*
				personal — *yous*
				possessive — *mines*
				relatives — *that*
				  who and *which*
				  frequency distribut-
				  ion, and omission
				  of relatives
				reflexives — *hissel,*
				  theirsels
				shadow pronouns
				additional occur-
				  rences of personal
				  pronouns
					personal — *we two,*
					  us, me, it
					possessive — *yours*
					interrogatives — *who?*
					  whose? which one?
					relatives — *who,*
					  whose, to
					  whom, where
					reflexives — *myself*
					  (etc), *himself*
					  (etc)

9	Demonstratives	adjectives
		pronouns
			non-standard *them*	non-standard *they,*
				  they yins
					items
					this, that, these,
					  those, in this way

10	Comparison	distribution in
		  former mechan-
		  isms
		double comparison
			comparative
			  adverbs
					items
					further, older than,
					a good deal more

11	Other aspects	articles
		adjectives
		conjunctions
		genitives
		emphasis
		typical tags
		style
			complement
			  sentences
			intrusive -*s*
				articles — addi-
				  tional occurrences
				discourse tags —
				  ken, like and *see*
				complementisers
				reference and func-
				  tion of relative
				  clauses
				wh- questions
				nane
				tenses in subordin-
				  ate clauses
					adjectives — items
					round
					straight
					askew
					brittle
					great
					genitives — items
					my father's boot
					this cow's legs
					particle — *enough*

discriminate between the geographical scope of each piece of work, that is, between those of a particular place, for which a closed token symbol has been used, and those of an area, for which a hatched token symbol has been used. Two areas, Ireland and Wales, are emphatically national, and they are further distinguished as hatched token symbols which are very large. These two surveys are discussed in separate papers in this volume. This cartographical technique has been extended to Map 9.5 in this volume (*last corn sheaf* — Scotland) where it was also necessary to state two separate orders of geography. Most of these studies are noted in Edwards/Trudgill/ Weltens (1984), referred to in note 4 and discussed above.

Figure 8.2 is a scheme which attempts to set out a number of 'abstract' distinctions which may be made from our present knowledge, from investigation and description, of regional syntax in Britain and Ireland. Basically, it comprises two intersecting axes, one vertical, distinguishing spoken from written English, one horizontal, distinguishing Standard from non-standard English. It remains to be settled whether regional syntax may be nationally identified with the non-standard.

A distinction is made between Scottish Non-Standard (ci.) and the rest of non-standard English in Britain and Ireland (cii.). More is probably known about Scottish English than any other regional variety. I know of no systematic study of non-standard written material elsewhere

(dii.) apart from the separate research projects of Caroline Macafee and myself on the Scottish (di.), although Graham Shorrocks has written about the representation of local speech in Lancashire dialect writing (Shorrocks 1978). It is well known, however, that Scottish English has always enjoyed a very special relationship to its literature, which is not found elsewhere. That is just one of many reasons why the Scottish is such a highly distinctive variety of English and which would justify the retention of the line between (ci./di.) and (cii./dii.).

Nonetheless, it is challenging to speculate whether (ci.) and (cii.) and (di.) and (dii.) could eventually be subsumed completely under (c.) and (d.), with the removal of the internal lines of division in the non-standard. As it happens, there are some good grounds for such speculation. Although the informants of Miller and Brown's survey were all from, or very near, Edinburgh, it cannot be claimed of everything that was recorded that it is local to Edinburgh or Central Scotland. This is particularly true of items which are unmistakable markers of discourse. (Even samples, let alone collections, of discourse are, of course, still extremely rare.) The paucity or absence of such items from written Scottish sources lends support to the view that they are indeed discoursal. Such items include numerous particle tags such as *like*, or *see*, or *ken*, which tend to occur at the beginning or end of a sentence (but which may or may not coincide with the beginning or end of an

Figure 8.2:   English Syntax in Britain and Ireland

a. Standard (Non-Regional) Spoken English (Quirk *et al.*)		b. Standard (Non-Regional) Written English (Quirk *et al.*)	
c. Non-Standard (Regional) Spoken English	ci. Non-Standard Scottish Spoken English (Miller/Brown)	di. Non-Standard Scottish Written English (Kirk; Macafee)	d. Non-Standard (Regional) Written English
	cii. Non-Standard Non-Scottish Spoken English (Cheshire; others)	dii. Non-Standard Non-Scottish Written English (?)	

utterance) and which usually have the function of promoting an adjacent constituent. The following examples from drama scripts (except 16a) may suffice to suggest their tenor:

(16a) See my man. See fish. He hates it.
(16b) Whit are they teachin ye like?
(16c) He's hopeless like.
(16d) . . . apart fae whit a send hame tae Maw like.
(16e) An yer sister look efter ye, like?

The description of spoken and written varieties of Standard English has centred on the activities of one remarkable man, Randolph Quirk, as Director, from its inception until 1983, of the Survey of English Usage at University College, London. Since 1975 this Survey has supported a sister project, the Survey of Spoken English at the University of Lund. Quirk's many activities include co-authorship with Jan Svartvik of Lund of *A Corpus of English Conversation* (Svartvik and Quirk 1980), based on the computer-stored London-Lund Corpus of Spoken English; co-authorship with Sidney Greenbaum, Jan Svartvik and Geoffrey Leech of *A Grammar of Contemporary English* (Quirk *et al.* 1972); the authorship of other more recent related publications and again co-authorship of the new *A Comprehensive Grammar of the English Language*. These grammars, although themselves not corpus-based, have all the same been informed by those minds which have been responsible for directing the development and application of corpus-based research. In all sorts of respects, these studies of unquestionably educated, usually middle-class, language may be compared with much of the work which is being currently undertaken on non-standard English throughout the UK. It is remarkable that our recent knowledge of the standard language has come largely from one person's initiatives, which have encompassed spoken and written English in a way which appears never to have been tackled in the regional non-standard.

One of the criteria usually applied to the separate identity of regional dialects is that, as varieties of the same language, they must be mutually intelligible. With pronunciation there is usually little difficulty, for one pronunciation may be substituted for another — SED recorded all cardinal, non-cardinal, numerous central and centralised vowels, a number of on-glides, and other variants all in the one word *stone*, yet none of this large set of variants is likely to be misheard or misunderstood, and, besides, it is easy for a speaker to repeat the word with a modified, probably more standardised, pronunciation. Lexis does not present a real difficulty for mutual intelligibility either. Words are never without a syntactic context which directs the listener towards their function, and even if a word is still in doubt, its meaning may be clarified by a synonym or other descriptive periphrasis.

Syntax, however, is far more significant as far as mutual intelligibility is concerned, for syntax contains such fundamental markers of the communicative system that no substitution or explanatory repetition is possible. Let us consider two interesting sets of examples, the first from Scotland, the second from the North of Ireland, both of which may not be restricted to these areas.

The first concerns the use of declarative syntax in sentences used as interrogatives, as in:

(17a) A: You're going for your lunch now?
        B: I'm sorry.
        A: Oh, you're not going for your lunch. I thought you were.

Character B in this exchange is a highly proficient non-native speaker, a university lecturer by profession, who has learned the rules of Standard English. He hears a declarative sentence, with a falling declarative intonation, and finds the utterance puzzling. He finds it difficult to respond and apologises. Scotsman, A, myself, hears the deferential apology and takes it to be a polite refusal. He is disappointed, and, on the assumption that his original utterance has been understood, seeks confirmation of this refusal. As it is not a rule of standard English to ask a question by making a statement without modifying the polar orientation of the intonation, communication breaks down. Examples from written Scottish texts are:

(17b) A: Ye gaun tae the canteen the day?
        B: Nae option . . . nae pieces.
(17c) A: Thought they are done that in Feegie.
        B: Aye, but that's maistly the drink . . .

Map 8.5: Regional Grammar in Britain and Ireland

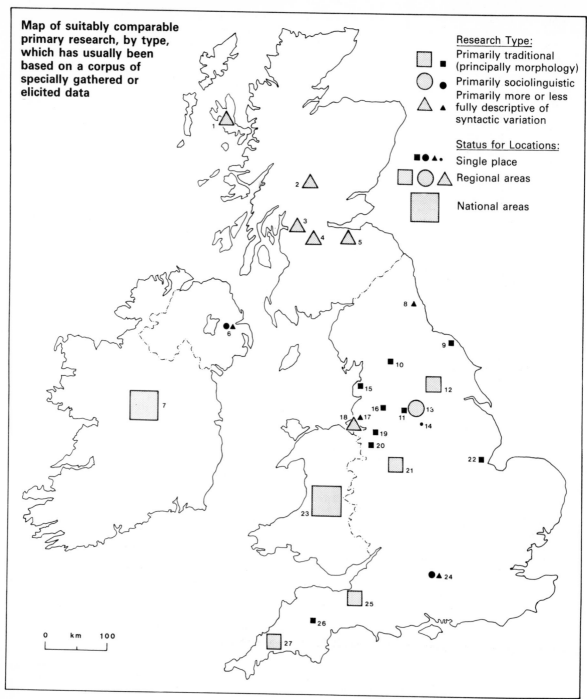

Map of suitably comparable primary research, by type, which has usually been based on a corpus of specially gathered or elicited data

Research Type:
■ Primarily traditional (principally morphology)
● Primarily sociolinguistic
▲ Primarily more or less fully descriptive of syntactic variation

Status for Locations:
■●▲• Single place
□○△ Regional areas
□ National areas

Key to Map 8.5: Regional Grammar in Britain and Ireland. Map of the major comprehensive and suitably comparable primary research, which has usually been based on a large corpus of specially gathered or elicited data of some kind, and by some methodology.

Entries are arranged under researcher.
1. A. Sabban — work in the Hebrides; cf. her *Galisch-Englischer Sprachkontakt*, Julius Groos Verlag, Heidelberg, 1982, Sammlung Groos no. 11, based on her University of Hamburg Dr. Phil. thesis.

2. A.J. Aitken — carefully impressionistic work pertaining to the whole of Scotland, which has been highly influential on most other work on Scottish English; see his 'Scottish Speech: a Historical View with Special Reference to the Standard English of Scotland', in A.J. Aitken and Tom McArthur (eds.), *Languages of Scotland*, Chambers, Edinburgh, 1979, pp. 83-118, and his two articles in Peter Trudgill (ed.), *Language in the British Isles*, Cambridge University Press, Cambridge, 1984.

3. C. Macafee — work in Central Scotland, particularly Glasgow, and on written sources; see her 'Characteristics of Non-Standard Grammar in Scotland', unpublished typescript, and her *Glasgow*, John Benjamins, Amsterdam, 1983, Varieties of English Around the World Text Series, vol. 3.

4. J.M. Kirk — work largely in Central Scotland primarily based on written sources, as a Survey of Scottish English Usage in progress; see his 'On Scottish Non-Standard English', *Nottingham Linguistic Circular*, vol. 10, no. 2, 1981, pp. 155-78, and his 'Linguistic Aspects of Twentieth-Century Written Scots', University of Sheffield PhD thesis, in preparation.

5. J. Miller and K. Brown (and others) — work in Central Scotland, particularly Edinburgh, based on continuous conversations and elicitative tests; see their Final Report to the SSRC on Grant no. HR5152, 1980, and their 'Aspects of Scottish English Syntax', *English World-Wide*, vol. 3, 1982, pp. 3-17.

6. J. and L. Milroy (and others, especially J. Harris and L. Policansky) — work in Belfast on a sociolinguistic survey of vernacular speech; see their Final Report to the SSRC on Grant no. HR5777, J. Milroy, *Regional Accents of English: Belfast*, The Blackstaff Press, Belfast 1981, and *Belfast Working Papers in Language and Linguistics*, vols. 1-6, 1977-82.

7. The Tape-Recorded Survey of Hiberno-English Speech, which is in progress and includes the collection of continuous conversations from throughout Ireland, most of which remain to be investigated; see paper 4 in this volume.

8. C. MacDonald — work in Newcastle-upon-Tyne: see her 'Variation in the Use of Modal Verbs with Special Reference to Tyneside English', unpublished PhD thesis, University of Newcastle-upon-Tyne, 1981. There appear to be no publications on grammar from the Tyneside Linguistic Survey.

9. H. Tidholm — work in North Yorkshire; see his *The Dialect of Egton in North Yorkshire*, Bokmaskinen, Göteborg, 1979, his University of Göteborg PhD thesis.

10. B. Hedevind — work in West Yorkshire; see his *The Dialect of Dentdale*, Uppsala, 1967, Studia Anglistica Upsaliensia, vol. 5, his University of Uppsala PhD thesis.

11. B.R. Dyson — work in West Yorkshire; see his 'A Synchronic Study of the Dialect of the Upper Holme in the West Riding of Yorkshire', 2 vols., unpublished PhD thesis, University of Leeds, 1960.

12. G. Melchers — work throughout Yorkshire; see her *Studies in Yorkshire Dialects*, 2 vols., Stockholm, 1972, Stockholm Theses in English, no. 9.

13. K.M. Petyt — work in West Yorkshire; see his '"Dialect" and "Accent" in the Industrial West Riding — A study of the changing speech of an urban area', unpublished PhD thesis, University of Reading, 1977, but cf. his *The Study of Dialect*, André Deutsch, London: 1980, and his *West Riding*, John Benjamins, Amsterdam: forthcoming, Varieties of English Around the World General Series.

14. J.D.A. Widdowson and G. Nixon — work in Sheffield and the surrounding area; see the archives of the Centre for English Cultural Tradition and Language, University of Sheffield, especially the pilot studies for the Survey of Sheffield Usage.

15. P. Wright — work in Fleetwood, Lancashire; see his 'Grammar of the Dialect of Fleetwood, Descriptive and Historical', 2 vols., unpublished PhD thesis, University of Leeds, 1955.

16. G. Shorrocks — work in Bolton, South Lancashire, now Greater Manchester County; see his 'A Grammar of the Dialect of Farnworth and District', unpublished PhD thesis, University of Sheffield, 1980, available from University Microfilms International, no. 8170023.

17. G. Knowles — work in Liverpool; see his 'Scouse: The Urban Dialect of Liverpool', unpublished PhD thesis, University of Leeds, 1974.

18. M. Newbrook — work on the Wirral; see his 'Socio-linguistic Reflexes of Dialect Interference in West Wirral', unpublished PhD thesis, University of Reading, 1982.

19. K. Flynn — work in Cheshire; see his 'A Grammar of the Dialect of Moulton (Cheshire)', unpublished MPhil thesis, University of Leeds, 1975.

20. P. Anderson — work in Cheshire; see his 'The Dialect of Eaton-by-Tarporley (Cheshire): A Descriptive and Historical Grammar', unpublished PhD thesis, University of Leeds, 1977.

21. P.H. Gibson — work in Staffordshire; see his 'Studies in the Linguistic Geography of Staffordshire', unpublished MA thesis, University of Leeds, 1955.

22. R. Brown — work in Lincolnshire; see his 'A Grammar of the Dialect of Great Hale, Lincolnshire', unpublished MPhil thesis, University of Leeds, 1969.

23. The Survey of Anglo-Welsh Dialects — work throughout Wales. See D. Parry (ed.), *The Survey of Anglo-Welsh Dialects*, 4 volumes: vol. 1: *The South-west*, 1977, vol. 2: *The South-east*, 1979, vols. 3 and 4, forthcoming, published by D. Parry; see also paper 3 in this volume.

24. J. Cheshire — work in Reading; see her 'Grammatical Variation in the English Spoken in Reading, Berkshire', unpublished PhD thesis, University of Reading, 1979, and her *Variation in an English Dialect*, Cambridge University Press, Cambridge, 1982.

25. O. Ihalainen — of the University of Helsinki, has conducted interviews of conversation (in Somerset) dealing with the personal histories of informants over the age of 64 which have been analysed in a number of short articles, most comprehensively in 'Relative Clauses in the Dialect of Somerset', *Neuphilologische Mitteilungen*, vol. 81, 1980, pp. 187-96.

26. M.B. Harris — work in Devon; see his 'The Phonology and Grammar of the Dialect of South Zeal, Devon', unpublished PhD thesis, University of Leeds, 1967.

27. M.F. Wakelin — work in Cornwall; see his *Language and History in Cornwall*, Leicester University Press, Leicester, 1975, and his *South-west English*, John Benjamins, Amsterdam, forthcoming, Varieties of English Around the World Text Series.

Miller and Brown's conversations produce further examples of this phenomenon:

(18a) A: So like you were left with three teachers there.
       B: Yeh.

Although, as they make clear, the example was intended to state how many teachers were left and did not have the typical Scottish interrogative intonation, nevertheless it was understood by a fellow Scottish participant in the conversation to be a question. Speaker A was checking out the facts, as it were, and B confirmed them.

(18b) So that was just like last weekend.

In example 18(b), in a discussion about hill-walking, the date of the walk is not made clear. From a previous reference the speaker guesses that it was the previous weekend. In this utterance he seeks to check his guess. It is an interrogative by intonation if not by its constituent syntactic structure. If tested as a cleft sentence, the meaning might be made clear by the rules of the standard language:

(18c) Was it just last weekend (that this happened)?

Declarative questions appear to be a feature of colloquial Standard English generally. In *A Grammar of Contemporary English* Quirk *et al.* state: 'Not all *yes-no* questions have subject-operator inversion. The declarative question is a type of question which is identical in form to a statement, except for the final rising question intonation:

(19a) You've got the exPLÓSive?
(19b) They've spoken to the amBÁSSador, of course?

Declarative questions have 'positive orientation' (or 'negative orientation')' (para. 7.61).
What distinguishes declarative questions in Scottish English, however, is the absence of this rising intonation. In their book *Questions of Intonation*, which is based on data from Edinburgh speech, Gillian Brown, Karen Currie and Joanne Kenworthy (1980) provide the following intonational transcriptions of declarative questions:

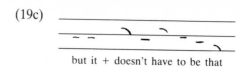

(19c)

but it + doesn't have to be that

The informant has asked the fieldworker whether it is important for the intonation survey to have equal numbers of male and female subjects. The fieldworker, one of the authors of the book, replies *we'd like a spread*. The informant then produces the utterance (19c) to which the fieldworker replies *no, not really*.

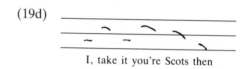

(19d)

I, take it you're Scots then

The informant has been talking to the fieldworker about the characteristics of the Scottish accent. A second fieldworker, who has been silent up until that point, remarks that when travelling abroad a Scottish accent can instantly be recognised. The informant then utters (19d). The second fieldworker replies *No, can you guess what I am? I'm very difficult, people are very confused about me.*

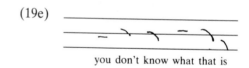

(19e)

you don't know what that is

The informant has been shown a photograph of Edinburgh and responds by saying *I just can't figure out which angle you're on at all*. The fieldworker points to a dome and utters (19e). The informant replies *No*.

As in (17b), (17c) and (18a), in each of (19c), (19d) and (19e) the interlocutor responds either affirmatively or negatively. Brown *et al.* conclude that the interlocutor interpreted the utterance as a question requiring an answer *yes* or *no* in spite of there being no formal marker, syntactic or intonational, of question function. They proceed to ask how it is that a participant in a conversation recognises that a question is being asked when an utterance is not formally marked as being a question. Perhaps the distinction question/statement is by no means as clear as is often suggested. At any rate, Brown *et al.* propose that what the speakers are producing in (19c), (19d) and (19e) are what could functionally be called 'try questions', that is they are trying out a hypothesis not only in the expectation that it is correct but also in the knowledge that they are also making a statement about what their interlocutor knows, thus thereby risking a contradiction. When an interlocutor recognises that a statement has been made about his domain of knowledge, Brown *et al.* argue, he feels free to accept or contradict it. He treats it as though it were a question. What Brown *et al.* find to be the crucial point at issue concerns who it is that is accepted by the participants as the repository of the relevant knowledge. Are the rules which decide this determined by the person who utters the falling intonation in a declarative question and expects to have it confirmed or not? In the case of (17a), A's intention was not understood. B was not in a position to confirm it. Therefore, the game could not be played on A's terms. All B can do is to apologise by appealing to the common arbiter of conventional politeness. I know myself that, on different occasions, I have been asked by other Scottish speakers to make clear whether I am telling or asking them something. These examples, with their dual focus of syntax and intonation, point to a number of fundamental aspects of effective communicative exchange about which we perhaps still know all too little, even though the following dance-hall exchange has become a familiar stereotype:

(19f) A: Are ye dancin?
       B: Are ye askin?
       A: Aye I'm askin.
       B: Well I'm dancin.

Unlike pronunciation, where repetition with greater or lesser modification is possible, or lexis, where substitution by other words or explanatory phrases is possible, it is not possible either to repeat syntax differently or to substitute for it in some other way. Each aspect of syntax is unique. If communication breaks down it may at best be clarified.

The second set of examples is taken from John Harris's work on Hiberno-English (Harris 1982) and shows how standard speaker and Ulster dialect speaker alike require to seek clarification where their syntactic systems do not coincide by mutually enquiring what the syntax actually means. These examples concern the relationships between tense/aspect and certain temporal references. They show that Hiberno-English differs in its choice of certain tenses from Standard English for reference to time which began in the past and is still continuing at the moment of speaking. Conversely, they show that the range of temporal reference in certain tense choices in each system is different.

(20) Standard Speaker: How long are you staying here?
      Ulster Speaker: Since Monday.

The regional dialect speaker understands the meaning of the tense here to refer to the past and replies accordingly, as happens, incidentally, in other languages, notably German (e.g. *Seit wann bist Du hier?*). When the dialect speaker asks the standard speaker the same question, the standard speaker responds to what he has heard with reference to the rules of the standard language and expresses a time in the future. This confuses the dialect speaker who has to have a second go to clarify what he meant by asking a different question altogether.

(21) Ulster Speaker: How long are you here, then?
      Standard Speaker: Well, I'm thinking of leaving next Thursday.
      Ulster Speaker: Oh, . . . I mean, . . . When did you get here?
      Standard Speaker: Just this morning, actually.

The request about length of time becomes a request to know when the time began. Thus a past tense, periphrastic *do* interrogative is used, which dialect and standard speakers both understand.

In these examples the confusion is clarified immediately. In the following set of exchanges it is carried on because what is said is generally not specific enough to block the communication flow. Only after the Standard speaker's second utterance does the Ulster dialect speaker, but not the standard speaker, become confused.

(22) Ulster Speaker: How long are you here, Mike?
      Standard Speaker: Oh, just a couple of days.
      Ulster Speaker: Funny I didn't bump into you before, isn't it?

Standard Speaker: Well, I only got in a couple of hours ago
Ulster Speaker: Uh? . . .
Standard Speaker: So, how are things anyway?

These examples show that syntactic systems are different in regional dialects from the standard language. They are not isomorphous. There is a structural mismatch of the verbal system. When an instance of one system is interpreted by the rules pertaining to another, confusion arises and the intended communication does not take place. The speakers do not have even a passive competence of each other's dialect. What is characteristic of local dialect is only isolated in the data by this communicative breakdown.

Thus these examples further show that non-standard and standard speakers do not have the polylectal competence it was once thought they did. Harris takes them as evidence for the claim that there is no structural identity underlying all types of English. In other words, there are different ways of producing the same referential effect, in this case, time, in different parts of the country.

From these Scottish and Irish examples we may draw a remarkable methodological inference. Whereas answers to questions in 'word list style' may once have formed a satisfactory discovery procedure for eliciting information about regional variation in syntax, collections of continuous free conversations have come to form the current prevailing practice. The question now is whether dialectologists should turn their attention to a methodology for analysing exchanges which are unsuccessful as communication. It is generally assumed that people converse without difficulty. But where they do not succeed linguistically, where there is a shortfall of meaning, is that where the frontiers of regional syntactic variation lie? May syntactic isoglosses stand for the boundaries of effective and efficient communication?

It is exciting to think that if we had enough regional information from throughout the UK about such patterns of variation as in the interrogative, in tense/aspect distinctions, or the modals, we could construct a set of multivariable symbols for syntax in each area and plot them on a map, with the result that the isoglosses which may be drawn between these

symbols may be interpreted as transitional areas — as the editors of *LAE* would have it — between fundamentally different communicative systems. They would in effect be *isolects*.

The problem of non-responses is not a new one. It has been known for some time that the definite article is omitted or inserted before certain classes of nominal heads, some in Scotland (cf. the entry for *the* in *The Scottish National Dictionary*), some in the North of England (see Shorrocks 1978), which are not so productive in the standard language. Questionnaire techniques, written or spoken, have usually presented informants with examples of the environment in which the definite article might have occurred. But they fall short of extracting an exchange between either dialect speakers, or dialect and standard speakers, to show whether the presence or absence of the article directly affects the meaning and understanding. Continuous conversation is likely to provide some commentary on the status of the variant. SED falls short of providing this information, except perhaps incidentally in the fieldworker's informal notes.

Let us consider the example of the second person pronoun. It appears to be universal in all varieties of English in Ulster that *you* is understood as a reference to only one person and no more. To refer to more than one person, everybody always has to say *youse*. It is a grammatical rule. Even the phatic leavetaking *see you* gives ready offence if uttered, even by an outsider, to a group of more than one person. I recall the following exchange I had with some Belfast youngsters who were annoying me by playing football on the private car park below the windows of the flat in which I live:

(23)   JMK: Will you please play your football in the park?
Boy: Why just me? Will you tell the others as well, mister?

Although this is a single anecdotal example, as are John Harris's examples, it highlights the value of data based on spoken exchanges, which provides the substance of the linguistic description. Lesley Milroy (1980) had a similar example concerning the use of this pronoun:

(24)   So I says to our Trish and our Sandra: 'Youse wash the dishes!' I might as well

have said 'You wash the dishes,' for our Trish just got up and put her coat on and walked out.

These commentaries in exchanges between dialect and standard speakers valuably discriminate regional shibboleths.

Such variation is, of course, by no means confined to the non-standard. Commentaries on language change and variation are commonplace in fictional writing of all kinds. Consider the following example from Kingsley Amis's *Jake's Thing* (1978: 9):

(25)   Now Dr Curnow shook his head a few times and swallowed. In the end he said, 'There's nothing I can do for you.'
'Oh, but surely you must have a —'
'No. The only way is for me to send you to someone.'
'That was rather what I —'
'Excuse me a second, would you please?'
Funny how it's got ruder to say please than not, Jake thought to himself as the doctor began to turn slowly through a small leather-bound book on his desk.

The question of interviewer's accent and the role of bi-dialectalism as an elicitative technique have already been raised in paper 4 of this volume, and I would only add that I doubt that mono-dialectal conversations are always methodologically preferable to the bi- or perhaps even poly-dialectal. After all, few would deny the permanent achievements of those dialectologists of English who were not themselves native English speakers. In their work Miller and Brown make an effort to defend mono-dialectalism as an external constraint on the elicitation of data which should be held constant. But whether one should hold the dialect, or some other external constraint, constant, is a profound matter of methodological procedure. I merely suggest that a further observer's paradox may reside in the fact that what he is observing (communication and breakdown) is the complete absence of what he believes he is observing (communication).

In the final part of this paper some formal implications of regional variation in the syntax of Britain and Ireland will be considered. I have already discussed a number of syntactic variants

which reveal contrasts between standard and regional, as well as between standard and non-standard, usage. Dialectologists, including myself (Kirk, 1981), have examined such variants as evidence for the existence of poly-lectal grammars. That is to say, although there were a great many systematic differences of syntax between standard and non-standard language in Scotland, they may all be explained, to borrow the jargon from transformational grammarians, in terms of late realisation rules of the same, deep, underlying and structurally identical system. And that these surface differences were superficial and did not amount to differences of deep grammar or of any abstract kind. Tense, or interrogation, or modality, or the pronouns, *qua* systems, *langue*, were not affected at any abstract level. Rather, the variation was restricted to the surface level, *parole*. Such was the nature of the variation occurring anyway in the standard language that the differences in the non-standard could be readily accounted for by an extension of the description of that variation. Of her findings concerning non-standard English in Reading, Jenny Cheshire has also said as much.

The evidence from the Scottish and Irish examples, where communication failed, forces me to reconsider that position. Harris (1982), challenges the view of polylectal grammars, which was first advanced about ten years ago by Charles-James N. Bailey (1973). The nature of the communication is of such a fundamental order that it cannot be explained in terms of late realisations of an identical deep system. For Harris, it is the deep systems of Ulster English and Standard English which are not identical, non-isomorphous, and which give rise to the breakdown in communication. His arguments remove a deep *v.* surface distinction on the grounds that such a distinction is not tenable in connection with the fundamental predicators of the logical systems (such as mood or polarity or temporal reference). In the above exchanges, (20-2), Ulster and Standard Anglo-English speakers were responding to their own coherent systems.

It is by reference to their own coherent systems of some of his student informants that Peter Trudgill also argues against the notion of polytectal grammars (Trudgill 1983). If speakers have polylectal grammars, then it would follow that they would find as acceptable all such variants of a grammatical variable as might readily occur from area to area. For the idea behind the notion of polylectalism was that it should incorporate, as a model of competence, not simply a few but all varieties of a particular language, but also, by showing how interrelated the varieties or lects of a language were, it should prove that a speaker's passive competence far exceeded his active. To test this hypothesis Trudgill presented a test of sentences from several UK varieties of English to some 111 university-based informants, largely students. It contained the following sentences:

(26a) Look — is that a man stand there? (East Anglia)
(26b) My hair needs washed. (Scotland)
(26c) I'm not sure — I might could do it. (Scotland)
(26d) She love him very much. (East Anglia)
(26e) Where's my book? — Ah, here it's. (West Highlands of Scotland)
(26f) Wait a minute — I'm now coming. (East Anglia)
(26g) Had you a good time last night? (Scotland)
(26h) It's dangerous to smoke at a petrol station without causing an explosion: petrol is very inflammable. (South Wales)

Informants were asked to state whether these sentences were acceptable to them as sentences of English. Remarkably high scores were returned that these sentences would not be acceptable. If they had a polylectal competence, it certainly did not extend to accepting these sentences, in the way the proponents of poly-lectalism would have us believe. From an active competence in their own dialect there did not emerge a passive competence for others. Yet sentences (26a-h) are typical examples of variation in regional syntax, and I have listed their areas of provenance alongside them. There is nothing spurious about the examples. Trudgill concludes that native speakers of English are not able to employ their passive competence in making grammaticality judgments about forms which they do not use themselves but which are habitually used by speakers elsewhere in the country or by members of the same class. Thus, for Trudgill at least, polylectal competence is a

myth; he maintains that there is no one single competence for English. Rather, speakers have their individual competences which have been developed by their permanent characteristics and other such features as exposure to, and tolerance for, variants of syntactic variables not shared by, or familiar to, themselves. That speakers all have their own competences in the language is borne out by the examples from Scotland and Ireland in that the breakdown in communication represents a difference in linguistic competence between regional and standard speakers.

Whether or not there are polylectal grammars, and no matter how we may consider variation in regional syntax as evidence for linguistic competence, these matters require much further careful investigation and cannot be resolved within this paper. Syntax is the central vehicle for the transmission of meaning and in any study of it these larger underlying issues are never far away. In this respect, too, the study of syntax is different from lexis and pronunciation.

The use of tests to elicit further information on an already known syntactic variable is of course a further research technique which has been used in some of the recent 'sociolinguistic' and 'variationist' studies included in Map 8.5, but most notably, perhaps, by those engaged on research on the standard language. Quirk and Svartvik (1979: 207) have written that it was never envisaged that any corpus, necessarily finite, would of itself be adequate for a comprehensive description of English grammar. This is no less true of those corpora on which descriptions of regional grammar are based. Quirk and Svartvik go on to say that, from the outset of the Survey of English Usage, elicitation tests with native subjects were envisaged as an essential tool for enlarging upon corpus-derived information and for investigating features not perhaps found in the corpus at all. These question tests are a very different matter from the SED questionnaire. For a start, they are only devised after considerable investigation of the local grammar has been carried out. Moreover, they are useful in providing quantitative information, often as confirmation, about behaviour or preferences of usage. Dialectologists cannot fail to benefit from elicitation tests, with much greater use likely to be made of them in future. A range of interesting tests, their results, and some of what the authors call 'the puzzlingly tantalising issues' which these tests lay bare, are discussed in Quirk and Rusiecki (1982).

The present paper has reviewed the contribution to the study of regional syntax made by SED as well as the advancements in methodology and description since. Although recent studies have concentrated on particular areas or places, they have contributed considerably more information about syntactic variation, with which comparisons across the whole of Britain and Ireland are increasingly possible. These new studies have not been slow to describe the complexities of syntactic data and have already identified new forms which have regional dialect implications. From these studies we may begin to draw up a profile of the touchstones of variation. Despite these achievements, however, very little real collecting of comparable spoken data in anything approaching sufficient abundance appears to have been done, or at any rate been made available, as coherent pieces of description. The recent and methodologically innovatory studies strongly suggest that spoken interactive data might be primarily characteristic of its medium, and thus more characteristic of its social variety (as non-standard) than of its area (as regional). To my knowledge, the only comparable data to Miller and Brown's Scottish conversations is that stored in the archives of the Survey of Spoken English at the University of Lund, a survey of emphatically educated, middle-class, non-regional, standard language.

The study of regional syntax presents formidable, complex and truly tantalising problems. Comparison with traditional lexical onomasiology and semasiology is unproductive. Syntax is far from being monolithic — its norm is heterogeneity. It is hoped that this paper demonstrates how challenging it is to investigate and describe regional syntax. The richness of the rewards for the dialectologist, however, make syntax an unquestionably exciting pursuit.

Notes

1. A version of this paper was read at the University of Oslo on 13 September 1983. I am grateful to Professor Stig Johansson for his kind invitation and for giving me ready access to the Brown Corpus and Lancaster-Oslo/Bergen Corpus during my stay. I am indebted to Professors A.J. Aitken and John Widdowson for many helpful suggestions.

2. Reviews of *The Linguistic Atlas of England* include: Burgess, A. *The Times Literary Supplement*, 27 October 1978, p. 1255; Diensberg, B. *Anglia*, vol. 101 (1983), pp. 462-8; Dodgson, J. McN. *Geographical Journal*, vol. 145 (1979), pp. 151-2; Howard, P. *The Times*, 6 September 1978; Kjellmer, G. *Moderna Språk*, vol. 77 (1983), pp. 81-4; McKee, G. *Yorkshire Post*, 7 September 1978; Moulton, W.G. *General Linguistics*, vol. 20 (1980), pp. 151-63; McDavid, R.I. *American Speech*, vol. 56 (1981), pp. 219-33; Quirk, R. 'Dialect Maps' *Books and Bookmen*, vol. 24 (1979), p. 44; Ross, A.S.C. *The Times Educational Supplement*, 15 September 1978; Russ, C.V.J. *Verbatim* (1979), pp. 7-10; Southard, B. *Journal of English Linguistics*, vol. 15 (1981), pp. 53-62; Speitel, H.-H. *Zeitschrift für Dialektologie und Linguistik*, in preparation; Trudgill, P. *Journal of English and Germanic Philology*, vol. 79 (1980), pp. 425-8; Wells, J.C. *The Times Higher Education Supplement* 1 December 1978; Wells, J.C. *The Journal of the International Phonetic Association*, vol. 9 (1979), pp. 39-43.

3. I am grateful to Dr Gunnel Melchers for permission to redraft her map.

4. Two versions of this study are to appear as (i) Edwards, V.K., P. Trudgill and B. Weltens, *The Grammar of English Dialect*, a Report to the ESRC Education and Human Development Committee, 1984, to which reference has been made here, and as (ii) Edwards, V.K. and B. Weltens, 'Research on non-standard Dialects of British English — Progress and Prospects', in W. Viereck (ed.), *Focus on: England* (John Benjamins, Amsterdam, forthcoming).

5. I am grateful to Professor P. Trudgill, Dr J. Cheshire and Dr J. Miller for permission to re-present their work in this way. It is worth noting that a grammar based on the *SED* is currently being prepared by Dr K. Forster of the University of Erlangen-Nürnberg, who spent a sabbatical year, 1980-1, at Leeds, investigating all the fieldworkers' Incidental Material. (Hitherto, the fullest, although brief, account based on the *SED* questionnaire responses is M.F. Wakelin, *English Dialects* (Athlone Press, London, 1972), chapter 6, in which the remark quoted in paragraph one was made.)

6. I am grateful to Mr Stewart F. Sanderson, then Director of the Institute of Dialect and Folklife Studies, University of Leeds, for permission to photocopy the section on grammar in the unpublished theses to which I refer, and to Professor M.B. Harris for a copy of his University of Leeds thesis.

References

Aitken, A.J. 'The Present State of Scottish Language Studies', *Scottish Literary News*, vol. 2 (1972), pp. 34-44

Allen, H.B. *Linguistic Atlas of the Upper Midwest*, 3 vols. (University of Minnesota Press, Minneapolis, 1973-6)

Amis, K. *Jake's Thing* (Penguin, Harmondsworth, 1978)

Anderson, P. 'The Dialect of Eaton-by-Tarporley

(Cheshire): A Descriptive and Historical Grammar', 2 vols. unpublished PhD thesis (University of Leeds, 1977)

Bailey, C.-J.N. *Variation and Linguistic Theory* (Center for Applied Linguistics, Arlington, 1973)

Brown, G., K.L. Currie, and J. Kenworthy. *Questions of Intonation* (Croom Helm, London, 1980)

Chambers, J.K. and P. Trudgill. *Dialectology* (Cambridge University Press, Cambridge, 1980)

Cheshire, J. 'Grammatical Variation in the English Spoken in Reading, Berkshire', unpublished PhD thesis (University of Reading, 1979)

—— *Variation in an English Dialect* (Cambridge University Press, Cambridge, 1982)

Francis, W.N. *Dialectology: An Introduction* (Longmans, London, 1983)

Harris, J. 'The Underlying Non-identity of English Dialects: A Look at the Hiberno-English Verb Phrase', *Belfast Working Papers in Language and Linguistics*, vol. 6 (1982), pp. 1-36

Hughes, A. and P. Trudgill. *English Accents and Dialects* (Edward Arnold, London, 1979)

Ihalainen, O. 'Grammatical Changes in Somerset Folk Speech', paper presented at the Third English Historical Linguistics Conference, Sheffield, 1983

Jespersen, O. *A Modern English Grammar on Historical Principles*, Part V, (Ejnar Munksgaard, Copenhagen, 1940)

Kirk, J.M. 'On Scottish Non-Standard English', *Nottingham Linguistic Circular*, vol. 10, no. 2 (1981), pp. 155-78

Krogvig, I. and S. Johansson. '*Shall, Will, Should* and *Would* in British and American English', *ICAME News*, no. 5 (1981), pp. 32-56

McIntosh, A. *Introduction to a Survey of Scottish Dialects* (Thomas Nelson, Edinburgh, 1952)

Melchers, G. 'Modal Auxiliaries in Regional Dialects', in *Papers from the Scandinavian Symposium on Syntactic Variation*, ed. S. Jacobsen (Almqvist and Wiksell, Stockholm, 1980), *Stockholm Studies in English*, vol. 52

Miller, J.E. and E.K. Brown. *Syntax of Scottish English* SSRC End of Grant HR5152 Report, 1980

—— 'Aspects of Scottish English Syntax', *English World-Wide*, vol. 3 (1982), pp. 3-17

Milroy, J. *Regional Accents of English: Belfast* (Blackstaff Press, Belfast, 1981)

Milroy, L. 'Applications of Sociolinguistics: Analysing Communicative Breakdown', paper presented at the Third Sociolinguistics Symposium, Walsall, 1980

Murison, D.D. 'A Survey of Scottish Language Studies', *Forum for Modern Language Studies*, vol. 3 (1967), pp. 276-85

Orton, H. 'An English Dialect Survey: Linguistic Atlas of England', *Orbis*, vol. 9 (1960), pp. 331-48

Orton, H. *et al. Survey of English Dialects (B) Basic Material*, 4 vols., each in 3 parts (E.J. Arnold, Leeds, 1962-71)

Orton, H., S. Sanderson and J. Widdowson (eds.) *The Linguistic Atlas of England* (Croom Helm, London, 1978)

Petyt, K.M. *The Study of Dialect: An Introduction to Dialectology* (André Deutsch, London, 1980)

Quirk, R. and J. Rusiecki. 'Grammatical Data by Elicitation', in J. Anderson (ed.), *Language Form and Linguistic Variation — Papers dedicated to Angus McIntosh, Current Issues in Linguistic Theory*, vol. 15 (John Benjamins, Amsterdam, 1982), pp. 379-94

Quirk, R. and J. Svartvik. 'A Corpus of Modern English', in H. Bergenholtz and B. Schaeder (eds.), *Empirische Textwissenschaft Aufbau und Auswertung von Text-Corpora* (Scriptor, Konigstein, 1979), pp. 204-18

Quirk, R., S. Greenbaum, G. Leech, J. Svartvik. *A Grammar of Contemporary English* (Longmans, London, 1972)

Séguy, J. *Atlas Linguistique et Ethnographique de la Gascogne* (Institut d'Etudes meridionales, Toulouse, 1954-73)

Shorrocks, G. 'The Phonetic Realisation of the Definite Article in Lancashire Dialect, and its Representation in Dialect Writing', *The Record*, no. 256 (1978), pp. 13-14

—— 'A Grammar of the Dialect of Farnworth and District', unpublished PhD thesis (University of Sheffield, 1980)

Svartvik, J. and R. Quirk (eds.) *A Corpus of English Conversation* (CWK Gleerup, Lund, 1980), Lund Studies in English, vol. 56

Trudgill, P. 'Sociolinguistics and Linguistic Theory', in his *On Dialect* (Blackwell, Oxford, 1983), pp. 8-30

Wakelin, M.F. *English Dialects: An Introduction* (Athlone Press, London, 1972)

Weltens, B. 'Non-standard periphrastic *do* in the Dialects of South-West Britain', *Lore and Language*, vol. 3, no. 8 (January 1983), pp. 56-64

9

Linguistic Atlases and Vocabulary: The Linguistic Survey of Anglo-Irish

P.L. HENRY

The names applied to nations and national languages, being so largely a product of historical accident, are hardly of prime importance to linguistic geography. What this subject requires is clarity of reference, and terms however partial or defective at the point of origin tend in this semantic area to acquire a clear definition through time. The names *Deutsch* and *Dutch*, though originally one, are today unambiguous; the role of the *Franks* in the formation of French language and civilisation may be controversial, but the application of the word *French* is not. *Gael* may well reflect a form of Welsh *Gwyddel* in the sense 'wild'; *Welsh* and *Slav* may show a close connection with words for 'slave'; but what these three names denote today is not in doubt.

The name *Anglo-Irish* for the English literature and language of Ireland had no serious rival until the 1960s. The introduction at this time of *Hiberno-English* for the language alone appears due on the one hand to a vague feeling that *English* should appear more centrally in the title of the linguistic discipline and on the other to the strategic interests of University Departments of English which might welcome a clearer brief for their labours. The newer term has never been properly motivated, which is a pity, not so much on account of any gain in clarity which we might expect in the use of names, as for the information which we would doubtless glean about the stance of scholars vis-à-vis their subject. For this reason let us hope that those who might wish to substitute *Cymro-English* for *Anglo-Welsh* will be more explicit.

The present writer has more than once proposed a solution to the disorder created in this way — without being able to elicit either dissenting opinion or conformable usage. The argument is as follows: the introduction of the name *Hiberno-English* as a global term for the language is unnecessary since Anglo-Irish has hitherto served unambiguously for the language as for the literature. In respect of both these areas the term *Anglo-Irish* is justified as names are rarely justified: it points to the creation in modern rural Ireland of a *new language* based upon Irish or Gaelic and absorbing linguistic resources chiefly lexical from outlying forms of English; that is to say, a mixed language mainly Irish in syntax and phonology with an appreciable and increasing English vocabulary and accidence. Yeats, Synge, Lady Gregory and the others found here a ready vehicle for a literature which in correspondence with the language has an essentially Irish character though modified and eked out by English. A ready specimen of it is found in the colloquial language of Patrick Kavanagh's *The Green Fool* and nothing can be more suggestive than the linguistic position of this major Irish poet who writes a sensitive Standard prose while thinking and speaking in a dialect, as it would appear, straight out of Irish. He compares the people of his own South-east Monaghan parish to those of Connemara (p. 309): 'They spoke Gaelic and yet I felt that the English-speaking peasants of my own country were nearer to the old Gaelic tradition'. He himself was approached, as a traditional Irish poet might be, to work a satire on an aggrieved man's neighbours (p. 327): 'I want ye to make a ballad on them, a good, strong, poisonous ballad . . . I'll give ye the facts, and you'll make the ballad . . .' (He told me which of them had bastard blood in their veins and which of them had been accused of theft) . . . 'That should make the bones of a good ballad.' The accounts of *áer* 'satire' in Irish manuscript sources could be usefully compared to this. The colloquial language of the book, in fact, offers an index to a whole civilisation and it is not surprising that it should be required reading for students of Irish folklore; of particular interest are the superstitions, which recall Pasternak's account of rural Russia in his *Dr Zhivago*.

An obvious role remains for *Hiberno-English*: in principle it should be applied to varieties of colonist English which owe least to their Irish environment and in which the historical relation with the mother country has some claims to being immediate and direct. In practice most of this variety will show some affinity with *Anglo-Irish*: if it did not, we should be dealing with split communities. Hiberno-English can include all the more 'standard' varieties whether of the schools, the towns, the media or the pulpit.

Modern Ireland since the seventeenth century shows an actively bilingual scene with major phases of linguistic assimilation. It seems to follow that research on the English language in modern Ireland is not so much a branch of English *philology* as of *linguistics* and that the traditional approach via English historical phonology may in a given case falter and peter out into tatters of reservation and conjecture. This is particularly to be expected where the realities underlying the names *Anglo-Irish* and *Hiberno-English* are confused, the latter name alone used and phenomena of Anglo-Irish provenance given the traditional historical treatment.

Some terms found in the oldest stratum of recorded Irish have passed into Anglo-Irish and English generally. Familiar from the archaic Irish *rosca* or 'rhetorics' are the two epithets of the fighting champion, *bulid* 'splendid' and *bras, brais* 'champion-like, great'. The connotation is originally poetic and allusive as we can see from such further epithets of the hero as *tonn anfaid*, literally 'storm wave'. Modern British and Ulster dialect and colloquial American retain the meaning 'fine' in the adjective *bully* while the more widely current substantives *bully* and *bully-boy*, 'tyrannical fellow', show the expected pejorative development found also in *brash*, 'hasty, insolent', etc. The dictionaries offer the meanings 'impetuous, quick-tempered, rash' for

Scottish Gaelic *bras, brais* and for Scots *brash*.

A military confrontation between the two civilisations involved at first in this commerce is recorded for the year 1586. Alastair mac Somhairle of the Clan Donnell of the Isles, captain of a troop of gallowglass, was followed and overtaken by an English troop under Captain Merriman in Inishowen, Co. Donegal. Alastair stepped forward in traditional style to challenge the rival leader to single combat, but Merriman did not take up the challenge. Instead, a 'lusty gallowglasse', representing himself as leader of the English stepped into the breach. Alastair killed him and was thereupon attacked and wounded by Merriman. Fighting then became general, Alastair was killed and his head spiked and set up on the battlements of Dublin Castle.

This case, which aroused much rancour, can serve to characterise the confrontation between the Tudor and the Gaelic spirit at the time: on the one hand the old and rather ingenuous concept of fair combat between champions so well attested in Norse and Irish literature; on the other, a modern, Machiavellian design and policy of conquest by total war. The clash of interests between the two countries is also reflected in the representation of Irish characters by English playwrights of the seventeenth and eighteenth centuries: the plays in question often show a virulent racial prejudice which tends to diminish their value for the linguistic record.

From the important movement of Scottish mercenaries to Ireland between the thirteenth and the seventeenth centuries derive the surnames *Gallogly, Gologly* from *mac Gallóglaigh*, literally 'son of the foreign soldier' (*gall-óglach*) and *Gallagher* from *Ó Gallchobhair*, literally 'descendant of foreign aid' (*gall-chobhair*). Shakespeare's *kerns and gallowglasses* (*Macbeth* I ii 13) for light and heavy infantry, respectively, are borrowed from sixteenth-century warfare in Ireland and are strictly inapplicable to eleventh-century Scotland.

One of the surest sources of Scots mercenaries were the so-called *broken clans*, that is, clans which had no chief able to find security for their good behaviour, and *broken men* who had no feudal protector or who were outlawed for crime. *Broken* also means, according to *SND* (*broken*, pp. 1. adj., 2) a ruined person, a bankrupt, or one in the direst poverty (cf. colloquial English *broke*). The interesting thing about this semantic development is that it parallels Old Ir. *bongim*, 'I break', to which belongs the old past participle *bocht*, recorded only in the meaning 'poor'. Scots legal usage of the sixteenth and seventeenth centuries as reflected in *broken clans(men)* appears to supply the missing term in the early semantic development of Ir. *bocht* from 'broken (physically)' to 'poor', namely 'broken legally, deprived of legal rights (and so prone to destitution)'.

While in its vocabulary and syntax Anglo-Irish naturally preserves a good deal of Elizabethan English usage, the parallels between the latter and modern Irish are numerous and striking. The following specimens are from *Hamlet*: I i 102, *by strong hand*, Ir. *le láimh láidir*, 'by violence'; cf. American colloquial *strong arm*, 'enforcers, racketeers'; III iii 334, *While the grass grows the steed starves*, Ir. *mair a chapaill, is gheobhair féar* = Anglo-Irish proverb *Live, horse, and you'll get* (or *ate*) *grass*, i.e. If you live, etc; II ii 356, *Do the boys carry it away? . . .* 'win the day?', cf. earlier Ir. *beirid* 'carries off, excels, wins'; I v 172, *To put an antic disposition on*, cf. Ir. *cuirim orm* 'I put on, assume'. Other prepositional phrases such as *meet with* and *fall out* are paralleled by Ir. *buailim le*, literally 'I meet with', *thuit sé amach*, literally 'it fell out'; so are expressions invoking good fortune: IV v 40, *God 'ield you!*, Ir. *go ngnóthaí Dia dhuit!*; I iii 56, *My blessing with thee!* Ir. *beannacht leat!*

Lexical material for the Linguistic Survey of Anglo-Irish is gathered orally by investigators plying the Linguistic Questionnaires in the field and also by way of a postal Lexical Questionnaire (Henry 1958). In both cases the information sought is of the rural, old-fashioned type with the emphasis on *concreta* such as birds and animals, implements and their parts, social and geographical phenomena. The rate of change in the rural community over the last twenty years has been rapid and a way of life then moribund has now for the most part become extinct. Hence Lexical Questionnaires now issued may in some cases gather mere vestigial recollections of extinct customs, so that for a fuller display one needs to take account also of earlier collections such as those of the Irish Folklore Commission, and local monographs.

The Linguistic Surveys of England, Scotland, Wales and the Irish-speaking districts of Ireland have amassed and presented a prodigious amount of material in the form of word lists and of mapped items displaying local distribution. But this great work is obviously only a beginning, for the analysis of the material is nowhere taken to be part of the display, and the reader is left to puzzle out meanings and relations as best he can. Inevitably also, perhaps, each survey tends to look like a closed and rather exclusive system ignoring the facts outside its narrower ambit. Whereas the expectation must rather be that the pre-Celtic, Celtic and Germanic peoples of the British Isles have greatly contributed to one another in the concepts and terms of their civilisations and that the individual surveys need to be compared and collated in order to identify and assess semantic and historical relationships and to reaffirm paths of contact which are outside the purview of the individual survey.

With this end in view, we proceed to consider briefly the responses recorded in Ireland and Britain for two particular items. The first is the prolific *smallest and weakest piglet of the litter* (Map 9.1), for which material is available from all the surveys. It appears to be a straightforward and uncomplicated item. Features of a general kind to be expected are the application of the term to other weaklings, animal or human; a preponderance of diminutive forms; the use of personal names for the weakling piglet; a number of nonce or unverified forms (which we leave out of account); and a number of baffling forms.

The English term *rut* recorded for Staffordshire, has established itself at the expense of Irish terms in Leinster and the Midlands. Ulster *crowl*, *crowlie* of obscure origin, dominate the centre of North-east Ulster, while some forms of Ir *deoraí*, AIr *jorry* etc. are scattered around the crescent from Down to Derry. In South-west Ulster, *crile*, a variant of *crowl*, is found (Braidwood, 1974) and in Donegal and North Connacht *arc*, *arcán*, *earc*, *earcán*. *Arc* is an established Middle Ir. variant of *orc* 'pig' (cf. Latin *porcus*); whereas *earc* is from earlier *erc* 'lizard' etc.; but the two forms mingle to denote the weakling piglet; and diminutives in *-án*, *-achán*, *-adán*, *-in* are freely found, particularly in south Mayo. *Droich*, apparently by metathesis from Sc. *duerch*, 'dwarf', is recorded chiefly in Donegal together with *dreoilín* (AIr *drawlyeen*), *dreoilí* (AIr *drawlye*), *dreolán*, properly 'wren'. Under *droille* Traynor (1953: 89) attaches the second of these forms to a word **draoille* 'dregs'

Map 9.1: *Smallest and Weakest Piglet of the Litter — Ireland*

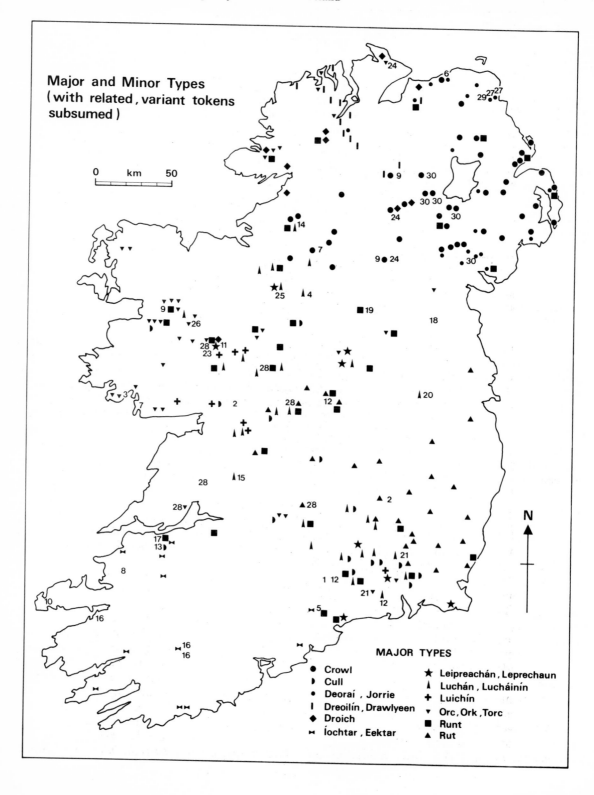

Major and Minor Types (with related, variant tokens subsumed)

MAJOR TYPES

●	Crowl	★	Leipreachán, Leprechaun
ꭰ	Cull	⅄	Luchán, Lucháinín
•	Deoraí , Jorrie	+	Luichín
Ɩ	Dreoilín, Drawlyeen	▾	Orc, Ork, Torc
◆	Droich	■	Runt
⋈	Íochtar , Eektar	▲	Rut

Key to Map 9.1

Smallest and Weakest Piglet of the Litter — Ireland

Tokens of major types

orc, ork; orcán, orkaun; orcachán, arc, earc, ark; arcán, earcán, arkaun; earcachán, arkahaun, earcadán, arkadaun; earcáinín, arkauneen; aircín, arkeen; torc, torcán, tarc, taircín

crowl, crowlie, crile, crilie

cull, cull-án

dreoilín, drawlyeen; dreoilí, drawlie; dreolán, dhreolan

íochtar (neidín), eektar, íochtairín

luichín, luchóg, luichín áil, loughinaul, luch áilín, lough awley

leipreachán, leprechaun, larachán, larahaun, lorgadán, lúrachán, lurachán, luraigín, luchán, luchinín

rut, rut-ín

runt

luchán, lucháinín

deoraí, jorrie

droich

Tokens of minor types

1. abhac
2. bainbhín, baniveen
3. craitheadh an mhála
4. daniel
5. díthriúch
6. doirb, dorbie
7. doherty, dorothy
8. dríodar
9. dwarf
10. fíothal
11. gárlach
12. groudie
13. iarmhar, eervar
14. méarnóg
15. moirt, murt
16. neddy, nedlin, neidín
17. pet
18. rantin
19. rawnie
20. seán, shawn
21. siabhra
22. scrapings of the pot
23. síóg
24. shakins of the poke
25. slinkeen
26. scearachán
27. snoddie
28. suck, suckie, suck-ín
29. ablach
30. copp, cappie, copney

given by Quiggin (1906: 47), without noticing that this form is a genitive case in his source. The forms *dreoilín* and *dreolán* render the argument superfluous. The Mayo form *darrol* from Ir. *dearóil*, *deireóil* 'miserable, wretched' recorded for the smallest piglet by Joyce (1910: 246) suggests that *dreoilín*, 'wren', is a derivative of this word. To the forms *copp*, *copney*, *cappie* found to the south and west of Lough Neagh, cf. Dinneen *copánach*, 'a little pig fed on milk from a saucer', and Monaghan *capánach*, where *capán* can mean 'saucer'.

The form *luchán*, which is not recorded as a diminutive of *luch*, 'mouse' beside *luchóg* and *luichín*, is found from Sligo to Kilkenny. It is probably a form of the highly variable *leipreachán*, 'leprechaun' which is recorded also in our meaning as *larachán*, *lorgadán*, *lúrachán* and *luraigín*. Two other occasional responses for the weakling piglet, namely *síóg*, 'fairy' and *siabhra*, 'elf' do offer evidence for a connection with the otherworld. The *SED* matches this in Cornish *widden*, *piggy-widden* and Kentish *Anthony*.

Of the remaining forms some indicate smallness or thinness as *dwarf*, *abhac*, 'dwarf', Ir. *ránaí*/AIr *rawny* and *runt* which tends to occur sporadically as a standard term. The Galway form *luichín áil*, literally 'little mouse of the litter', has a variant *luch áilín* with transference of *-ín*. This is written *Lough awley* by the correspondent. It is no doubt an Anglo-Irishism, since the addition of *-ín* to a genitive is peculiar. Besides, the correspondent writes of the piglets as *awleys*, which shows a further independent Anglo-Irish development. Other residual forms express the notion of 'dregs'; cf. *scrapings of the bag*, *poke shakins*, *iarmhar* = remnant, *íochtar* = bottom, *íochtar neidín* 'bottom of the nest'. Or they represent personal names as *Daniel*, *Dorothy*, *Seán*, *Neddy*, *Nedlem*. In these last two forms we have association of *neidín*, 'little nest' with the personal name, *Ned*. A few of the residual forms are pet names, such as *suck*, *suck-ín*.

The characteristic Ulster responses *Droich* (*Droit*) and *Crowl* occur also in Scotland and partly in northern England.

In Scotland there has been some commerce in terms for the weakest piglet between the Gaelic and the English-speaking areas. The Inveraray term *seota* with pre-aspirate on the North-west European pattern [ʃoχtə] is an adaptation of Scots *shot* as in Perth and Argyllshire; whereas Scots *eeshan* in the North-east area of the Firths of Moray and Dornoch is from Gaelic *isean* as in Lewis, Sutherland and Inverness where the further specification *deireadh lìn(e)*, i.e. '(weak-

Map 9.2: *LAS* vol. 1, map 65: *The Youngest of a Brood*

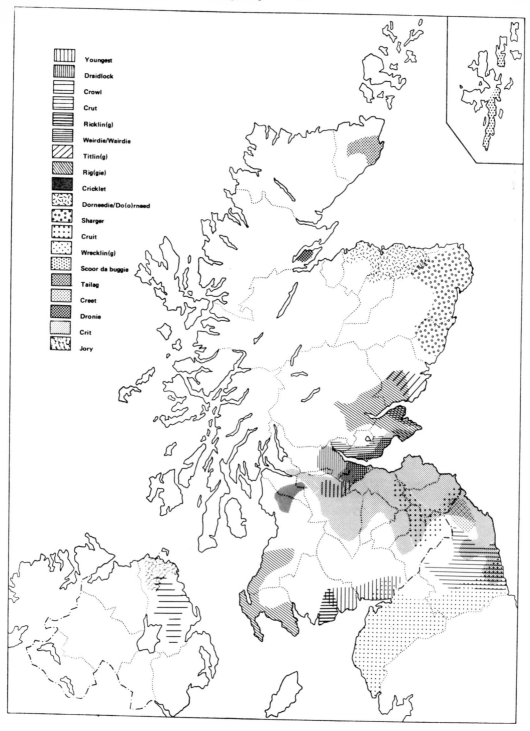

Map 9.3: *LASID*, map 34: *smallest pigling of a litter*

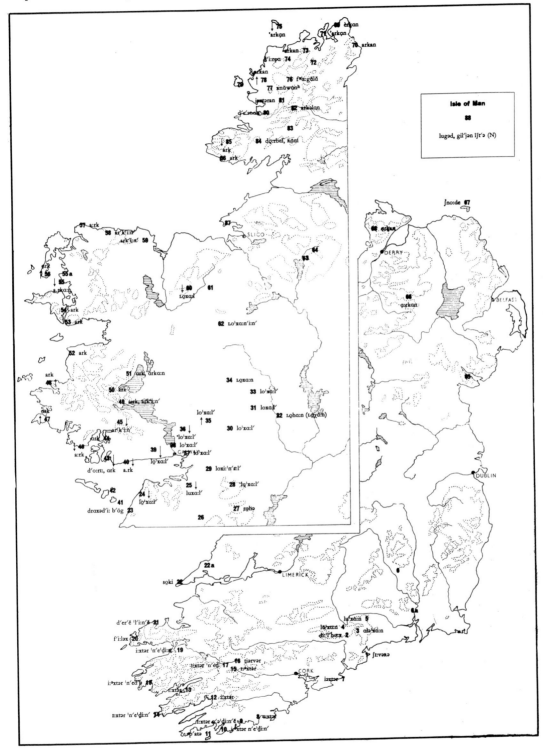

ling) of the end of the litter', is added (Wagner 1969: p. 190 (Map 34) reproduced here as Map 9.3; cf. *LAS* vol. 1, pp. 281-2 and p. 110: Map 65, reproduced here as Map 9.2). Scots *carneed* and *dorneed* from Nairn and Moray appear to contain *nid*, genitive of *nead*, 'nest' as second element; *corr* 'an undersized or diminutive animal' and *doirb*, 'diminutive or insignificant creature or person' appear to be the first elements. *Doirb* with the suffix -*ie* occurs at Ardara (Map 9.3: point 84) and at Portrush, Co. Antrim, (Map 9.1). Scots *shargar* in Aberdeen and Kincardineshire is from Gaelic *seargair*.

In Scots *poke shakins* from Ayrshire, with many variants of it elsewhere in Scotland, and *croitheadh a' phocáin* from Fanad, N. Donegal (Map 9.3: point 69) are one and the same concept, identically expressed. Fanad also has *deireadh díne*, literally 'last of the generation or litter', to which compare West Kerry *deire líne* (Map 9.3: point 21) and Scottish Gaelic *deireadh lín(e)* mentioned above. A similar approach is seen in *banbhán an bhalláin deiridh*, literally 'little bonham of the last tit' (West Donegal, Map 9.3: point 80), elsewhere in Ireland *earcán balláin deiridh*.

The responses for Wales (cf. Thomas 1973: 261) may be subdivided as follows: (a) English borrows: *cwlyn* in the North and North-west, cf. English *culling*; *ratlin* in a small area at the junction of Montgomeryshire and Denbighshire, cf. English dialectal *ratlin* in neighbouring Shropshire; (b) terms indicating diminutive size: as *bach y nyth*, literally 'the small one of the nest', in Lleyn and the West Midlands, and *cranc(yn)*, *crenc(yn)*, 'dwarf weakling' sporadically in the South; (c) the epithet denotes 'dregs' in *gwaddodwyn* from near the sources of the Aeron, Teifi and Usk, and *tin y nyth*, literally 'bottom of the nest', in the North-west Midlands and North Anglesey; (d) the sense 'beggar' appears to inhere in *cardot(w)yn* south of the Dyfi and of the higher reaches of the Severn, but there is much variation in the group to which it belongs.

In spite of structural and semantic similarities to the *SED doll* and *darling* groups, *dilling*, which is well represented in the centre of England, appears to be originally distinct. *OED* cites *dillin* in the sense *mignon* from Salesbury's Welsh dictionary of 1547, and Lloyd-Jones gives the meanings 'jewel, ornament; beloved' for early Welsh *dillyn*. This term may have been

applied to the pet piglet.

Cornish *widden* and *piggy-widden* contain the Cornish adjective *gwyn* (later *gwidden*) in the sense 'sacred', a meaning which inheres in the corresponding Irish word *finn* in the earliest instances of it. Welsh and Cornish *gwyn* and Ir. *finn* otherwise commonly mean 'white'. The weakest piglet was a sacred animal and belonged to the clergy in the Middle Ages. It was often dedicated to St Anthony the hermit, whence the English dialect forms *anthony*, *anthony-pig*, *tanthony* for it (Wakelin 1975: 199-200). a curious analogy with this is provided by the Irish word *deiseálán* for the best piglet at Waterville, County Kerry (*LASID*, vol. II, p. 203). According to Dinneen, *deiseálán* means a certain natural turn of the hair on the head of some persons and on certain parts of the bodies of animals. In Anglo-Irish it is called a *cow's lick* and is deemed auspicious: *deiseal* means 'righthandwise', connoting the auspicious course of the sun. The abstract *deiseálánaí* expresses the condition of having the *cow's lick*, which in the case of a piglet is found near the small of the back. The maxim runs *Tóg an banbh ina bhfuil an deiseálánaí*, 'Rear the bonham with the cow's lick', as it is bound to thrive. Through these examples from the Celtic fringe glimmer shreds of the elder faiths of Britain and Ireland.

Maps 9.4, 9.5 and 9.6 concern the *last corn sheaf cut at harvesting*, a complex and absorbing item for which the material is much less readily available. Its era was that of the sickle rather than the scythe and the evidence from Ireland, Scotland and Wales suggests that the customs connected with it were in decline by the second last decade of the nineteenth century. *LAS* vol. 2, Map 60 (reproduced here as Map 9.4) shows returns for this item from Scotland, Northern Ireland, Northumberland and Cumberland. As the coverage for Scotland is concentrated on the eastern and south-western periphery, we have thought it helpful to map the information assembled by Frazer (1890; 1963) and MacLean (1964) in order to fill out the picture for the Islands and Highlands. Rather more is known of the customs connected with this feature in Scotland than in Ireland generally, and we shall take the Scottish evidence into account from the beginning. We start by considering the more significant general aspects of the feature and proceed then to the illustrative detail.

Three of the more important facets of this

Map 9.4: *LAS* vol. 2, Map 60: *Last corn sheaf cut at harvesting*

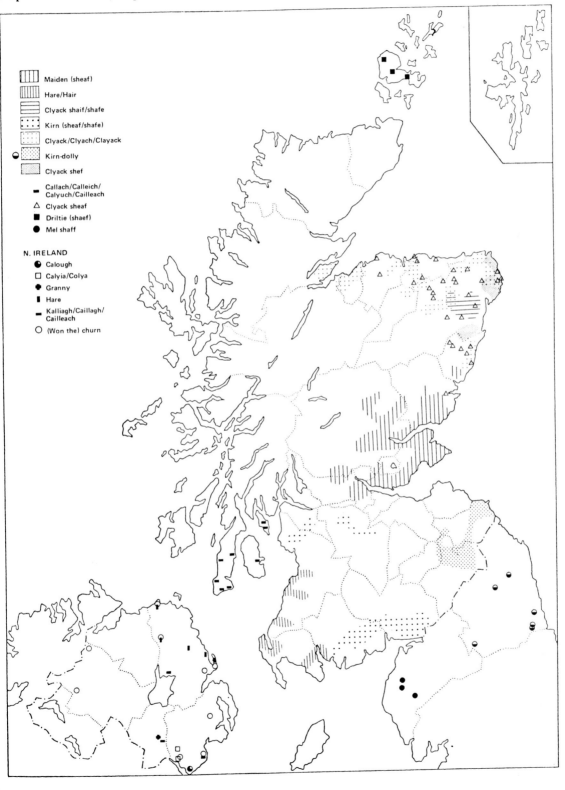

feature are: (a) the last sheaf can symbolise the dying harvest and give rise to characteristic — and often divisive — customs. This is typically the case with the *cailleach* ('old hag') and *Gobhar Bhacach* ('lame goat') in the Western Isles of Scotland, where the last sheaf is so named; but names and customs tend to vary and overlap, and *cailleach* may be used where the customs belong to class (b): here the last sheaf can serve as a talisman for future fertility and the names *Maiden*, *Bride*, for example, themselves bespeak a festive spirit vibrant with the sense of renewal and increase. Terms such as *kirn-dolly* and *kirn-baby* show how natural it is to adapt a last sheaf so conceived into the figure of a girl or a doll. A third point worth remembering is that the Harvest celebration (Harvest Home, Harvest Supper) is closely associated with the last sheaf. Map 9.6 contains locations at which the term for the last sheaf is also applied to the Harvest Home, and one at which the term for the Harvest Home is *Kirn*.

The last sheaf may have an animal reference, usually to the hare. In Ireland one is then said to *hunt* or *chase* or *put out* the hare or rabbit, an event concomitant with the fall of the last sheaf, which is their final lurking place. The sheaf may alternatively have a human reference, either *cailleach*, 'old woman', or *Old woman, Old*

Maid, Granny. Stories of the witch-hare, found widely throughout Ireland, suggest that these two aspects are related; euphemisms or taboo names such as *the one we were looking for*, *what the cobbler threw at his wife* tend to support the suggestion of a supernatural background in the use of the terms *hare* and *witch-hare* in Ireland. The concepts of *cailleach* and *hare* are reflected in the following two associated groups of responses for the last sheaf; to the cailleach group belong: *Cailleach Fómhair* ('Harvest Hag'), *Cuid na Cailli* (The Hag's Share), *Carlin* ('Old Woman'), *Granny*, *Hag*, *Old Hag*, *Old Woman*, *Old Maid*, *Seanchailleach* ('Old Hag'), *Seanbhean* ('Old Woman'); to the *Hare* group belong: *Dornán an Ghirria* ('The Hare's Handful'), *Faogadh an Ghirria* ('The Hare's Remnant'), *Girria* ('Hare'), *Hare's Sheaf, Hare Gone Sheaf, Hare's Bite, Hare's Tail, Hare's Seat, Hunt the Hare, Kitty the Hare, Luíochán* ('Lying in wait'), *Nead an Ghirria* ('The Hare's Lair'). Other animals, birds and fish which lend their names to the last sheaf are: the rabbit, hog, cow, swallow and *piardóg* (crayfish).

By such association of ideas as we have suggested above, the last sheaf may be thought to bring either misfortune or fortune (MacLean 1964: 195):

Key to Map 9.5

Last corn sheaf — Ireland

Tokens of major types
cailleach, cailleach fómhair
churn
Euphemisms
girria, giver
hag
hare, hare gone sheaf, hare's bite, hare's sheaf, hare's seat, hare's tail, hunt the hare, kitty the hare
head, harvest head, head sheaf

Tokens of minor types
1. buinneach
2. blade, blade's sheaf
3. band
4. bunoc
5. cuid na cailli
6. carlin
7. cow
8. the cursed sheaf
9. deoch a' dorais
10. dornán an ghirria
11. dwarf sheaf
12. fangle
13. faogadh an ghirria
14. girria, giver
15. granny
16. an gráinnín mhullaigh
17. hog
18. last
19. luíochán
20. mil searrach
21. nead an ghirria
22. old hag, old maid, old woman
23. piardóg
24. plump
25. punann bundúin
26. rabbit, rabbit's bed, rabbit's sheaf
27. an rubaillín (earabaillín) caol
    an driobaillín (earabaillín) deiridh
28. seanchailleach
29. seanbhean, sealbhán
30. swallow
31. scríobadh an chrúiscín
32. taoibín
33. women's corn, women's sheaf
34. who-shall

Map 9.5: *Last corn sheaf* — Ireland

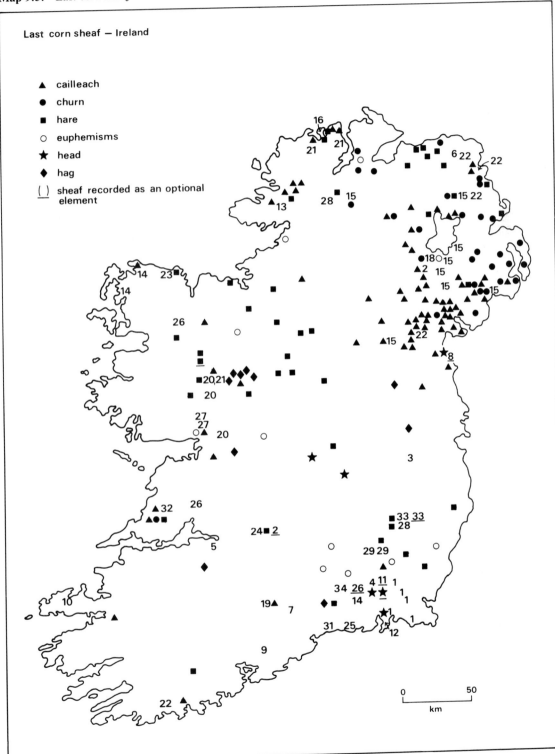

Last corn sheaf — Ireland

▲ cailleach

● churn

■ hare

○ euphemisms

★ head

◆ hag

( ) sheaf recorded as an optional element

Map 9.6: *Last corn sheaf* — **Scotland: major and minor responses from printed sources**

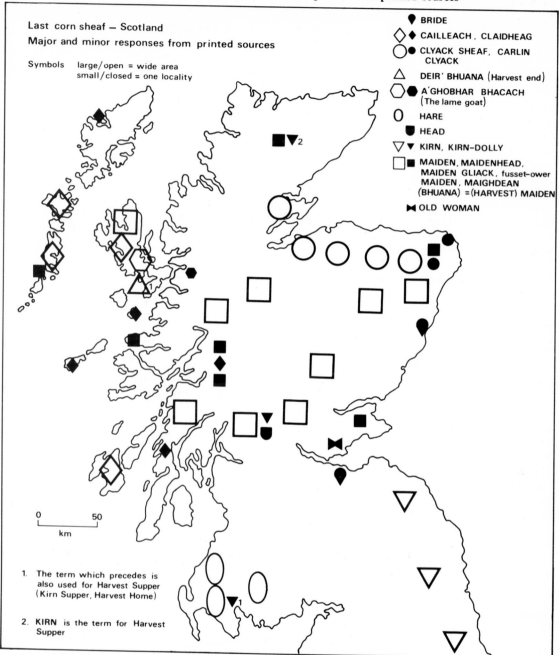

Last corn sheaf — Scotland

Major and minor responses from printed sources

Symbols   large/open = wide area
           small/closed = one locality

● BRIDE

◇ ◆ CAILLEACH , CLAIDHEAG

○ ● CLYACK SHEAF, CARLIN
      CLYACK

△ DEIR' BHUANA (Harvest end)

⬡ ● A'GHOBHAR BHACACH
      (The lame goat)

0 HARE

⬛ HEAD

▽ ▼ KIRN, KIRN–DOLLY

◻ ◼ MAIDEN, MAIDENHEAD,
      MAIDEN GLIACK, fusset–ower
      MAIDEN, MAIGHDEAN
      (BHUANA) =(HARVEST) MAIDEN

⋈ OLD WOMAN

0 _____ 50
    km

1. The term which precedes is
    also used for Harvest Supper
    (Kirn Supper, Harvest Home)

2. **KIRN** is the term for Harvest
    Supper

In South Uist the *cailleach* was sent from person to person in a township according as they finished the harvest and the last person had to keep it and had to feed it, as it were, through the winter. The belief was common in the last century that misfortune overtook the person on whom the *cailleach* was inflicted, he would lose some of his stock or even he himself would die. In certain areas in the west the *cailleach* was much feared and during harvest time certain people remained on guard all night in case the *cailleach* was sent to them. One informant from Eochar in South Uist stated that the *cailleach* was made of *cuiseagan ruadha*, dockens, and dressed up in old woman's clothing and was given slippers to wear. Another informant from the same island stated it was given some head-dress. The *cailleach* was sent not only from crofter to crofter, but also from township to township and from farm to farm. A farmer in Cill Donann in Eigg sent the *cailleach* to his neighbour in Laig across the island. A servant riding on a swift, black mare brought the sheaf and placed it on a wall near the victim's house. He was seen and fled, pursued by the angry farmer who fired several shots at him but missed. That took place towards the end of the eighteenth century. In the late sixteenth century Clanranald in South Uist sent a messenger on horseback from Ormicleit to Geirinish. The *cailleach* was left in Geirinish in a patch of standing corn. The messenger was seen, pursued and killed within one half-mile of his own township. Had he gone a half-mile further he could have been safe. In the last century, however, in Uist, the sending of the sheaf gave rise to nothing more than an occasional outburst of vituperative verses about the *cailleach*, reviling her as if she were an ugly old woman.

The sheaf actually sent to taunt a neighbour need not be the last sheaf cut, and a dressed-up figure was sometimes used in its place.

The auspicious or 'sonsy' counterpart of the *cailleach* is the *Maiden* (*Maighdean Bhuana*, *Bride*). As Sir James Frazer puts it (1963: 536):

In some parts of the Highlands of Scotland the last handful of corn that is cut by the reapers on any particular farm is called the *Maiden*, or in Gaelic *Maidhdeanbuain*, literally 'the shorn maiden' [rectius *Maighdean Bhuana*, 'the

Harvest Maiden']. Superstitions attach to the winning of the *Maiden*. If it is got by a young person, they think it an omen that he or she will be married before another harvest. For that or other reasons there is a strife between the reapers as to who shall get the *Maiden*, and they resort to various stratagems for the purpose of securing it. One of them, for example, will often leave a handful of corn uncut and cover it up with earth to hide it from the other reapers, till all the rest of the corn on the field is cut down. Several may try to play the same trick and the one who is coolest and holds out longest obtains the coveted distinction. When it has been cut, the Maiden is dressed with ribbons into a sort of doll and affixed to a wall of the farmhouse. In the north of Scotland the *Maiden* is carefully preserved till Yule morning, when it is divided among the cattle 'to make them thrive all the year round'. In the neighbourhood of Balquhidder, Perthshire, the last handful of corn is cut by the youngest girl on the field, and is made into the rude form of a female doll, clad in a paper dress, and decked with ribbons. It is called the Maiden, and is kept in the farmhouse, generally above the chimney, for a good while, sometimes till the Maiden of the next year is brought in. The writer of this book witnessed the ceremony of cutting the Maiden at Balquhidder in September 1888. A lady friend informed me that as a young girl she cut the Maiden several times at the request of the reapers in the neighbourhood of Perth. The name of the Maiden was given to the last handful of standing corn: a reaper held the top of the bunch while she cut it. Afterwards the bunch was plaited, decked with ribbons, and hung up in a conspicuous place on the wall of the kitchen till the next Maiden was brought in. The harvest-supper in this neighbourhood was also called the Maiden; the reapers danced at it.

Gaelic *cailleach* was borrowed into Scots as *clyack* and this found its way back as *claidheag*. The *clyack(-sheaf)*, *Maiden* and *Maighdean Bhuana* share much the same traditions (MacLean, 1964: 197):

The Clyack-sheaf, according to one account from the North-East, was much smaller than an ordinary sheaf and was given to the favourite horse. It was made into a female figure and given a drink of ale, but the informant states that he had only seen this once. Another account, presumably from Buchan, states that the Clyack was either known as the *Maiden* or the *Carlin Clyack*, according as the harvest was early or late. An account from Banff states that the Clyack was dressed up to resemble a girl of the agricultural community. It remained in the kitchen till New Year's morning, when it was undressed and shared out among the animals. When the sheaf was brought home the harvesters were treated to 'Meal and Ale', oatmeal, whisky and sugar or syrup, made thick. A ring was put in it and the finder would be married before the next harvest. Dr. Gregor also states that the sheaf was named according as the harvest was early or late. In Corgarff, Aberdeenshire, when all the crop is cut before St. Michael's Day, 29th September, it is called a *maiden gliack*, but if the crop is cut later, the sheaf gets the name of 'a fusset-ower maiden' i.e. deluded or betrayed maiden. The man who cuts the last sheaf in a delayed harvest, marries a widow or unchaste woman, and if a woman cut it, she marries a widower or unchaste man. One other important point he makes is that the Clyack-sheaf was not allowed to touch the ground when being bound. Another account from Aberdeen says that the sheaf was divided among the stirks on New Year's Day. In Kincardineshire, the sheaf was kept till Christmas and given to a cow in calf, and another account says that it was kept till Old Christmas Day and given to the best cow in the byre.

Deir' Bhuana, *Maiden* and *Kirn* (*Churn*) each occur in the double application 'last sheaf' and 'Harvest Home'. In the case of *kirn* (*churn*) it is easiest to assume that 'Harvest Home' is the primary meaning and the other due to association with it. *Kirn-dolly* and variants show an application of the last sheaf for decorative purposes at the Harvest Feast.

To judge from its distribution on the map, *cailleach* appears to have been the most widely used native name for the last sheaf in Ireland. North-east Ulster is a main area of innovation, with *churn* strongly represented in East Down and Antrim; but *cailleach* persists in the upper reaches of the Lagan, and its clustering in South-east Ulster is impressive. A. Gailey's map (1972: 10) has a rather similar coverage for Ulster, with less in the North and North-west, while his coverage for *hare* and *churn* is fuller than ours. *Hare* was the term used in the South-west corner of Scotland across the Channel, in Wigtown, Kirkcudbright and South Ayrshire, whereas *churn* is not recorded. G.B. Adams (1962: 10) would spell this *chirn* and his map of this item includes an instance of *corn-dolly* near Ballinderry in South-west Antrim.

South Leinster is another area of interest and the variety of names in Kilkenny and Wexford is surprising. The Wexford term *buinneach* is no doubt a derivative of *buinne* 'sprouting; sprout', etc. *Ag teacht i mbuinneadh*, literally 'coming into growth, springing up', is said of the growing corn. *Bunac* is clearly a bad spelling — for *buinneach*, it may be.

In the following brief review of the terms for the last sheaf in Ireland we must confine ourselves to the elucidation of the more or less obscure items. The term *blade* (North Armagh) is cognate with L. *flos*, Ir. *bláth* 'flower' and the sense 'swelling out, blooming' appears appropriate to the last sheaf. The term *band* as in hay band also suits the plaited sheaf. *Deoch a dorais* (Clonmult, East Cork), common in the sense 'stirrup-cup', can have the double reference to the completion of the task and to the subsequent celebration or drink. Other terms which refer to the end of the task are *Giver* (Mullinavat, South Kilkenny) so-called, according to the correspondent, from the giving-up (i.e. completion) of the work; and *punann bundúin*, literally 'bottom sheaf' (Tramore, Co. Waterford). *Last* (North Armagh), glossed 'What the cobbler threw at his wife' has the devious character of a taboo term. In Ballyshannon, Co. Donegal it runs 'What the cobbler killed his wife with' and also in Kirkcudbright with *shoemaker* for *cobbler*. A euphemism of the type 'The one *or* the grain I *or* we were looking for (all day)' has been recorded from the following places in Co. Kilkenny: Coon, Castlecomer; Mullinahone, Dunamaggan, and Tullaroan; from The Harrow and Cranford near Gorey in Co. Wexford, and from Ballymurphy in Co. Carlow. The Galway form *mil searrach*, if reliable, means 'honey of foals'. *Piardóg* 'crayfish' from the North Mayo coast could be pictorially appropriate to certain forms of the last sheaf. *Sealbhán* (Kilkenny) may be related to the meanings 'herd, flock' etc. offered by Dinneen, in the sense that the last sheaf can be a symbol of fertility. *Taoibín* (Clare) may stand for *taoibhín* 'a small addition'.

A quick glance at the data available for Wales and England can provide some comparative insights. In one corner of South-west Wales, comprising Pembrokeshire, South Cardiganshire and West Carmarthenshire, the last sheaf was known by the names *y wrach* ('The Hag'), *Y Gaseg Fedi* ('The Harvest Mare'), *Y Gaseg Ben Fedi* ('The End of Harvest Mare') and (in South Pembrokeshire) *The Neck* (Peate: 1930; 1971). Throwing the last sheaf on to a neighbour's land was practised in Wales as in Scotland and Ireland.

The terms *kirn* or *kern* are recorded for the last sheaf in Northumberland, Durham and Yorkshire, and *Harvest Queen* in Northumberland and Cambridge. The figure made from the last sheaf was known in the North of England as *Kern Baby* and as *Ivy Girl* in Kent. In Hertford-shire and Shropshire the sheaf was called *the mare* and a ceremony with ritual wording called *crying the mare* was practised in these counties when the sheaf had been cut and the harvest finished. In Devon and Cornwall the last sheaf was called *the neck* as in South Pembroke and a similar ceremony called *crying the neck* was practised. The Wexford forms with *head* appear to be related to these *neck* forms. A response from Templeorum, Co. Kilkenny for the last sheaf, recorded in the form *Who shall* may in view of the practices mentioned be the opening of a ritual question at the ceremony of cutting the last sheaf. The Kilkenny informant's sentence *This is the who-shall* is in fact explained by him as the beginning of a conjectural question *Who shall cut the cailleach* (*deal the final hand of cards*)? etc., for which information and for many Kilkenny references I am indebted to my colleague Dr S. Ó. Maoláin, as also to Dr N. Mac Conghail for some Irish material.

References

Adams, G.B. 'The Chirn', *Ulster Folklife*, vol. 8 (1962), pp. 10-14

Braidwood, J. '*Crowls* and *Runts*: Ulster Dialect Terms for "The Weakling of the Litter" ', *Ulster Folklife*, vol. 20 (1974), pp. 71-84

Dinneen, P. *An Anglo-Irish Dictionary* (Irish Texts Society, Dublin, 1927)

Frazer, J.G. *The Golden Bough*, 2 vols. (Macmillan, London, 1890)

—— *The Golden Bough*, abridged edn. (Macmillan, London, 1963)

Gailey, A. '*The last sheaf* in the North of Ireland', *Ulster Folklife*, vol. 18 (1972), pp. 1-33

Henry, P.L. 'A Linguistic Survey of Ireland: Preliminary Report', *Lochlann*, vol. 1 (1958)

Joyce, P.W. *English as We Speak it in Ireland* (The Talbot Press, Dublin, 1910: rep. Wolfhound Press, Portmarnock, Co. Dublin, 1979)

Kavanagh, Patrick, *The Green Fool* (Brian and O'Keeffe, London, 1971)

MacLean, C.I. 'The Last Sheaf', *Scottish Gaelic Studies*, vol. 8 (1964), pp. 193-207

Mather, J.Y. and H.-H. Speitel. *The Linguistic Atlas of Scotland:* Scots Section, 2 vols. (Croom Helm, London, 1975-7)

Peate, I.C. 'Corn Customs in Wales', *Man*, vol. 30 (1930), pp. 151-5

—— 'Corn Ornaments', *Folklore*, vol. 82 (1971), pp. 177-84

Quiggin, E.C. *A Dialect of Donegal* (Cambridge University Press, Cambridge, 1906)

The Scottish National Dictionary, ed. W. Grant and D.D. Murison, 10 vols. (The Scottish National Dictionary Association, Aberdeen and Edinburgh, 1929-76)

Thomas, A. *The Linguistic Geography of Wales* (University of Wales Press, Cardiff, 1973)

Traynor, M. *The English Dialect of Donegal* (The Royal Irish Academy, Dublin, 1953)

Wagner, H.H. *A Linguistic Atlas and Survey of Irish Dialects*, vol. 4 (Institute for Advanced Studies, Dublin, 1969)

Wakelin, M.F. *Language and History in Cornwall* (Leicester University Press, Leicester, 1975)

10

Linguistic Maps: Visual Aid or Abstract Art?

R.K.S. MACAULAY

'The map appears to us more real than the land' (D.H. Lawrence)

Linguistic atlases are expensive to produce and consequently even more expensive to purchase so that the consumer is entitled to ask: What am I getting for my money? The answer is not always clear, and to some extent it will depend upon the kind of mapping adopted. This article will examine different kinds of visual presentation and discuss their respective merits. First of all, it is necessary to distinguish between those atlases that present the basic material in map form and those atlases that map material that is presented in a different form elsewhere. In the first category are *The Linguistic Atlas of New England* (Kurath *et al.* 1939-43) and Manuel Alvar López's *Atlas lingüístico y etnográfico de Andalucía* (1961) in which whole words are written at approximately the location of the speaker whose response was recorded by the fieldworker. Obviously, this is a very expensive method since all the material must be mapped by hand, and the decision to map whole words means that a great deal of redundant information is included. Unfortunately, such maps are also the most difficult to read and the least rewarding to consult since the patterns of distribution do not quickly emerge. Kurath (1972: 21) himself admits that it is easier to work from lists than from maps in attempting to establish dialect boundaries or identify the characteristics of a speech area. Thus it is not surprising that the volumes of *LANE* have been little used for further studies, as the preface to the second printing bemoans.

The recent atlases based on the SED and LSS materials, however, map material that is

presented in list form also. Since the information is already available, the question that then arises is: what purposes do the maps serve? In this connection it is useful to note the distinction drawn by Chambers and Trudgill (1980: 29) between *display* maps which simply map the responses and *interpretive* maps which attempt to make a more general statement. *Phonological Atlas of the Northern Region* and *Atlas of English Sounds* provide good examples of display maps, especially the latter since it sometimes employs more than one colour. In these atlases a distinctive symbol is used to represent a particular variant at each location. Since the form of the symbols has been ingeniously designed to show certain relationships, these maps are fairly easy to read once the system of symbols has been mastered. Map 10.1 is an example of this and shows how the form of the symbols reflects a grouping of related variants with the horizontal bars indicating a high front vowel, the circles a diphthong, and the vertical bars a low vowel. A map such as this may suggest an interpretation but it makes no explicit statement.

The maps in *The Linguistic Atlas of England* and *A Word Geography of England*, on the other hand, show isoglosses which reflect decisions about where the lines should be drawn. For example, in Map 10.2 (*LAE*: Ph 69b) it would have been possible to include Yorkshire in the [ɛ] area and draw an isogloss running from Norfolk to Cheshire showing the area to the north as predominantly [ɛ], with [a] as an alternative in many locations and occurring as the main variant in a much smaller area than Map 10.2 suggests. The maps in *LAE* provide isoglosses for single words, morphological forms

Map 10.1:   *AES*, p. 9: ME /ī/, *died* (p.p.)

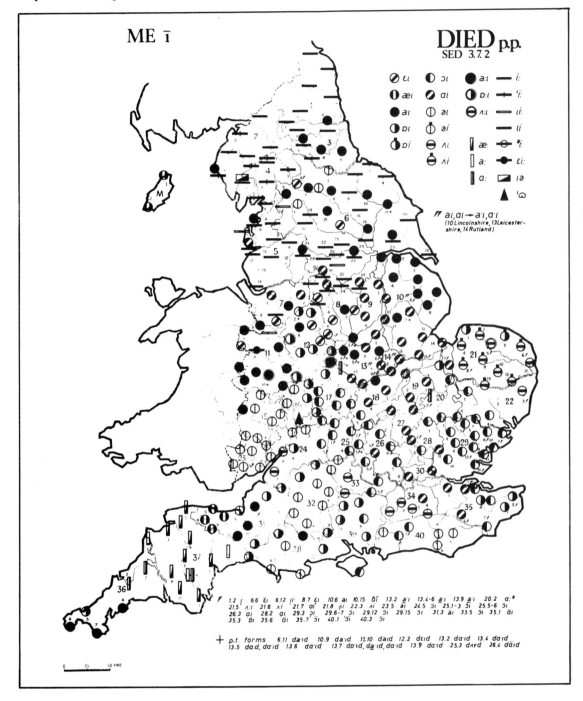

Map 10.2: *LAE: Ph 69b: make*

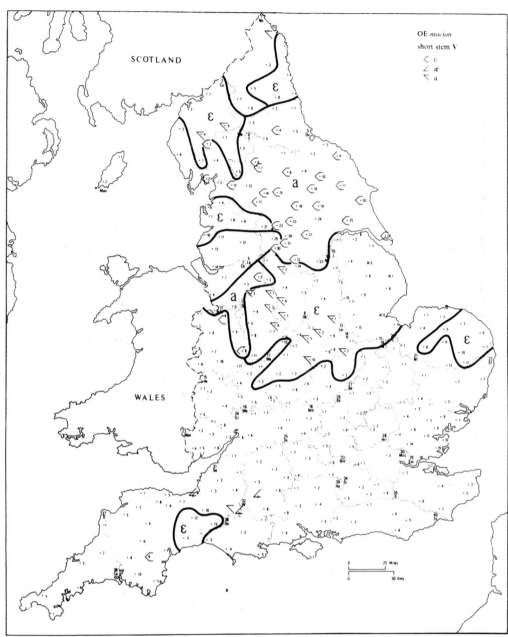

ε: 1Nb 5, 21Nf ⁺5/⁺12 under ε

ι 13Lei ⁺2

-MAKING- 31So ⁺11; -MAKER 31So ⁺11;
    MAKE 2prpl 6Y ⁺6, 21Nf11; 3prpl 12St ⁺5,
    21Nf10; imp 6Y ⁺15/⁺25/⁺32, 12St ⁺3,
    31So 12; ndg 8Db ⁺6, 10L 8, 12St ⁺6;
    MAKE(S) 3prsg 1Nb 2, 2Cu 1, 3Du ⁺4,
    4We ⁺2, 6Y ⁺14/⁺19/⁺25, 8Db ⁺2/⁺7,
    10L 3/6, 11Sa ⁺8, 12St ⁺5/11, 13Lei ⁺10,
    33Brk 5; MAKING prp 5La 1, 6Y ⁺20,
    11Sa ⁺8, 12St ⁺2, 21Nf 3; vbl n 21Nf 8

mj- 1Nb 4/6, mι- 31So ⁺11

or syntactic patterns. (In some cases, where there are two phonological features to represent, e.g. a vowel and a consonant, two maps are provided for a single word.) Many of these maps necessarily reflect arbitrary decisions about where to draw the isoglosses (cf. Francis 1978: 224-7), a fact which presumably need not bother anyone unduly since the information is there for reinterpretation if one wishes to do so. The difficulty arises when an attempt is made to combine the information from different maps, even for the reflex of a single ME sound, since the reasons for drawing isoglosses for one item in the word class may differ from the reasons for doing so for another item in the same word class. Francis (1978: 229) in his review of WGE hypothesised that the isoglosses were drawn 'to show the widest extent of the nonstandard', and the editors of LAE confirm that this was indeed Orton's general practice. This makes it particularly regrettable that the editors of LAE have not included any composite maps showing the distribution of the reflexes of a particular sound across the word class, since the editors would be aware of the places where arbitrary decisions had been made. It is somewhat paradoxical that Kolb and his associates include 23 'collective maps' of this kind in AES but since these are display maps it is still necessary to use this information as the basis for drawing interpretive maps showing the major isoglosses, even though the pattern is sometimes clear, as in Map 10.3 (AES: 227). At other times the situation may be too complex to make a collective map satisfactory. In this case, there is probably too much detail to make the map easily interpretable and it might have been better to combine some of the variants to present a more coherent distribution. Nevertheless, the ingenuity with which so much information is presented is quite impressive.

Thus both LAE and AES leave the reader with the task of combining information from different maps in order to interpret the evidence that is presented. This situation presumably results from the preoccupation of dialect geographers with description rather than explanation, something which Trudgill (1974: 216-17) deplores. Mather and Speitel, however, in the first two volumes of the Linguistic Atlas of Scotland make even greater demands on the reader. Instead of using lines to mark isoglosses, Mather and Speitel use different kinds of shad-

ings and claim (1975: 21) that the isoglosses can be inferred from the boundaries of the patterns that result. However, it is clear that what Mather and Speitel have done is very different from the task performed by the editors of LAE, as examination of Map 10.4 (LAS vol. 1, Map 14) for the word splinter will show. This is a good example of the ingenuity with which the maps in LAS have been constructed: eleven different responses are mapped and the areas in which there is a concentration of a particular response are clearly outlined. Yet the boundaries of the shaded portion are not isoglosses as ordinarily understood. If they were, they would erroneously indicate that skelf does not occur north of Angus, although there are 42 occurrences of skelf (out of a possible total of 361, not counting Orkney and Shetland) and while 11.6 per cent is not a high density it is not negligible either. Moreover, Mather and Speitel have been scrupulous in not combining responses that are different though possibly related. In this case, if skelb, skelve, skilf, etc. are counted along with skelf (and it has to be remembered that LAS contains the responses to a postal questionnaire, not forms recorded by a fieldworker), then the proportion of responses for this group for the mainland counties north of Angus rises to over 30 per cent. An alternative to Mather and Speitel's methods of mapping would have been to group hypothetically related items together and attempt to bring out the pattern of distribution more clearly. For example, in this case, stab and stob can probably be safely grouped together, as can spell and spale. Spelk and spilk would also appear to be related but spilk essentially is restricted to a small area in Caithness and its distribution does not seem to be related to that of spelk. Spelk and spilk are therefore best treated as distinct forms, as is splice. This would reduce the list of items to be mapped to six. There is no reason to map splinter since the respondents were asked to supply the local word for it and it should, for the purposes of mapping, be treated as a 'nil' response. This is true of all the stimulus words in both questionnaires because they must be assumed to be familiar to the respondents, otherwise they could not be expected to identify the local equivalent. With only six responses to map the task becomes simpler, as Maps 10.5 and 10.6 show. Moreover, there is a difference between the skelf/skelb/skelve group and the

Map 10.3:　*AES*, p. 227: ME /ŭ/ collective map 1

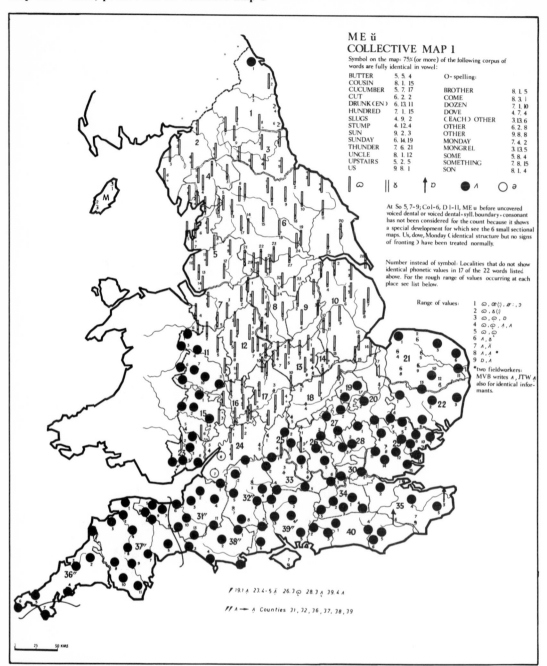

other five. It is clear that the former group occurs throughout mainland Scotland and the relevant question is not where it occurs but with what density. Accordingly, the representation of this set of responses will require some indication of relative percentages showing the proportion of respondents who supplied this form. The other five responses are more restricted in their occurrence and it is possible to draw heteroglosses showing the limits of their distribution.

Map 10.4: *LAS* vol. 1, map 4: *splinter*

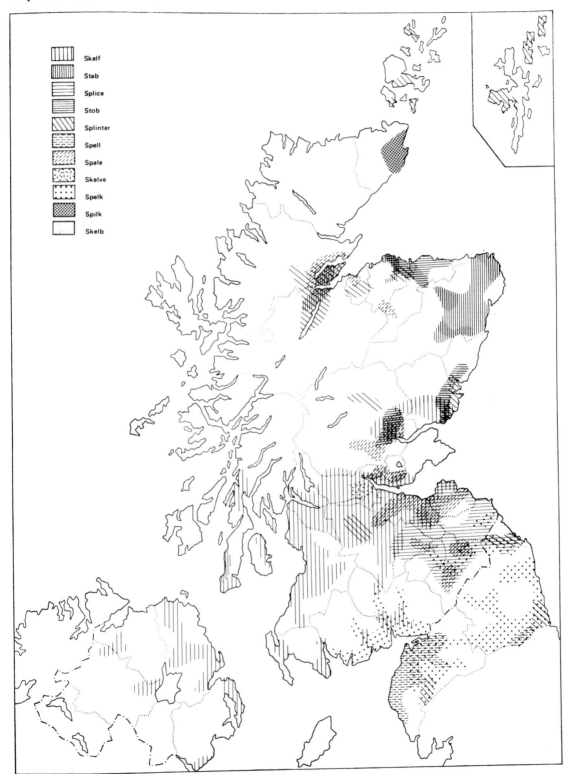

Map 10.5: *Splinter*: **Alternative Local Responses**

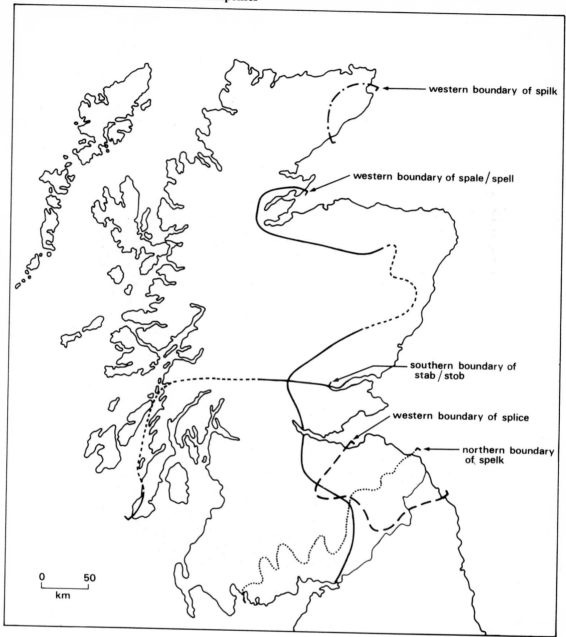

Map 10.6: *Skelf*: Percentage Tokens of Occurrences in Scotland

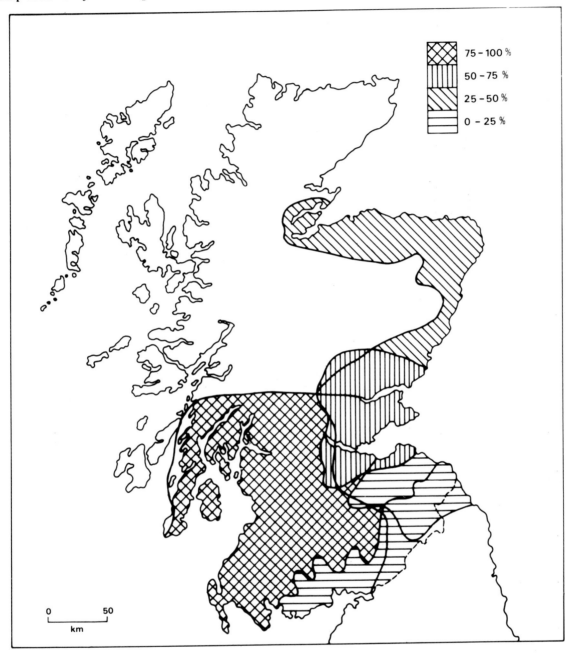

The results can be seen in Map 10.6 which also incorporates the relevant heteroglosses of Map 10.5. This map contains much less information than Map 10.4 and it is also based on assumptions that may turn out to be unjustified but it is probably easier to read. The important point is why anyone would prefer Map 10.4 to Map 10.6 or vice versa. The answer will naturally depend upon the purpose of the atlas: for whom are these expensive volumes designed? As Francis (1978) in his review of *WGE* pointed out, this is a question to which the answer is far from obvious.

One might begin by considering the purpose of maps in general. One obvious purpose is to provide a guide for travellers so that they will be able to find out where they are and how they can get to their chosen destination. In any literal sense linguistic maps do not have this function. It is highly unlikely that any linguist of the future, armed with *LAS* vol. 1, taperecorder and a grant for mileage and *per diem* expenses, will attempt to locate the respondent (or the descendants of such) who produced the *hapax legomenon* of *currie wawpit* for 'left-handed' in Fife. Nor is it very likely that *LAS* vol. 1 will serve as a kind of *Guide bleu* for linguistically enlightened tourists seeking to explore interesting relic areas. Instead, the purpose of linguistic maps is presumably to present information of the kind shown in maps which display the average rainfall or distribution of population in a particular area. Such maps are produced as teaching tools or as means of conveying information to non-experts in a form that is fairly easy to grasp. How successfully have linguistic atlases performed this function? Atlases of the type of *LANE* and Alvar López's *ALEA* have probably not been very successful. The information contained in these volumes is much less accessible than in the Basic Material volumes of *SED* or in the index to *LAS* vol. 2. Far from being a visual aid the maps are probably a barrier to grasping the pattern of distribution and it seems very unlikely that anyone nowadays would attempt this kind of mapping. Given the sorting power of computers, basic information is much better stored in a form that is suitable for machine processing than in conventional map form. In fact, one of the priorities must be to carry out Orton's desire to have the *SED* data coded for machine-processing, if this has not already been done. Then, and probably not until then, will it be possible to ask the kind of questions that might provide answers that would be worth mapping. For all their magnificence and despite the hard work and ingenuity that has gone into them, it must be admitted that *LAE*, *AES*, the *LAS* volumes and the others are disappointing. The most obvious weakness lies in the almost total lack of analysis. The editors in each case are extremely knowledgeable about the material and would have been in an excellent position to develop genuinely interpretive maps. That they have not done so presumably follows from a strict view of the dialect geographer's role as limited to the collection and presentation of data. But the maps in *LAE*, *AES* and *LAS* are not a primary source of information; they are derivative and consequently redundant unless they add something which is not contained in the lists of material. Even their use as a teaching tool is limited by the narrow range of information contained in each map; a few maps are useful to illustrate the phenomenon of regional variation to a class, but several hundred seems an excessively large number. If the maps are of limited appeal to the layman, perhaps they are valuable for the expert. Again, the answer is probably in the negative. By consulting the maps, a scholar can obtain some indication of what to look for in the lists, but further analysis must be based on the lists themselves rather than on the maps. A written description of the distribution of the responses would have been at least equally as effective though it would have been aesthetically less attractive. In comparison with the recent atlases of British speech, Allen's *Linguistic Atlas of the Upper Midwest* (Allen 1973-76) is superficially a dreary affair which is likely to grace few coffee tables, though it contains a great deal of information in accessible form. In contrast, *AES*, for example, is elegant almost to the point of ostentation and provokes appreciative comments from casual visitors but it is hard to use for analytical purposes. It is doubtless churlish to look such magnificent gift horses in the mouth (and I ought to confess that most of the atlases I own are review copies) but the more I study these handsome volumes the more frustrated I feel at their editors' self-denying stand on interpretation. There is even something disturbing about the uniformity of format in each atlas, almost as if a decision to use one form of mapping necessarily excluded any others. One is inclined to wonder whether

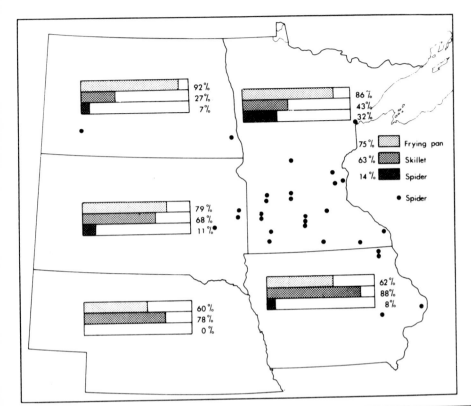

Map 10.7: *LAUM*, fig. 14.4: *frying pan*

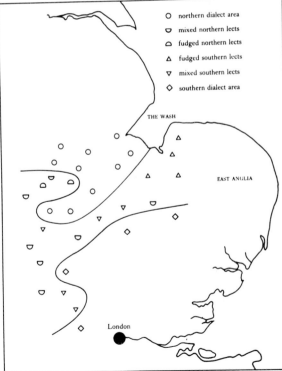

Map 10.8: Transition Zone between East Anglia and the East Midlands: Distribution of Lectal Types

the editors belong to different schools of art: Kolb and his atelier could be Symbolistes, Mather and Speitel Impressionists, while Orton's school fittingly appears to follow the firm, clean line of William Blake.

What are the alternatives? One example that has already been mentioned is Allen's *LAUM* where the use of maps is limited to comparatively few illustrations, generally indicating proportion of use. Map 10.7, for example, indicates the distribution of the words for *frying pan*. This is not a particularly impressive-looking map but along with the accompanying textual description it provides a great deal of information clearly and concisely.

A more interesting illustration of what might be done is provided by Chambers and Trudgill (1980) in their analysis of the reflexes of ME ŭ in words such as *butter*, *duck* etc. in the East Midland counties and East Anglia. Chambers and Trudgill obtained their figures by tabulating the responses for all 65 items in the *SED* Basic Material containing reflexes of ME ŭ, thus bringing together information that appears in different sections of the Basic Material volumes. They are able to show that between the clearly northern speakers with [ʊ] for ME ŭ and the clearly southern speakers with [ʌ] for ME ŭ, there is a transition zone where there is variation among the speakers. The details of their analysis need not be repeated here, but the important point is that they were able to classify the speakers in the transition zone into several categories on the basis of their responses. Chambers and Trudgill have labelled the southern line of the transition zone, which can be seen in Map 10.8, as the *base* and the northern line as the *beach head* since the change in progress is moving northwards (i.e. [ʌ] is replacing [ʊ], not the other way round). Chambers and Trudgill's treatment of ME ŭ is one illustration of how quantified data can be presented visually in a form which is fairly easy to grasp. This information would be very hard, if not impossible, to glean from either *LAE* or *AES*.

Chambers and Trudgill also give examples of how social differences in the use of a linguistic feature can be mapped if there is a spatial dimension to the distribution. Map 10.9 shows the distribution of uvular /r/ in western Europe according to the concept of 'educated speech'. The map shows the diffusion of uvular /r/ from

Paris as a prestige feature in which the innovators are 'educated speakers'. The map also illustrates another point made by Chambers and Trudgill that innovations need not spread continuously like an oil spill but may 'jump' from one urban centre to another.

A linguistic map, however, can be only as good as the material it is based on. The published materials of SED and LSS provide no information on social differences such as education or social class, though *LAS* provides information on the age and place of birth of the respondents in addition to the birthplaces of the respondents' parents. This latter information can be used to eliminate 'unreliable respondents' (Macaulay, 1979) and it could also be used to plot changes over 'apparent time' if certain words are cited only by older respondents. In general, however, the published SED and LSS materials provide evidence only of geographical distribution with little differentiation among the respondents. Given these limitations, what can be extracted from the materials that it would be appropriate to map?

One obvious approach is to extend Chambers and Trudgill's treatment of the reflexes of ME ŭ to other linguistic variables. In their book, they also deal with the reflexes of ME ă, but there are probably a number of other variables that could be fruitfully investigated in this manner. One might be the distribution of initial /h/ and another possibility would be the voicing of initial voiceless fricatives in the South-West. In fact, however, wherever individual maps in *LAE* or *AES* show different distribution for the reflexes of a single sound in different words, the existence of variability becomes apparent, though it will not always indicate a sound change in progress. For example, the *LAE* phonological maps reproduced here as Maps 10.10 and 10.11 show the distribution of a final voiced velar stop after the velar nasal in *tongue* and *tongs* respectively. Leaving aside the occurrence of such forms in Kent, there is a considerable difference between the two maps as regards the distribution of the velar stop in the West Midlands. One possible explanation might be that the phonetic context is different, since in *tongs* the context for the velar nasal (stop) is not word-final. This may indeed be the explanation, but these two words are not the only ones recorded in the SED responses in which a velar nasal (stop) occurs in word-final position.

Map 10.9: Uvular /r/ in Europe

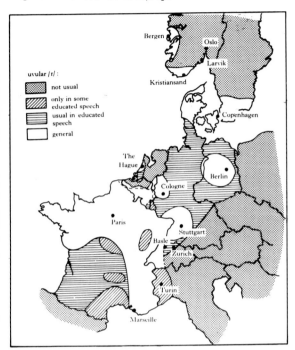

Map 10.10: *LAE*: Ph 242: *tongue*

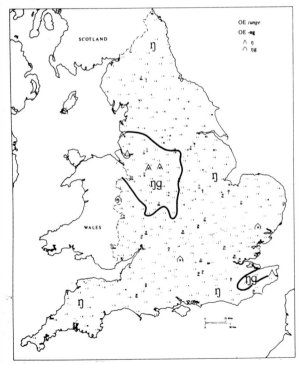

Map 10.11: *LAE*: Ph 243: *tongs*

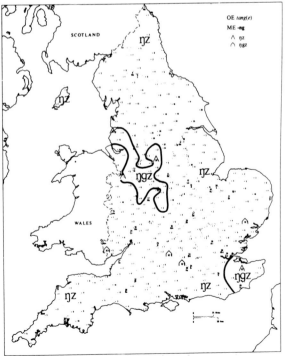

Among the responses widely given by West Midland respondents there are also the following: *string*, *wrong*, *Spring*, *among* (not generally supplied by respondents in Shropshire), *rung*, *bing*, and *daddy long-legs*. There are also a number of words which occur more sporadically.

Since the number of possible contexts for final voiced stops after velar nasals varies from location to location, it is necessary to calculate their occurrence as a percentage rather than simply listing the number of occurrences. When this is done, it is clear that there is a relatively small area in East Central Staffordshire with 100 per cent occurrence of stops. This area extends from Alton (18.3) in the North to Lapley (18.8) and Edingale (18.9) in the South. This area includes Cannock for which Heath (1980) reported that 80 per cent of his respondents used a velar stop after a velar nasal and a further 6 per cent used a velar stop variously. Surrounding this innermost area in which the velar stop is used categorically by SED respondents, there is a larger area ranging from Charlesworth (15.1) in the North of Derbyshire, West as far as Audlem (17.5) in Cheshire and Kinnersley (19.4) in Shropshire, as far East as Sutton-on-the-Hill (15.7) and as far South as Himley (18.11) in

Staffordshire and Nether Whitacre (23.1) in Warwickshire. Within this larger area voiced velar stops occur after velar nasals with a frequency of at least 70 per cent. Surrounding this 70 per cent plus area, there is an even larger area in which the velar stop is found after velar nasals with a frequency of from 25 per cent to 60 per cent. This does not extend further North than the 70 per cent plus area but it extends as far West as Hanmer in Flintshire, as far East as Stonebroom (15.5) in Derbyshire, and as far South as Cradley (27.8) in Herefordshire. There are three small pockets in which final velar stops after nasals are found with a frequency lower than 25 per cent. The largest of these is in West Shropshire (19.3, 19.5, 19.6, 19.7) and the other two larger villages of Brimfield (27.3) in Herefordshire and Hanbury (27.5) in Worcestershire.

The mapping of these figures suggests that East Central Staffordshire is a relic area in which the occurrence of the voiced velar stop after nasals occurs regularly although the feature is receding in the surrounding area so that its distribution is limited to the northern West Midland counties (and a small area in Kent). This distribution is shown in Map 10.12.

Map 10.12:   Percentage Occurrences of Final Voiced Velar Stops in the West Midlands

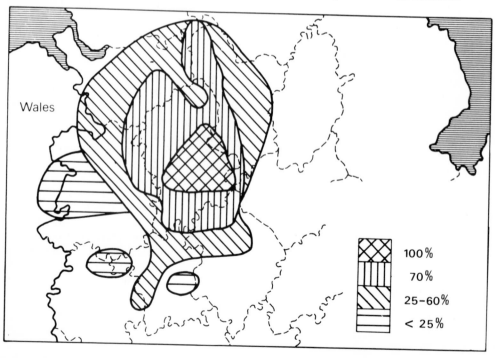

Another approach would be to start with a hypothetical dialect boundary and test it against the evidence provided by the surveys. This is what Speitel (1969) and Glauser (1974) did in examining the Scottish-English border. Both Speitel and Glauser were able to show quite convincingly that the political border has clear linguistic correlates. Since the English spoken on either side of the border developed from a single variety, the differences must have arisen as a reflection of nationalist feelings in which language functions as an identifying characteristic (Fishman 1972; Macaulay 1973). It is likely, however, that other significant dialect boundaries arise because there are geographical areas smaller than countries that produce similar language loyalty.

One of the curious features of both SED and LSS is that they present their results in terms of the political units known as counties. On the face of it, there may seem no reason to believe that county boundaries will coincide with dialect boundaries, and the counties have now even ceased to function as administrative units of local government. On the other hand, it is likely that county names will continue to resonate for a variety of reasons: Middlesex County Cricket Club, Devonshire cream, Yorkshire pudding, and so on. Such labels help to reinforce the 'mental maps' (Gould and White 1974) that contribute to our perception of the world we live in. An interesting exercise would be to take any two bordering counties and investigate the extent to which linguistic differences coincide with the old administrative boundaries. One would expect that in some cases the linguistic boundaries would be much more clearly marked than in others and that this difference would correspond to some estimate of the sense of identity held by the inhabitants of the counties.

For example, Ayrshire is a Scottish county with a strong sense of identity perhaps because of its long history of settlement, having become a single administrative unit at the beginning of the thirteenth century. Many powerful families, such as the Bruces and Stewarts, were connected with it, and its towns of Ayr and Irvine flourished as major centres of Scottish commerce until the sixteenth century. Later, Ayrshire was to become identified with the poetry of Robert Burns and to a lesser extent with the novels of John Galt. It is perhaps significant that Ayrshire is the only southern Scottish county to appear as prominently as Midlothian in the mental maps collected by Gould and White from school-leavers in Inverness and Kirkwall (Gould and White 1968: 171-2). Since the first two *LAS* volumes deal only with vocabulary, it is not possible to make strong claims about the strength of the dialect boundary but it is interesting that there are a number of items which are clearly marked as Ayrshire words. In *LAS* vol. 1 for example, *stimpit* or *stimpart* is given by over 40 per cent of the respondents in Ayrshire for map 22 'quarter of a peck' but there are only six similar responses from the rest of Scotland. Two of the respondents from outside of Ayrshire who gave this response were actually born in Ayrshire and a third had an Ayrshire mother. There are many other examples of atypical responses that can be explained on grounds of birthplace or parentage, suggesting that the lexical data from the two postal surveys may in fact be fairly reliable. Other Ayrshire words in *LAS* vol. 1 are *linn* for map 28 'slate pencil' (really a Kilmarnock word), *garnel* (*rope*) for map 56 'straw rope', *crow fricht* for map 57 'scarecrow', *sheep's tartles/turtles* for map 63 'sheep's dung', and *pishmole* for map 76 'ant'; in *LAS* vol. 2 there are *shelmonts* for map 57 'horizontal frames laid over a cart for carrying hay', *glaiks* for map 58 'instrument used for twisting straw ropes', and *tummel the cran* for map 80 'head over heels'. In addition, there are many examples of words that are shared by Ayrshire with neighbouring counties on one side but not on the other (Macaulay 1979). A fuller investigation involving more than lexical data would be necessary to establish the point but on the basis of the *LAS* volumes there is at least a *prima facie* case for claiming that Ayrshire is a distinct dialect area.

There are other ways in which the survey materials of SED and LSS could be imaginatively and creatively used to present a clearer picture of linguistic variation in Great Britain and some of them are illustrated in this volume. In future years, no doubt, there will be interpretive atlases of value to students and scholars alike. Meanwhile, I am grateful for the elegant works of art that grace my coffee table and intrigue my visitors.

References

Allen, H.B. *The Linguistic Atlas of the Upper Midwest*, vols. 1-3 (University of Minnesota Press, Minneapolis, 1973-6) (*LAUM*)

Alvar López, M. *Atlas lingüistico y etnográfico de Andalucía* (Universidad de Granada, Granada, 1961) (*ALEA*)

Chambers, J.K. and P. Trudgill. *Dialectology* (Cambridge University Press, Cambridge, 1980)

Fishman, J. *Language and Nationalism* (Newbury House, Rowley, Massachusetts, 1972)

Francis, W.N. Review of H. Orton and N. Wright, *A Word Geography of England* in *American Speech*, vol. 53 (1978), pp. 221-31

Glauser, B. *The Scottish-English Linguistic Border: Lexical Aspects* (Francke, Bern, 1974) (Cooper Monographs, no. 20)

Gould, P. and R. White. 'The mental maps of British school leavers', *Regional Studies*, vol. 2, (1974) pp. 161-82

Heath, C.D. *The Pronunciation of English in Cannock, Staffordshire — A Sociolinguistic Survey of an Urban Speech-Community* (Blackwell, Oxford, 1980) (Publications of the Philological Society, vol. 29)

Kolb, E. *Phonological Atlas of the Northern Region* (Francke, Bern, 1966) (*PANR*)

Kolb, E., B. Glauser, W. Elmer, R. Stamm. *Atlas of English Sounds* (Francke, Bern, 1979) (*AES*)

Kurath, H. *Studies in Area Linguistics* (Indiana University Press, Bloomington, 1972)

Kurath, H. *et al. Linguistic Atlas of New England*, 3 vols. in 6 parts (Brown University Press, Providence, 1939-43, reprinted AMS Press, New York, 1972)

Macaulay, R.K.S. 'Double standards', *American Anthropologist*, vol. 75 (1973), pp. 1324-37

—— Review of *The Linguistic Atlas of Scotland vol. 2* in *Language*, vol. 55 (1979) pp. 224-8

Mather, J.Y. and H.-H. Speitel. *The Linguistic Atlas of Scotland*: Scots Section, 2 vols. (Croom Helm, London, 1975-7) (*LAS*)

Orton, H. 'Editorial Problems of an English Linguistic Atlas' in L.H. Burghardt (ed.). *Dialectology: Problems and Perspectives* (University of Tennessee, Knoxville, 1971), pp. 79-115

Orton, H. and N. Wright. *A Word Geography of England* (Seminar Press, New York and London, 1975) (*WGE*)

Orton, H., S. Sanderson and J. Widdowson (eds.). *The Linguistic Atlas of England* (Croom Helm, London, 1978) (*LAE*)

Speitel, H.-H. 'An Areal Typology of Isoglosses: Isoglosses Near the Scottish Border', *Zeitschrift für Dialektologie und Linguistik*, vol. 36 (1969), pp. 49-66

Trudgill, P. 'Linguistic Change and Diffusion: Description and Explanation in Sociolinguistic Dialect Geography', *Language in Society*, vol. 3 (1974), pp. 215-46

PE1700 .S7 1985   c.1
                                           100106 000

Studies in linguis... ograph

3 9310 00071564 7
GOSHEN COLLEGE-GOOD LIBRARY